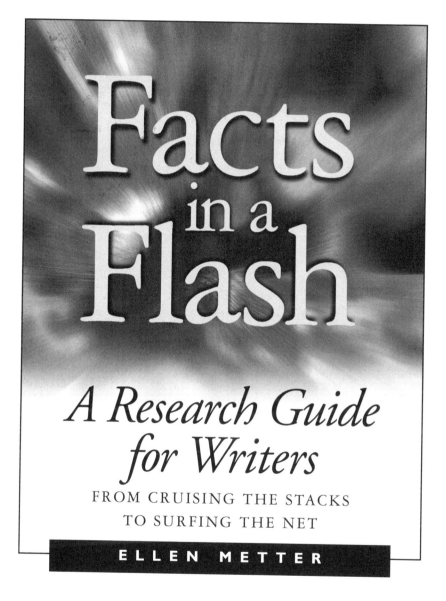

Facts
in a
Flash

A Research Guide for Writers

FROM CRUISING THE STACKS
TO SURFING THE NET

ELLEN METTER

WRITER'S DIGEST BOOKS
CINCINNATI, OHIO

Other fine Writer's Digest Books are available from your local bookstore or direct from the publisher.

Visit our Web site at www.writersdigest.com for information on more resources for writers.

To receive a free weekly E-mail newsletter delivering tips and updates about writing and about Writer's Digest products, send an E-mail with "Subscribe Newsletter" in the body of the message to newsletter-request@writersdigest.com or register directly at our Web site at www.writersdigest.com.

03 02 01 00 99   5 4 3 2 1

Library of Congress Cataloging-in-Publication Data

Metter, Ellen.
    Facts in a flash : a research guide for writers / by Ellen Metter.—1st ed.
        p.   cm.
    Includes bibliographical references and index.
    ISBN 0-89879-910-4 (alk. paper)
    1. Authorship Handbooks, manuals, etc. 2. Research—Methodology Handbooks, manuals, etc. 3. Bibliography—Methodology Handbooks, manuals, etc. 4. Reference books—Bibliography Handbooks, manuals, etc. I. Title.
PN146.M47   1999
001.4—dc21   99-39517
                                                                              CIP

Edited by David Borcherding, Michelle Howry, and Jennifer Lile
Designed by Sandy Kent
Cover design by Brian Roeth
Production coordinated by Rachel Vater

ACKNOWLEDGMENTS

Thank you to Louise Gangler-Treff, for proofing the law and government documents chapters when her plate was already sloshing over the edges; to the editors of *Facts in a Flash*, David Borcherding, Jennifer Lile, and Michelle Howry; to Danny Walker of Denver Public Library for helping me understand patents; to Jack Heffron of Writer's Digest, a long overdue thank-you for coediting *The Writer's Ultimate Research Guide* and supporting this type of book; to Roseanne Biederman, another overdue thank-you to for ably coediting *The Writer's Ultimate Research Guide*; to Stan Oliner, Sue Maret, Ellen Greenblatt, Eveline Yang, and Kerranne Biley for sharing their expertise with me; to David Hammond, for being the best neighbor in the universe; to Dan Organ, for being patient; to my family: Harriet Sasso, Dave Delaney, Sarah Delaney, Lisa and Claudia Ritter, Rich Metter, Ainsely Burke, Daniel Burke Metter, Bette, Larry, Jolie, and Mike Sasso, Barb, Gerald, and Alana Metter, and my mom, Mallery Sasso; to my honorary family: Laura, Sylvia, and Phil Goodman, Elaine Jurries, Valerie Miller, Gary Hutchison, Norman Sanford, April Allridge, Susan and Ricardo Norton, Kathleen Smith and the great people at the Auraria Library.

ABOUT THE AUTHOR

 Ellen Metter is a research librarian and bibliographer at the Auraria Library, which serves three institutions of higher education: the University of Colorado at Denver, Metropolitan State College of Denver, and the Community College of Denver. She holds a Master of Information Science degree from Drexel University in Philadelphia, and she received the Excellence in Librarianship Award from the University of Colorado at Denver in 1999.

Metter has written articles for *College & Research Libraries News, Wilson Library Bulletin, Research Strategies, Colorado Libraries, American Association of Higher Education Bulletin* and *Nexus.* She has contributed a research report for the National Writer's Association, and was interviewed by the *American Writer's Review* about her first book for Writer's Digest, *The Writer's Ultimate Research Guide.* She lives in Denver, Colorado.

CONTENTS

CHAPTER 5

Background and Statistics Research . . . 112
Finding Definitions, Topic Summaries, Overviews, and Statistical Data

CHAPTER 6

Experts and Quotations . . . 165
Locating Experts and Using Their Words to Enhance Yours

CHAPTER 7

Biographical and Autobiographical Research . . . 188
Learning of the Lives of the Famous and Infamous

CHAPTER 8

Historical Research . . . 211
Finding Details of Different Eras

CHAPTER 9

Cultural Research . . . 240
Uncovering the Mores of Populations Around the World

CHAPTER 10

Geographical Research ... 265
Weather, Maps, and Geographical Details

CHAPTER 11

United States Legal Research ... 277
Finding the Law

CHAPTER 12

Business Research ... 312
Information About Companies, Industries, and the Economy

CHAPTER 13

Authorship Research . . . 358
The Business and Pleasure of Writing

APPENDIX A

Commercial Online Database Vendors . . . 380

APPENDIX B

Periodical Indexes . . . 389

So Many Formats, So Little Time

The print, phone, and online materials presented in this book are intermingled in single lists. I've chosen not to separate them, as other research books have done, for two reasons: (1) Many resources are now available in multiple formats (i.e., a particular title might be available in book format, on CD-ROM, and also on the Web); and (2) it makes sense to list items based on their research usefulness rather than arbitrarily separating them by format.

When, a particular resource is available in multiple formats, the book publication information will be mentioned first, followed by an indication that it's on CD-ROM, the Web, and/or as a subscription database through a commercial online service provider.

An example of a multiformat resource:

CorpTech Directory of Technology Companies. Woburn, MA: Corporate Technology Information Services. Annual. Also available on CD-ROM, at http://www.corptech.com, and as a subscription database via Corporate Technology Information Services, DataStar, and OneSource.

This directory identifies U.S. manufacturers and developers of technology products, including those involved in artificial intelligence, biotechnology, computer hardware and software, defense systems, robotics, and transportation.

Criteria for Inclusion

In the case of Internet sites, databases of substance that are available at no cost represent the majority of sites included—free or inexpensive availability was a major consideration. If a Web site is listed you can assume it's free unless otherwise indicated.

Since I'm tired of reading "link-happy" books that recommend every Web site remotely related to a topic, whether it's exceptional or mediocre, I've tried to avoid that route. Instead, the focus is on *meta* sites that lead you to many resources, or to a site or two that are representative of the many available for a subject.

This book also describes databases from major commercial online system vendors such as DIALOG, Ovid, and OCLC. Most of the databases offered by these companies would be out of the financial range of an individual subscriber (unless you're listed at http://www.forbes.com, the Web page that lists the Forbes 400 Richest People in America). These databases are ones likely to be available at no charge via your local public or academic libraries. Commerical providers of online services mentioned in this book are listed in Appendix A. Call them to see if a local library subscribes to their database or for costs of subscribing.

The print resources included are those that are either commonly found in larger public and academic libraries or lesser known specialized texts, useful for many research purposes. Since I guessed that Writer's Digest Books wouldn't consider a forty-five-volume edition of *Facts in a Flash*, I've tried to pick the most representative resources possible for all kinds of research needs.

Index is Indispensable

Please use the detailed back-of-the-book index to help you find particular subjects and titles. Although the table of contents is lengthy, it's a pale substitute for the index. Because of the nature of the subject matter, there's great crossover between chapters—and I hate to think of anyone laboriously picking through chapters to find a tiny bit of information you remember reading.

If you have comments on *Facts in a Flash*, contact me via E-mail at emetter@ carbon.cudenver.edu.

Portions of this book were derived from *The Writer's Ultimate Research Guide* (Writer's Digest, 1995), though these sections have been completely revised and updated.

CHAPTER I

Know Your Research Options

Using a Combination of Computers, Hard Copy, and People

"The way to do research is to attack the facts at the point of greatest astonishment."

—Celia Green

Research: Why Do It?

There's plenty of room in the world of research for opinion. But opinion supported by facts has more impact and credibility. Researchers and professional writers need accurate statistics, authoritative quotations, historical background, scholarly conjecture, biographical tidbits, arcane facts, and detailed explanations of every process, theory, concept, methodology, and function imaginable. Research adds authority and color to writing.

Few writers, including fiction writers, can enchant their readers with pure imagination unspeckled with reality. For example, nothing irks mystery readers more than to read of the bloodcurdling slaying of an eighteen-year-old damsel by a method they know would have done little more then muss her hair. The facts need to be there.

Facts and data can be elusive, but once you learn fundamental techniques for searching proficiently and know where you should be able to find what you need, you'll be able to increase your efficiency—and more times than not, find facts in a flash.

Choosing the Best Method

The information you need is out there and this book will lead you to some of the best sites online, the choicest crannies in libraries and bookstores, and most useful phone numbers and online discussion groups.

Knowledge of online research, hard copy research, and expert research will get a writer/researcher to just about any information needed. Why choose one method over another?

Accuracy

All research methods—online, expert, and hard copy—may yield accurate results. Certain indicators help insure that you're reading or hearing accurate information. Ask yourself a few questions when evaluating the validity of your information source:

Does this information come from a reputable organization?

Whether reading an article, newsletter, book, Web site, or whatever, find out which publisher or organization is behind it. For example, a publisher such as the Rutgers University Press will likely publish books that contain "accurate" information, or, at the very least, well-considered theories. Alternately, self-published tomes can be produced by anyone willing to invest a few thousand dollars.

Has the information been reviewed by editors, scholars, or other experts in the field?

In the world of scholarship the peer-review process is a mainstay. A peer-reviewed journal is one whose editors send submitted manuscripts to outside reviewers who are experts in the manuscript's topic. These experts, specialists in their given field, then comment on the quality of the content, often challenging the author to better substantiate certain claims or to go further with a thesis. And the reviewers often find rather amazing mistakes!

Even as a casual reader of articles in my personal "expert" field (information gathering techniques), I'm often startled by the blatant inaccuracies I read in magazines and newspapers about libraries and the Internet. My first thought is, "Well, there's another bit of wrong information flung out there for the unsuspecting reader to absorb." And of course I'm not aware of all the inaccuracies *I'm* absorbing reading articles that are not in my field.

I don't expect you to do all your reading from only peer-reviewed resources—life just wouldn't be as enjoyable if you did. But in your *research*, I recommend you tap the most reputable resources you can.

Is the individual providing the information a true expert,
well qualified to comment on a particular subject?
Both the glory and degradation of the Internet can be traced to this fact: Anyone can plop anything they want onto it. Does the author know what he or she is talking about? Sometimes it's hard to say. I'm the first to admit that pristine credentials do not guarantee flawless writings. For example, consider that the "Unabomber's Manifesto" was written by a man with a mathematics Ph.D. from the University of Michigan and an undergraduate degree from Harvard. (Although his math papers were probably fine.)

All information should come with a "Buyer Beware" tag. If time allows, check your facts in more than one resource. Librarians certainly don't check each fact in every book they buy for veracity or each idea in every tome for its usefulness. Books go out of date but they remain on the shelves as historical works. Studies are debunked, but the original research is still on the shelf. Celebrities fib about their age and that might appear in a reputable biography. The written word isn't always the gospel truth.

Write Down Where You Found It

No matter what your information resource, always document where you found your data. Students need to list this information either in footnotes or reference lists (a.k.a. bibliographies), and professional writers may need to show editors the resources they used in their research. And if you ever need to refer back to a document that you don't have a copy of, you'll be very glad you kept good notes. Many a frustrated writer has come to my reference desk, plopped down a photocopied page and said, "I have no idea where I got this from." Though it's usually possible to track it down, it can take a while. Always jot down the particulars while you've got the resource in your hand or on your screen.

Convenience
Online information is nearby and bundles needed resources together.
Once you have a computer set up at home with your favorite Web sites and search engines bookmarked for easy use, it's incredibly convenient to just shuffle over to your computer chair and begin searching.

Signing up with a large commercial Internet service can also be convenient because of the variety of information it offers. A service such as CompuServe will not only get you to the Internet, but also give you access to databases, full-text journals, and unique services that they lease.

Commercial databases, like the Web-based *Electric Library* at http://www .elibrary.com, are similarly attractive, offering a convenient "package" of information. *Electric Library* may be found at some libraries but is also inexpensive enough to allow individuals to subscribe. *Electric Library* is a database that includes just a bit of everything: full text from selected magazines, newspapers, books, radio and TV transcripts, and even pictures. The *Electric Library* may be all the dabbling researcher will ever need. For more serious or varied research, *Electric Library* is a stop along the way.

It's convenient to pull a book off a shelf when you know how to efficiently find it.
A library or bookstore is convenient once you become familiar with techniques for finding what you need. Sometimes I'll sit in my office for an hour trying to find a fact on the Internet (and failing), when I know full well which book in the library I'm sitting in has the answer. If you already know where your answer is in a book, sometimes the best choice is to go get it. And one of the conveniences of a single book or magazine: No electricity, batteries, or solar power required.

Cost
Libraries are a bargain for the patron.
Statistics from 1995 show that library operating expenditures per capita ranged from an annual cost of one dollar in New York to fifty dollars in West Virginia. And library resources don't come cheap. I routinely purchase reference books for an academic library that cost hundreds of dollars. Commercial databases may cost tens of thousands of dollars. Having access to these research riches for literally pennies a day continues to be the bargain of the millennium.

Electronic resources can be a bargain.
Internet access can also be quite inexpensive, costing less per month than cable TV. This price is rather fabulous considering the ability to both chat with and cull information from the international community. For example, an E-mail to New Guinea costs no more than an E-mail to New Hampshire.

Watch out for hidden costs in electronic resources.

Access to premier online information resources can add to your tab. And access to full-length book information is currently spotty at best.

Hours can be eaten up quickly when you're online. If you're not signed up with a service that offers unlimited hours for a flat fee, be careful that you don't surf away the grocery money.

Will there come a time when every Web site you would ever want to visit will be free? I'd say no. Advertising can cover many, but not all, expenses. As an example, look at cable TV. Subscribers may buy in at a variety of levels, with "premium" channels costing more. And that cost is over and above the money cable pulls in from advertising and pay-per-view offerings.

Though some pages you access on the Web are slapped up with little cost, others, such as commercial databases, can only be created and maintained at a rather astounding expense. Luckily, many terrific Web destinations can be accessed for no fee, and libraries continue to subscribe to the most useful fee-based sites.

Archiving

Preservation isn't the Internet's strong point.

There are innumerable times when researchers need information more than a few decades old. Perhaps it's information from an 1898 *New York Times*, a 1960s article from *Life* magazine, or a book released by a French publisher in 1942 that is only available in five U.S. libraries. These items are not full text online. I'll guess that the older *New York Times* will be at some point, *Life* magazine— maybe—but the book? Never. The bottom line: You'll find significantly larger collections of older research material in libraries. But, as my former boss was fond of saying, there's probably more future than there is past.

The Internet is new in comparison to libraries and the written word. This newness is part of the reason there's little information that is archived permanently and few indexes that extend back more than a few decades.

Another reason for poor online archiving: economics. Since fewer people use older information than current information, it doesn't make good money sense for a specific journal to archive it's holdings online beyond a few years.

Yet another reason is pure flakiness. The instability of the majority of Web sites also wreaks havoc on maintaining older information. Some sites disappear overnight due to lack of funding or interest, and that's that. At least when a library cancels a journal subscription they get to keep the older editions they already purchased.

Still, some sites on the Internet consider their archival records to be of utmost importance. A database called *JSTOR (The Journal Storage Project)* is a compilation of full-text scholarly journals with holdings going back to the inception of each journal—and some go back to the early 1900s. Still, this database represents a handful of journals, and it's available on the Web only through a costly subscription fee (though your local library may subscribe to it). *JSTOR's* combination of scholarly and older material spells little economic promise, which is why this project was created and is supported by academic and philanthropic groups.

Libraries specialize in archiving.

Libraries have, since their inception, been repositories of the earliest editions of journals and books. Larger ones have made an effort to collect, usually in microform format, editions of writings that existed before publicly maintained libraries were the norm.

With the prevalence of so much information in electronic format, however, some archiving has been compromised. For example, my library purchased a financial database for years on CD-ROM with the promise that we would be able to keep our older disks. Now that no current technology will play the older disks, we're only glad we kept them because they sure look nice on the library Christmas tree. But the last researcher who hoped to search an older disk was anything but pleased.

Another archiving conundrum for libraries involves the advent of full-text journals online. Can libraries safely drop their subscriptions to the paper editions of these journals and be sure there will always be an archive of back issues to refer to online? Especially since "full text" often doesn't mean that all the journal's contents, cover to cover, are online. The jury is out on that one.

Standardization of Terminology

Capital punishment or death penalty? Which words should you use?
It's not clear-cut when you use the Web.

When you look at a record for an item on a library catalog, you can be certain that at least one individual examined that item and made decisions, based on standardized cataloging rules, regarding its overall description and which subject headings to assign to it. On the Net, the majority of indexing is accomplished with indexing software programs, with no standardization between programs. The automatic indexing of Web sites makes searching on the Web far more of a guessing game when it comes to choosing search terminology.

Web search engine creators are competitive, leading to more variety instead of more standardization in search terminology and techniques.

Since each search engine on the Net wants to be the one search engine that people use, they have no reason to hold hands and share standards with other search engines. As commercial entities, they want to be perceived as unique and offering different advantages to attract customers.

There are pros and cons regarding this competition among search engines. On the con side, it can drive researchers crazy. A common and appropriate complaint about the Internet is that it is, overall, messy.

The pro side of the nonstandardization between Web search engines? It allows the creators of search engines to continually bring forth new ideas on the best way to access information. With no rules to confine them, they can experiment with different methods of best matching the mind of the researcher to the information he or she is seeking. Hopefully, ultimately, the best of the methods will float to the top and then be more or less standardized across the Web. This is already occurring informally. As one search engine rolls out its latest upgrade, seven other engines quickly unveil a virtually identical option.

Standard terminology is used in libraries, hard copy periodical indexes, and better quality online subscription databases.

Library catalogs, commercial databases, and print periodical indexes all have specified controlled vocabulary by which they classify the contents of their databases or indexes. By knowing the preferred terminology of a certain database or index, you can more efficiently choose words that describe your topic. If I know that *capital punishment* is the preferred terminology, then I won't bother typing *death penalty*. The controlled vocabulary is usually in the thesaurus or index and can usually be found as an online option or, sometimes, as a separate printed resource.

Libraries also share records representing the items they own.

Libraries have an efficient method for sharing the information they've cataloged, using a distributed cataloging infrastructure. That means when one library catalogs a book based on established cataloging standards, the record produced can be shared with many other libraries. This cooperative process, facilitated by the Online Computer Library Center (OCLC) and the Research Libraries Group (RLG) in the U.S., is emblematic of the nonprofit nature of libraries.

Ease of use
Both online and print research methods can be easily learned.
Searching the Internet and other online systems is deceptively simple. It's easy to throw a few words into a search engine and have some sort of result rush back. Often you're lucky and pull up some wonderfully relevant information. And sometimes you keep pulling up the Yemen the Clown home page even though you're trying to learn of the economic climate in Yemen. Once you learn the most commonly used online search techniques, discussed in chapter two, and start perusing help screens, the Internet becomes a simple and effective research tool.

Libraries, like the Internet, are deceptively simple. Researchers will toodle around forever at online library catalogs without any actual plan in mind. Sometimes that works just fine, and sometimes it's a colossal waste of time. Once you understand the basic arrangement of most libraries and frequently used search techniques, both outlined in chapter two, libraries are more than manageable. And hopefully, an incredibly helpful librarian is on hand to lend assistance if needed.

Being schooled in interviewing techniques makes interviewing easy.
What could be difficult about talking directly to an expert on the phone, in person, or online? Plenty, such as not having all your questions prepared beforehand or having an expert who has a lot of information in his head but is not very talented at translating it for the layman. Professional writers and aspiring professional writers would be well served to read some books and articles on interviewing techniques, including *Creative Interviewing* (Allyn & Bacon, 1997), *Interviews That Work: A Practical Guide for Journalists* (Wadsworth Publishing, 1991), and *Interviewing Practices for Technical Writers* (Baywood Publishing, 1991).

Browsing a book is easy.
Sometimes it's simpler to thumb through a print compilation than an online one. As you flip from one printed page to the next, certain numbers or words catch your eye and you can stick your fingers in at least three sections of the book while you check back and forth between pages.

And of course, you can't balance a computer on your head to practice good posture.

Space and speed considerations
Bits and bytes don't take up much space.
The typical unabridged print encyclopedic set runs in excess of twenty printed volumes. If you have space for a computer and its accessories, you can get an encyclopedia online or on CD-ROM, the latter having the ability to store the equivalent of 275,000 double-spaced typed pages.

Top quality connections make online searching fast.
The speed of your modem and/or the way you're connected will dictate the speed of your Internet searching. If you find the going is slow, increase your speed by turning off the graphics. Most Web browsers give you the option of loading text without pictures.

It's easy to waste time online.
If it turns out that what you need is full text online, great—you found some facts in a flash. Just don't beat a dead computer. If you're online for a while and you've used the techniques you learned in this book and still aren't coming up with anything, move on! Weary people often come to the library with stories of having spent five hours on the Internet when what they needed was in the library, and vice versa.

It's also worth mentioning that even when items are available full text online, they aren't always fast to load. Some take many minutes to "open" and then are awkward to look through, and they're usually too long to make printing desirable.

Libraries can be fast.
After you've read this book you'll be able to pop into a library and at minimum know where to best begin. If your question is tricky, you should grab—figuratively, of course—the closest librarian to help you get started.

Timeliness
If it's new, it's probably on the Net or a commercial online database.
Books aren't the place to look for something that happened last week, yesterday, or ten minutes ago. Many months or longer may pass before a final manuscript is published.

It's becoming common for the news on the Internet to "scoop" the television and radio media, or at minimum, to simultaneously transmit the information. This makes the Internet a top resource for timely information.

Some of the timely online information is not available for free. There are

Start Early

Whenever possible, *give yourself time to do your research.* Perhaps the book you need isn't on the shelf and needs to be ordered through a bookstore or interlibrary loan. You find that the article you need from a 1949 medical journal has been neatly razor bladed out by a royal moron, and it's not available online. Maybe the site you need on the Web is under construction and not available. Or your Internet service provider is providing you with nothing but busy signals. Research has stumbling blocks. But if you give yourself time, these minor setbacks won't phase you. Additionally, you may need more time than you think as you make discoveries along the way that take you in a different direction than you'd originally intended.

online databases, for example, that update stock prices constantly. They're not free and they're not inexpensive.

Another advantage to having information in electronic format is the fact that it can be updated more easily. If three numbers in a 333-page book need to be corrected—forget about it. You'll never know until a second printing—if there is one. Online, the errant figures would be gone and replaced as soon as they were discovered.

The first information you find isn't always the best.

Finally, keep in mind that the most in-depth, carefully considered, and overall accurate information will likely be found in follow-up materials that didn't have to be produced in a rushed manner or were shored up with the complete facts once those facts were gathered.

Interconnected information
You can click from subject to subject online.

The Web, with its hypertext capabilities, is rather incredible when it comes to linking information resources. A well-constructed Web site will not only supply information on a particular topic, but also recommend links to other sites on that topic.

New library catalogs do more to connect information than ever before. Catalogs mounted on the Web at your library may allow you to seamlessly move from that catalog to the Internet and on to commercial databases that your library subscribes to.

Print resources also lead to related resources.

Interconnected information is available through print resources, but it's not very flashy. The references at the end of articles, book chapters, and books lead you to related writings and experts. But then it takes some legwork to follow up.

Experts recommend other experts.

It's rare that you'll talk to one expert who can't recommend a follow-up interview with another expert. Ask them.

Serendipity

Despite the following hundreds of pages of advice on how to do efficient information gathering, I'll admit that one of my favorite methods of finding information is through serendipity—that is, stumbling upon gems of information by chance. Browsing is a great research method if you have the time.

Print surfing.

Browsing the aisles of a library or bookstore at random is so enjoyable it's amazing that it's free and legal. When browsing in a library I do recommend doing a little "structured browsing" by at least starting at the location of a known and desired book, placing you in the subject area you're interested in.

Net surfing.

Browsing is also appealing on the Web. Since almost all Web pages have pointers to other Web pages, you can easily jump from intriguing page to intriguing page. On the down side, I often discover that an hour has elapsed and I have jumped twenty pages ahead to sites that satisfy my entertainment needs but not my research needs! The Net can be downright *entrancing*.

Reproducibility
More copying possibilities using electronic information.

On a PC you have many options for saving and reproducing the information you're staring at on a Web page or another online resource. In addition to being able to get a hard copy printout, you can also save it to disk or hard drive to edit,

snip, reformat, or browse at your leisure. You may also have the option of
E-mailing the text to a colleague or yourself for examining or downloading later.

Books are clunky when it comes to reproducing.
A book? Well, of course you can photocopy pages, and you can scan printed text
into a computer, but such computer peripherals are not universally available in
homes or libraries at this point.

Cutting, pasting or copying text manually is a tedious business. Cutting and
pasting and copying text using a computer is a time-saving endeavor that insures
greater accuracy when quoting a passage within your writing. For this book I cut
and pasted the Internet addresses into the text to be sure I didn't mistype them.

Comprehensiveness
Not everything is on the Internet.
Believe me. It's not. There *are* myriad gems and incredible opportunities for
connecting with experts, and sometimes you find just what you need there, but
not everything is on the Internet—especially not everything serious researchers
need. And the number of "dead links"—i.e., links to sites that no longer exist—
is downright infuriating.

Not everything can be found in a library.
Now that statement seems easier to believe, doesn't it? The public is aware of the
limitations of even the largest library collection.

Remember that the same limitation does apply to the Internet, experts, trusted
colleagues, and bookstores. If you want to access the known information in the
universe, don't restrict yourself to one method of research.

CHAPTER 2

Research Techniques and Strategies

An Overview

"My sources are unreliable, but their information is fascinating."

—Ashleigh Brilliant

B eing savvy to basic research methods and the structure and content of online and print information repositories will be the foundation of your information-gathering efforts. That means when you have a research question (and want reliable information), you'll know where to look for it and how to get to it. This chapter examines libraries, online library catalogs, and the Internet.

Different Types of Research Facilities

Libraries and research centers are everywhere. Different types cater to specific populations and excel in different subject specialties. Choose the ones best suited for the topic you're pursuing.

Public Libraries. Public libraries build their collections based on the interests of the community they serve. For example, the New York Public Library makes sure they carry the weekly newspaper *Back Stage*, covering theater, television, and motion picture events and opportunities, and Denver Public Library's Western History Department subscribes to the *Western Livestock Journal*.

Unfortunately, many sparsely populated communities can only support libraries with small collections. Fortunately, with the proliferation of online systems such as *WorldCat*, a database which lists the holdings of libraries worldwide, you or your librarian can usually determine which library in your state, the country, or the world, owns the material you need. You can then borrow materials from around the globe via your library's interlibrary loan service at low cost or no cost.

Commercially based information delivery services will also obtain obtain such material for a fee. Check for such services in print or online telephone directories under Information Services or Information Retrieval Services, through the *Burwell World Directory of Information Brokers* (also available on the Web at http://www.burwellinc.com), or the Association of Independent Information Professionals home page at http://www.aiip.org.

Academic Libraries. Like public libraries, academic libraries serve their community—their campus community. The materials they select support the curriculum of their institution. So, for example, a university that supports a master's program in education should have a good collection of materials related to curriculum development and behavioral problems in schools.

Academic libraries also carry specialized scholarly journals that focus on academic topics. Such resources are essential for student researchers since professors will normally insist that much of their work come from such journals.

Visit a College Library
Whether or Not You're a Student

Though there is some crossover in the holdings of academic and public libraries, academic libraries focus on collecting materials of a scholarly nature, i.e., specialized materials written by educated experts in the field. Since you'll often need such specialized information, investigate academic libraries whether or not you're enrolled at a college. Many are open to the public.

Many college and university libraries allow members of the public to use the library at no charge. Other academic libraries charge a small annual fee, and some, like Princeton University Library, charge a rather princely sum. (At the time of this writing the cost at Princeton was $18 a week or $150 a year for access to the library, and a $380 annual fee for both access and borrowing privileges.)

Special Libraries. Special libraries exist in museums, government agencies, societies, research centers, businesses, hospitals, churches, and associations. With their tight subject focus, such libraries may be just what you need for a particular project. For example, a library at a botanical garden would have horticultural materials, and the library of a hiking society would offer resources on outdoor recreation safety and techniques.

Many special collections are open for browsing, some only lend their materials through interlibrary loan, and some are completely closed to the public. Still, why not follow my mother's advice when it comes to libraries that are closed to the public: "Ask! What can it hurt?" A polite phone call or a succinct letter will often gain you entrée or, at the very least, advice.

Special Collections/Archives. Special collections and archives of materials may also be found within academic and public libraries. Libraries receive gifts of special collections ranging from rare books, personal libraries and belongings of celebrities or scholars, diaries, art objects, correspondence, short runs or first editions of books, locally significant writings, photographs, posters, and paintings. For example, the Chicago Public Library maintains the Chicago Blues Archives, a repository of audio and visual recordings, promotional materials, and other artifacts related to blues music. The University of Maine's library is the recipient of materials from author Stephen King, including drafts and galleys of his published writings and typescripts of his unpublished works.

The archival records of the agencies of the U.S. government are housed in the National Archives and Records Administration (NARA), National Archives Building, Seventh St. and Pennsylvania Ave. NW, Washington, DC 20408, Phone: (202)501-5400, URL: http://www.nara.gov. For more NARA information see chapter eight.

Finding Libraries: Online and Print Guides

The print directories below point you to the kind of library you need in terms of specialized collections or convenient geographic location.

American Library Directory. 2 Volumes. New Providence, NJ: R.R. Bowker. Annual.

> A geographically arranged guide to all types of libraries in the U.S. and Canada. Each entry supplies contact information, size of staff and holdings, subject interests, and special collections.

Official Museum Directory. The American Association of Museums. New York: R.R. Bowker. Annual.

> This directory profiles over seven thousand U.S. museums and organizations such as aquariums, nature centers, historical societies, planetariums, and zoos. Many of them have specialized library collections, including the Museum of Tobacco Art & History in Nashville, Tennessee, which includes a library of books and articles relating to tobacco, and the Fire Museum of Maryland in Lutherville with a 480-volume library.

Subject Collections. 7th edition. Lee Ash. New York: R.R. Bowker, 1993.

> Writing about Mark Twain? *Subject Collections* names eighteen states with

collections brimming with Twain material. Investigating poultry breeding? Libraries in Iowa and Massachusetts can help you out. Arranged under almost nineteen thousand subject headings, this directory pinpoints North American libraries specializing in different research areas. See also the annually produced *Directory of Special Libraries and Information Centers* (Detroit: Gale) with over twenty-three thousand pointers to special collections.

Most libraries have their catalogs online on the Web or accessible via telnet or dial-in connections. Two online pointers to libraries are the *Libweb: Library Information Servers via WWW* at http://sunsite.berkeley.edu/LibWeb/usa-pub .html, where you can search by type of library (e.g., public, academic, or special), and designate specific regions; and the *Yahoo! Libraries* section at http://www .yahoo.com/Reference/Libraries, a page that supplies pointers to public, academic, and special libraries in such subject areas as Performing Arts, Sports, Latin American Studies, Native Americans, Health, and Lesbian, Gay and Bisexual Resources, just to name a few.

A notable online library is *The Library of Congress* at http://www.lcWeb.loc .gov. The Library of Congress, 200 years old in the year 2000, began its life with a collection of books acquired from Thomas Jefferson. This Washington, DC-based library exists to make information available to Congress, other government agencies, and the people of the U.S. The vast Library of Congress catalog is searchable at its Web page along with special collections that contain some full-text documents and photographs. The Library of Congress is the largest repository of recorded knowledge in the world, collecting and cataloging materials in all areas except technical agriculture and clinical medicine, which are covered by the *National Agricultural Library* (http://www.nal.usda.gov) and the *National Library of Medicine* (http://www.nlm.nih.gov) respectively.

How Libraries Are Arranged

Though every library has its unique points, there are universal elements in most U.S. libraries. Familiarize yourself with these common aspects so any library will look familiar.

Classification schemes

The two major subject classification systems used by libraries are the Dewey decimal system and the Library of Congress classification system (LC system). These systems place the millions upon millions of books, videos, CDs, tapes, and

Library vs. Bookstore

When looking for printed materials, sometimes a bookstore is the best source and sometimes a library. Keep these factors in mind when deciding where to go:

- A bookstore may carry the newest and most popular reference books. A library keeps books around for researchers even when they've lost their cachet for the buying public.
- A bookstore will have the best selection of the newest books and most outrageous titles. Many libraries eschew "fringe" publications such as materials written by New Age publishers or the extremely conservative or exceedingly liberal press.
- Books with common elements may be placed in different areas of a bookstore or library. At a library, the catalog helps you identify those sources, and indexes are available to help you piece together information from thousands of magazines and newspapers, both historic and modern.

other items in logical order. Both systems use letter/number combinations to create a unique "address" for each book, referred to as the call number, and insure that items on like topics are found near each other.

The Dewey decimal system, invented by Melvil Dewey in 1876, is a classification system that divides materials into ten major subject groups. It is most often found in school and public libraries. The Dewey call number assigned to each library item starts with a three-digit number, with each number grouping representing a particular subject area.

Here's a list of the subjects associated with each numerical grouping in the Dewey system:

The Dewey System

000-099	General Works, including bibliographies, encyclopedias, library science, journalism, and publishing materials
100-199	Philosophy and psychology, including metaphysics, epistemology, logic, and ethics
200-299	Religion and mythology
300-399	Social sciences, including statistics, political science, economics, law, commerce, education, and customs
400-499	Language and linguistics

500-599	Natural sciences and mathematics, including physics, astronomy, chemistry, earth and life sciences, and zoology.
600-699	Applied sciences, including engineering, medicine, home economics, agriculture, and manufacturing
700-799	The Arts, including architecture, drawing, painting, photography, sports, recreation, and performing arts
800-899	Literature and rhetoric
900-999	History, biography, and geography

So, you'd go to the 200s to stroll through the religious tomes, and if you were in the mood for philosophy you'd head for the 100s.

Most academic and research libraries use the Library of Congress classification system, or LC system. This system was originally created to organize the Library of the Congress of the United States, and it's more expandable and flexible than the Dewey system. A series of one to three letters at the beginning of each call number represents different subject areas.

Library of Congress Headings

A	General works, including encyclopedias
B	Philosophy, psychology and religion, including logic, parapsychology, aesthetics, and ethics
C	Auxiliary sciences of history, including archaeology, numismatics, epigraphs, heraldry, genealogy, and biography
D	History, general and Old World
E	History, United States (General)
F	Local U.S. history and history worldwide
G	Anthropology, geography, and recreation, including cartography, oceanography, folklore, customs, sports, and dancing
H	Social sciences, including statistics, economics, finance, transportation and communication, commerce, and sociology
J	Political science and public administration
K	Law
L	Education
M	Music
N	Fine arts, including architecture, sculpture, drawing, painting, printmaking and engraving, and woodwork
P	Language and literature, including how-to books on writing

Q	Science, including mathematics, astronomy, physics, chemistry, geology, natural history, botany, zoology, anatomy, physiology, and microbiology
R	Medicine (The National Library of Medicine [NLM] uses W for Medicine and related subjects. Major medical collections often use the NLM scheme.)
S	Agriculture
T	Technology, including industrial engineering, mining, building construction, photography, handicrafts, and home economics
U	Military science
V	Naval science
Z	Bibliography and library science

Each call letter expands further with different combinations of letters and numbers designating particular subjects. In the LC system you'll find those religion and philosophy books you were trolling for in different sections of the B area.

Here's an example of a call number in both the Dewey and LC systems for William Zinsser's renowned book, *On Writing Well: An Informal Guide to Writing Non-Fiction* (New York: HarperPerennial, 1998): In LC the Zinsser book can be found at PE1429.Z5, while in Dewey it's at 808.042Z66on. Though call numbers for the same item may vary from library to library since catalogers have some leeway in each cataloging system, call numbers for a specific title are generally the same from library to library.

Library Hopping

Familiarize yourself with several of your local public, special, and academic libraries. Discover which subjects they excel in and what special services or remote access they offer. Becoming familiar with them now will save you time later.

Librarians

Call them what you will: librarians, cybrarians, information intermediaries or even "Hey, you." Librarians are information experts and hold master's degrees in information studies, information systems, or library science. Ideally, this group keeps up with cutting edge information sources, search techniques, and technology. Consult with a librarian whenever you feel unsure of where to begin or how to continue with your research. A librarian will often have an interesting recommendation or two.

Reference books and reference databases

The majority of the print resources recommended in this book are **reference books**, the kind you refer to for definitions, statistics, subject overviews, concise biographical information, addresses, facts, laws, court cases, and chronologies of events. Reference books include encyclopedias, almanacs, dictionaries, handbooks, chronologies, directories, yearbooks, atlases, and gazetteers.

Familiarize yourself with the LC call number or Dewey decimal section of your library's reference collection that represents your area of interest. For example, if you're a psychology major, browse the reference books in the BFs in LC or the 150s in Dewey. If you're writing an article in the field of music, visit the M section for LC or the 780 area for Dewey. The right reference book can save you hours of time by synthesizing related information in one place. It may help uncover "hidden" information difficult to identify through a catalog or index.

Many Titles and Databases Are Alike

You won't find every print or online resource I recommend in every library you enter. But don't yell at the librarians. Tell them the resource you're interested in. They'll let you know if they have another source that's nearly identical. The publishing world is nothing if not repetitive.

Online Library Catalogs

Remember card catalogs? Or maybe you've at least seen them in the movies! In the card catalog, each card represented one book. The catalog allowed you to look up books by author, title, or subject. Though a few bemoan the loss of that multidrawered monstrosity (see the article "Discards" from *The New Yorker*, April 4, 1994, v.70, n.7, p.64+), I don't rank in their numbers. When it comes to library catalogs, online is better.

Online library catalogs are available to you in libraries and from your home or office via either a dial-in connection, a telnet connection, or on the Web. Ask your library what remote options they offer.

Your library may refer to the catalog as a PAC, which stands for public access catalog, or an OPAC, for online public access catalog. Many libraries name their system with an acronym or a catchy name. For example, the library catalog for the *Metropolitan State College of Denver* at http://www.cudenver.edu/public /library is called Skyline and the online system for *Drexel University* in Philadelphia is called Dragnet, http://www.library.drexel.edu.

Unlike card catalogs, which generally led you to only one format of information (e.g., only books or only films), online catalogs tend to identify most or all of a library's holdings in one database: books, films, magazines, government publications, videos, CDs, and other electronic and media formats.

Searchable elements in online library catalogs

Online catalogs are easy to use. Just like the old card catalogs, you can still search by author, subject, or title, though different systems use different terminology. In one catalog the term AUTHOR may be preferred, while in another you'd use NAME to perform the same search. Subject searching might be called TOPIC or WORD searching. These catalogs are designed to be simple to master after using the system a few times. If you think you'll be using a particular online system often, learn the advanced searching techniques. Shortcuts will allow you to dump the easy menus and work faster.

Online catalogs also enable you to go beyond the choices of author, title, and subject searching. Other search possibilities may include limiting your search by date; confining your search to a particular material format, like maps or videos; finding materials in a foreign language; searching for resources from a particular publisher; and combining the author's name and subject words to pull up information.

Each resource in an online catalog is represented by a **record**. Common elements in a record for a book, for example, include:

- Title.
- Author(s), editor(s), or illustrator. The author's name is usually followed by his or her birth date and then death date if applicable.
- Publisher's city, publisher, year published.
- Number of pages.
- Whether or not there are any illustrations, indicated by the abbreviation *ill.* This is handy to know when you must locate a book that has pictures in it.
- Sometimes, a summary of the topic of the book, or, a practice that is becoming more common, a list of the chapter titles in the book.

- Call number and/or code that gives the physical location of the book.
- A listing of words that describe the contents of the book. This section will usually be labeled: subject headings, entries, descriptors, or terms.

Online searching techniques: persuading the catalog to find what you need

One of the great advantages of searching any online system is the ability to quickly link two or more concepts, something that was awkward in the days of the card catalog. Most online systems allow you to do **Boolean** searching, that is, combining words in ways that exclude some keywords and include others so you can come up with the perfect brew for finding information on your subject.

Common Boolean search strategies may be illustrated by using the terms AND, OR, and NOT. For example:

Subject: You need some quotes from baseball players. So you try the Boolean operator AND for your search. In the online catalog you type:

baseball and quotes

The AND guarantees you'll pull up all records that have both the word BASE-BALL and the word QUOTES in it. The system will reject any record that does not have both concepts in it.

Illustrated, here's what that search looks like:

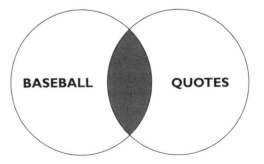

The shaded area represents the sources you want which are those containing both concepts you selected. When I did this search in *Clevnet*, the Cleveland Public Library's online catalog at http://www.cpl.org, I received a list of seven titles, including *Baseball's Greatest Insults* (New York: Simon & Schuster, 1984)

and *Baseball's Funniest People* (New York: Sterling, 1997).

Subject: You realize that some quotations from baseball players might also show up in general sports quotation books. So you do a more encompassing search, integrating the Boolean operator OR into the search by typing:

> (baseball or sports) and quotes

Now the system will perform your request in the parenthesis first, and create a set of all records that mentions SPORTS or BASEBALL. It then combines that new set with the word QUOTES, finding only those sports or baseball books that have quotes in them. Visually, that search would look like this:

When I entered this search into *OhioLink* at http://olc1.ohiolink.edu/search/, an online system that searches fifty-six Ohio library catalogs, I pulled up twenty-eight items. Some were just baseball quotation books and some were sports quotation books such as the *Dictionary of Sports Quotations*, (Routledge & K. Paul, 1987).

Subject: You want information about Paul Simon, the politician, not Paul Simon the musician. Using the Boolean operator NOT will tell the system to exclude records containing certain keywords. So you might try this NOT search:

> paul simon not music

Be careful with NOT searches. They may be useful in narrowing down a search if you get too many records, but they might also get rid of records you really want. Personally, I rarely do NOT searches.

Some databases "assume" an AND. That is, if you type in two words next to each other, say POVERTY CITIES, it assumes you want to do the Boolean AND operation and will search for all records that have both those words occurring in

Search by Organization or Call Number

When searching an online catalog remember that an "author" of a publication may actually be an organization. You may guess, for example, that the Department of Transportation has compiled statistics you're looking for. So, if the online system you're using is capable of a combined author/subject search you would do a search combining the phrase DEPARTMENT OF TRANSPORTATION and the word STATISTICS.

Another handy way to search online is call number searching, and here's a scenario to illustrate why: Let's say you're searching a library's catalog online, from your home, and, by doing a keyword search, you come up with a wonderful book on your topic. Knowing that books on similar topics are shelved next to each other you think, hmmmm, I wonder if there are other useful books on the shelf near the book I found? By searching by the call number of the promising book, the system lists all books that show up in order before and after that book, in effect, allowing you to browse the shelves of a distant library on your screen.

the record, no matter where in the record they occur. Other systems will not assume an AND and will instead check for the exact phrase POVERTY CITIES, which is not what you want at all! If it doesn't find those two words in the exact order they appear, right next to each other, it will report zero results. Always check the directions for the database you're working on so you know what operations are assumed and which you must apply.

A note concerning AND, OR, and NOT: Unfortunately, there's no widespread standard insisting that all publishers of search software use the same Boolean search terms. Thus, any number of commands will perform the operations I just described. I've seen the term ANY used for OR, and the + symbol for AND. As long as you understand the Boolean searching concepts, it doesn't really matter what they're called; you'll be able to do a precise search for what you need. Read the instructions for the system you're using.

Natural language is not quite a reality

Have you ever seen the Hepburn/Tracey classic film *The Desk Set*? In that fanciful flick, Spencer Tracey, as the computer programmer, creates a computer he calls Emerac, a.k.a. Emmy. Emmy can answer **natural language** queries, that is, questions formulated the way we speak naturally. Though the movie is decades old,

I'm afraid we still aren't quite at the natural language stage yet.

If you type in the question WHAT'S THE POLITICAL SITUATION IN NICARAGUA?, you probably won't retrieve much of the information you're after. First the computer will throw away the **stop words** it detects, meaning words that occur so frequently that the database is designed to ignore them so as not to slow the search process. Two examples of stop words are *the* and *in*.

Thus, in our hypothetical search, the system looks up the words WHAT'S, POLITICAL, SITUATION, NICARAGUA, finding records that contain all four of those words. I tried this search on *Marqcat*, the library catalog for Marquette University's Memorial Library in Wisconsin (telnet to libus.csd.mu.edu). The system had no books with all four of the nonstop words and only one with two of them: WHAT'S and NICARAGUA. The book title retrieved, *Journalism: Stories From the Real World*, was irrelevant to my topic. The word WHAT'S was from a chapter in the book called "So, What's Your First Question?" and the reference to NICARAGUA was from a chapter in the book called "Doing the Legwork in Nicaragua."

This doesn't mean Marquette University students should complain bitterly to their librarians that they are bereft of books about Nicaragua. My next search, when I ignored natural language words, was more fruitful. I did a keyword search using the two words that most clearly described my topic: POLITICS and NICA-RAGUA. The system then sought titles that contained those two words; I received more than 150 titles, with a number of the newest ones being very relevant.

There have been advances with natural language systems. If you find a database that purports to support one, read the help screens.

Free searching vs. controlled vocabulary: choosing words to feed the online catalog

Using any keywords you like when searching an online catalog is **free searching**— you throw in a word and hope it shows up somewhere. Once you get a few good records using the free-search method, look at the part of the record that lists **subject headings**, which may also be called **terms**, **entries**, or **descriptors**. Those are the words that describe the contents of the resource. Use one of the words or word phrases listed to find even more materials on your subject.

For example, let's say you're looking for books dealing with methods for quitting smoking. You try a keyword search in your library's online catalog by typing in SMOKING QUITTING. You get only one record for a book called *The Enlightened Smokers Guide to Quitting* (Rockport, MA: Element, 1998). Though

Well-Chosen Subject Words for Online Searching

When searching online, it's often wiser to use just a few keywords. Putting in too many keywords may inadvertently lose relevant records as the system tries to find records that match every word you've submitted.

that sounds interesting, you'd like to find more books on the topic. Looking at the part of the record that designates the descriptors, you find these four phrases that describe the book: SMOKING—CESSATION PROGRAMS, CIGARETTE HABIT, TOBACCO HABIT, and MIND AND BODY.

So you go back and try one or more keyword searches with these new word combinations. Trying a search with the phrase CIGARETTE HABIT brings up many useful titles, including *Cigarettes: What the Warning Label Doesn't Tell You.* This book gives you another idea for a keyword search since the subject descriptor portion lists a new possibility: TOBACCO TOXICOLOGY.

This is an example of a search using **controlled vocabulary**, the practice of referring to listings of standardized terminology that you'll use to search with. The descriptors listed on each online catalog record come from a standardized list called the Library of Congress Subject Headings, or the LC Headings.

The LC Headings are collected in a multivolume set of books—simply a big list of the words used in card and online catalogs throughout the U.S. Since it's difficult to choose the best term or phrase for your search in our world of synonyms, a quick flip through these volumes will lead you to the best search terms for a particular subject. For example, other phrases found in the LC Headings related to the subject of quitting smoking include SMOKING— PSYCHOLOGICAL ASPECTS, SMOKING—PHYSIOLOGICAL ASPECTS, and PASSIVE SMOKING.

LC Headings are available in most libraries. I must admit that more often than not I simply use the method I outlined in the smoking example: Take a guess at a subject heading, then pull official subject headings from pertinent records that appear.

Other tips on subject searching in an online library catalog
Search the right database.
A library's online system may consist of more than the catalog to that library's holdings. There may be a few, a few dozen, or a few hundred other databases

Be a Walking Thesaurus

Always think of varied ways of describing your topic. For example, if you're doing research on the death penalty, remember that it may also be referred to as *capital punishment*. A quick look in the *Library of Congress Subject Headings* also suggests *executions and executioners, death row,* and *hanging.* This tip is especially relevant when doing Internet searching where controlled vocabulary is a hit-or-miss affair.

available. For example, at the library I work for, any one of our in-house terminals connects to over three hundred databases and the Internet. So be certain you're in the database you mean to be in—they often look similar.

Try a narrow topic, but if you can't find it, think of a broad one.
You may be more familiar with the advice: Narrow your subject—focus! And that's good advice. But broad searching can unearth items others have left on the shelf. For example, let's say you're writing an article about the question of the legalization of marijuana, coming up on a town ballot. You want articles or books discussing the pros and cons. You try a search on the online catalog using the words MARIJUANA and LEGALIZATION. You come up with five books, all checked out.

At this point you could curse the other researcher who has the books, or you could try a broader search, using the words DRUGS and LEGALIZATION. Books you find under the broader heading will likely have a chapter on marijuana, or at least some insight into the pros and cons of legalizing any unlawful narcotic.

The Internet Defined
The **Internet**, or **Net**, is a network of separate computer networks worldwide, some tiny, some huge, all interconnected, and all able to "speak" to each other. **Internet service providers** (ISPs), make it possible for you and your personal computer to tap into this network of networks.

Though the Internet had its roots in the 1960s, its popularity rocketed beyond the academic and research world with increasingly common use of the **World Wide Web**. The **Web** or **WWW** has made the Internet friendly by adding graphics, sound, and motion and allowing quick access to related information links.

Uniform Resource Locators—URLs

Just as Dewey Decimal and Library of Congress call numbers act as the address for items in a library catalog, a **Uniform Resource Locator** or **URL** is the address of a World Wide Web location. Most URL's start with *http://*. This stands for **hypertext transfer protocol**, the protocol by which computers exchange information on the Web.

Other information in the URL includes the host's name, which is the name of the computer or server location from which the information is being received, a two- to three-letter designation for the type of server it's on or what country the server is located in, the directory path, often followed by one or many subpaths, and a file name. So, for example, in the URL for accessing the section of the *Mental Health Net* site, dealing with mental depression, the uniform resource locator http://www .mhnet.org/guide/depress.htm is interpreted as: *http* stands for hypertext transfer protocol; *www* stands for World Wide Web site; *mhnet* is the name of the host site; *org* indicates that this site is sponsored by a nonprofit organization; *guide* is the name of one of the subpaths for this site; *depress* is the file name; and *htm* indicates that the whole shebang is written in hypertext markup language.

In the United States, six commonly used three-letter codes designate the type of server or **domain**:

.com—commercial

.edu—educational

.gov—government

.net—network

.org—non-profit organization

.mil—military

Examples of each:

Ben & Jerry's Homemade, Inc.—http://www.benjerry.**com**

University of Southern California—http://www.usc.**edu**

The Peace Corps—http://www.peacecorps.**gov**

The U.S. Army—http://www.army.**mil**

Alternate Access, Inc. (an Internet service provider)—http://www.aa.**net**

United Way of America—http://www.unitedway.**org**/

International addresses (for sites originating in non-U.S. countries) may have a two-letter code at the end of the server/location, such as, .uk for the United Kingdom and, .au for Australia.

Case-Sensitive URLs

URLs may be case sensitive—meaning it *does* matter if you don't capitalize a letter that should be capitalized. So if a URL is presented with some of the letters capitalized, be sure to capitalize them when you type them in.

Gopher, telnet, dial-in, and FTP

Before the dawn of the Web, text-based Internet was the only game in town. Text-based just means that you search for the same information you now find on the Web, only without any graphics or hypertext links. You can still search the Internet in text-only through software such as Lynx.

Before the hypertext capabilities of the Web, **gopher servers** were used to navigate the Internet. Each gopher server is a menu listing of subjects and each subject leads to related subject menus—basically, the text version alternative to pointing and clicking with a mouse. These menus ultimately lead to text-based Internet sites, i.e., documents online with no interactive hypertext or shimmering graphics.

Some organizations are still mounting text-only on the Internet available via gophers because of the time-saving advantage of not needing to first convert the text into an HTML format that will then be Web ready. However, most gopher servers are now closing. But some sites persist, and if you're referred to one you can connect to it through an Internet service provider, through telnet (see below), or via a Web browser. On the Web, a URL that takes you to a gopher site starts with *gopher://* instead of the usual *http://*.

When using the Internet, you'll likely encounter a few additional situations that are holdovers from the time when Internet was only text-based. You'll sometimes see a resource identified as a **telnet** site. By typing in the telnet address of a remote computer server, you can access certain databases, including library catalogs and full-text documents. For example, the online catalogs for The Alliance, a group of Colorado libraries, may be accessed by telnetting to the telnet address pac.coalliance .org. When you telnet, you're literally logging on to another computer.

You'll usually have the ability to telnet through software provided by your Internet service provider. There will be some sort of telnet prompt unique to the software you're using where you type in the telnet address. Most World Wide Web browsers automatically connect you to telnet sites when you type in *telnet://*

before the telnet address. So, using the Colorado libraries alliance as an example, I'd type *telnet://pac.coalliance.org* into my Web browser. This sets the telnet software into motion and allows me to connect. If there was no telnet software in place, a message would appear to alert me to that. Telnet destinations are shrinking as sites move exclusively to the World Wide Web, but excellent telnet destinations are still available. And during the times the Web slows to the pace of paint drying, I use the telnet option to reach my library and its commercial databases.

You may also **dial-up** to remote databases. When you dial-up (or dial-in, as it's sometimes called), you enter a location's phone number into your computer's communication software, and the modem phones that computer to connect to it. For example, in addition to being able to telnet into the Colorado library catalogs mentioned previously and being able to access them on the Web, you can also dial-in to them at (303)758-1551. Most new computers now have the communications software and modem built in.

You may learn that a particular document of interest can be **FTP**'d. FTP stands for **File Transfer Protocol**, a program that's designed to pull a file stored on one computer and transfer it to another. The files may be documents or software. Many servers allow an **anonymous FTP**, where you don't need a special password to the computer where the document is stored but instead type *anonymous* when asked for your name. How do you FTP a document? Via the major Web browsers (see p. 42), you need only type *ftp://* before the FTP address to connect to sites. There are also FTP client programs that allow you to FTP documents. Two popular ones are WS_FTP for Windows and Fetch for Macintosh systems.

What's Available on the Internet?

The Internet is a mini-universe of human thought, intellect, foible, and ephemera. For authors, the Net can be seen, at minimum, as a gold mine of ideas waiting to be excavated. Following are major categories of services and destinations of most interest to researchers. Specific sites and options will also be listed under appropriate headings in the chapters that follow.

Home pages for associations, organizations, companies, and agencies

The **home page** is the starting point on a Web site—akin to the cover of a book, its table of contents, and the welcome wagon rolled into one. A Web site is usually comprised of numerous Web pages.

The question is no longer *what businesses and organizations have Web home pages*, but *which do not?* And the answer to that question: fewer and fewer. Well-conceived home pages for nonprofit and for-profit organizations will supply most or all of the following: a history of the organization, including biographical information of employees or members; a description of services, goals, and projects; full-text documents related to the organization; career, internship, or volunteer opportunities; answers to frequently asked questions (referred to as **FAQs**); graphics of products or offerings; information on how to contact the organization; and links to related sites. I've used organization home pages to:

Check a company's financials

Find a university's class offerings

Learn of a museum's internship opportunities

Look at a restaurant's menu

Examine the seating chart for a theater

E-mail and discussion groups

E-mail is a valuable research tool. Being able to rapidly, inexpensively exchange written messages with experts worldwide is a terrific way to gather information. Tapping into groups of experts via online discussion groups increases the potential for gathering information.

You can join online groups that discuss particular topics or just check the current and archival discussions that such groups have had. Online discussion groups go under monikers such as listservs, electronic conferences, forums, special interest groups, discussion groups, newsgroups, and bulletin board services.

Some online groups, like **listservs**, require you to subscribe to be able to participate. Once you subscribe, the "conversations" of the group members automatically appear in your E-mail. You can read them, delete them, and if you choose, reply either to an individual or to the entire list.

Joining a listserv or other mailing group is easy. There are two basic E-mail addresses associated with each listserv. One address is used for system operations such as subscribing or unsubscribing to the list; the other is the one you'll use to send messages to the members of the list once you've joined. A common beginner error is to send a subscription request message to the entire list of readers.

Listserv is actually the type of administrative software that helps make it simpler to maintain these online groups. Since the program "understands" certain commands sent to it, such as the subscribe and unsubscribe messages, a live person doesn't have to acknowledge each new member and manually register them.

Other administrative software for online groups are known as **listproc** and **majordomo**.

The typical format for subscribing to a listserv is to send an E-mail message to the **SYSOP**, or systems operator. That's the address used for subscribing. The address will follow this format: listserv@hostname. Leave the subject header blank and put only the following words in the body of the message:

> subscribe[space]nameoflistserv[space]yourname

For example, when I joined a listserv for business librarians called Buslib-L, I sent a message to the system address listserv@idbsu.idbsu.edu, and put the following in the body of the message:

> subscribe buslib-l ellen metter

The subscription format varies as seen in the following sample mailing lists. What topics do listservs and other discussion groups cover? Just about anything you can imagine—even if you have a creative and colorful imagination! Just a few examples:

Adoption-Reform List. A forum for the discussion of legal issues surrounding adoption. To join, send *subscribe adoption-reform yourfirstname yourlastname* in the body of an E-mail message to listserv@maelstrom.stjohns.edu.

Descartes-L. Discussion of Rene Descartes' philosophy. To join, send *subscribe descartes-l your name* in the body of an E-mail sent to listserv@bucknell.edu.

Ferret-L. Participants exchange information about pet ferrets. To join, send a message to Ferret-L-Request@cunyvm.cuny.edu. In the body of the message, put your name and say you'd like to join.

Physics. For talk of anything related to what the list owner refers to as the "accepted" study of physics. To join, send the words *subscribe physics* in the body of an E-mail sent to listproc@u.washington.edu.

To find discussion groups focusing on certain subjects of interest, check these Web pages:

CataList: The Official Catalog of Listserv Lists.
   http://www.lsoft.com/lists/listref.html
Directory of Scholarly and Professional E-Conferences.
   http://www.n2h2.com/KOVACS/
Liszt: The Mailing List Directory. http://www.liszt.com
Tile.Net. http://tile.net/listserv/

Once you subscribe you'll receive instructions on how to mail messages to the entire list, how to temporarily halt the in-flow of messages if you go on vacation, and how to access the list archives, if they are maintained. Save those.

I've found listservs and other discussion groups to be helpful when I know I have a question that would be easy to answer if the right person could see it. For example, I once needed to track down customer service videos in the field of recreation. Using Liszt: The Mailing List Directory, I found SPRENET, a listserv of recreation professionals nationwide. I joined the group and politely put out my query, letting the list know of the resources I checked before asking for their expertise. Not only did I get great responses, I was able to share my answers with others in the group who were interested.

If you're joining a list simply to ask a question, explain in your message that you've done some preliminary work first. The subscribers to listservs are often busy professionals who are happy to assist with the tough questions but less tolerant of those who pop on the list hoping the listserv people will do their work for them. If you have time, "lurk" on the list for a while, i.e., see what types of topics the list addresses and how they tend to deal with those issues. Each list has a personality, you might say, and you'll quickly get a sense of the acceptable parameters for participation.

Listserv Overload!

Many listservs generate an avalanche of messages that automatically appear in your E-mail. Don't be surprised if you open your E-mail after joining a few listservs and find a hundred or more messages waiting for you. I enjoy the convenience of listservs because they simply appear in my E-mail, but I've gotten into the habit of quickly deleting the messages that don't look promising.

Like listservs and other mailing lists, **Usenet newsgroups** are online discussion groups covering topics in all categories from the serious to the absurd, from the genteel to the raunchy.

The **Usenet**, a worldwide computer network where newsgroups are hosted, was created as a place for the first Net techies to exchange ideas and just chat. Newsgroups don't automatically pop into your E-mail; you go to them. Newsgroups are accessed through software known as a **newsreader**, usually supplied by your Internet service provider. Most Usenet newsgroups are easily accessible through many Web search engines. Newsgroup participants can browse through archival and ongoing messages or **posts**, reading the commentary and joining in when desired.

The letters at the beginning of the newsgroup moniker let you know what general category it falls into. Some examples:

alt "Alternative" topics, with some but not all being outside the mainstream. *Alt* designated groups don't have a moderator like most groups.

bionet Biology-related topics.

comp Computer-related subjects.

misc Miscellaneous categories.

rec Recreation, hobbies, pastimes.

sci Science-related subjects.

soc Social, societal issues.

Sample newsgroups whose topics are obvious by their names:

alt.politics.homosexuality

comp.human-factors

sci.environmental.waste

To find newsgroups appropriate to your topic, use sites on the Web created for just such a purpose, including *Deja News* at http://www.dejanews.com/ or *Usenet Info Center Launch Pad* at http://sunsite.unc.edu/usenet-i/home.html.

And finally, online discussion groups are attached to any number of Web pages. If you find a site representing something you're interested in, there may be a chat group associated with that page. The link to the chat group will be prominently displayed.

Cyber-libraries

Most libraries' online catalogs can be accessed remotely through the Web, via a telnet address, or by dialing in, as discussed earlier in this chapter. It's convenient to search a library catalog before you actually go to a library; when you get there, you'll be ready to grab what you need. Searching the catalogs of faraway libraries is a handy way of discovering what items necessary to your research you might order through interlibrary loan.

Two URLs that were already mentioned but bear repeating will bring you to Web-based library catalogs:

Libweb: The Library Information Servers via WWW.
    http://sunsite.berkeley.edu/LibWeb/usa-pub.html
Yahoo! Libraries Section at http://www.yahoo.com/Reference/Libraries

Two databases, *WorldCat* and *Eureka*, don't search specific library catalogs, per se, but search vast catalogs of information and identify which libraries around the world own a particular item. Such catalogs used to be available for behind-the-scenes library use only, to aid with the cataloging of books and to assist interlibrary loan departments in finding libraries they could borrow material from. Now they're available in many libraries for public use. They're not free on the Web—ask your library if they subscribe. These databases are also wonderful places to check if that idea for a book you're thinking of writing has ever been executed by anyone else. (Sometimes you'll find that your idea has been taken but hasn't been updated in forty-five years. Bingo. Also use the Library of Congress catalog mentioned previously for this type of search.)

Full-text periodicals online: electronic journals and E-zines

Quite a bit of the full-text from magazines, journals, newspapers, newsletters, and newswires is floating about on the Web in a number of different forms. Some periodicals exist only in an online format, like *The On-line Journal of Ethics* at http://condor.depaul.edu/ethics/ethg1.html, and some are the electronic version of print periodicals, such as the newspaper *The LA Times* at http://www.latimes.com. Full-text articles are also included as part of commercially produced indexes such as the *General BusinessFile ASAP* and the *General Science Abstracts Full Text*.

For pointers to E-zine sites and more information about online periodicals, take a look at chapter four under Finding Full-Text Magazines and Journals Online.

Full-text books online: E-Texts

Though only the tiniest fraction of a fraction of all books ever published in paper are online, those available are known as **E-texts** or **electronic texts**. Most books online are either those whose copyright has expired or books from new authors available for a fee. Some publishers and authors have experimented with putting entire books online at no charge, finding that in some cases the placement of the book's full text on the Web actually stimulates sale of the print edition. You'll also find many instances of the first chapter of books being available electronically, which interests the reader in wanting to read more. Another common practice is to place the supplement to a book online.

One major attempt at gathering E-texts online has been done by Project Gutenberg. The Project Gutenberg site is the repository of classic books that are no
longer covered by copyright and are in the public domain, such as *Aesop's Fables*,
The Return of Sherlock Holmes, and *Walden*. Project Gutenberg has a goal of
placing ten thousand texts online by the year 2001. Pointers to E-texts on the
Web include:

European Literature. http://www.lib.virginia.edu/wess/etexts.html.
   Texts in Western European languages other than English.
The On-Line Books Page. http://www.cs.cmu.edu/books.html
Oxford Text Archive. http://firth.natcorp.ox.ac.uk/ota/public/index.shtml
Project Gutenberg. http://www.gutenberg.net.

Miscellaneous Web offerings

Many kinds of information available on the Web that won't be discussed in-
depth in this book are worth a mention, including:

Bookstores

Though I love browsing real, live, dusty bookstores, I also enjoy the ease of
ordering a book online. Sample sites:

Amazon.com. http://www.amazon.com
Booksmith. http://www.booksmith.com
Midnight Special Bookstore. http://read.msbooks.com/MSBooks
   /homepage.html
Tattered Cover Book Store. http://www.tatteredcover.com
VarsityBooks.com. http://www.varsitybooks.com
   Reduced price college textbooks

Also try *BookWebs CIBON: Comprehensive Independent Booksellers Online Network* at http://www.bookWeb.org/bookstores/ from the American Booksellers
Association, or *Acses* at http://www.acses.com—both pointers to numerous online
book shops.

Internet relay chats and other multiuser environments

Internet relay chats, also known as **IRCs**, **chat groups**, **chat rooms**, and **chats**,
allow you to schmooze online in "real" time, akin to a conference call via the
telephone. Though many of these chat sites are used for entertainment, their use
is blossoming among researchers recognizing the advantages of real-time discus-

sions with others in geographically disparate places. Different chat **channels** focus on different topics, with new topics often spontaneously created.

Since subtle meanings may be lost during online chatting and even more so in a group discussion, chat participants use **emotes**, which are descriptions of what the participant is "doing" in reaction to a comment or in combination with a reply. Emotes indicate what their body language or sheer presence would indicate if the group were physically together. Some emotes include *listen, chortle, yawn, wink, bow,* and *cackle.* Participation in chat groups takes practice. I find them awkward, but thousands disagree as evidenced by the number of participants displayed online at any given moment. Chat environments that provide visuals are in their infancy; I think that's the innovation that will make chats universally used.

You can find chat channels on the opening pages of most search engines, including Yahoo! and Hotbot. Special Web sites that will get you to chat areas include:

Looksmart Yack. http://looksmart.yack.com

Chat Seek: The Chat Only Search Engine. http://www.chatseek.com

Web Chat System. http://pages.wbs.net/Webchat3.so?

Other multiuser environments go a step further than IRCs in that they create a virtual environment using verbal descriptions of space and dictating parameters of movement and behavior. This medium was originally the province of players of the role-playing game Dungeons and Dragons, the "spaces" participants played in were known as Multiuser Dungeons, or Muds. Now that Muds are also used for other purposes, they are often referred to as Multiuser Domains. One guide to Muds is *The Mud Connector* at http://www.mudconnector.com. Other virtual environments showing up in academic applications are Moos, Mud Object Oriented.

Classified ads

Classified ads on the Internet run the gamut from homes for sale to help wanted. They may be updated more rapidly than print ads. Ads appear in numerous locations on the Web, including the online versions of traditional newspapers such as *The Denver Post* at http://www.denverpost.com, and newsgroups dedicated to selling, buying or trading items, like alt.auto.parts.wanted.

Images and graphics

Though most of the images and graphics on the Web are copyright protected, some photographs and animated files are available in the public domain. Clip art Web site locations include *The Clip Art Connection* at http://www.ist.net/clipart /index.html and *Public Domain Images* at http://www.pdimages.com.

The search engine *Arriba Vista*, http://www.arribavista.com/, is an image search engine, where you can search for an image by keyword, such as HOME-LESS, or by a category, such as CORPORATE. Once you find an image, Arriba will also identify the original page on the Net it was pulled from. An image search can also be done in the Pictures and Sounds section of the *Lycos* search engine at http://www.lycos.com/picturethis/.

To find specific images you can also use the image function on the search engine *AltaVista* at http://altavista.digital.com. Typing *image:filename* pulls up Web pages with images that have specific descriptive filenames. So, for example, if you need a nice picture of a kitty, type in *image:cat* in the AltaVista search engine to pull up sites featuring cat pictures. In *HotBot*, at http://www.hotbot.com, just mark the "images" box when you do a search.

At the time of this writing, a beta site for Virage's Video Cataloging technology, in partnership with AltaVista, created a searchable index of a video. Using this software you can jump around to specific parts of a video on the Web based on keyword searching. The beta test site, featuring the video and transcript of the Clinton grand jury testimony of August 17, 1998, was, and hopefully still is, at http://video.altavista.com/cgi-bin/avsearch. If not, try the *Virage* home page at http://video.altavista.com/virage/.

Personal home pages

Some personal home pages represent individuals interested in promoting their businesses, while others want to share their hobbies or scholarly pursuits. Then there are those that seem like little more than narcissistic exercises of interest only to the page creator and his or her mother. A tilde (~) somewhere in the URL usually indicates that a Web page is operated through a personal account.

Personal home pages can be valuable. Page creators often fill their pages with links to sites of interest to them. There have been times when I found a terrific link because somebody in some little town linked it to his home page. Though many personal pages won't be found with search engines, some will. A search engine dedicated solely to searching personal home pages is Ahoy! at http://ahoy .cs.washington.edu:6060/.

Shareware and freeware

You can download free and inexpensive software programs from the Web. They range from action-packed 3-D games to packages that help you do your taxes. With **shareware**, you download the program and then give it a trial run. If you like it and keep it, you're "on your honor" to pay for it. Programs known as **freeware** are actually free and may be distributed at no charge because the creator is simply interested in sharing it, or it may act as a promotional tool for a commercial endeavor.

Downloading from the Internet always brings the possibility of computer viruses that can literally destroy your computer. If you download from the Web, be sure you have virus detection software. Whenever possible, if the file isn't too big, download to a floppy disk first and then run it through a virus detection scan. Also, downloading shareware is not always the most straightforward of operations; if you're not a techie yourself, you may want to take one to a very nice dinner and have her nearby when you try your first download.

Shareware links appear on the opening pages of most search engines. Other places to find shareware on the Net include the *Shareware Directory* at http://www.sharewaredirectory.com, or *Shareware.com* at http://www.shareware.com.

Shopping

The Internet accepts plastic. Products on the Internet include traditional L.L. Bean–type companies (http://www.llbean.com) which have always offered merchandise via catalogs; offerings of collectibles, such as the rock music and film memorabilia site *Rock and Real Memories* at http://www.beatlemaniashoppe.com; as well as individuals offering custom-made items such as quilts, like the site at http://www.quiltsmith.com.

Postcards

Postcard sites let you create semipersonalized Web postcards. Sites offering free postcards include:

Blue Mountain Arts. http://www.bluemountainarts.com/
Eastman Kodak Company. http://www.kodak.com.
   Click "Picture This Postcards."
Poteidaia Post Office. http://www.randar.com/postcard/
   Xena/Hercules Postcards.
Web Weaver U.S.A. http://www.Webweaverusa.com/postcard.html

Travel reservations

To book airplane flights or make hotel reservations try *Microsoft Expedia* at http://www.expedia.com, *Travelocity* at http://www.travelocity.com, or *The Trip.com* at http://www.thetrip.com.

Searching the Web: Using Web Browsers and Search Engines Effectively

World Wide Web browsers are the software applications that allow you to search the Web and enjoy its graphical and hypertext offerings. When using a Web browser, type in a particular URL, press the enter key, and away you go.

The most frequently used browsers are Netscape Navigator, presented as part of the Netscape Communicator package, and Microsoft's Internet Explorer. Some ISPs supply their own browser, unique to their company. Two typical browser features that are useful to researchers include bookmarks and file folders.

Choosing and organizing favorite Web sites

Don't type in the URL of your favorite Web site every time you want to access it. Setting **bookmarks**, as they're called on Netscape, or designating **favorites**, as they're referred to on Explorer, stores URL addresses, allowing you to quickly find and click on your most used sites.

Some people's bookmark sites are as packed as a thirty-year-old address book, one that's fallen apart and been taped together in a jumbled fashion. These junk drawer bookmarks can be organized using **file folders**. Once you have a few dozen sites bookmarked, you'll be fortunate if you can recall the precise name for any of them. So, organize by subject. Using file folders, you can name groupings of URLs by appropriate subject headings. For example, some of my file folder names include Bookstores, Library-Related, and Fun.

When you pop into Netscape or Microsoft's Internet Explorer, you also have the option of choosing which Web site you'd like to be greeted by. I've changed mine based on projects I've been working on, different times of the year, or pure whim. In Netscape Communicator, choose "edit" from the top pull-down menus and then "preferences" to set your preferred opening page. In Explorer choose "view" then "options" and then "navigation."

Using search engines

". . . Although Web search tools often appear to be quite sophisticated and complex, they are actually remarkably simple. This is *not* to say that they are simple to use well, but rather that none of them do as much as Web searchers tend to think they do. Not one of them searches the entire Web—or even comes close to it. None of them achieve the flexibility and power of traditional commercial database vendors like DIALOG. Unlike a library catalog, no search engine provides or utilizes a controlled vocabulary or an authority file to standardize access to information sources.

". . . By and large—Web search engines are the result and embodiment of ongoing automated processes designed to perform 'quick and dirty' collecting and indexing of Web pages."

—*Authoritative Guide to Web Search Engines.* Susan Maze, David Moxley, and
Donna J. Smith. New York: Neal Schuman Publishers, 1997.

Search engines, a.k.a. **Web searchers** and **search directories**, are essential in helping you find what you need on the Web. They allow you to either pick from categories of subject headings or, like online library catalogs and other commercial online databases, submit a word or phrase that describes the information you want. These search engines then retrieve lists of hypertext links representing different Web sites.

No search engine searches the Web completely. Although some Web pages on these search engines are selected by humans, all search engines use software programs known as **robots**, a.k.a. **'bots**, **spiders**, **worms**, **ants**, **fish**, **crawlers**, or **intelligent agents**, to retrieve Web pages and index them. These robots may be directed to find specific keywords found in the URL, the title, the text, or a hidden portion of the document that contains **metatags**, keywords and descriptions of Web pages chosen by its author; or instructed to gather Web pages from specific types of sites.

Search directories supply subject guide access, like Yahoo! and Magellan. At Yahoo! and Magellan, live indexers evaluate Web sites and place them in a hierarchical subject tree, going from the general to the specific. Such subject trees may begin with a broad subject such as art and then branch out to a subcategory like photography, then offer a link to photography galleries and collections, and so on. Such structures may lead the researcher to excellent pages—perhaps even the cream of the crop. But great sites may also be missed.

A more flexible method of searching, though more likely to bring in the ugly with the lovely, is offered by most Web search engines, allowing researchers to find Web pages by typing in words or phrases that describe their topic, just as online library catalogs and commercial databases are searched. But the results are not as consistent as those produced in online library catalogs and commercial databases for several reasons.

Because the of the massive size of the Web and its shifting contents, every site cannot be cataloged by a human being. To index on such a large scale, the operators of the search engines rely on automatic indexing software, mentioned earlier, to make the Web pages it has gathered—usually millions of them—accessible to the searcher. The automatic indexing software accurately indexes some pages but inaccurately pinpoints others, resulting in some strange search results.

Facts in a Flash

What to Do When the Web Address Seems Wrong

It's inevitable, unfortunately, that some of the Web addresses I supply in this book will be defunct when you go to find them. Sometimes a site seems to be gone but actually, the address has just changed a little. So, go back and put just the beginning part of the URL in (the part ending in *edu, com, org, gov, mil,* or *net*). Many times this will bring you to the opening page where you can click to the section you want.

Also, this book includes Web addresses listed at the end of sentences, meaning a period (.) may appear at the end. A URL never ends in any type of symbol other than a forward slash (/), though it does not *have* to end in a slash.

Familiarize yourself with the advanced workings of several engines. If you don't get the expected results in one search engine, try another. Also, go into the "help" documentation offered by each product. They should at minimum alert you to the syntax and features of that search tool. Become extremely familiar with at least two; learning the most advanced capabilities of the search engines you choose will increase your chances of retrieving useful results.

Here's an example of the vastly varied lists of sites retrieved by different search engines. I was looking for ideas on how to enjoy a vacation in Miami. I did a quick-and-dirty search by just typing in the two words MIAMI TOURISM. This search brought these opening lists of results in the following search engines:

AltaVista. http://www.altavista.digital.com.

Found 1,825,040 sites. The first site was a useful Miami tourism page sponsored by Air France. The second site was a link to a story about a Miami tourism coordinator receiving an award. Not useful. Others on the opening page linked to tourism in different areas of Florida and a Miami tourism page in French.

Excite. http://www.excite.com.

Found 424,655 sites. The page opened with just what I wanted: a little map of Miami and pointers to all types of tourism information from http://city.net.

WebCrawler. http://www.webcrawler.com.

Found 24,648 sites. There were several immediately useful links such as *Miami Information Access* at http://miami.info-access.com/. Others got me to Miami information in a more roundabout way, such as the link for the Miami Project to Cure Paralysis.

Yahoo! http://www.yahoo.com.

The search retrieved two Yahoo categories, the first a bull's-eye: Recreation: Travel: Convention & Visitors Bureaus: U.S. Cities: Miami.

Useful results were pulled from all of the search engines using a simple search. There was virtually no overlap between top-ranked results for each engine. The moral: If you don't like what you find in one search engine, try another.

Search engine conventions

Web search engines share many commonalties. The ones offering subject categories list those categories. You then click on the appropriate categories and subcategories to find Web pages.

All search engines also provide a box or boxes in which you type your search request. Once you submit the search you'll either be told you retrieved "0" hits or that you got a certain number of hits. The first ten or so will be displayed in citations consisting of the URL and either a brief description of the Web page it represents or the first few sentences of that Web page. Clicking on the URL, which will be highlighted, is how you'll connect to the Web page.

Common search engine search methods:

Simple Searching and Advanced Searching. A search engine's home page may simply show a tantalizing box to drop keywords into or you may have the option of clicking on an icon or area labeled something along the lines of "Advanced" or "Power Searching" to fully reveal your search options. Click it! Also check the general "help" documentation to see which conventions to use when using the general search page as opposed to the advanced search page. Conventions may or may not overlap.

Boolean Searching on the Net. Many search engines encourage the use of natural language queries. As mentioned earlier in this chapter, a natural language query is one in which you would input a sentence such as WHAT IS THE MEANING OF LIFE? Though there have been innovations in natural language searching on the Web, it's still flawed. Being familiar with Boolean searching is essential.

Boolean searching, explained earlier in this chapter, is available in all search engines. To quickly reiterate, Boolean searching lets the researcher combine words and phrases in such a way that the search software pulls up the most relevant resources. Connecting words or phrases with AND retrieves sites containing both words or phrases specified, e.g., TUDOR AND ARCHITECTURE; combining words with OR pulls up sites that have at least one of the words or phrases specified, e.g., CAPITAL PUNISHMENT OR DEATH PENALTY; and combining words with NOT ignores any documents that contain the word or phrase following NOT, e.g., PYTHON NOT MONTY.

Some search engines use the actual words AND, OR, and NOT for Boolean searching while others use such search connectors such as $+$, $-$, $/$, and & to perform the same type of searches. Note: Search engines often require that the Boolean search terms be capitalized—sometimes the operation will not work if the terms are not capitalized. Examples of AND, OR, and NOT searching in different search engines:

AltaVista and HotBot:
In advanced mode:

> AND or &
> OR or |
> AND NOT or ! in AltaVista; NOT or ! in HotBot

In general mode:

> Putting a plus sign ($+$) in front of a word indicates that the word *must* be retrieved, so the search: $+$FATS $+$EXERCISE in the general search would be equivalent to FATS & EXERCISE in the advanced search. Putting a minus sign ($-$) in front of a word indicates that the word must not appear in a document.

Excite:

Use:

> AND
> OR
> AND NOT

Excite can also use the aforementioned plus (+) and minus (−) operations, and additionally has a power search page with different search options.

Yahoo!:

Yahoo!'s Search Options page lets you specify, by checking a choice, if you want to do an AND or OR search. It also accepts the plus (+) and minus (−) convention.

Plus Sign Searching

The plus sign (+) as used in search engines is worth a second mention. I urge you to use it. Many search engines use the plus-sign convention, that is, putting a + in front of a word to indicate that the word must be included in the final results of a search. This convention is available in many search engines. I use it constantly to pull up more accurate results. Thus, instead of typing BRONCOS FOOTBALL, I type + BRONCOS + FOOTBALL. Without the plus signs I could pull up some records that mention only football—not the Broncos.

Phrase Searching. This concept can make or break your search: You need to be sure a search engine is searching a phrase *as* a phrase. If you don't take that precaution, it often ruins the search. For example, if I'm searching for the phrase BILL GATES and I don't specify that I only want to search those two words together, in that particular order, then I may also retrieve sites that refer to *Bill* Smith, expert at building fences, and *gates*. The most widely used method for restricting a search to a phrase search is by enclosing the search in quotation marks, e.g., "BILL GATES." But check to see if your preferred engine uses a different method (the quotation marks may be misinterpreted if they are not the correct method for phrase searching in that engine). I frequently combine phrase and plus sign searching, e.g., + TRIAL + "BILL GATES."

Relevance Ranking. Different search engines rank their results based on criteria determined by that engine. Each engine follows a ranking algorithm determined by the engine's developers, placing varying degrees of importance on whether the keywords requested fall in a page's title, body, URL, or metatags. This ranking is generally done automatically when you enter a search, though some engines require particular action, unique to each search engine, to activate a ranking search. A **score**, usually expressed as a percentage, will often appear next to each site the engine retrieves. For example, if 100% appears next to the first site listed, it indicates that the engine is positive this site meets all the requirements of your search and that you should be blissfully happy with the contents. The 100% indicates that one or both of the keywords appeared everywhere that the algorithm deemed most important. For example, Yahoo! says that documents matching more occurrences of a keyword will be ranked higher than those with fewer; documents matching words found in the title area are ranked higher than those found in its body or URL, and categories matching higher up in the Yahoo! tree hierarchy are ranked higher than those deeper in the hierarchy.

Case Sensitive. Generally, search engines aren't case sensitive and will look for results that are capitalized, all lowercase, or any combination thereof. But there are some quirks in different systems. For example, if you capitalize a word in Alta Vista, you'll only find sites that contain that word in a capitalized form. If you submit a word in lowercase, it will search for that word in both upper- and lowercase.

Truncation. Using **truncation**, also known as **stemming** or a **wild card**, allows you to quickly search variations of a word without typing in every variation. For example, if the wild-card character is $ then performing the search COMPUTER$ will tell the search engine to look for any words with the word *computer* as its root. Thus COMPUTER$ will retrieve any document with the words: computer, computers, computerized, computerization, computer-aided, etc. Truncation options are also available in virtually all library catalogs and commercial online databases. Not all search engines have truncation, so check their help screens to see if they do. Three search engines that use an asterisk (*) as wild cards are AltaVista, HotBot, and Yahoo!

No Need to Type http://. In both Netscape Navigator and Microsoft's Internet Explorer, there is no need to type the *http://* when you type in a URL. The http:// is considered a default, so you can just start typing in the address after the http:// point. For example, if I were going to the page for *Box Office* magazine, I'd simply type *boxoff.com*. Though this may seem like a negligible savings of time, you'll come to appreciate it! If the URL starts with *Telnet://*, *FTP://*, or *gopher://* you'd need to type that in.

Language. You may retrieve results where the majority of sites are in a language you do not speak. Look for an on-screen option limiting the search by language, offered by most search engines. This will allow you to limit the results to only the language you wish to retrieve.

Domain Limiting. Domain limiting allows you to only retrieve sites designated by particular domains, i.e., edu, com, gov, org, mil, or net. In HotBot and AltaVista you limit to domain using the format *domain:domainname*. For example, to limit a search to educational sites, you'd search for DOMAIN:EDU and probably combine it with a keyword. So your search might be SEMICONDUCTORS AND DOMAIN:EDU to find mention of the word *semiconductors* only in educationally related Web pages. In *HotBot*, at http://www.hotbot.com, you can also limit to a specific domain by going into the section labeled "more search options."

Be Suspicious of Zero Results

If you retrieve zero results from a Web search, consider several possibilities, including typos, the need for fewer keywords, or choosing different keyword(s). Be sure you use alternate spellings, e.g., *color* and *colour*, or *nonprofit* and *non-profit*. Also, one of the words you selected may be a **stopword**—a word that occurs so frequently that the system has been set to never search it. Common stopwords on the Web and other online databases are *the, a, be,* and *to. HTML* is a stopword on HotBot.

Proximity/Adjacency Operators. Proximity searching, another feature widely available on the Web and in commercial online databases, specifies the nearness of one keyword to another. For example, proximity searching could limit a search to finding two words in the same sentence, paragraph, or within a certain number of words apart from each other.

In AltaVista the word NEAR or the tilde symbol (~) finds documents containing both specified keywords within ten words of each other. So the search MARKET NEAR SHARE would pull up pages containing the phrase MARKET SHARE in them or containing a sentence such as *Computext's **share** of this enormous **market** is 40%.*

Choosing Keywords. On the Web it's important to be a living, breathing thesaurus, able to guess which words are likely to retrieve what you need. When you do find one excellent resource, scan its contents to see what words are used. It will present new keyword possibilities to you.

> **Finding the Relevant Part of a Web Page Quickly**
>
> The "find" feature is important to anyone doing research on the Net. You can quickly find out where a specific word or phrase appears on a Web page by using this feature, available on both Internet Explorer and Netscape Navigator. Just press the *ctrl* key simultaneously with the letter *F* key (or, pull down the "edit" choice from your tool bar and choose "find"). This retrieves a search box that you type your word or phrase into. When you press the *enter* key you'll find the cursor has moved to and highlighted the word or phrase you're seeking.

Date Searching. Date searching is not always advisable on the Web. The date you find may be the page's copyright date or simply the date some small item was updated. And many pages of interest have no date at all. Still, search engines do usually offer the choice of limiting by date, so try the feature with my *caveat emptor* in mind.

HotBot offers the option of limiting your search to only those pages that have changed in the last three or six months. Though that change may be awfully insignificant, the fact that the page was tweaked at all means someone thinks it's still viable.

Search Engine Bells and Whistles. More and more, search engines are fashioning themselves to be destination spots as opposed to simply jumping-off points. They are cramming their opening pages with links to the latest news, stock market quotes, sports scores, television schedules, movie listings, and offers for free E-mail. They list broad subject channels, allowing you to select those sites you'd like sitting on your computer desktop for quick access. You may choose your favorite search engine based solely on the offerings on the opening page. That's certainly valid, but I do urge you to familiarize yourself with at least one other search engine.

Choosing Search Engines and Directories

These are Internet pages that present a selection of search engines and directories, including those that specialize in newsgroups, gopher sites, and other miscellaneous destinations. Two such meta pages are:

All-in-One Search Page. http://www.allonesearch.com
All Known Search Engines. http://www.primenet.com/~rickyj/index.html

Specific engines and directories include:
AltaVista. http://www.altavista.digital.com
Argus Clearinghouse. http://www.clearinghouse.net
Excite. http://www.excite.com
GoTo. http://www.goto.com
HotBot. http://www.hotbot.com
Infoseek. http://www.infoseek.com
Looksmart. http://www.looksmart.com
Lycos. http://www.lycos.com
Magellan Internet Guide. http://www.magellan.excite.com
MSN Web Search. http://www.home.microsoft.com
Northern Light. http://www.nlsearch.com
Snap! http://www.snap.com
WebCrawler. http://www.Webcrawler.com
Yahoo! http://www.yahoo.com

Meta search engines

SavvySearch at http://www.savvysearch.com is an example of a **meta search engine**, (also known as a **metacrawler**, **multisearch**, **parallel search** or **mega-search engine**), a searcher that queries multiple search engines in one shot. Just remember if you apply any advanced search techniques in your search, each engine being searched may interpret the search differently. Still, I do sometimes choose meta search engines and have retrieved valuable sites. Meta engines include:
DogPile. http://www.dogpile.com
     Allows you to "fetch" instead of search!
Mamma. http://www.mamma.com
MetaCrawler. http://www.go2net.com
MetaFind. http://www.metafind.com
Profusion. http://www.profusion.com

Keeping up with the Net

Why don't I simply tell you which search engines are the best? Because new ones appear often and innovations occur rapidly. Beyond keeping your ears open, there are numerous print and nonprint methods for staying as up-to-date as any one

What Are the Joneses Searching?

A fascinating site is at the WebCrawler Search Voyeur, a ticker tape-like banner of the search words Internet users are entering on to WebCrawler. (No names or locations of those searching are available.) It's at http://webcrawler.com/SearchTicker.html.

carbon-based life form can be with the whims of the Web:

Boardwatch Magazine. http://www.boardwatch.com

A reviewer calls *Boardwatch* "one of the most intelligent (as well as opinionated) Internet-related magazines available." *Boardwatch* editors recommend a subscription to the print edition, reminding readers that "you still can't take our Web site to the bathroom with you."

CNET: The Computer Network. http://www.cnet.com

CNET follows the pulse of the high tech companies, products, and happenings, with general news articles, product appraisals, and avenues for chatting with other CNET members. CNET goes well beyond the Net, so non-techies may find it a bit too much. Register to become a user (for free) at http://www.cnet.com; this gives you access to all areas of CNET and enables you to receive their free E-mail newsletter.

Free Pint. http://www.freepint.co.uk/

Free Pint is a free monthly E-mail newsletter from the U.K. that spotlights new quality Web sites and search techniques for specific topics.

Internet Scout Project: Scout Reports. http://www.scout.cs.wisc.edu/scout/

The Scout Reports alert you to new Web sites or significant changes of note in existing sites. Begin an E-mail subscription, at no charge, to any of the subject-specific reports covering science and engineering, business and economics, and the social sciences. Also browse archival issues at their Web site.

Librarian's Index to the Internet. http://sunsite.berkeley.edu/InternetIndex/

This search engine features two links to new sites: New This Week and Last Week.

Netsurfer Digest. http://www.netsurf.com/nsd/

E-mailed to you weekly, Netsurfer Digest is a guide to interesting news, places, and resources online. It covers a mix of scholarly, professional, and just-for-fun sites and news. Register for your free subscription at http://www.netsurf.com/nsd/subscribe.html.

Search Engine Watch. http://www.searchenginewatch.com

This site contains expert advice on all aspects of search engines including construction, history, innovations, and search worthiness. The Search Engine Watch page can be accessed at no charge, but those who subscribe for $44 per year (at the time of this writing) get additional information, a preview of upcoming articles, and access to a zipped version of the site.

Wired Magazine. http://www.wired.com/wired/

One colleague calls this magazine the perfect example of modern nonlinear reading. With its many sidebars, illustrations, and graphics, the print version of *Wired* looks like a hard copy of an MTV video. *Wired* describes its mission as "chart(ing) the impact of technology on business, culture, life."

Yahoo! What's New. http://www.yahoo.com/new

This page lets you browse new sites added to Yahoo!, listed by subject category.

There are also Web directories that carry selective Web sites only, each rated for its content, including *Britannica* at http://www.britannica.com. Many libraries also maintain such lists of recommended Web sites, such as the *Auraria Library's Cool Net Sites* at http://carbon.cudenver.edu/public/library/reference/cool.html.

Choosing an Internet Service Provider: Options

With the assistance of an Internet service provider (ISP), you can connect to the Internet once you have a computer, communications software, and as fast a modem as possible. The modem and communications software lets you dial-in via telephone lines to the ISP's host computer, your portal to the Internet.

A popular choice is a SLIP/PPP account, ranging from about twenty to thirty dollars per month. SLIP/PPP stands for Serial-Line Internet Protocol/Point-to-Point Protocol. It's a method for connecting directly to the Internet via phone lines. High-speed digital lines known as ISDN lines (Integrated Services Digital Network) are another option for impressively fast access.

Traditional telephone lines may become the less favored or obsolete option for connecting to the Internet as fast cable modems come into use.

There's also the option of having direct access to the Net by purchasing a T1 or T3 data connection, but the cost is high, usually in the thousands of dollars per month.

There are two major types of ISPs. There are companies that solely help you link to the Internet. Using these companies will likely get you a Web browser, E-mail, and software to enable you to access telnet locations, do file transfers, and connect to Usenet groups. Then there are the commercial online services that provide all of the above along with a variety of databases and special-interest discussion groups they create, maintain, or lease.

As a point of history, such services as America Online and Prodigy actually began their lives as insular services that simply let you get to the unique online databases and services they created or leased. Originally, you couldn't even get to the Internet when using a big commercial online service. Now, of course, these companies emphasize the Internet end of their online offerings.

Here are some points to consider when choosing an Internet service provider:

- The ISP should be willing to give you at least a limited demo period, at minimum a few days, at no charge.
- Ascertain it's a *local* call to connect to the ISP. Providers with toll-free connections usually have surcharges. If you plan to travel and use your provider in other areas, try to find a company with local numbers in multiple areas or inexpensive access to toll-free numbers.
- Check to be sure there is reliable, live help available at least during traditional business hours. If you know you're going to need it beyond the nine-to-five work day, there are providers that will help you twenty-four hours a day, seven days a week.
- Seek word-of-mouth recommendations.
- Look for at least 5MB of storage for your account if you think you'll be actively using E-mail, retrieving files, and searching the Web.
- Make sure the ISP can well support the type of computer you have.
- If you want to create a personal or business Web page, make sure you can do so with your ISP. Find out what fees are involved.
- If you don't want to be faced with busy signals, find a company with a good ratio of users-to-phone lines, with an 8:1 ratio being acceptable. During the demo period try to connect during times when you would normally use the service to be sure you actually can connect.
- You shouldn't pay a start-up fee.
- There may be fees for access to commercial databases offered through the ISP. This is a justified additional cost, though keep in mind you may be able to access some of those commercial databases through your local library.
- Find out the details regarding canceling the service. Will you receive a

Smithsonian

GIFT SAVINGS CERTIFICATE

Return this card to give a SMITHSONIAN Magazine subscription

11 issues only $39 - SAVE 49%

Please enter this subscription... ☐ as a gift. ☐ for me. ☐ as a gift and for me.

My name: _____
(Please Print)

Street _____

City _____

State/Zip _____

Gift for: _____
(Please Print)

Street _____

City _____

State/Zip _____

☐ Bill me. ☐ I've enclosed $_____.

Savings are from $6.99 newsstand price. Smithsonian is usually published 11 times a year, but may occasionally publish combined issues, which count as two issues. Add $13 for each Canadian and $26 for each other foreign order. Member discounts may vary. Ninety-nine percent of dues allocated for magazine. Please allow 6-8 weeks to receive your first issue.

A007SL

Visit our website
www.smithsonianmag.com

BUSINESS REPLY MAIL

FIRST-CLASS MAIL   PERMIT NO 50   PALM COAST FL

POSTAGE WILL BE PAID BY ADDRESSEE

Smithsonian Institution
P.O. BOX 420300
PALM COAST, FL   32142-9959

refund if you cancel mid-month or mid-year, or are you tied in to a certain amount of time?

• Flat rate service for unlimited time online is an attractive offer since you don't need to monitor the clock.

Following is a list of four well-known commercial online services. They all offer basic ISP services and usually some special services, such as access to commercial databases or specialized discussion groups. Call for the latest information.

America Online (800)827-6364. http://www.aol.com

CompuServe (800)848-8199. http://www.compuserve.com

Microsoft Network (800)386-5550. http://www.msn.com

Prodigy (800)776-3449. http://www.prodigy.com

Befriend a Techie

I hear writers and students complain of the problems they have had becoming familiar with the technical workings of the Internet. I know I'm fortunate to have a job where an automations expert is a few doors away and can literally hear my whimpers for help. Though much of the Net is now simple, some operations are still baffling. So take an Internet basics class at your local college or continuing education facility. Get a buddy while you're there so you have someone to commiserate with. Or connect with a computer science major at a local community college and give him or her a small hourly wage and lunch to help you with your questions.

Of course there are hundreds of choices beyond the big ISPs, with many offering superb services and reasonable prices. How do you choose a specific provider? Here are some methods for locating and judging Internet service providers:

• Visit a computer store or two and ask what services they recommend.

• There is probably a local computer newspaper in your area with ads for ISPs. Check with your neighborhood bookstore.

• See if your library carries the *Boardwatch Directory of Internet Service Providers.* Or order a copy for about ten dollars from the *Boardwatch* home page at www.boardwatch.com/. It's updated quarterly. The *Boardwatch* ISP Locator is also free at the Boardwatch home page.

- Look under *Internet* in your phone book's yellow pages. There will be a good-size list of Internet access providers to choose from. Ask them some of the questions outlined earlier in this chapter.
- Browse the ads in magazines like *Wired, Boardwatch*, and computer magazines.
- If you're a college student, consult with the campus computer service. Chances are your college offers free or inexpensive E-mail/Internet access.
- If you have access to the Web, check *The List* (http://www.thelist.com), a listing of ISPs worldwide along with what services they offer, prices, and phone numbers. Also check the *ISP Finder*, which lists ISPs by area code, at http://ispfinder.com/cfdocs/isplist/isparea.cfm.
- You can also ask for opinions via Usenet newsgroups such as alt.internet .services.
- Another option for connecting to the Internet is via Web TV. Web TV puts the Internet on your television set, allowing you to manipulate it with a remote, wireless keyboard. Check your local computer/electronics store or their Web site at http://www.webtv.com.

CHAPTER 3

Government Research

Free and Inexpensive U.S. and
International Resources

"Government is too big and too important to be left to the politicians."

—Chester Bowles

U.S. Government Publications

The U.S. government is the most prolific publisher in the world. Though dozens of specific government publications and Internet sites appear throughout this book in appropriate subject areas, this chapter highlights the unique aspects and multisubject usefulness of government publications overall. Publications covering all subject fields are created by both official U.S. government agencies and organizations whose services have been contracted by the government.

Just a few examples of government titles to illustrate their subject variety:

- A poster, *Humane Handling of Animals: It's the Law*, from the Animal and Plant Health Inspection Service of the U.S.D.A.
- A booklet from the National Cancer Institute, *What You Need to Know About Breast Cancer.*
- A book, *Heart of the Storm: The Genesis of the Air Campaign Against Iraq*, written by a colonel of the U.S. Air Force.

And of course the U.S. government publishes the type of publications you'd probably expect, such as laws, treaties, regulations, environmental impact statements, and congressional hearings and reports. Government "documents" may be books, pamphlets, guides, transcripts, reports, maps, periodicals, cookbooks, proceedings, posters, directories, press releases, newspapers, surveys, and, well, you get the picture. Oh, yes—and pictures. Some libraries use the phrase government publications, realizing that documents is a misleading moniker.

Why am I writing a separate chapter on government materials, since many will be examined in the following chapters? A few aspects unique to government documents earn them a chapter:

- The majority of government publications aren't found in general bookstores, so you won't come across most of them by browsing at the local Barnes & Noble.
- The government produces an avalanche of statistics covering an impressive range of topics. In fact, they're the largest producer of statistics in the world. You may find a statistic quickly by going to a government Web page or grabbing a government publication. Being aware of the types of statistics you're likely to find from state, local, and international agencies will assist you when you need numbers.
- Libraries generally house their government documents collections in areas separate from their general collections. This can result in people overlooking their riches. It's still not common to have all government publications integrated into a library's online catalog, so if you want to know what's available, techniques in this chapter will help you.

Government depository collections

A good percentage of the publications released by government entities are available through **depository libraries**. The Federal Depository Library Program was established by Congress more than a century ago to ensure that the American public had access to government information. Depository publications are those seen as having educational value or interest for the public.

There are 1,400 U.S. libraries eligible to receive U.S. depository documents at no charge. These are referred to as **government** or **federal depository libraries**. It's very likely, if you live in the U.S., that one or more are close to your home.

Nondepository government publications—those not given to depository libraries—include those created for administrative purposes and seen as having little educational value, items created for "official use" only, materials classified in the interest of national security, or those that simply don't get into the distribution system.

About half the depository libraries are academic libraries—yet another reason, as mentioned earlier, to familiarize yourself with nearby college libraries. To locate depository collections, ask your librarian or check the depository library locator Web page at http://www.access.gpo.gov/su_docs/dpos/adpos003.html.

Some of those 1,400 libraries choose to be full depositories, receiving every item offered through the depository program, while others are selective or partial depositories. For example, the library I work in has opted to select only those documents most pertinent to the students on campus, which means we receive about fifty to sixty percent of the documents available. A publication like *Cattle and Sheep Outlook Yearbook* wouldn't be useful to us because we don't have an agricultural program. But even libraries without depository status carry some of the more widely used government publications.

Full and partial depository libraries often house their government publications in a separate section of the library and are cataloged by yet another system of classification: the **Superintendent of Documents classification system**. The number/letter combination assigned to each source is referred to as the **SuDoc number**.

The SuDoc classification system works differently than the LC or Dewey system. Instead of arranging items by subject, items arranged by the SuDoc system are grouped by the agency that issued them. The first letter(s) in a SuDoc number tells which agency produced the item.

Superintendent of Documents Classification System:
Major Agency Designations

A	Department of Agriculture
AE	National Archives and Records Administration
C	Department of Commerce
C3	Bureau of the Census
D	Department of Defense
E	Department of Energy
ED	Education Department
EP	Environmental Protection Agency
GA	General Accounting Office
GP	General Printing Office
HE	Department of Health and Human Services
I	Department of the Interior
J	Department of Justice
L	Department of Labor
LC	Library of Congress
NAS	National Aeronautics and Space Administration
NS	National Science Foundation
P	Post Office
PREX	Executive Office of the President
S	Department of State

SBA	Small Business Administration
SI	Smithsonian Institution
SSA	Social Security Administration
T	Department of the Treasury
TD	Department of Transportation
VA	Department of Veterans Affairs
X,Y	United States Congress
Y3	Congressional Commissions and Independent Agencies
Y10	Congressional Budget Office

So if you roam through the L section of shelves arranged in SuDoc order, you'll find publications from the Department of Labor with such titles as *The Monthly Labor Review* and the *Employer's Pocket Guide for Teen Worker Safety.* If you walk through the E section, you'll locate resources published by the Department of Energy such as *The Domestic Alternative Fuel Vehicle Outlook* and *Photovoltaics: Basic Design Principles and Components.*

As you might guess, a classification system that arranges material by the producing organization can play havoc with the concept of placing subject-related items together to assist browsing researchers. Though it may seem the publications produced by one agency would be pretty much on the same subject, it isn't always so. Agencies do research in diverse areas. For example, the publication dealing with kidnapping called *International Parental Child Abduction* is classified near the brochure titled *You and Your Passport* because they're both published by the Department of State.

If particular government publications are in demand, a library sometimes re-catalogs them under a Dewey or LC call number so the item will be in subject order with other highly used materials.

The amount of government information being placed on the Internet is exciting. Government sites on the Web are among the most substantive free resources you'll find. The majority are absolute gold mines of information, not just superficial starting points.

Many government depository items have, in the last number of years, been distributed to libraries in microform format instead of paper format. Microform (filmed copies of the publications) was seen as a less expensive way to distribute and store a large number of documents. But it's not the most convenient format for researchers to work with, and many depository libraries and their patrons were less than ecstatic. The placement of some of the most highly used and sought after government publications on the Web is a welcome development—if you have access to the Internet, of course. And here's a plug for libraries: I recommend you support Internet access at libraries so government information is easily accessible to all.

Government bookstores

The Government Printing Office (GPO) prints, binds, and sells the publications of the Congress and other executive departments and agencies of the federal government. The GPO also administers the federal depository library program, distributing publications to government depository libraries at no charge.

Though many government publications will be accessible at your library, you can also choose to be the proud owner of government titles. The GPO operates twenty-four U.S. government bookstores throughout the United States. Each store carries at least 1,500 of the government's highest demand print and electronic publications, and they will order items they don't have in stock. GPO usually has about twenty-thousand print and electronic titles available.

Government Printing Office Bookstores Listed by State

Alabama	O'Neill Building, 2021 N. Third Ave., Birmingham, AL 35203 Phone: (205)731-1056, Fax: (205)731-3444
California	ARCO Plaza, C-Level, 505 S. Flower St., Los Angeles, CA 90071 Phone: (213)239-9844, Fax: (213)239-9848
	Marathon Plaza, Room 141-S, 303 Second St., San Francisco, CA 94107 Phone: (415)512-2770, Fax: (415)512-2776
Colorado	1660 Wynkoop St., Suite 130, Denver, CO 80202 Phone: (303)844-3964, Fax: (303)844-4000
	Norwest Banks Building, 201 W. 8th St., Pueblo, CO 81003 Phone: (719)544-3142, Fax: (719)544-6719
District of Columbia	1510 H St. NW, Washington, DC 20005 Phone: (202)653-5075, Fax: (202)376-5055
	U.S. Government Printing Office, 710 N. Capitol St. NW, Washington, DC 20401 Phone: (202)512-0132, Fax: (202)512-1355
Florida	100 W. Bay St., Suite 100, Jacksonville, FL 32202 Phone: (904)353-0569, Fax: (904)353-1280
Georgia	First Union Plaza, 999 Peachtree St. NE, Suite 120, Atlanta, GA 30309 Phone: (404)347-1900, Fax: (404)347-1897

Illinois	One Congress Center, 401 S. State St., Suite 124, Chicago, IL 60605 Phone: (312)353-5133, Fax: (312)353-1590
Massachusetts	Thomas P. O'Neill Building, Room 169, 10 Causeway St., Boston, MA 02222 Phone: (617)720-4180, Fax: (617)720-5753
Maryland	U.S. Government Printing Office, Warehouse Sales Outlet, 8660 Cherry Lane, Laurel, MD 20707 Phone: (301)953-7974, Fax: (301)953-8995
Michigan	Federal Building, Suite 160, 477 Michigan Ave., Detroit, MI 48226 Phone: (313)226-7816, Fax: (313)226-4698
Missouri	120 Bannister Mall, 5600 E. Bannister Rd., Kansas City, MO 64137 Phone: (816)765-2256. Fax: (816)765-8233
New York	Federal Building, Room 2-120, 26 Federal Plaza, New York, NY 10278 Phone: (212)264-3825, Fax: (212)264-9318
Ohio	Federal Building, Room 1653, 1240 E. Ninth St., Cleveland, OH 44199 Phone: (216)522-4922, Fax: (216)522-4714 Federal Building, Room 207, 200 N. High St., Columbus, OH 43215 Phone: (614)469-6956, Fax: (614)469-5374
Oregon	1305 SW First Ave., Portland, OR 97201-5801 Phone: (503)221-6217, Fax: (503)225-0563
Pennsylvania	Robert Morris Building, 100 N. Seventeenth St., Philadelphia, PA 19103 Phone: (215)636-1900, Fax: (215)636-1903 Federal Building, Room 118, 1000 Liberty Ave., Pittsburgh, PA 15222, Phone: (412)395-5021, Fax: (412)395-4547
Texas	Federal Building, Room IC50, 1100 Commerce St., Dallas, TX 75242 Phone: (214)767-0076, Fax: (214)767-3239 Texas Crude Building, 801 Travis St., Suite 120, Houston, TX 77002 Phone: (713)228-1187, Fax: (713)228-1186
Washington	Federal Building, Room 194, 915 Second Ave., Seattle, WA 98174 Phone: (206)553-4270, Fax (206)553-6717
Wisconsin	Reuss Federal Plaza, Suite 150, 310 W. Wisconsin Ave., Milwaukee, WI 53203 Phone: (414)297-1304, Fax: (414)297-1300

Freedom of Information Act (FOIA) and the Privacy Act of 1974

Not every glorious word produced by government organizations is distributed to libraries through the federal library depository system. Many agency files, internal documents and the like may or may not be available for public consumption. If

Shopping for Government Goodies Online or on the Phone

You can browse the offerings of GPO bookstores and order online by using the *Sales Product Catalog* (known until recently as the Publications Reference File), located at http://www.access.gpo.gov /su_docs/sale.html. The Sales Product Catalog indexes public documents currently for sale by the GPO as well as forthcoming and recently out-of-print publications. Government publications can also be purchased through the GPO order desk between 8 A.M. and 4.P.M. eastern standard time, Monday-Friday, Phone: (202)512-1800, Fax: (202)512-2250.

you think a government agency has a document you need, FOIA can help.

The Freedom of Information Act (FOIA) was enacted in 1966 to assure, within reasonable constraints, that records in the possession of U.S. government agencies and the executive branch would be accessible to U.S. citizens. FOIA established the doctrine that citizens have a *right* to know and they no longer must prove a *need* to know when requesting a document. FOIA doesn't apply to documents of elected officials of the federal government, those who receive federal contracts or grants, tax-exempt organizations, or state and local governments.

The Privacy Act of 1974 is related to FOIA in that it assists individuals in obtaining access to federal agency records about themselves. Additionally, the Privacy Act also restricts the wholesale distribution of personal information.

Neither FOIA or the Privacy Act guarantees that a citizen can look at any federal record. However, the laws do give citizens the right to request any information and to receive a response to the request. If the request is denied, a reason for the denial must be supplied.

Most government-related home pages have a FOIA section that points the reader to information regarding how to make a request for records. The *Freedom of Information Act Clearinghouse* on the Web at http://www.citizen.org/litigation /foic supplies the text of the act, its amendments, a citizens guide to obtaining federal information under the act, and a listing of administrative and legal contacts at federal agencies who assist those requesting information. You can also contact the Clearinghouse at P.O. Box 19367, Washington, DC 20036, Phone: (202)588-7790.

Finding government publications with databases and indexes

Traditionally, the majority of government documents owned in depository libraries haven't been found in the library's catalog. The massive amount of government documents published made the task of cataloging each and every piece virtually impossible for the typical library. That meant the researcher had to rely heavily on specialized print resources that aided in finding government information.

Now that online catalogs are common, it's finally affordable and feasible for more libraries to include government documents on catalogs along with their other library holdings. Still, documents are not yet universally included in library catalogs, so when you visit a depository library in search of government publications, ask if all the publications are listed in the catalog. Meanwhile, quite a few other options exist for locating government materials.

The *Catalog of U.S. Government Publications*, on the Web at http://www .access.gpo.gov/su_docs/dpos/adpos400.html, is an online index to all government publications distributed to full government depository libraries from 1994 to the present. When searching by subject, title, or organization, this database pulls up records that describe the publication(s) found, indicates which libraries in your area own the item, and gives you the SuDoc number needed to retrieve it from the shelf.

The Catalog of U.S. Government Publications is also available online through the FirstSearch commercial online system, where it is called the *GPO Monthly Catalog*, indexing materials back to 1976. This database is also available online for no charge from the CARL Corporation at telnet://database.carl.org (choose the option "Open Access Databases") under the name *Government Publications* (it also indexes materials from 1976 through the present). It's also available through the Information Access Company on a CD-ROM called the *Government Publications Index*.

The print edition of the Catalog of U.S. Government Publications, titled *The Monthly Catalog to Government Publications*, is available in most larger libraries and indexes depository and nondepository government publications spanning 1895 to the present. Publications marked with a black dot (•) should be at all full depository libraries.

Other Ways of Searching for Government Materials

The Federal Bulletin Board. http://www.access.gpo.gov/su_docs/fedbbs.html.
    Also available at telnet://fedbbs.access.gpo.gov or dial-in: (202)512-1387.

The Federal Bulletin Board is an index to thousands of federal agency documents available free to download.

FedStats: One Stop Shopping for Federal Statistics. http://www.fedstats.gov

Use FedStat to locate statistical publications residing on more than seventy federal agency Web sites.

GovBot: Database of Government Web Sites. http://www.business.gov/Search_Online.html or http://ciir2.cs.umass.edu/Govbot/

With GovBot you can search online government Web pages using key-words. I've found a rather stunning array of publications when searching Gov-Bot, since it dives deeply into documents I never would have thought of looking for. Many of the results are "bad hits," but the good ones make wading through the junk worthwhile.

Government Information Xchange. http://www.info.gov

The Government Information Xchange offers a grab bag of links to popular government Web destinations.

Government Information Locator Service (GILS). http://www.access.gpo.gov/su_docs/gils/gils.html

Designed as the "card catalog" for all executive branch government information, GILS is the name for a network of databases. Each government agency mounts its own database listing the electronic and print resources it produces that are available to the public. Through the GILS interface, you can search all these agencies at once, discovering which agency has what document.

A subject search pulls up records representing pertinent items, just as an online library catalog does. Each record supplies a title, the department that produces the document or nonprint item, a description of the item, and either ordering information or a Web link that will take you to the document.

This all sounds terrific as I describe it, but, at the time of this writing, GILS was still cumbersome, with results that may seem less than straightforward to the typical user. (Since government databases seem to rapidly improve, I hope it will be better by the time you try it.)

Guide to Popular U.S. Government Publications. 5th edition. Frank W. Hoffmann. Englewood, CO: Libraries Unlimited, 1998.

Updated every few years, this book is a listing of highly requested materials produced by departments and agencies of the federal government. It's arranged in subject order under such diverse headings as Consumer Information and Protection; Grants; and Posters and Decals.

InfoMine. http://lib-www.ucr.edu/search/ucr_govsearch.html

InfoMine points to all manner of government-related Web resources, including databases, electronic journals, electronic books, bulletin boards, listservs, online library card catalogs, articles, directories of researchers, and more.

NTIS: National Technical Information Service. http://www.ntis.gov/

NTIS gathers and indexes government-sponsored writings covering U.S. and international scientific, technical, engineering, and business-related research. (It's worth noting that the U.S. government sponsors more research and development than any other in the world.) As a self-supporting agency of the Department of Commerce, NTIS is mandated by law to cover its expenses by the sale of these research publications, so only a small percentage of NTIS publications are given to depository libraries.

NTIS has almost 400,000 entries from recent years on its free Web site (http://www.ntis.gov/) and more than three million items in its repository. The subjects of these publications vary greatly, as seen in these sample titles: *Achieving Aeronautics Leadership* from NASA and *Economic Feasibility of Biochemical Processes for the Upgrading of Crudes and the Removal of Sulfur, Nitrogen, and Trace Metals From Crude Oil* from the Department of Energy. NTIS also indexes data sets and software programs produced by government-backed agencies and companies.

To more fully search the NTIS holdings, use the *NTIS Database* available on CD-ROM and through several commercial vendors. NTIS publications from 1975–1996 are also indexed in the *Government Reports Announcements and Index (GR&I)*, a print index available in many libraries.

The *National Audiovisual Center*, a database listing titles of federally developed audiovisual/media training and education materials, is also searchable at the NTIS Web site. Sample titles include: *Arson Prevention in Our Churches*, a video from the Federal Emergency Management Agency, and *Swahili: Basic Course*, twenty audiocassettes accompanied by text from the Department of State.

NTIS also maintains *FedWorld* at http://www.fedworld.gov, billed as "a comprehensive central access point for searching, locating, ordering, and acquiring government and business information."

U.S. Government Periodicals Index (USGPI). Bethesda, MD: Congressional Information Service. 1993–present. Also on CD-ROM and as a subscription database via the Congressional Information Service.

USGPI is an index to about 180 periodicals produced by the U.S. government with such titles as *Civil Rights Update, FDA Medical Bulletin,* and *Animal*

Welfare Information Center Newsletter. These magazines and journals aren't always indexed elsewhere, so this resource supplies a way to tap the multisubject contents of these periodicals.

Identifying specific government organizations and agencies

Why does the U.S. government publish in a such a plethora of subjects? Because the government is comprised of numerous and diverse agencies whose mission is to collect and dispense data and conduct research needed to support or debunk policies, enforce law, and to further learning.

Check the annually produced *United States Government Manual*, published by the GPO and available at virtually all libraries, for descriptions and contact information for agencies of the legislative, judicial, and executive branches, as well as quasi-official agencies and other boards, commissions, and committees. Online, the manual can be found at http://www.access.gpo.gov/nara/nara001.html.

Your phone book also contains local numbers for federal agencies in the federal government section. Another print directory of addresses and phone numbers (this one commercially published and available at many libraries) is the *Government Phone Book USA: A Comprehensive Guide to Federal, State, County, and Local Government Offices in the United States* (Detroit: Omnigraphics) containing more than 100,000 U.S. government contacts.

Following are descriptions of major departments and agencies of the U.S. federal government along with contact information. In the narratives, only sample unique elements of their Web pages are described. Virtually all the government Web sites supply:

- The agency's mission statement
- Description of their programs, projects, and activities
- Statistics generated by or related to the agency
- Laws, rules, or regulations related to the organization's mission
- Biographical information about the agency's leadership
- Job-seeker information
- Either the full text or ordering information for publications generated by the agency
- Links to related Web pages

The phone numbers listed are general information numbers for the federal

Finding Government Studies on the Web

I f you read the newspaper or listen to the radio you probably hear snippets of information attributed to government studies and reports. When you read or hear of a particular government agency's publication that you're interested in, check the agency home page. The full text of the publication may be there.

offices. Check in your phone book's government pages to see if a local number is available. You'll likely get faster service via the local contact.

Legislative branch

Congressional Budget Office (CBO), Second and D Streets SW, Washington, DC 20515, Phone: (202)226-2621, URL: http://www.cbo.gov/

This office supplies the House and Senate members with evaluations of the economic impact of the federal budget. Check the CBO site for *The Monthly Budget Review*, historical budget data, and economic projections.

General Accounting Office (GAO), 441 G St. NW, Washington, DC 20548, Phone: (202)512-3000, URL: http://www.gao.gov/

The GAO is the investigative arm of Congress, charged with examining matters relating to the receipt and disbursement of public monies. They perform audits and evaluations of government programs and activities. The GAO home page contains links to the agency's reports, testimony, policies, and decisions of the comptroller general, the head of the GAO.

United States House of Representatives, Washington, DC 20510, Phone: (202)224-3121, URL: http://www.house.gov/

This congressional site lets you find data on your state representatives, including just how they've voted on various issues and a schedule of House activities. Also on this site is a link to the Internet Law Library, further described in chapter eleven.

United States Senate, Washington, DC 20510, Phone: (202)224-3121, URL: http://www.senate.gov/

Browse the Senate page for recent legislative actions, information on senators, Senate leadership, Senate committees, and the Senate's history, procedures, and terminology.

Judicial branch

Federal Judicial Center (FJC), Thurgood Marshall Federal Judiciary Building, One Columbus Circle NE, Washington, DC 20002-8003, Phone: (202)273-4000, URL: http://www.fjc.gov/

The FJC conducts research on the operation of federal courts and conducts continuing education programs for federal judges, court employees, and others. The FJC page has links to a variety of federal court rules and opinions.

Supreme Court of the United States, United States Supreme Court Building, One First St. NE, Washington, DC 20543, Phone: (202)479-3000, URL: http://supct.law.cornell.edu/supct/index.html

The Web page for the Supreme Court offers the Court's calendar for the current term, a schedule of oral arguments, biographies for present and past justices, and all Court opinions from May 1990 to the present.

United States Sentencing Commission, Suite 2-500, South Lobby, One Columbus Circle NE, Washington, DC 20002-8002, Phone: (202)273-4500, URL: http://www.ussc.gov/

This commission develops federal criminal sentencing policies and practices. The *Federal Sentencing Guidelines Manual* is available on their Web page.

Departments

Department of Agriculture (USDA), Fourteenth St. and Independence Ave. SW, Washington, DC 20250, Phone: (202)720-2791, URL: http://www.usda.gov/

The USDA endeavors to create and expand markets abroad for agricultural products; works to slow and alleviate hunger, poverty and malnutrition; participates in efforts to protect natural resources; oversees rural development projects; and runs inspection and grading services to ensure quality standards for the U.S. food supply. The USDA home page brings you to their many agencies, including the Farm Services Agency, Foreign Agricultural Service, Food and Nutrition Service, Food Safety and Inspection Services, Animal and Plant Health Inspection Service, Forest Service, Natural Resources Conservation Service, Rural Utilities Service, and the Rural Housing Service.

Department of Commerce (DOC), Fourteenth St. between Constitution and Pennsylvania Avenues, Washington, DC 20230, Phone: (202)482-2000, URL: http://www.doc.gov

The DOC Web page supplies entrée to Web locations for the units of the department, including the Bureau of Export Administration, the Bureau of Economic Analysis, the Bureau of the Census, the Economic Development

Administration, the International Trade Administration, the Minority Business Development Agency, the National Oceanic and Atmospheric Administration, the National Telecommunications and Information Administration, the Office of the Inspector General, the Office of the Secretary, the Patent and Trademark Office, the National Institute of Standards and Technology, the National Technical Information Service, and the Office of Technology Policy. There is also a link to Stat-USA, a database containing trade and economic data from fifty federal agencies, further discussed in chapter twelve.

Department of Defense (DOD), Office of the Secretary, The Pentagon, Washington, DC 20301-1155, Phone (703)545-6700, URL: http://www.defe nselink.mil

The DOD home page, called Defense Link, leads you to Web pages representing the U.S. Army, Navy, Air Force, Marine Corps, Coast Guard (part of DOD in time of war, otherwise part of the Department of Transportation), the Secretary of Defense, and the Joint Chiefs of Staff.

Department of Education, 600 Independence Ave. SW, Washington, DC 20202, Phone: (202)401-5986, URL: http://www.ed.gov

The Department of Education promotes educational excellence and works to ensure equal access to education for all Americans. Its Web page presents education priorities of the current administration, grant opportunities, and links to educational research facilities and the data they generate.

Department of Energy (DOE), 1000 Independence Ave. SW, Washington, DC 20585, Phone: (202)586-5000, URL: http://www.doe.gov

The DOE supplies energy-related technical information and scientific and educational support for the attainment and maintenance of efficient energy use, diverse energy sources, a strong economy, good environmental quality, and a secure national defense. On the Web, the DOE page connects to such offices and programs as the Office of Civilian Radioactive Waste Management, the Federal Energy Regulatory Commission, and the Office of Nuclear Energy, Science, and Technology. The DOE Information Bridge provides access to more than two million full-text pages of research and development reports.

Department of Health and Human Services, Information Center, 200 Independence Ave. SW, Washington, DC 20201, Phone: (202)619-0257, URL: http://www.os.dhhs.gov/

The Health and Human Services home page is a gateway to sites for the Administration for Children and Families, the Administration on Aging, the Agency for Health Care Policy and Research, the Agency for Toxic Substances and Disease Control, the Centers for Disease Control and Prevention, the Food and Drug Administration, the Health Care Financing Administration, the Health Resources and Services Administration, the Indian Health Service, the National Institutes of Health, and the Substance Abuse and Mental Health Services Administration.

Department of Housing and Urban Development (HUD), 451 Seventh St. SW, Washington, DC 20410, Phone: (202)708-1422, Hotline: (800)347-3735, URL: http://www.hud.gov

HUD oversees programs dealing with U.S. housing needs, including fair housing and community development. The HUD Web site offers consumer information on topics such as buying, owning, and renting a home; dangers in the home; and housing discrimination. Homes for sale by HUD are also listed on this page, and you can use HUD's mortgage calculator to find out how much home you can afford.

Department of the Interior, 1849 C St. NW, Washington, DC 20240, Phone: (202)208-3171, URL: http://www.doi.gov

The Department of the Interior manages U.S. public lands and minerals, national parks and wildlife refuges, and Western water resources. It also honors federal trust responsibilities to Native American tribes. The Web pages for the eight bureaus of the department can be accessed at this site: the Bureau of Indian Affairs, the Bureau of Reclamation, the Bureau of Land Management, the Minerals Management Service, the National Park Service, the U.S. Fish and Wildlife Service, the U.S. Geological Survey, and Surface Mining Reclamation and Enforcement.

Department of Justice (DOJ), Constitution Ave. and Tenth St. NW, Washington, DC 20530, Phone: (202)514-2000, URL: http://www.usdoj.gov/

The DOJ acts as the nation's police officer and lawyer. A few of the sites searchable via this home page are the Drug Enforcement Administration, the Federal Bureau of Investigation, the Executive Office for the United States Attorneys, the Office of the Inspector General, the Bureau of Prisons, the United States Marshals Service, and the Immigration and Naturalization Service. The mugs of the FBI's, DEA's, and U.S. Marshal's most-wanted criminals also adorn this site.

Department of Labor (DOL), 200 Constitution Ave. NW, Washington, DC 20210, Phone: (202)219-5000, URL: http://www.dol.gov

This federal agency is charged with helping assure that the workplace is safe and discrimination-free and that wages and pensions are fair. The DOL also offers job training programs, with particular outreach to groups such as older Americans, youths, members of minority groups, and the disabled. The *Small Business Handbook*, a guide to labor laws and regulations, is full text on their Web page.

Department of State, 2201 C St. NW, Washington, DC 20520, Phone: (202)647-4000, URL: http://www.state.gov

As the advisory organization for creation and implementation of foreign policy, the Department of State makes recommendations to the president regarding U.S. foreign relations. They gather and analyze international data, participate in the negotiation of treaties and agreements, and represent the U.S. at the United Nations and dozens of other international organizations. Their Internet page contains a wide variety of comments and analysis on topics such as counterterrorism, women's issues, and general relations between the U.S. and nations worldwide.

Also, visit the Department of State Web site for help with foreign travel questions. You'll find information regarding passports, visas, embassies, and consulates, and answers to commonly asked questions regarding living abroad.

Department of Transportation (DOT), 400 Seventh St. SW., Washington, DC 20590, Phone: (202)366-4000, URL: http://www.dot.gov

At the DOT home page you can connect to the Bureau of Transportation Statistics, the Federal Aviation Administration, the Federal Highway Administration, the Federal Railroad Administration, the Federal Transit Administration, the Maritime Administration, the National Highway Traffic Safety Administration, the Saint Lawrence Seaway Development Corporation, the Surface Transportation Board, the Coast Guard (administered by DOT in time of peace), and other links related to the creation of U.S. transportation policy.

Department of the Treasury, 1500 Pennsylvania Ave. NW, Washington, DC 20220, Phone: (202)622-2000, URL: http://www.ustreas.gov

The treasury manages the government's finances; offers support and input regarding economic, financial, tax, and fiscal policies; oversees the manufacture of coins and paper currency; and has law enforcement functions, including protection of the financial systems and the nation's political leaders. The diverse groups in this agency include the Bureau of Alcohol, Tobacco and Firearms, the Bureau of Engraving and Printing, the Federal Law Enforcement Training Center, the Internal Revenue Service, the U.S. Customs Service, the U.S. Mint, and the U.S. Secret Service. Also visit the treasury home page to find IRS tax forms online and to find the public debt (click on "Site Map"), which was $5,504,211,009,027.55 when I accessed it. (Hey, I'll kick in the fifty-five cents. . . .)

Executive branch

Office of Management and Budget (OMB), Executive Office Building, Washington, DC 20503, Phone: (202)395-3080, URL: http://www.white house.gov/OMB/

The OMB assists the president in the preparation of the U.S. federal budget and oversees its administration in executive branch agencies. You'll find the United States Budget on the OMB home page along with circulars and bulletins containing fiscal instructions or information issued to federal agencies.

Office of National Drug Control Policy, Executive Office of the President, Washington, DC 20503, Phone: (202)395-6700, URL: http://www.white housedrugpolicy.gov/

This office coordinates efforts at the federal, state, and local levels for controlling drug abuse. They also devise strategies for anti-drug activities. Their strategies and goals can be examined on their Web page. Data on drug use are also available.

Office of Science and Technology Policy (OSTP), Old Executive Office Building, Washington, DC 20502, Phone: (202)395-7347, Fax: (202)456-6022, URL: http://www.whitehouse.gov/OSTP.html

OSTP provides expert advice to the president in all areas of science and technology for policy, budget, and research purposes. There are four divisions: Environment, Science, Technology, and National Security and International Affairs. Policy statements, fact sheets, remarks from the president and vice president, press releases, and other policy documents are searchable and retrievable on this page.

Office of the United States Trade Representative (USTR), 600 Seventeenth St. NW, Washington, DC 20508, Phone: (202)395-3230, URL: http://www.ustr.gov/

This office has the task of formulating trade policy and directing trade negotiations for the U.S. Agreements negotiated by the USTR are full text at this site.

The White House, 1600 Pennsylvania Ave., Washington, DC 20500, Phone: (202)395-7250, URL: http://www.whitehouse.gov/

Visiting the White House online brings you to biographical data on the president and vice president, a guide to finding resources produced by the federal government, a virtual tour of the White House, and the opportunity to view historic photographs and listen to speeches.

Selected independent establishments and government corporations

African Development Foundation, 1400 Eye St. NW, Washington, DC 20005, Phone: (202)673-3915, URL: http://www.adf.gov

This foundation works to alleviate poverty and promote sustainable development in Sub-Saharan Africa. Funding eligibility requirements are posted on their home page.

Central Intelligence Agency (CIA), Washington, DC 20505, Phone: (703)482-1100, URL: http://www.odci.gov/cia/

The CIA digs up foreign intelligence related to national security and conducts counterintelligence activities. Their Web site contains the full text of the statistic-packed *World Fact Book* and the *Handbook of International Economic Statistics*.

Commission on Civil Rights, 624 Ninth St. NW, Washington, DC 20425, Phone: (202)376-8177, URL: http://www.usccr.gov

The Commission on Civil Rights collects and analyzes information related to discrimination or denial of equal protection based on race, color, religion, sex, age, disability, and national origin. Locate regional commission offices and instructions for filing a complaint are at their Web site.

Consumer Product Safety Commission (CPSC), Information and Public Affairs, East West Towers, 4330 East West Highway, Bethesda, MD 20814, Phone: (800)638-2772 or (301)504-0580, URL: http://www.cpsc.gov

The CPSC develops safety standards for consumer products and informs the public of product hazards and the comparative safety of different products. They supply online access to publications that discuss such issues as children's safety, indoor air quality, recreational safety, and poison prevention. Recalls of products are also posted on their Web page.

Corporation for National and Community Service, 1201 New York Ave. NW, Washington, DC 20525, Phone: (202)606-5000, URL: http://www.cns.gov/

Engaging Americans in national service initiatives, a.k.a. volunteering, is the goal of the Corporation for National and Community Service. They administer AmeriCorps, Learn and Serve America, and the National Senior Service Corps. Look for details about each group and instructions for joining at the corporation home page.

Environmental Protection Agency (EPA), 401 M St. SW, Washington, DC 20460, Phone: (202)260-7751, URL: http://www.epa.gov

The mandate for the EPA calls on them to battle environmental pollution in cooperation with state and local governments. On the EPA Web site you can locate facts and data relating to environmental issues; environmental stories and information geared to children; descriptions of programs, research, and grant opportunities; and listings and information about nationwide EPA offices and research facilities.

Federal Communications Commission (FCC), 1919 M St. NW, Washington, DC 20554, Phone: (202)418-0200 or (888)225-5322, URL: http://www.fcc.gov.

Developing and implementing policy related to radio, television, telephone, telegraph, cable, satellite, and items such as pagers, is the job of the FCC. A few points of interest on their home page include orders and actions of the FCC, notices of proposed rulemaking, and fees imposed for licenses and other FCC services.

Federal Deposit Insurance Corporation (FDIC), 550 Seventeenth St. NW, Washington, DC 20429, Phone: (202)393-8400, URL: http://www.fdic.gov.

The FDIC insures bank and thrift deposits up to $100,000, and checks that state-sponsored banks not part of the Federal Reserve System are complying with consumer protection laws and running fiscally sound institutions. Their page on the Net contains news of interest to the banking industry, laws and regulations applicable to financial institutions, and information for consumers in regard to financial institutions.

Federal Emergency Management Agency (FEMA), 500 C St. SW, Washington, DC 20472, Phone: (202)646-4600, URL: http://www.fema.gov/

FEMA works with state and local governments in developing disaster preparedness programs that protect life and property in the event of a catastrophe, and mitigate the loss and recovery process after such an event. Find tips on disaster preparedness and reports of disasters and their follow-up on their home page.

Federal Reserve System, Board of Governors of the Federal Reserve System, Twentieth St. and Constitution Ave. NW, Washington, DC 20551, Phone: (202)452-3000, URL: http://www.federalreserve.gov

This is the central bank of the United States. The Federal Reserve System supervises and regulates U.S. banking functions. Their Web page contains documents directed to both consumers and those in banking.

General Services Administration (GSA), General Services Building, Eighteenth and

F Streets NW, Washington, DC 20405, Phone: (202)708-5082, URL: http://
www.gsa.gov

GSA has the job of supplying work space, security, furnishings, supplies, and equipment for federal employees. Learn how to buy discarded government property such as cars, office furniture, and laboratory equipment on their Web site.

Inter-American Foundation (IAF), 901 N. Stuart St., Arlington, VA 22203, Phone: (703)841-3800, URL: http://www.iaf.gov/

The Inter-American Foundation awards grants to promote social and economic development in Caribbean and Latin American nations. Learn about the IAF Fellowship program on their home page.

National Aeronautics and Space Administration (NASA), 300 E St. SW, Washington, DC 20546, Phone: (202)358-1000, URL: http://www.nasa.gov/

NASA conducts research related to flight both within and beyond the Earth's atmosphere. The NASA home page offers connections to Web sites for NASA Centers, including the Jet Propulsion Laboratory in California, the Kennedy Space Center in Florida, and the White Sands Test Facility in New Mexico. Information regarding how to become an astronaut is also supplied, along with daunting figures: There are about twenty openings every two years and about four thousand applicants for those openings.

National Foundation on the Arts and Humanities, 1100 Pennsylvania Ave. NW, Washington, DC 20506, Phone: (202)682-5400

The foundation fosters national activity and progress in the humanities and arts and includes the *National Endowment for the Arts* (http://arts.endow.gov/), the *National Endowment for the Humanities* (http://neh.fed.us), the *Institute of Museum and Library Services* (http://www.imls.fed.us), and the Federal Council on the Arts and Humanities, which coordinates the activities of the two endowments and related federal programs.

National Labor Relations Board (NLRB), 1099 Fourteenth St. NW, Washington, DC 20570, Phone: (202)273-1000, URL: http://www.nlrb.gov

This organization upholds the tenets of the National Labor Relations Act, protecting such options as an employee's right to organize, and preventing unfair labor activities on the part of employers, unions, or employees. The NLRB Rules and Regulations are full text on the Internet.

National Railroad Passenger Corporation (AMTRAK), 60 Massachusetts Ave. NE, Washington, DC 20002, Phone:(202)906-3000, URL: http://www .amtrak.com

AMTRAK was created to develop the potential of rail travel for intercity passenger transportation. Check schedules and fares, and make reservations online.

National Science Foundation (NSF), 4201 Wilson Blvd., Arlington, VA 22230, Phone: (703)306-1234, URL: http://www.nsf.gov

NSF fosters science and engineering research and education. News about current trends in all areas of science and engineering is on their Web page.

National Transportation Safety Board (NTSB), 490 L'Enfant Plaza SW, Washington, DC 20594, Phone: (202)314-6000, URL: http://www.ntsb.gov

This independent federal agency investigates every civil aviation accident and major railroad, highway, marine, pipeline, and hazardous material mishap. Both statistics and descriptions of NTSB-investigated accidents are located on their Web page.

Nuclear Regulatory Commission (NRC), 11555 Rockville Pike, Rockville, MD 20852, Phone: (301)415-7000, URL: http://www.nrc.gov

The NRC licenses and regulates nonmilitary use of nuclear energy. They strive to protect the health and safety of the populace and the environment. Check their Web site for the daily events report of incidents regarding nuclear facilities.

Peace Corps, 1990 K St. NW, Washington, DC 20526, Phone: (202)606-3886, Toll-Free Recruitment Phone: (800)424-8580, URL: http://www.peacecorps .gov/

What a laudable mission the Peace Corps has: "to promote world peace and friendship." Look for essays written by Peace Corps volunteers on their Web site.

Securities and Exchange Commission (SEC), 450 Fifth St. NW, Washington, DC 20549, Phone: (202)942-4150, URL: http://www.sec.gov

The SEC keeps an eye on the securities industry, making sure investors are being treated fairly under the law and the market is adhering to regulations. From the SEC site on the Web you can connect to EDGAR: Electronic Data Gathering, Analysis, and Retrieval, the place to look when seeking financial information about publicly traded companies (see chapter twelve).

Small Business Administration (SBA), 409 Third St. SW, Washington, DC 20416, Phone: (202)205-6533, URL: http://www.sba.gov

The Small Business Administration supports the start-up of small business enterprises nationwide. Local SBA offices in every state are all listed on the SBA Web site.

Social Security Administration, Office of Public Inquiries, 6401 Security Blvd., Room 4-C-5 Annex, Baltimore, MD 21235-6401, Phone: (410)965-7700, URL: http://www.ssa.gov

This administration manages the U.S. social insurance program. Some of the top-ten services listed on the SSA Web page include issuing personal earnings and benefit estimates statements, a statement of your lifetime earnings and an estimate of future benefits; current cost-of-living data; and instructions regarding replacing, correcting, or changing your name on your social security card.

United States Information Agency, 301 Fourth St. SW, Washington, DC 20547, Phone: (202)619-4700, URL: http://www.usia.gov/

This agency works to increase understanding and acceptance of U.S. policies by the populace of other countries, and to increase communication by U.S. citizens and institutions and their overseas counterparts. In other countries the agency is known as the U.S. Information Service. Find links to information about *Radio Free Europe*, *Voice of America*, and the Fulbright Exchange Program at their Web site.

United States Postal Service, 475 L'Enfant Plaza SW, Washington, DC 20260, Phone: (202)268-2000, URL: http://www.usps.gov

This is the place that handles processing and delivering of a great portion of U.S. mail. Going to their Web page is similar to going to the post office. You'll find zip codes, a postage calculator, change of address forms, and new stamps. Order stamps twenty-four hours a day at 1-800-STAMPS24. If only there was a slot in the computer where you could drop your packages. . . .

Census Data

On their home page at http://www.census.gov, the stated mission of the Bureau of the Census is to be the preeminent collector and provider of timely, relevant, and quality data about the people and economy of the United States. This section offers an overview of the type of information the bureau collects and the terminology they use when presenting it.

The federal government is mandated by the U.S. Constitution to count the population every decade, and it has done so since 1790. The decennially conducted Census of Population and Housing is the most comprehensive demographic survey in the U.S., including data relating to population, socioeconomic characteristics, and housing.

Government Information via Meta Links and a Toll-Free Number

For an extensive online listing of U.S. government Web pages, try any of the following meta sites:

- The *U.S. Federal Government Agencies Page* at http://www.lib.lsu.edu/gov /fedgov.html
- The *Federal Web Locator* at http://www.cilp.org/fed-agency/fedwebloc.html
- *Federal Government Resources: Executive Branch* at http://www.lib.umich.edu/libh ome/Documents.center/federal.html
- *Yahoo!: Government Agencies* at http://www.yahoo.com/Government/U_S__ Government/Agencies/ (there are two underscores after the capital letter *S* and before the word *Government*)
- The *America Anywhere* directory, part of the *Official U.S. Government Blue Pages* at http://www.bp.fed.gov

Don't know which agency to contact? Call the Federal Information Center toll free at (800)688-9889 from 9:00 A.M. to 8:00 P.M., weekdays.

The latest fully published decade census at the time of this writing is the now almost ancient 1990 census. The bureau does issue interim reports that update some of the decennial information, albeit based only on sample populations, or, in some cases, projections.

The 1990 census was the most accurate census to date since such issues as accounting for the homeless population were considered. Also, for the first time, researchers could retrieve a good amount of census data for areas as small as a city block for the entire nation.

For the 1990 census, every U.S. household was asked to fill out a brief survey called the *short form*. Additionally, 17 percent of all households, representing a sample population of the U.S., answered additional questions on the *long form*.

The first census in 1790 asked six questions: name of the head of the household, number of free white males over sixteen and under sixteen, number of free white females, number of slaves, and all other persons not heretofore mentioned. Here are the items of information gathered in the 1990 census:

Data derived for the 1990 census from the short form (all households)
Population Items: the respondent's relationship to householder, sex, race, age, marital status, ethnic origin, family size, household size, family type, household type, and number of persons in a unit.

   Housing Items: type/size of building, number of rooms in a unit, large acreage or commercial use, unit rented or owned, presence of mortgage, value of property if owned, monthly rent, meals included in rent, vacancy status and reason for vacancy, duration of vacancy, and number of persons per room.

*Additional data derived for the 1990 census from additional
questions on the long form (17 percent of households)*
Population Items: school enrollment, educational attainment, state or country of birth, citizenship and year immigrated, language spoken at home, ability to speak English, ancestry/ethnic origin, where resided five years ago, veteran status/period served, disability, children ever born, current employment status, hours worked per week, place of employment, travel time to work, persons in car pool, year last worked, industry/employer type, occupation/class of worker, self-employed, weeks worked last year, total income by source, poverty status, and type of group quarters.

   Housing Items: type of structure, plumbing facilities, use of property as a farm, source of water, method of sewage disposal, year structure built, year householder moved into unit, type of heat and heating fuel, cost of utilities and fuel, kitchen facilities, number of bedrooms, number of bathrooms, presence of telephone, number of cars, vans, and trucks, amount of real property taxes, property insurance costs, monthly mortgage payment, taxes/insurance in mortgage, second mortgage payment, condominium status, condominium fee, mobile home shelter costs, and total housing costs.

   Combining and cross-tabulating this data answers some interesting questions. For example: How many Hispanic women have a commute to work that takes more than an hour? How many bathrooms, on average, are there in homes where the income is over $40,000? In what percentage of U.S. homes is the Arabic language spoken? Census data begs for questions like those.

   Census data can be retrieved for quite a variety of discrete geographic areas. This is useful to the researcher who, for example, wants average monthly rent prices for a particular neighborhood and not just a county. Census information is compiled for what are called political geographies and statistical geographies, though not every piece of data is available for all permutations of geographies.

Political geographies supply data for any of these politically defined areas: all of the U.S., states, possessions, congressional districts, counties, voting districts, and American Indian/Alaska Native areas.

Statistical geographies designate areas based on specific criteria. Sample area designations for statistical geographies:

- *Urbanized Areas* (UAs), defined as those having at least 2,500 people.
- *Rural Areas*, those having less than 2,500 inhabitants.
- *Metropolitan Statistical Areas* (MSAs) include one or more counties with a total population of more than fifty thousand. An MSA is usually named after the city in the area with the highest population, e.g., the Boston MSA will include surrounding communities.
- *Primary Metropolitan Statistical Areas* (PMSAs), smaller areas within MSAs with populations of at least one million.
- *Consolidated Metropolitan Statistical Areas* (CMSAs), groups of adjacent PMSAs.
- *Census Tract*, neighborhoods within metropolitan areas of about four thousand people.
- *Block Numbering Areas* (BNAs), neighborhoods outside of metropolitan areas.

So where do you find this terrific data? All full-depository libraries and many of the 1,400 partial-depository libraries contain print and electronic census publications. These publications are available in many formats, including books, maps, news releases, microfiche, and in electronic format. The publications tend to be geographically oriented, with, for example, separate volumes for different states.

Decennial census information was available on CD-ROM for the first time for the 1990 census. Often used are the census CD-ROMs called Summary Tape Files (STFs), containing data organized in easy-to-browse tables. Alternately, PUMS data (Public Use Microdata Samples) are not organized into tables and, with some knowledge of statistical packages such as SPSS or SAS (which allow the manipulation of statistical data), you can do some fancy cross-tabulations. STFs meet the needs of most users.

There are two STF series for the 1990 census on CD-ROM available in many libraries and on the Web at http://govinfo.kerr.orst.edu/index.text.html through the Government Information Sharing Project from Oregon State University. The STF 1 series covers answers supplied by 100 percent of all respondents. The STF 3 series covers the 17 percent sample that answered the wider variety of questions. Discs are further broken down into A, B, C, and D discs, each offering different geographic level coverage (though they won't be identified as such on the Web version).

For the 2000 census expect the Internet to be the primary repository of census data. There will also be CD-ROM products, but fewer and smaller printed reports than in 1990.

Historic Census Data on the Net

If you're seeking census data from years gone by, two hundred years of statistics can be pulled from the *Historical U.S. Census Browser* at http://icg.fas.harvard.edu/census/. Choose data from any census, from 1790 through 1970.

The census home page

There's a wealth of statistics on the census home page, accessible in numerous ways. The Census Bureau site can be searched by way of an A-Z alphabetical directory of titles and subjects representing data found in publications from the census. Sample headings include Aging, Fathers as Care Providers, Journey to Work, and Sales and Inventories—Retail. In cases where full-text publications are not available online, ordering information is supplied. It's also possible to do a general word search by subject.

Pointers to decennial census data can be found under the "Data Access Tools" heading on the Census Bureau home page. Sample access tools include Map Stats, which leads to both STF 1 and STF 3 information for the state and county level. Just choose a state and then either select "State Profiles" or click on a particular county on the state's map. Access this information directly at http://www.census.gov/datamap/www/index.html.

Also under the "Data Access Tools" choice is the TIGER Map Server. TIGER Maps are high quality, detailed maps of anywhere in the United States, created by using public geographic data. Read more about TIGER Maps in chapter ten.

Beyond the decennial census

In addition to producing the Census of Population and Housing, the Census Bureau conducts nine economic censuses, conducted in years ending in two and seven and covering construction industries, finance, government, manufacturing, mineral industries, retail and wholesale trade, service industries, and transportation. The Department of Agriculture conducts the agricultural census.

The Census Bureau also produces ongoing surveys, updating much of the data produced in its ten-year and five-year censuses on a monthly, quarterly, annual, or irregular basis. Additionally, the bureau has its hand in the international arena, compiling current statistics on U.S. foreign trade, including import, export, and shipping data.

The names of dozens of census experts and their Washington, DC, phone numbers are listed at http://www.census.gov/main/www/ask.html. Census experts can also be reached at state data centers. State data centers exist in every state to provide training and technical assistance in accessing and using census data, and they produce population estimates and projections for their state. Find your local data center listed at http://www.census.gov/sdc/www/ or in your local phone book's federal government section listed under the Department of Commerce, then listed under Census.

State Government Information
State libraries

Some states have created depository programs similar to the federal government depository program. These programs usually arrange for the distribution of state agency documents to the official state library as well as other libraries designated as state depositories. Since there is quite a range of state agencies, there is also quite a variety of information at state libraries, including business, housing, history, and state surveys and statistics of all sorts. The *Library of Congress State Libraries Page* at http://lcweb.loc.gov/global/library/statelib.html lists home pages of state libraries, or find the URL in the upcoming list.

State home pages and phone numbers

A fabulous amount of information is available via the individual state home pages on the Web. Home pages for each state of the United States are filled with laws, facts, figures, and links related to the state's economy, demographics, educational and health systems, tourism, government issues, people, community events, and more. For example, on the North Dakota home page I was able to find the names, backgrounds, and recent political activities of North Dakota lawmakers and how to contact them; I learned of the current condition of major roadways around the state; examined the daily lunch menu for the Westhope Public School (which notes that all meals are served with milk, bread, peanut butter, and honey); and I was able to download the sheet music for the "North Dakota Hymn."

Following is a listing of state Web pages and phone numbers for each state's information office and state library.

AL   http://www.state.al.us
        State Library: (334)213-3900, Information Office: (334)242-8000
AK   http://www.state.ak.us
        State Library: (907)465-2921, Information Office: (907)465-2111
AZ   http://www.state.az.us
        State Library: (602)542-4159, Information Office: (602)542-4900
AR   http://www.state.ar.us
        State Library: (501)682-1527, Information Office: (501)682-3000
CA   http://www.state.ca.us
        State Library: (916)654-0174, Information Office: (916)322-9900
CO   http://www.state.co.us
        State Library: (303)866-6900, Information Office: (303)866-5000
CT   http://www.state.ct.us
        State Library: (203)566-4777, Information Office: (203)566-2211
DE   http://www.state.de.us
        State Library: (302)739-4777, Information Office: (302)739-4000
DC   http://www.dchomepage.net/dcmain/index.html
        Main Library: (202)727-1101, Information: (202)727-1000
FL   http://www.state.fl.us
        State Library: (850)487-2651, Information Office: (850)488-1234
GA   http://www.state.ga.us
        State Library: (404)657-6220, Information Office: (404)656-2000
HI   http://www.state.hi.us
        State Library: (808)548-4775, Information Office: (808)546-2211
ID   http://www.state.id.us
        State Library: (208)334-5124, Information Office: (208)334-2411
IL   http://www.state.il.us
        State Library: (217)782-7596, Information Office: (217)782-2000
IN   http://www.state.in.us
        State Library: (317)232-3675, Information Office: (317)232-1000
IA   http://www.state.ia.us
        State Library: (515)281-4118, Information Office: (515)281-5011
KS   http://www.state.ks.us
        State Library: (913)296-3296, Information Office: (913)296-0111
KY   http://www.state.ky.us

	State Library: (502)564-8300, Information Office: (502)564-3130
LA	http://www.state.la.us
	State Library: (504)342-4923, Information Office: (504)342-6600
ME	http://www.state.me.us
	State Library: (207)287-5600, Information Office: (207)582-9800
MD	http://www.state.md.us
	State Library: (410)974-3914, Governor's Office: (410)974-3901
MA	http://www.state.ma.us
	State Library: (617)727-2590, Information Office: (617)722-2000
MI	http://www.state.mi.us
	State Library: (517)373-5400, Information Office: (517)373-1837
MN	http://www.state.mn.us
	State Library: (612)296-3398, Information Office: (612)296-6013
MS	http://www.state.ms.us
	State Library: (601)359-6850, Information Office: (601)359-1000
MO	http://www.state.mo.us
	State Library: (314)751-3615, Information Office: (314)751-2000
MT	http://www.state.mt.us
	State Library: (406)444-3115, Information Office: (406)444-2511
NE	http://www.state.ne.us
	State Library: (402)471-3189, Information Office: (402)471-2311
NV	http://www.state.nv.us
	State Library: (702)687-5160, Information Office: (702)687-5000
NH	http://www.state.nh.us
	State Library: (603)271-2144, Information Office: (603)271-1110
NJ	http://www.state.nj.us
	State Library: (609)292-6220, Information Office: (609)292-2121
NM	http://www.state.nm.us
	State Library: (505)827-3800, Information Office: (505)827-4011
NY	http://www.state.ny.us
	State Library: (518)474-5355, Information Office: (518)474-2121
NC	http://www.state.nc.us
	State Library: (919)733-2570, Information Office: (919)733-1110
ND	http://www.state.nd.us
	State Library: (701)328-2490, Information Office: (701)328-2000
OH	http://www.state.oh.us
	State Library: (614)644-7061, Information Office: (614)466-2000

OK	http://www.state.ok.us
	State Library: (405)521-2502, Information Office: (405)521-2011
OR	http://www.state.or.us
	State Library: (503)378-4274, Governor's Office: (503)378-3111
PA	http://www.state.pa.us
	State Library: (717)787-5718, Information Office: (717)787-2121
RI	http://www.state.ri.us
	State Library: (401)277-2473, Information Office: (401)277-2000
SC	http://www.state.sc.us
	State Library: (803)734-8666, Information Office: (803)734-1000
SD	http://www.state.sd.us
	State Library: (605)773-3131, Information Office: (605)773-3011
TN	http://www.state.tn.us
	State Library: (615)741-2764, Information Office: (615)741-3011
TX	http://www.state.tx.us
	State Library: (512)463-5455, Information Office: (512)463-4630
UT	http://www.state.ut.us
	State Library: (801)466-5888, Information Office: (801)538-3000
VT	http://www.state.vt.us
	State Library: (802)828-3261, Information Office: (802)828-1110
VA	http://www.state.va.us
	State Library: (804)786-8929, Information Office: (804)786-0000
WA	http://www.state.wa.us
	State Library: (360)753-2041, Information Office: (360)753-5000
WV	http://www.state.wv.us
	State Library: (304)558-2041, Information Office: (304)558-3456
WI	http://www.state.wi.us
	State Library: (608)264-6534, Information Office: (608)266-2211
WY	http://www.state.wy.us
	State Library: (307)777-7283, Information Office: (307)777-7011

When seeking information about a particular state, searching that state's home page is a great choice. If you need information regarding several states, go to one of the meta sites that make it easy to jump from one state to another, including: *NASIRE StateSearch.* http://www.nasire.org/ss

NASIRE StateSearch hotlinks to over twenty subject categories of interest which in turn link to specific states. Some of the categories: auditors, criminal justice, economic development and commerce, education, employment services, energy, environment and natural resources, regulation and licensing, state home pages, and transportation.

Piper Resources: State and Local Government on the Net. http://www.piperinfo.com

In Piper, the researcher clicks on the name of a state to link to Web sites of interest, including the state's home page, state directory, statewide offices, agencies, departments, counties, cities, and sites related to the state's legislative, judicial, and executive branches.

Then there's a page which is not only useful, but also has some zing: *50 States and Capitals* at http://www.50states.com/ does link to some official state government pages, such as each state governor's page. Additionally, this site quickly supplies the answers to dozens of "What's the state bird" type questions. Thus, the Connecticut resource page informs you that the state bird is a robin and then links you to a color photograph and encyclopedic essay about the dear little fellow.

The *U.S. Census Bureau* home page, at http://www.census.gov, also offers quick access to state data via Map Stats, mentioned earlier. Click on "Data Access Tools" to visit the Map Stats page where you'll find links to economic, population, and social data for states, counties and congressional districts corralled for easy retrieval. The Map Stats links point to the specific data you're seeking in such publications as the STF 1 and STF 3 census series and the publications *State Government Finances* and *County Business Patterns.* Map Stats also displays a map of each state carved neatly into counties, and supplies links to the state data center home page for all states.

Carroll's Directories are good examples of print directories that list thousands of useful state government phone numbers. Carroll Publishing produces directories listing contact information for federal, state, county, and municipal agencies and personnel. The directories are available in print, on CD-ROM, and online by subscription. Titles in the series include:

Carroll's State Directory—supplies contact information for over 37,000 key executive, legislative, and judicial officials.

Carroll's Municipal Directory—covers more than 35,000 elected, appointed, and career officials in 7,800 cities, towns, and villages.

Carroll's County Directory—provides contact information for over 28,000 key officials in nearly 3,100 counties, boroughs, and parishes nationwide.

Carroll's Publishing also offers *Carroll's State Pages* at no charge at http://www.carr

ollpub.com/States/stateopener.html. *State Pages* supplies, for each state, links to pages for the governor and staff, to pages for U.S. congressional members from that state, to the state's official home page, and to other state government pages.

Public records from state and local government agencies

Many public records generated by agencies at the state and local government level are available for perusal by the public. Some local documents, such as the minutes from a city council meeting, may be printed in the town newspaper. However, most documents from government bodies below the state level (i.e., city and county documents), are only available at a variety of city offices, and you need to go to the source to obtain them.

What are deemed "public records" can't be summed up in a few words or even a few paragraphs since it varies tremendously from state to state. For example, while some states offer access to criminal histories and worker's compensation records, other states grant no access or restricted access. Michael Sankey and Carl R. Ernst, editors of the book *Find Public Records Fast: The Complete State, County, and Courthouse Locator* (Tempe, AZ: Facts on Demand Press, 1998), list categories of records you're likely to find accessible, including:

- Basic contact information for an individual or organization, even if someone has an unlisted phone number
- Case information about companies and people who have filed for bankruptcy protection
- Information culled from financial transactions of individuals or companies
- Data about licensed drivers
- An individual's educational background
- Environmental hazards information
- Civil litigation in municipal, state, or federal courts (though records may be closed at the discretion of the judge)
- Years of service and rank in the military service
- Facts concerning the ownership, transfer, value, and mortgaging of real property
- Records of involuntary liens
- Vital records, including birth, death, marriage, and divorce; voter registration records; and worker's compensation records.

Though records may be public, this doesn't mean they will always be supplied without charge. There may be search, copying, and/or certification fees. There are also many private companies whose business is the purchase and maintenance of databases of government records. These businesses specialize in resale of this information. Working with these companies may be an efficient fee-based option for finding public records. You can locate such firms at http://www.brbpub.com /prrn/, the *Public Record Retriever Network*, a Web guide to firms that specialize in retrieving local and state government records.

To make your initial phone contact, either use one of the aforementioned state information phone numbers, check for phone numbers in your telephone book government pages, or check a print directory, such as the *Government Phone Book USA: A Comprehensive Guide to Federal, State, County, and Local Government Offices in the United States* (Detroit: Omnigraphics. Annual).

I also recommend looking at *The Sourcebook of State Public Records: The Definitive Guide to Searching for Public Record Information at the State Level* (Tempe, AZ, 1997) by Michael Sankey. Arranged by state, it supplies contact information for agencies such as the State Department of Health Statistics for access to birth certificates and death records and the Secretary of State for corporate information. Much more than just a directory of phone numbers, this guide describes how and when most offices listed make records available to the public and the type of information you're likely to find. The 400 + pages in this book makes it quite obvious that laws governing availability of different public records vary greatly from state to state.

Other titles that will assist you in the public records search process include *Public Records Online: The National Guide to Private and Government Online Sources of Public Records* (Tempe, AZ: Facts on Demand Press, 1999) and *Naked in Cyberspace: How to Find Personal Information Online* by Carole Lane (Wilton, CT: Pemberton Press, 1997).

Only a tiny percentage of local public records are online at no charge. The home page for *BRB Publications* at http://www.brbpub.com, a publisher specializing in public records research, presents a handful of links to online public records and invites researchers to keep checking the page for updates.

International Government Publications

As the global village expands, so do the international offerings in libraries and on the Net. Try these meta sites to find Web-based international data:

Foreign Governments. http://www.library.nwu.edu/govpub/resource/internat /foreign.html

   Arranged by country, these pages hotlink to government-related home pages such as the country's central bank, office of statistics, and various departments/ministries, such as the Ministry of Foreign Relations, Finance, Defense, Education, External Affairs, and Economics.

The International Local Government Home Page. http://www.world.localgov.org

Use this site to link to Web locations for municipal governments worldwide. Though far from comprehensive, it should grow over time.

International Organizations. http://www.library.nwu.edu/govpub/resource/internat/igo.html

An A-Z guide to international organizations. Some sample organizations listed include Asia-Pacific Economic Cooperation, the European Union, the Food and Agricultural Organization, INTERPOL, the North American Free Trade Agreement Secretariat, the Pan-American Health Organization, the United Nations Development Programme, and the World Tourism Organization.

Each public, academic, or special library's international holdings will reflect the interests of their constituency. Check your library's catalog to see what they have. You may be surprised. Though library holdings in the area of international materials are generally unique to the particular library, there are two special collections of international materials: materials from the European Union and from the UN. Though any library may gather materials in these areas, libraries designated as depositories will have the most extensive collections.

A complete listing of EU libraries can be found at http://www.eurunion.org/infores/index.htm, and a good jumping-off point for information about the EU can be found at their home page at http://www.eurunion.org. Check http://www.un.org/MoreInfo/Deplib/usa.htm for a listing of United Nations depository libraries worldwide. Most larger libraries, and especially federal depository libraries, will also have a substantial collection of UN and UN-related publications. The *United Nations* home page is located at http://www.un.org.

To bone up on just what types of publications flow from foreign governments, browse through the *Guide to Country Information in International Governmental Organization Publications* (Bethesda, MD: Congressional Information Service/GODORT, 1996). This guide identifies periodicals, books, and other publications emanating from international government organizations. Publications are first divided by geographic area and then by twenty-five subject categories that include agriculture, children, crime, economic affairs, education/training, environment/natural resources, human rights, international trade, laws/treaties, media/communications, and women.

Also of interest from the same publisher is the *Guide to Official Publications of Foreign Countries* (2nd edition, 1997), which cites documents in nineteen categories, including laws and regulations, economic affairs, development plans, central bank publications, budgets, census, health, labor, education, court reports, environment, human rights, and status of women.

CHAPTER 4

Contemporary Research

Unearthing Articles, Transcripts, Conference Papers, and Dissertations

"You should always believe what you read in the newspapers, for that makes them more interesting."

—Rose Macauley

Articles appear in print and online newspapers, magazines, journals, and newsletters, collectively referred to as either periodicals or serials. Each type of periodical has unique qualities appropriate to different types of research.

Journals: Geared to Experts in Particular Fields

Are there ever inaccuracies in journals? Absolutely. But journals have processes in place to insure the highest likelihood of freedom from errors.

Journals contain research studies, news, or information of interest in a particular field written by experts in that field. *The Journal of the American Medical Association (JAMA)*, written by medical professionals, is an example. Authors of journal articles have a sophisticated level of understanding of the topic they're writing about, and claims and opinions are substantiated with the results of studies, surveys, or other scholarly investigation. Journals are often published by university publishers or special associations, like the American Psychological Association.

As mentioned in chapter one, journal submissions are peer reviewed or refereed, meaning that a panel of experts in the field evaluated the article for accuracy. Articles that don't pass the peer-review process might be rejected outright or the editor might request substantial revisions.

A Journal by Any Other Name Is Just as Accurate

The word *journal* is not part of the title of all journals. Examples of no-journal-in-the-title journals include *Phi Delta Kappan*, which publishes articles concerned with educational research, service, and leadership, and *The Lancet*, a journal of medical science and practice. One way you can distinguish between a magazine and a journal is by the presence of a bibliography at the end of each article. Journals provide a listing of references the authors used in their research. That's not something you'd find at the end of a feature in *Glamour* magazine. Another quick way to determine that you're holding a scholarly journal will be the lack of advertisements featuring trim women hawking makeup, style, and sneakers. Scholarly journals will either have no advertisements or only specialized ads, e.g., dental equipment in a dental journal.

Some extremely specialized journals require authors to pay substantial fees to have their writing published in them. This is often seen in the sciences where publication in a peer-reviewed journal is a common method for an author to both share information and achieve recognition for his or her research. With relatively small audiences, these important journals couldn't afford to survive without being subsidized in some manner.

The writer of a journal article expects a certain level of expertise in the reader. The writing may contain more jargon. If you're not an expert in the topic, either read some basic articles or book chapters to get up to speed on a topic or keep a dictionary near that's geared to the subject at hand (a physics dictionary or literary dictionary, for example).

Magazines: Geared to the General Reader

Magazines contain popular articles that are usually shorter and less authoritative than journal articles. These are the kind of periodicals that you see in supermarkets, like *GQ*, *Good Housekeeping*, or *Reader's Digest*. Articles in popular magazines tend to be written by journalists, as opposed to experts on the subject of the article.

Since many magazine articles are written by nonexperts, they're usually easy to understand. The writers take the time to learn a subject unfamiliar to them, and then pass on to the reader what they've learned. Therefore, magazine articles may be the place to start when you want to familiarize yourself with a topic.

Also, since journalists are expert writers, the articles they produce will probably be written more clearly and smoothly then those written by subject experts. Mavens in their subject field are not always expert at sharing that information with others. Professional writers specialize in making complex topics digestible for the layperson.

If you're a college student, you may only be able to use a few popular periodicals; faculty usually insist that much of the information you gather come from journals.

Newspapers

You'll find information on just about any subject in the typical newspaper. Think of your local paper. In the last year it included comprehensive articles on health, scientific breakthroughs, political issues, and the lives of local heroes.

Newspapers often write on the fly, releasing breaking news with only sketchy details. If possible, look for several articles from a paper on a particular topic. Note how the facts increase day by day and certain retractions and corrections are noted.

Specialized newspapers contain frequently updated information on a particular topic. Examples include *The Financial Times*, which covers company and industry information, and *The Chronicle of Higher Education*, which keeps tabs on educational concerns in higher education.

Newsletters

Newsletters focus on specialized topics. They may be produced for the employees of a certain firm, members of an organization, or participants in a particular industry.

Examples of newsletters include *The Ghost Trackers Newsletter* (Ghost Research Society, P.O. Box 205, Oaklawn, IL 60454-0205), which investigates paranormal phenomena, and *For Fish Farmers* (Mississippi Cooperative Extension Service, P.O. Box 9690, Mississippi State, MS 39762), addressing the concerns of fish farmers. Try the directory *Newsletters in Print* (9th edition. Detroit: Gale, 1997) for finding names, contact information, and descriptions of print and online newsletters in North America, and the *Newsletter Access* site on the Web at http://www.newsletteraccess.com/ for links and information for more than five thousand newsletters.

Newswires and daily news

Newswire services, also known as newswires or wire services, supply constantly updated news stories. You've no doubt noticed that your local newspaper articles

Periodicals on Every Subject Imaginable

The thousands of magazines, journals, newspapers, and newsletters published every year are all potential markets for your writing and opportunities for your research. The magazines you see at bookstores and in the supermarkets represent a fraction of the specialized and niche periodicals that exist. A well-known directory listing thousands of serials arranged by subject is *Ulrich's International Periodicals Directory* (New York: R.R. Bowker. Annual, plus supplements). The competitor to *Ulrich's* and just as useful is *The Serials Directory: An International Reference Book* (Birmingham, AL: EBSCO. Annual, plus supplements).

often sport the byline *by Associated Press*, a wire service. Newswires are the place to look for announcements trumpeting new products, press releases, company news, announcements from the scientific community, cultural and community events, and any breaking news story. Two newswires that offer information at no charge on the Web:

Associated Press. http://wire.ap.org. This site, called The Wire, displays the day's news from the Associated Press and supplies a search engine that will look through a week's worth of stories.

PR Newswire. http://www.prnewswire.com. Browse their Web site for timely news articles on all topics. PR Newswire stories are also accessible through a number of commercial database services, including Bloomberg Financial Markets, Bridge Information Systems, DIALOG, Dow Jones, NEWSEARCH, Predicast's, LEXIS-NEXIS, and others.

You'll never be far from current daily news stories on the Web since you can also grab them on the home page of virtually any search engine, such as *Lycos* (www.lycos.com) or *Excite* (www.excite.com). A link to the latest news will be clearly marked. Daily news is also reported via television and radio Web pages, including *ABC* at http://www.abcnews.com, *NBC* at http://www.msnbc.com, *CBS* at http://www.cbs.com, *FOX* at http://www.foxnews.com, *CNN* at http://www.cnn.com, *C-SPAN* at http://www.c-span.org, *BBC* at http://news.bbc.co.uk/, and *NPR* at http://www.npr.org.

You can also choose to have only the type of news you want gathered for you. One service that does this is *PointCast* at http://www.pointcast.com. Download their free software, indicate the type of news you want to follow, and PointCast will gather full-text publications pulled from hundreds of online newspapers, newswires, and other online services and have it available and constantly updated on your computer desktop.

Periodicals on the Shelf and the Net

Thousands of periodicals are published in print format. Traditionally, when libraries had accrued a few years of a print periodical, they would assure archival access to it in one of two ways: (1) They'd bind the issues together with a book binding, creating bound journals, or (2) They'd purchase back issues of the journal in a microform format, filmed copies of periodicals or other materials that are either in a roll, called microfilm, or flat, called microfiche. Microform both preserves the material and lets libraries and other researchers store large collections in relatively small spaces.

Though bound and microform formats are very much alive for the time being, they are being reevaluated in light of the Web. But until different producers of online periodicals make ironclad promises about access to archival materials—which few have—librarians are going to hesitate before throwing out those back issues.

Many publishers took the Internet plunge early while others are still just dipping their toes in. Few have completely abandoned print format in lieu of an online version. Plenty of full-text journals are now available on the Web and through other electronic means. They come in varied packages with widely ranging access options, some more useful to researchers than others.

The many varieties of online periodicals: E-zines and E-journals

- *Only Online.* Some periodicals on the Web exist solely in electronic format. They were born on the Web and they live on the Web. Many are free and some call for a fee.
- *In Print and Online.* Periodicals that began life in print may include only some of their full-text articles on the Web. Alternately, others not only offer all articles from recent issues, but also include additional online only features.
- *Not Really Online.* Many journals that appear to be online in reality have a home page that merely describes the print version and supplies subscription information.
- *Full-Text via Subscription Databases.* Full-text articles are also online via

dozens of commercial databases and indexes such as *The Health Reference Center*. A few, such as *Electric Library*, are within financial reach of most people, but most are expensive. Luckily, libraries routinely subscribe to online, full-text article databases, with many offering remote access.

- *Full-Text for a Fee.* Additionally, there are online indexes you search for free on the Web, such as the *Northern Light Special Collection* at http://www.nlsearch.com/, *UnCover* at http://uncWeb.carl.org, and *The New York Times* archives at http://www.nytimes.com/, which then charge you a fee to retrieve the full text of an article you want.

Using Periodical Indexes: Efficiently Finding the Article You Need

When you want to find an article on a particular subject or one written by a certain author, use a periodical index. Periodical indexes exist in both print and electronic format. For contemporary research (the mid- to late-1980s on), you'll likely choose indexes in electronic format.

Just as a book index leads you to specific sections of a book, a periodical index leads you to the contents of hundreds of periodicals. Instead of painstakingly browsing journals one at a time to find an article on, say, schizophrenia, simply look in a periodical index such as *PsycInfo* that points to psychology articles. By looking under the subject SCHIZOPHRENIA in either the electronic or print versions, you'd pull up hundreds of articles dealing with schizophrenia.

In a nutshell: Indexes let you find articles by subject or author. When you look up a subject in an index you'll first get a list of citations to articles in different magazines, journals, and/or newspapers about that subject. Commercial electronic indexes now frequently supply the full text of the article you've found online. If the article isn't online, the citation gives all the information you need (including title of the article, author, name of the periodical, volume, issue, pages, and date) to actually go find that article in a library or order it through interlibrary loan or an information broker.

Here's an example of a citation that appeared under the subject heading Right to Die in a volume of the print format of the *Social Sciences Index*, a periodical index that helps you find articles on topics in the social sciences, including sociology, crime, psychology, and economics.

Paging Dr. Death: the political theater of assisted suicide in Michigan. S.P. Fino and others. bibl *Polit Life Sci* v16 p87-103 Mr. 97

First the title of the article, *Paging Dr. Death: the political theater of assisted suicide in Michigan*, is listed, then the author *S.P. Fino* who wrote this article with *other* authors. The *bibl* indicates there is a bibliography.

Notice the name of the journal is abbreviated: *Polit Life Sci*. Print indexes often use abbreviations to save space. The key-to-the-abbreviations page, either in the front or the back of the index, tells you what the full name of the journal is. In this case it is *Politics and the Life Sciences*, Volume 16. Luckily, online indexes rarely abbreviate the name of the journal. Note that journal articles can be rather long; this one, on pages 87-103, is fifteen pages. The final abbreviation, *Mr. 97*, stands for March 1997.

All Journals Are Not Available Full-Text Online

Although librarians are as pleased as the next guy about full-text journals being available on commercial indexes and the Web, we're not so happy to break the news that not all journals are available full-text online. Perhaps public pressure and creative economics will allow this to happen. Not yet.

Online indexes spell the disappearance of most periodical indexes in print format. Though print indexes are still available and up-to-date in most libraries, many print subscriptions are being quietly canceled as researchers realize the advantages of online indexes, including being able to search large time periods quickly and to search two or more keywords at one time.

Choosing indexes based on the type of article you need

Some articles offer quick, simple subject treatments. Others supply in-depth, detailed coverage. Let's say you're looking into causes of stress. Your choices range from popular articles, such as the article from *Redbook* magazine titled "How Stressed Are You? A Personalized Test" (January 1998, v.190, n.3, p.90), to scholarly treatments of the topic, such as the article "Anger Expression and Cardiovascular Reactivity to Mental Stress: A Spectral Analysis Approach" found in the journal *Clinical and Experimental Hypertension* (July-August 1997, v.19, n.5-6, p.901-911).

So, how do you know which index will get you to the kind of article you're looking for? Appendix B of this book will help. Arranged by subject, it lists subject-specific indexes in print and online. You'll see some indexes specialize in identifying scholarly material in a particular field, such as *Sociological Abstracts*. Others, like *General Reference Center* or *Readers' Guide to Periodical Literature*, are best used to find information on popular topics from well-known magazines like *Time, Fortune,* or *Ebony*. Other indexes mix scholarly material with popular material and even throw some books into the mix. As you familiarize yourself with local libraries you'll discover which indexes they subscribe to are best suited to your topic and which are available via remote access.

Often, a multisubject index is a great place to start. Though there's crossover between the holdings of these indexes, I usually check a few of them since I almost always find a gem or two in one that I didn't find in another.

Multisubject indexes

Academic Search Elite. EBSCO. Available as a subscription database via EBSCOhost. Indexes articles from thousands of journals. About half are full text online.

Access. Evanston, IL: John Gordon Burke, 1975–present. Covers magazines not covered by the *Readers' Guide to Periodical Literature*, as well as regional and city magazines.

Alternative Press Index. Baltimore, MD: Alternative Press Center, 1969–present. Also available on CD-ROM and as a subscription database via NISC. Index to "nonmainstream" publications such as *American Atheist* and *Socialist Review.*

ArticleFirst. Dublin, Ohio: OCLC, 1990–present. Available as a subscription database on FirstSearch. Electronic index to over 12,600 full-text articles, some free, some for a fee.

Canadian Periodical Index. Detroit: Gale, 1938–present. Index to English and French language periodicals from the U.S. and Canada.

Contents1st. Dublin, Ohio: OCLC, 1990–present. Available as a subscription database on FirstSearch. Online index to the tables of contents of over 12,600 periodicals.

Electric Library. Wayne, PA: Infonautics Corp. http://www.elibrary.com. A Web-based minilibrary of full-text documents from magazines, newspapers, newswires, radio and television transcripts, and chapters from reference books. Search citations at no charge and retrieve full text for a fee.

The Essay and General Literature Index. New York: H.W. Wilson, 1933–present.

Also available on CD-ROM and as a subscription database via WilsonWeb.
Indexes essays and articles contained in collections of essays and miscellaneous
works such as conference proceedings.

Expanded Academic Index. Foster City, CA: Information Access Company,
1980–present. Available on CD-ROM and as a subscription database via
InfoTrac. Online index to 1,400 scholarly and general-interest journals.
About half the articles are full-text online.

¡Informe! (Revistas en Español). Foster City, CA: Information Access Company.
Current plus two years. Available on CD-ROM and as a subscription
database via Infotrac. Electronic index to periodicals in Spanish. Half are
full-text online.

Magazine Index Plus/ASAP. Foster City, CA: Information Access Company.
Available on CD-ROM and as a subscription database via Infotrac. An index
to popular and general-interest magazines with selected full-text online.

Northern Light Special Collection. http://www.nlsearch.com/. Free Web-based
index to thousands of periodicals. There's a small fee for pulling up the
full text of articles.

Periodical Abstracts. Dublin, Ohio: OCLC, 1986–present. Also available on
CD-ROM and as a subscription database via FirstSearch. Provides indexing
for 1,500+ general and academic journals with full-text available for many
of the articles.

What's an Abstract?

An abstract is a short description of a piece of writing, such as
an article or conference paper, for example. Some periodical
indexes have the word *abstract* in their title, such as *Criminal Justice
Abstracts*, which means that the index will, at minimum, provide a summary paragraph about the article you want.

Poole's Index to Periodical Literature. Gloucester, MA: Peter Smith, 1802–
1906. One of the earliest periodical indexes covering periodicals on a wide
variety of subjects.

Project Muse. http://muse.jhu.edu/muse.html. *Project Muse* subscribers have
access to the full text of the 40+ scholarly journals in the humanities,
social sciences, and mathematics from the Johns Hopkins Press.

ProQuest Discovery and *ProQuest Research.* Ann Arbor, MI: Bell & Howell.

Multisubject online indexes. The former is geared to public libraries and the latter to academic. About half the items are full-text online.

Readers' Guide to Periodical Literature. New York: H.W. Wilson, 1890– present. Also available on CD-ROM and as a subscription database through WilsonWeb. Indexes popular magazines. The full-text version has selected full text available.

SIRS Researcher. Boca Raton, FL: SIRS, 1988–present. Also available as a subscription database via Infotrac. Contains thousands of full-text articles from newspapers, magazines, journals, and government publications.

UnCover. Denver: The UnCover Company, 1988–present. Also available at http://uncWeb.carl.org or telnet://pac.coalliance.org. Choose "UnCover" under the "Free Databases" selection. Free online index to article citations and tables of contents from over seventeen thousand scholarly journals and popular magazines. Full-text articles can be ordered for a fee.

Vertical File Index. Bronx, NY: H.W. Wilson, 1932–present. Index to material published in unusual formats, such as pamphlets, charts, posters, maps, and other inexpensive paperbound items. Ordering instructions for each item are included.

Newspaper Indexes. Since general newspapers cover all topics, newspaper indexes are also multisubject indexes. For a listing of indexes that cover multiple newspapers, check Appendix B.

Finding Electronic Journals by Subject

If you know the name of a journal, magazine, newsletter, or newspaper on the Web, you could simply use your favorite search engine to find the publication by doing a search by the periodical's name; unfortunately, this method has a substantial failure rate.

The sites below will guide you to particular E-journal titles and/or help you discover new titles by searching by subject. These sites will not, however, assist you in searching the contents of E-journals; they let you identify an entire publication by subject. From there you can usually link to the publication and search that single issue.

Ecola Newsstand. http://www.ecola.com/

Ecola Newsstand supplies links, by region and broad subject headings, to over six thousand Web newspapers and magazines worldwide. Ecola selects only those publications that are maintained by paper-printed publications, supply English language content, and offer unrestricted access.

Newspapers on the Web

A terrific page for locating newspapers with any presence on the Web, maintained by the *American Journalism Review*, is *AJR Newslink* at http://www.newslink.org/news.html. AJR Newslink can be searched by geographic area worldwide or by name of newspaper. So it's just as simple to tap into the *Irish News* (http://www.irishnews.com) from Northern Ireland as it is the *Trentonian* (http://www.trentonian.com) from New Jersey's capital city. Lists of papers can also be generated for major metropolitan areas, dailies, non-dailies, business, alternative, specialty, and campus newspapers at this site. Other sites connecting to newspapers include the *Columbia Journalism Review* at http://www.cjr.org/database/papers.asp and *AILEENA* at http://www.aileena.ch/. Newspaper directories in hard copy are listed in chapter thirteen under Market Directories.

Electronic Journal Access. http://www.coalliance.org/ejournal/

Search on this well-organized site by journal title or LC subject heading. Instead of moving directly to the E-journal from the title chosen, this site supplies a useful intermediate record that gives an overview of the E-journal's features, helping the researcher decide if the next click will be a fruitful one. These records describe the intent of the journal, frequency of publication, whether or not it is peer reviewed, and publisher contact information.

E-Journal. http://www.edoc.com/ejournal/

E-Journal presents different periodical categories to choose from, including academic and reviewed journals, college or university publications, E-mail newsletters, magazines, newspaper, print magazines, and online publications focusing on business, finance, or politics. There are then further subject breakdowns within each of these categories.

Also, try a search on a search directory such as Yahoo! by combining the word NEWSLETTER with a subject word of your choice and see what you get.

Locating Hot Topics to Write About
Compilations of current events

The titles below synthesize and analyze current, controversial issues. Use them to generate ideas for your writing topics and as resources for your writing. Older issues will reveal topics that have been too long ignored and are ready to be examined again.

CQ Researcher, formerly titled *Editorial Research Reports*. Washington, DC: Congressional Quarterly, 1924–present. 48/year. Also available online for a fee from Congressional Quarterly.

Four times a month, the *CQ Researcher* issues a report on a topic of current interest. Past reports have covered gay rights, high-speed rail, Americans' feelings about the institution of marriage, and the Peace Corps. Each report gives background on the topic, includes a chronology of major events surrounding the issue, and quotes opposing viewpoints from experts. Also from this publisher is *CQ Weekly*, focusing on current activities on Capitol Hill.

Editorials on File. New York: Facts on File, 1970–present.

What are people thinking about? Concerned about? What's occupying their thoughts to such an extent that they take time to write to newspaper editorial pages to vent their feelings? *Editorials on File* reproduces editorials and editorial cartoons culled from over 150 U.S. and Canadian newspapers. Each topic covered is prefaced by a brief summary of the events that stimulated the editorials. A subject index makes it simple to find opinions on particular topics.

Opposing Viewpoints—SOURCES. Series. St. Paul, MN: Greenhaven Press.

Each volume in this ongoing series focuses on an issue of debate, presenting materials culled from magazines, journals, books, newspapers, and position papers representing opposing views on controversial topics. The differing views are placed back-to-back to create a running debate. Some topics covered in the series include assisted suicide, biomedical ethics, capital punishment, immigration, media violence, and tobacco and smoking.

Taking Sides: Clashing Views on Controversial Issues. 4th edition. Danbury, CT: Grolier Educational, 1997.

Taking Sides is a twenty-one-volume set presenting differing viewpoints on topical issues. Sample topics include: Have public schools failed society? Can public television survive without funds? Should drug use be legalized? Two volumes in this compilation also delve into modern analysis of historic events and actions with such questions as: Was Antebellum Reform motivated primarily by humanitarian goals? Was the Mexican War an exercise in American imperialism?

Dissertations and theses: new ideas from seasoned students

Students studying for masters' degrees in any field usually complete their requirements by writing a thesis, and doctoral students winding up their Ph.D. programs must complete a dissertation. These writings often contain original, breakthrough work, or a new approach to problems and ideas that have been previously studied.

Consider a few recent dissertation titles: "Vocal Abuse In Singers: Causes, Prevention, Remedies and Cures" (Bruce Alan Cain, Ph.D. in Music, Northwestern University, 1998), and "The Relationship Between Employed Women's Stressors and Anger: The Moderating Role of Her and Her Husband's Coping Styles" (Cynthia A. Shelton, Ph.D. in Psychology, Kent State University, 1997).

The most comprehensive index to dissertations, commonly found in academic libraries, is *DAI: Dissertations Abstracts International* (Ann Arbor, Michigan: University Microfilms, 1973–present). *DAI* is available in print, on CD-ROM, and online through CompuServe, DIALOG, DataStar, OCLC, and Ovid subscription online systems. *DAI* cites a large percentage of the doctoral dissertations accepted in North America since 1861. Since 1988, dissertations from fifty universities in Great Britain have also been included. Dissertations are also listed on the commercial database *WorldCat*, though not as comprehensively as in *DAI*.

Neither *DAI* nor *WorldCat* supply the full text of theses and dissertations online. There are four ways of obtaining full-text dissertations and theses:

- Bell & Howell Information and Learning, the publisher that compiles *Dissertations Abstracts Index*, also sells copies of the materials listed, both in print and in microform format. They range in price from about thirty to seventy dollars. Order by calling Bell & Howell's Dissertation Hotline at (800)521-3042 or (800)521-0600, ext. 3781.
- Order a thesis or dissertation through your library's interlibrary loan service. At least one copy of the work is usually maintained by the library of the university or college the student attended. Sometimes the library won't allow these publications to be loaned out if they own just one copy.
- Contact the writer of the dissertation and see if she has a copy to loan. Often the person is willing. You can only hope she lives in the area where she went to college! Call phone information at 555-1212 preceded by the area code for the location, or try some of the online phone directories recommended in chapter six.
- If you can go to the library at the school the writer got his degree from, the publication should be there. As far as other libraries owning the work: rare, but possible.

Bibliographies

Bibliographies, not to be confused with biographies, are lists that recommend research resources on a particular subject. Sometimes, bibliographies are the result of an author's research on a particular aspect of a topic. After writing a book, article, or encyclopedia entry, the author will collect all of the titles of the resources used and list them at the end of the writing.

Other times, those interested in a particular subject will simply compile book-length bibliographies as the goal of their research. They hope other researchers will use the information they recommend to continue burrowing into the subject. Bibliographies may list books, articles, films, sound recordings, special library collections, newsletters, associations, references to unpublished materials, and anything else that might help researchers identify the information that exists on their topic.

One interesting bibliographic series that may stimulate ideas is the *Bibliographic Index* (H.W. Wilson, 1937/42–present). Arranged by subject heading, the *Bibliographic Index* cites bibliographies with at least fifty references that show up in books, pamphlets, magazines, and journals, or that are published separately. Examples from the index include, under the heading Soyfoods, the *Soy Yogurt: Bibliography and Sourcebook*, 1934–1993, which includes original interviews and unpublished archival documents, and under Mentally Handicapped Children, pages 411–418 of the book *Children With Mental Retardation: A Parent's Guide*.

Conference proceedings

Where do flocks of scholars, enthusiasts, and experts gather at least once or twice a year to discuss new developments in their field? At conventions, conferences, professional meetings, and trade shows.

Just as there are indexes to the contents of periodical articles, there are indexes that enable researchers to search for conference papers by subject. Two are:

PapersFirst. On OCLC's FirstSearch, 1993–present, updated monthly. An online index to citations of papers presented at worldwide meetings, conferences, expositions, workshops, congresses, and symposia.

ProceedingsFirst. On OCLC's FirstSearch, 1993–present, updated twenty-four times a year. An online index to over nineteen thousand citations of every congress, symposium, conference, workshop, and meeting received at the British Library.

Once you've identified the name of a conference paper or proceeding you want to peruse, there are a few ways of obtaining them. Some transcripts of conference proceedings, though not many, are now showing up free on the Web. Check the home page of any association likely to hold a conference you'd be interested in; they'll have links to either the transcripts themselves or, more likely, to ordering information.

You can check local library catalogs, but chances are probably slim that your library owns a dazzling number of conference proceedings. Order conference papers and proceedings through a library's interlibrary loan service or a fee-based information broker.

To contact an organization directly regarding their conference proceedings or tapes, use *The Encyclopedia of Associations* or call the toll-free phone directory at (800)555-1212 to obtain numbers for organizations you think maintain toll-free numbers.

If you'd like to attend, gather information from, or locate experts through a particular type of convention but don't know which specific organizations might be involved, try these print directories: *Directory of Conventions* (New York: Successful Meetings Databank. Annual), *World Meetings* (New York: Macmillan. Quarterly), *Encyclopedia of Associations* (Detroit: Gale. Annual). Or try these online directories: *EXPOguide* at http://www.expoguide.com/shows/shows.htm; *TSCentral* at http://www.tscentral.com; and Eventline, available as a subscription database via DIALOG, DataStar, EINS, or OCLC's FirstSearch, a directory of conventions, conferences, symposia, trade fairs, and exhibits worldwide scheduled between the present time through the twenty-first century.

Browsing through periodical indexes to generate ideas

As discussed above, indexes and abstracts lead you to articles on hundreds of different subjects. They can also lead to hundreds of ideas for a topic. Browse through indexes that feature articles from popular magazines to discover what topics are hot. College students can then synthesize ideas from the existing writing and expand upon the ideas presented; freelance writers can brainstorm an untried angle. Also, look through that same index, only in an edition that's fifty years older. What was hot then? Is it time to revive it? Follow up on it?

Freelance writers will find it especially interesting to browse the citations of scholarly indexes and abstracts for ideas. These references represent articles in specialized, scholarly publications. But often the subjects of these articles touch on ideas that would be of interest to the public at large. Find those articles and make the ideas readable and accessible. Different writers can produce polar opposite pieces on the same subject.

Transcripts of Speeches and Broadcasts

Information first presented in the spoken word is now often captured in the written word. It's possible to find transcripts of many speeches and presentations from conferences, banquets, or other special events, and transcripts of radio and television broadcasts. Having a chance to slowly pore over the written words of a political debate, for example, can be fascinating. It offers a closer look at words that may have flown by the ear, and the opportunity to pull interesting quotations.

Commercial databases containing full-text transcripts

Programs that supply transcripts tend to be news programs, talk shows, and documentaries. Commercial indexes that supply the full text of numerous broadcasts include:

Electric Library. Wayne, PA: Infonautics. http://www.elibrary.com

In addition to supplying full-text reference books and periodicals, *Electric Library* subscription online system also offers transcripts from a variety of television and radio shows, including: ABC programs such as *20/20*, *Good Morning America*, and *World News Tonight With Peter Jennings*; shows from CNNfn (CNN Financial Network) such as *Moneyline*; NPR programming, including *All Things Considered* and *Fresh Air*; and MSNBC offerings, such as *MSNBC Professional.*

LEXIS-NEXIS. Dayton, Ohio: LEXIS-NEXIS. http://www.lexis-nexis.com

Some of the program transcripts on the commercial LEXIS-NEXIS system come from ABC News, CNN, CNN Financial Network, and National Public Radio.

Transcripts on radio and television web pages

You'll have mixed luck locating transcribed broadcasts on the Web pages maintained by media companies. Some worthwhile stops include:

CNN: Cable News Network. http://www.cnn.com

Search the CNN Web page by keyword for full-text transcripts from many CNN broadcasts. Video and audio segments can also be viewed by downloading the needed plug-ins. The number of days, years, or months that transcripts are available on this page varies for different CNN programming.

MSNBC. http://www.msnbc.com

Choose "On Air" from the home page choices to locate select transcriptions of NBC's cable and network offerings, including *Dateline, Today, Nightly News With Tom Brokaw, Meet the Press, Imus on MSNBC, InterNight, The Big Show With Keith Olbermann, News With Brian Williams,* and *Time & Again.* To find the transcripts, click on a particular show and then choose "archives." A few dozen transcripts are offered for each show, with topics ranging from a

Dateline show titled "Egg Freshness," to a *Today* segment called "Birth Order: Does It Shape Your Personality?"

PBS: Public Broadcasting System. http://www.pbs.org

The Web site for PBS offers transcripts from programs such as *The News-Hour With Jim Lehrer, NOVA,* and *Frontline.* Choose "search" from the home page and do a keyword search (for example: OKLAHOMA CITY or MARI-JUANA). Though many transcripts are free, some need to be ordered for a fee from Strictly Business, (913)649-6381.

Television News Archives: Vanderbilt University. http://tvnews.vanderbilt.edu/

Since 1968, the Television News Archive has recorded, abstracted, and indexed television news broadcasts from ABC, CBS, and NBC. Videotapes of programs can be borrowed from Vanderbilt but the searchable abstracts on their Web site also contain useful information. Contact information: Vanderbilt Television News Archive, Vanderbilt University, 110 21st Ave. South, Suite 704, Nashville, TN 37203, Phone: (615)322-2927, Fax: (615)343-8250, E-mail: tvnews@tvnews.Vanderbilt.edu.

Voice of America. http://www.voa.gov

The goal of *VOA* is to communicate U.S. policy, news, and events to the rest of the world via the radio. Either listen to or read up to a weeks worth of reporting from *VOA* correspondents on this Web page.

The Speech and Transcript Center at http://gwis2.circ.gwu.edu/~gprice /speech.htm is a meta site of pointers to audio and text versions of speeches on the Web. There are links to historical speeches from business executives; radio and television broadcasts; U.S. city, state, and federal government officials; and representatives of international government and organizations.

Buying transcripts

If you'd like to bypass the no-charge options and quickly get your hands on a transcript, call one of the major transcription companies and make your purchase. The cost of transcripts hovers between five and seven dollars, though shipping and handling on rush orders can raise that price significantly.

Burrelle's Transcripts, Department I, Box 7, Livingston, NJ 07039-0007, Phone: (800)777-8398 or outside the U.S.: (801)374-1022, E-mail: burrelle@aol .com, URL: http://www.burrelles.com

Sample programs transcribed by Burrelle's: *48 Hours, 60 Minutes, CBS Evening News, CBS This Morning, Face the Nation, Osgood File, Dateline NBC,*

Meet the Press, NBC Nightly News, (NBC) Today, Charles Grodin, Rivera Live, Tim Russert, C-Span's Booknotes, The 700 Club, InterNight, Montel Williams, and *Oprah.*

Federal News Service (FNS), Phone: (800)211-4020, E-mail: info@fnsg.com, URL: http://www.fnsg.com

FNS supplies same day verbatim transcripts of words spoken by American and Russian leaders on matters of official government policy and other issues of the day. They cover all presidential statements; briefings at the White House and State, Defense and Justice Departments; speeches and press conferences of policymakers and spokespersons; and speeches by foreign dignitaries visiting Washington congressional hearings. FNS Moscow provides verbatim text in English of speeches, press conferences, and interviews with Russia's political and economic leaders. Search the FNS site by keyword.

800-All-News, 1535 Grant St., Suite 390, Denver, CO 80203, Phone: (800) ALL-NEWS (255-6397), E-mail orders: Web-orders@800-ALL-NEWS.com, URL: http://www.800-all-news.com

The search engine on HyperScribe's home page will help you quickly locate descriptions of programs transcribed by HyperScribe, or call their toll-free number and tell them what you need. Some of the programs covered by HyperScribe include: *Adam Smith's Money World, The Charlie Rose Show, Frontline, Nova, Washington Week in Review,* and *Wall Street Journal Report.* HyperScribe also sells videotapes of programs.

Strictly Business, P.O. Box 12803, Overland Park, Kansas 66212, Phone: (913)649-6381

Strictly Business transcribes PBS programming, including *The NewsHour With Jim Lehrer.* At the time of this writing they were planning on launching a Web page.

Speech collections and indexes

Speeches and interviews are plentiful in libraries and on the Web. Type in the word SPEECHES in your library's online catalog or on an Internet search engine along with subject keyword(s) or the name of the person, e.g., GLORIA STEINEM SPEECHES, FEMINISM SPEECHES, or NATIVE AMERICANS SPEECHES.

You'll locate speeches in print, audio, and video. If you only want to hear the speech, put the word SOUND (for sound recording) or VIDEORECORDING after your search terms in a library catalog. For more general collections of oratory,

Worth a Visit: The Museum of Television and Radio

Whether you want to watch Lucille Ball get into mischief or Dick Cavett interview Rudolph Nureyev, you can do it at the Museum of Television and Radio. The museum has thousands of radio and television broadcasts but no transcripts. Visitors may stop and start programs as needed while viewing. In New York the museum is located at 25 W. Fifty-second St., New York 10019, Phone: (212)621-6800 for daily information on scheduled activities or (212) 621-6600 for other information; In California: 465 N. Beverly Dr., Beverly Hills, 90210—Phone: (310)786-1025 for daily information or (310)786-1000. Also see http://www.mtr.org.

combine the word SPEECHES with a word such as GREAT or HISTORY.

Local newspapers sometimes include the full transcript of orations important to the area they serve, and national newspapers may include transcriptions of important speeches. Check the newspaper indexes listed in Appendix B.

A useful index which, unfortunately, has not been updated since 1982, is the *Speech Index: An Index to Collections of World Famous Orations & Speeches for Various Occasions: 1966-1980* (4th edition. New York: Scarecrow Press, 1982.) *Speech Index* is a guide to the speeches of famous orators of all eras that have been reprinted in books, indexed by speechmaker, title, or subject.

The following books of collected speeches contain the transcripts of talks from events ranging from fund-raising dinners to presidential inauguration ceremonies.

Voices of Multicultural America: Notable Speeches Delivered by African, Asian, Hispanic, and Native Americans, 1790-1995. Deborah Gillan Straub, ed. Detroit: Gale, 1996.

Over 230 full-text speeches from 130 speakers fill this volume. Just a few of the subjects covered include: desegregation, ethnic stereotyping, protest speeches, and repatriation of Native American remains and artifacts.

Representative American Speeches: The Reference Shelf Series. New York: H.W. Wilson, 1937–Present. Annual.

Speeches in these volumes represent current issues and social trends in America. Some examples from the 1996–1997 edition include remarks in Congress by Senator Carol Moseley-Braun regarding a rash of church burnings and the legislation needed to curb them, and a speech by teacher Claudia Hopkins to the Rotary Club in Tupelo, Mississippi, regarding the idea that

learning is dependent upon a personal connection between teacher and pupil.
Vital Speeches of the Day. New York: The City News Publication Co., 1934–
present. Published twice monthly.

Vital Speeches presents texts of addresses of contemporary leaders of public
opinion in the fields of economics, politics, education, sociology, and business.
Sample speeches from *Vital Speeches* include: "Market Capitalism: The Role
of Free Markets" by Alan Greenspan, delivered to the Annual Convention of
the American Society of Newspaper Editors in May 1998, and "From Lip
Service to Real Service: Reversing America's Downward Service Spiral," a
speech to the Chief Executive Club of Boston by Jim Kelly. *Vital Speeches* is
indexed by speech topic and speechmaker in many periodical indexes, including *ABI-Inform, General Reference Center, PAIS, Readers' Guide to Periodical
Literature,* and others.

Weekly Compilation of Presidential Documents. Washington, DC: Office of the
Federal Register, National Archives and Records Administration, 1965–
present. Also available at http://www.access.gpo.gov/nara/nara003.html,
1995–present.

This source contains statements, comments, speeches, and other presidential materials released by the White House. Examples of contents include:
remarks by the president at formal dinners (for example, a dinner hosted by
François Mitterand in Paris), statements when greeting organizations (such as
the National Council of La Raza), presidential proclamations, and transcripts
of news conferences and radio addresses.

CHAPTER 5

Background and Statistics Research

Finding Definitions, Topic Summaries, Overviews, and Statistical Data

"Everybody is ignorant, only on different subjects."

—Will Rogers

There are times when you just need to get a grip on a topic—to learn the background of an event you mention in your writing, in preparation for an interview with an expert, or to gear up for the in-depth research you'll do later. Similarly, you'll often need to pull specific statistics or facts to add authority or perspective to your writing and presentations. Using dictionaries, encyclopedias, almanacs, fact books, and articles are great ways of familiarizing yourself with varied subjects and gathering scattered data.

Lingo: Using Specialized Dictionaries to Learn Unfamiliar Terminology

Often, the first challenge of learning a new subject is becoming familiar with the special words used in that subject area. There are special dictionaries that define the jargon of any discipline or profession. Here are just a few sample titles to show the variety available:

The Sailing Dictionary. (2nd edition. Dobbs Ferry, NY: Sheridan House, 1992). Sample definition: "*Quant*—A long pole with a fork or disc at the lower end, used to propel a small boat (quanting) by pushing on the bottom."

The Facts on File Dictionary of Military Science (New York: Facts on File, 1989). Sample definition (excerpt): "*Mae West*—A brightly colored inflatable life jacket first worn for emergency use by American pilots during World War II flights over water."

To locate specialized dictionaries in your library, do a keyword search in the library's online catalog using a word describing your topic and the term DICTIONARIES. For example: AERONAUTICS DICTIONARIES, NUTRITION DICTIONARIES, or PSYCHOTHERAPY DICTIONARIES.

Often, you'll need to choose broad subject headings when looking for specialized dictionaries. For example, a small library that doesn't have a biology dictionary may have a general science dictionary containing the terms you need. Some broader search examples: RELIGION DICTIONARIES (instead of BUDDHIST DICTIONARIES), SPORTS DICTIONARIES (instead of FOOTBALL DICTIONARIES), and BUSINESS DICTIONARIES (instead of REAL ESTATE DICTIONARIES).

The quality of dictionaries on the Web is mixed. While authoritative resources have definitely made their way online, others are mounted by hobbyists and contain only brief definitions with no quality control in sight. You can use the subject words recommended earlier in a Web search (DICTIONARIES and the topic word), but your results won't be as consistent as on a library catalog. You'll also have success on the Web by combining a keyword with the word DICTIONARY (singular instead of plural) or GLOSSARY.

Sample titles of dictionaries on the Web include *The Political Dictionary* at http://www.fast-times.com/political/political.html, *InvestorWords: The Biggest, Best, Investing Glossary on the Web* at http://www.investorwords.com/, and *Ice Hockey Glossary* at http://www.firstbasesports.com/glossaries/hkygl.htm.

Internet meta sites to dictionaries of all sorts, including English language, foreign language, and special topic, include:

A Web of On-Line Dictionaries.
   http://www.facstaff.bucknell.edu/rbeard/diction.html
Yahoo!: Reference: Dictionaries. http://www.yahoo.com/reference/dictionaries

Of note is the OneLook Dictionary at http://www.onelook.com. OneLook looks for the definition of a word by simultaneously searching hundreds of dictionaries it has links to. To see a list of the subject-specific dictionaries that OneLook searches, just click on "Special Subjects."

Finding Facts and Statistics Using Multisubject Resources

When looking for statistics or general facts, start by perusing one or more of the print and electronic resources that compile information on multiple subjects.

Since most are easily accessible, they're an easy and often fruitful place to start when looking for just about any statistic.

General encyclopedias

Even as a librarian, I forget just how much information is contained in a good, general encyclopedia set. Elements presented in most encyclopedias include biographies of well-known people; a wide spectrum of statistics, historical surveys, and contemporary information on different topics, organizations, and events; explanations of complex concepts in terms understandable to the layman; and photographs, drawings, diagrams, maps, and other illustrations that complement the text and further the reader's understanding of a topic.

Facts in a Flash

Use the Back-of-the-Book Index for Unearthing Facts

Many statistics aren't found in statistical compilations—they're just in general, run-of-the-mill books. For example, a general book that discusses capital punishment would most likely quote statistics dealing with the death penalty, and a book about divorce will likely list figures for marriage breakups. Always use the index in the back of a book to find a tiny bit of hidden information—don't just rely on the table of contents in the front.

Also apply the advice about using back-of-the-book indexes to multivolume reference sets such as encyclopedias. Though the major subjects are in alphabetic order in the set, useful data is hidden within each subject area. For example, a student I was working with couldn't find the concept of *heart rate* in *The Encyclopedia of Human Biology* (2nd edition. 9 Volumes. New York: Academic Press, 1997). I realized she was just looking under *H* for *heart* in the main volumes. Once we looked under *heart rate* in the index volume, we located mentions of *heart rate* in several sections.

Of course this example illustrates an advantage of electronic versions of encyclopedias: When you type in a word, it will find all occurrences of the word whether the word is at the head of a section or buried in a paragraph. (This can also be a drawback since jumping to a word or phrase in any context can bring you to places you don't want to be!)

All libraries own one or more encyclopedic sets in print, and many offer electronic versions online. Check with your library to see if they also offer an online version to remote users, so you can use it at home.

A CD-ROM encyclopedia with periodic updates is a worthwhile investment for any computer owner. As librarian and writer Walt Crawford says in *Online Magazine*, January 1998, "most households are better served by $30-$50 CD-ROM encyclopedias updated every year or two than by massive $600-$1,500 print encyclopedias that the households will never update."

Though free, multisubject encyclopedias on the Web don't generally have the breadth and/or editorial control of commercially available encyclopedias, they're worth a look. General Web encyclopedias at no charge include:

Encarta Online. http://encarta.msn.com/EncartaHome.asp Encarta Online, from Microsoft, includes the contents of the Encarta Concise Encyclopedia, an abridged version of *Encarta Encyclopedia on CD-ROM.* The print equivalent to the complete Encarta is the Funk & Wagnall's encyclopedia.

Encyclopedia.Com. http://encyclopedia.com. Over 17,000 encyclopedic articles from the Concise Columbia Electronic Encyclopedia reside on this Web site.

Free Internet Encyclopedia. http://clever.net/cam/encyclopedia.html. This site brings you to links on the Web that supply encyclopedic entries on different topics.

Statistical compilations covering all subjects

Do you need to know the educational attainment level in different U.S. states? How about the number of families in the U.S.? And the number of children in each? Or the average expenditures on fresh fruit by race and age? The data for all these diverse questions and hundreds of others can be found in one terrific statistical package: *Statistical Abstract of the United States* (Washington, DC: U.S. Bureau of the Census. Annual). This compilation of statistics gathered from government organizations and trade and industry groups is the first place to look for any statistic. *Statistical Abstract* should be available at every library in print or on CD-ROM, and the last few editions are on the Web at http://www.census.gov/.

In addition to *Statistical Abstract,* the following resources present statistics on numerous topics:

Gale Book of Averages. Kathleen Droste, ed. Detroit: Gale, 1994.

Did you know that you burn an average of 180 calories per hour doing housework? Or that the driest city in the U.S. is Reno, Nevada, with average yearly rainfall of 7.53 inches? The *Book of Averages* looks at averages of all kinds, for activities, consumption, manufacturing, costs, weights, life cycles, temperatures, and speeds.

Historical Statistics of the United States: Colonial Times to 1970. Washington, DC: U.S. Department of Commerce, Bureau of the Census, 1976. Also available on CD-ROM.

This is a two-volume compilation, commonly found in larger libraries, containing U.S. historical statistical data on subjects ranging from rape statistics to figures for men's shoe production. There are 12,500 time series included, mostly annual, of figures related to U.S. social, economic, political, and geographic development from 1610 to 1970.

Information Please. http://www.infoplease.com/

The Information Please publishers have established a free Web site that pulls statistics and facts from *The Columbia Encyclopedia, The Random House Websters College Dictionary* and their almanacs, including *The A&E Information Please Entertainment Almanac* and the *ESPN Information Please Sports Almanac.* Choose from dozens of subject headings or simply do a keyword search.

A Matter of Fact: Statements Containing Statistics on Current Social, Economic, and Political Issues. Ann Arbor, MI: Pieran Press. Also available on CD-ROM and as a subscription database via OCLC's FirstSearch, where it's called *FactSearch.*

A Matter of Fact/FactSearch presents statistical statements searchable by subject pulled from some one thousand newspapers; magazines; newsletters; congressional hearings and press briefings from the White House, State Department, and Department of Defense; and Australian, British, and Canadian Parliamentary Debates. Web links to free full text are frequently listed.

Price's List of Lists. http://gwis2.circ.gwu.edu/~gprice/listof.htm

Librarian Gary Price of George Washington University has done a stellar job of maintaining a Web page that points to listings and rankings of people, places, corporations, industries, activities, best-selling books, and anything else one might think to rank. Sample lists include 250 Richest Towns in America, On-Time Arrival Rankings by Major U.S. Air Carriers, and Ten Countries With the Highest Plant Biodiversity in Their Frontier Forests.

Statistical Resources on the Web. http://www.lib.umich.edu/libhome/Documents .center/stats.html

Maintained by the government documents center at the University of Michigan library, this site links to pages containing statistics for just about any topic.

World Almanac and Book of Facts. Mahwah, NJ: World Almanac Books. Annual. Also available on CD-ROM as part of Microsoft Bookshelf and Softkey's

Infopedia, and as a subscription database via OCLC's FirstSearch, *Electric Library*, and EBSCOhost.

With over a million features and facts, this is a mini-universe of information, highlighting both current and historical economic, social, and political events worldwide, supplying facts on every state in the U.S. and every country in the world, and providing basic facts such as weights, measures, and eclipses of the moon.

Statistical indexes covering all topics

Just as periodical indexes lead you to articles found in magazines, statistical indexes zero in on statistics buried in books, documents, and other nooks and crannies. A statistical index of note is *ASI: The American Statistics Index* (Washington, DC: Congressional Information Service, 1973–present. Monthly. Also available on CD-ROM and as a subscription database via *Statististical Universe*).

ASI—a goldmine of statistics—is a detailed subject index to statistics appearing in U.S. government publications. When using *ASI* you'll note that some items are marked by a black dot (•). This dot indicates that the item is owned by all full depository libraries—maybe your library. Two other monthly indexes produced by this publisher and complementary to *ASI* are *Statistical Reference Index (SRI)* and the *Index to International Statistics (IIS)*. *SRI* is a subject index to the statistics in a variety of publications produced by sources other than the U.S. government. *IIS* indexes and describes statistical publications from about one hundred international intergovernmental agencies around the world.

Finding statistics in articles

Articles are often where "fast facts" are waiting for you to find them—statements from experts, biographical information, a concise interpretation of a complex subject, or statistics. Many newly gathered statistics will appear first in periodical articles. Even if I find statistics in reference compilations, I sometimes follow up with articles where I may find newer figures and additional commentary. Use the statistical indexes listed earlier or the periodical indexes listed in Appendix B to locate figures and basic information from articles. For example, if I wanted to find statistics on the prevalence of gangs, I might choose the *Criminal Justice Abstracts* or a multisubject index like *UnCover*.

Keywords to use to find statistics online

When searching for statistics or facts by subject in a library catalog use a word describing the kind of statistics you want, or an area you'd like statistics for, combined with the word STATISTICS. To locate encyclopedic works that cover specific subjects and usually include statistics, combine your topic word with ENCYCLOPEDIAS or HANDBOOKS. Some examples: CALIFORNIA STATISTICS, CRIME ENCYCLOPEDIAS, or COMPUTER SCIENCE HANDBOOKS.

You can also match your keyword(s) with OPINION POLLS, PUBLIC OPINION, SURVEYS, or MISCELLANEA.

Techniques for searching online library catalogs will also work, though less consistently, on the Internet. If you do want to simply cast around for statistics and encyclopedias on the Internet using search engines, use any words you can think of that might show up in the type of document you hope to find. For useful jumping-off points, see Meta Sites to Reference Works on the Web later in this chapter.

Browsing the Reference Collection to Find Statistics

One effective way of finding specialized statistical directories in a library is by just browsing in the area of a library reference collection that represents your subject area. For example, compilations of health/medical statistics will be in the R section of the reference stacks in a Library of Congress arranged library, and in the 610-619 area of a Dewey library.

Using Encyclopedias, Guides, and Statistical Compilations

There are a myriad of choices when looking for fact and statistic reference works focusing on specific topics. I've listed representative online and print resources for dozens of subjects, along with search strategies.

Abbreviations and symbols

Acronym and Abbreviation Server. http://www.ucc.ie/info/net/acronyms/acro.html
Search for acronym translations at this site maintained by the University College of Cork. If you don't find one, it will be added to a list of stumpers so that kind and curious visitors to the page can offer a clue or solution.

Acronym Finder. http://www.AcronymFinder.com
A searchable database of common acronyms and abbreviations on all sub-

jects but with a focus on computers, technology, telecommunications, and the military.

Acronyms, Initialisms & Abbreviations Dictionary. 24th edition. 3 Volumes. Detroit: Gale, 1998.

Using this set, just look under an abbreviation (for example, *STB*) and see what it stands for (STB denotes a Bachelor of the Science of Theology degree). The last volume is the *Reverse Acronyms, Initialisms, & Abbreviations Dictionary* which enables the reader to look up the full name of an organization or a full title or word and find its abbreviation.

Symbols.com. http://www.symbols.com/

Over 2,500 Western signs and ideograms are displayed and described via this Web page. Search by the meaning of a symbol or use the graphic index to describe what the symbol you're seeking looks like.

Animals and Insects

See also: Nature/Environment

Grzimek's Animal Life Encyclopedia. 13 Volumes. Bernhard Grzimek, ed. New York: Van Nostrand, 1972–1975.

Grzimek's supplies information on the physiology and habits of birds, fish, amphibians, reptiles, insects, mollusks and echinoderms, lower forms, and mammals, along with illustrated color drawings and photographs. The mammals volumes have been updated in *Grzimek's Encyclopedia of Mammals* (5 Volumes, 1990). It is also available on CD-ROM from the National Geographic Society under the title *Mammals: A Multimedia Encyclopedia.*

Wildlife Web Animal Links. http://www.selu.com/~bio/wildlife/links/animals .html.

See this site for links to specialized sites on the Web dealing with wildlife issues and information about a daunting number of species.

To locate other encyclopedias on specific animals when searching a library catalog, combine the name of the type of animal, using the plural version, such as CATS, DOGS, HORSES, FISH, BIRDS, or ENDANGERED SPECIES, with the word ENCYCLOPEDIAS or the word HANDBOOKS.

Anthropology

See chapter nine

Art and Architecture

Architecture Virtual Library. http://www.clr.toronto.edu:1080/VIRTUALLIB/
ARCH/news.html

This Web page is a starting point for finding dozens of architecture-related destinations on the Web, including organizations, newsgroups, competitions, and educational information.

Grove Dictionary of Art. 34 Volumes. New York: Macmillan Reference, 1996. Also available as a subscription database via Grove Dictionaries, Inc.

Over 6,800 scholars from 120 nations took part in the creation of this widely hailed art encyclopedia. It covers all forms of the visual arts including painting, sculpture, architecture, graphic and decorative arts, and photography, from prehistory to the 1990s. It contains 15,000 images. Another major collection is the *Encyclopedia of World Art* (17 Volumes. New York: McGraw-Hill, 1959–1968. V.1-15, 1983, first supplement; 1987, second supplement).

Encyclopedia of Architecture: Design, Engineering, & Construction. 5 Volumes. Joseph A. Wilkes, ed. New York: John Wiley & Sons, 1988–1990.

The essays in this set examine architectural design, the regulations it's bound by, methods and materials of construction and engineering, and architecture education. Many photographs, line drawings, and graphs accent the lengthy entries. The lives and work of well-known architects are also included.

Essential Links to Photography. http://www.el.com/elinks/photography/

This meta site to photography pages points to such destinations as an online digital archive of photographs and photographic exhibits.

Virtually Visiting Museums

Museums worldwide maintain Web pages that display representative works from their collection. Two meta sites that lead to museum pages are *WWW Virtual Library: Museums* at http://www.comlab.ox.ac.uk/archive/other/museums/lists.html and *WebMuseum, Paris* at http://sunsite.unc.edu/louvre/.

Awards

To find books or listings of award winners and awards when searching a library catalog or the Web, use the word PRIZES or AWARDS with a keyword such as DESIGN, MUSIC, or SCIENCE.

Also search by names of familiar awards, such as ACADEMY AWARDS (film), EMMY AWARDS (television), GRAMMY AWARDS (music), NEWBERY MEDAL (children's book writing), NOBEL PRIZES (physics, chemistry, physiology, medicine, literature, economics, and the promotion of world peace), PULITZER PRIZE (journalism, letters, drama, and music), and TONY AWARDS (theater).

The Web is also an excellent choice when looking for mention of honors and recognition by community groups, small businesses, and other organizations. Use the same search terminology recommended for library catalogs.

Two print award compendiums of note are *Awards, Honors, and Prizes*, 14th edition (2 Volumes. Detroit: Gale, 1998), an international directory of award opportunities and their donors, for achievement in all fields, including arts and humanities, business, science, and the social sciences, and *World of Winners: A Current and Historical Perspective on Awards and Their Winners* (Detroit: Gale, 1992) which identifies winners of 2,500 awards in "all areas of human endeavor."

Careers

See also: chapter twelve

To locate detailed descriptions of jobs, look at specialized career guides. Find these guides by using a library catalog and doing a keyword search, matching the word that describes an occupational field along with the phrase VOCATIONAL GUIDANCE. It sounds archaic but it works. Some examples: SCIENCE VOCATIONAL GUIDANCE, MARKETING VOCATIONAL GUIDANCE, or SPORTS VOCATIONAL GUIDANCE.

Avoid using career descriptions that are too specific. For example, the phrase KINDERGARTEN TEACHER matched with VOCATIONAL GUIDANCE is too specific. You'd probably be more successful using the general wording TEACHERS or EDUCATION.

Some recommended sites for job hunters are *The Career Mosaic*, http://www.careermosaic.com, *The Monster Board*, http://www.monster.com, and *Job Options*, http://www.joboptions.com. Also, if you have a company or organization in mind to apply to, remember that many are now putting employment information on their company Web page.

Chemical Properties, Formulas, and Effects

See also: Poisons, Toxic Chemicals, and Dangerous Wildlife; and Science and Engineering

The Chemical Formulary: Collection of Commercial Formulas for Making Thousands of Products in Many Fields. New York: Chemical Publishing Company. Irregular.

Each volume of this growing set reproduces commercial formulas for many substances, including beverages, food, paints, cosmetics, cleaners, drugs, adhesives, plastics, and miscellaneous items such as dog shampoo and mildewproofer for leather goods.

The CRC Handbook of Chemistry and Physics: A Ready-Reference Book of Chemical and Physical Data. David R. Lide, ed. Boca Raton: CRC Press. Annual.

This handbook covers such information as basic constants, units and conversion factors, fluid properties, physical constants of organic compounds, and properties of the elements and inorganic compounds. Also covered are aspects of physics, including atomic, molecular, optical, nuclear, and particle physics.

Hazardous Chemicals Desk Reference. 4th edition. Richard J. Lewis, Sr. New York: Van Nos Reinhold, 1997.

By hazardous, this reference is referring to chemicals that are explosive, highly flammable or reactive. For each chemical presented, the author provides the molecular formula and weight, the properties, synonyms for the entry name, any cancer-causing suspicions surrounding the chemical, and a hazard rating.

The Merck Index: An Encyclopedia of Chemicals and Drugs. 12th edition. Rahway, NJ: Merck & Company, 1996. Also a subscription database via Questel-Orbit.

The Merck Index is an encyclopedia of chemicals, drugs, and biological substances, supplying descriptions of the preparation and properties of compounds, a listing of their trivial, generic, and chemical names, and explanations of their use, pharmacological properties, and toxicity.

Children and Youth

Gale Encyclopedia of Childhood and Adolescence. Jerome Kagan. Detroit: Gale, 1998.

This volume is directed to both specialists and students, covering the study of human development from birth through adolescence. Included are entries on theories, behaviors, and physical ailments related to children.

Statistical Record of Children. Linda Schmittroth, ed. Detroit: Gale. Biennial.

How many children are awaiting adoption? What percentage live in poverty? What's the percentage of children who are read to? If you're looking for answers to these types of questions about U.S. youth, give this volume a try.

Unicef, 333 E. 38th St., GC-6, New York, NY 10016, Phone: (212)686-5522

or (212)922-2620, Fax: (212)779-1679, E-mail: information@unicef.usa,
URL: http://www.unicef.org

UNICEF, part of the United Nations, works toward improving the living
conditions of children worldwide. Check their home page for such publications as *State of the World's Children* and *Progress of Nations*, focusing annually
on issues of concern and supplying statistical indicators of how children are
cared for worldwide. Their publications are also available in hard copy.

Youth Indicators: Trends in the Well-Being of American Youth. National Center
for Education Statistics. Washington, DC: U.S. Dept. of Education, Office
of Educational Research and Improvement. Annual. Also available at http://
nces.ed.gov/pubs/yi/index1.html.

Are modern-day kids in good physical shape? Are they proficient in science?
Youth Indicators is a statistical compilation of data on the world of young
people, including family structure, economic factors, extracurricular activities,
education, substance use and abuse, health, and values.

Other sites focusing on the well-being of children are *America's Children:
Key National Indicators of Child Well-Being* at http://childstats.gov/ac1998/
ac98.htm and *Kids Count Data Book: State Profiles of Child Well-Being* at
http://www.aecf.org and also available in print.

Crime

See also: Drug and Alcohol Abuse

Bureau of Justice Statistics. http://www.ojp.usdoj.gov/bjs/welcome.html

The Bureau of Justice Statistics, under the auspices of the United States
Department of Justice, produces a veritable storm of statistics on topics related
to crime, criminals, and law enforcement. Sample publications available on
the BJS Web page and in print at many libraries and at government bookstores
include:

Correctional Populations in the United States.
http://www.ojp.usdoj.gov/bjs/pubalp2.htm.

This reports looks at the number of inmates in local, state, and federal
jails, including those executed and those awaiting the death sentence.

Crime in the United States: Uniform Crime Reports for the U.S.
http://www.fbi.gov/crimestats.htm

Published by the FBI, this report presents annual statistics on U.S. crime rates, trends, and arrests.

Sourcebook of Criminal Justice Statistics.
http://www.albany.edu/sourcebook
A yearly publication supplying statistics on the characteristics of criminal justice systems, public attitudes toward crime, the nature and distribution of crimes and criminals, the judicial processing of criminals, and aspects of incarceration.

Also, visit the *Department of Justice* home page at http://www.usdoj .gov/ for links to publications and data at such sites as the *National Institute of Corrections* at http://www.nicic.org/inst/, the *Federal Bureau of Prisons* at http://www.bop.gov, and the *Federal Bureau of Investigation* at http:// www.fbi.gov.

Corrections Yearbook: Instant Answers to Key Questions in Corrections. South Salem, NY: Criminal Justice Institute. Annual.
Presents wide-ranging statistics dealing with probation, parole, jails, and public and private prisons.

Crime Investigation

Books and Internet sites of interest to both the professional crime investigator and the mystery writer include: *Latent Print Examination* at http://onin.com/fp/fp.html for information about examining fingerprints, palm prints, and footprints; *An Introduction to Forensic Firearms Identification* at http://www.geocities.com/~jsdoyle/ to learn how to determine if a bullet, cartridge case, or other ammunition component was fired from a specific firearm; and, in hard copy, the *Howdunit* series from Writer's Digest Books which includes titles such as *Scene of the Crime: A Writer's Guide to Crime-Scene Investigations, Police Procedural: A Writer's Guide to the Police and How They Work,* and *Private Eyes: A Writer's Guide to Private Investigating.* Also see the section under Death.

Drug Enforcement Administration (DEA), Department of Justice, Washington, DC 20537, Phone: (202)307-7977, URL: http://www.usdoj.gov/dea
The DEA home page supplies charts illustrating drug use statistics, photo-

graphs and descriptions of fugitives, and DEA program information.

The Encyclopedia of Police Science. 2nd edition. William G. Bailey. New York: Garland, 1995.

> *The Encyclopedia of Police Science* explains what U.S. law enforcers do on the job, describes notable police officers and departments, and details some of the stresses and pitfalls of working in such a dangerous profession.

Encyclopedia of World Crime. 6 Volumes. Jay Robert Nash. Wilmette, IL: CrimeBooks, 1990.

> This compendium details the activities of murderers and other ne'er-do-wells around the world, along with descriptions of law enforcement officials and victims. It also includes a dictionary of more than twenty thousand terms used by criminals and those in law enforcement, from ancient times through the 1980s.

Justice Information Center: National Criminal Justice Reference Service (NCJRS). http://www.ncjrs.org/.

> This site has links to documents, Web sites and listservs pertinent to all areas of criminal and juvenile justice. The NCJRS Abstracts Database at this site supplies summaries of more than 140,000 criminal justice publications, including federal, state, and local government reports, books, journal articles, and unpublished research.

Dance

International Encyclopedia of Dance. 6 Volumes. Selma Jeanne Cohen, ed. New York: Oxford University Press, 1998.

> This set contains entries on all forms of dance around the world, with selective entries on individuals involved in the art and more than two thousand illustrations.

Death

See *also:* Vital Statistics

Autopsy. http://worldmall.com/erf/autopsy.htm

> Pathologist Ed Friedlander has written this description of the autopsy process, and he supplies links to other sites for budding pathologists and murder novelists.

Cause of Death: A Writer's Guide to Death, Murder & Forensic Medicine. Keith D. Wilson, MD. Cincinnati, Ohio: Writer's Digest Books, 1992.

Part I of this volume, "Death and Dying," discusses the various stages one might go through when dying and the medical definitions of death. Part II, "Medical and Legal Procedures Related to Death," investigates the details of emergency room procedures, the steps involved in declaring someone legally deceased, what happens to the body after death, how the moment of demise might be determined, what's involved in an autopsy, and how to determine if a death was a murder or suicide. Part III looks at many causes of death, including electrocution, falling, and chronic illnesses.

Death to Dust: What Happens to Dead Bodies? Kenneth V. Iverson, MD. Tucson, AZ: Galen Press, 1994.

Some questions answered in this book include: How can a person be identified from partial or decomposed remains? How is a body prepared for embalming? How is a shrunken head prepared?

World Health Statistics. Geneva: World Health Organization. Annual.

Use this compendium to find detailed causes of death in nations worldwide, including specific diseases, and accidents caused by transportation vehicles, fire, drowning, suicide, homicide, and other means.

Drug and Alcohol Abuse

Encyclopedia of Drugs and Alcohol. 4 Volumes. Jerome H. Jaffe, ed. New York: Macmillan Library Reference, 1995.

Check this encyclopedia for articles written for nonspecialists on the effects of drugs and on alcohol and drug abuse in the context of social policy, politics, history, economics, scientific research, treatment, prevention, and law enforcement.

The National Clearinghouse for Alcohol and Drug Information (NCADI), P.O. Box 2345, Rockville, MD 20847-2345, Phone: (800)729-6686 or (301)468-2600, Fax: (301)468-6433, URL: http://www.health.org/index.htm

NCADI claims to be the "world's largest resource for current information and materials concerning substance abuse." Prevline: Prevention Online, is on this page and offers electronic access to databases and prevention materials that pertain to alcohol, tobacco, and drugs.

Office of National Drug Control Policy (ONDCP), Executive Office of the President, Washington, DC 20503, Phone: (202)395-6700, URL: http://www.whitehousedrugpolicy.gov/

This Web page supplies facts about ongoing efforts of the ONDCP to stem the use of illegal drugs along with data and discussion on narcotics use, production, arrests, treatment, descriptions of particular drugs, and related topics.

Economics

See also: chapter twelve for resources that point to U.S. and international economic indicators.

Encyclopedia of American Economic History. 3 Volumes. Glenn Porter, ed. New York: Charles Scribner's Sons, 1980.

The essays in this set examine classic economic theories and views, written for the "intelligent layperson."

The New Palgrave Dictionary of Economics. 4 Volumes. John Eatwell. London: Macmillan, 1994.

This resource defines such concepts as bioeconomics, intertemporal equilibrium and efficiency, and Taylorism. Noted economists are featured throughout.

Find numerous links to Web pages related to economics at *WebEc*, http://netec.wustl.edu/WebEc.html.

Education

National Center for Education Statistics. http://www.nces.ed.gov

NCES collects national and international educational statistics. Rather than supplying the three-mile-long URL for each of the publications listed below, I suggest you go to the home page and choose the most obvious search category—it's simple to search on this page. Sample publications available on the NCES Web site and in print at many libraries and at government bookstores include:

The Condition of Education.

A yearly statistical report covering enrollment, curricula, finance, student and faculty/staff characteristics, and other indicators relevant in assessing the condition of U.S. education for the elementary, secondary, and postsecondary levels.

Digest of Education Statistics.

Annual. A compilation of American educational statistics covering students, faculty, and staff for kindergarten through graduate school. Figures are provided for enrollments, finance and expenditures, population characteristics, and salaries.

QED's State School Guide. Denver: Quality Education Data. Annual.
Updated each year, this directory provides data on public, Catholic, and private schools and school districts. Each state and the District of Columbia has its own guide. Sample *QED* information includes: number of students and teachers in a district, discretionary dollars spent per pupil, brands of computers used, and name of each school's principal and librarian.
World Education Report. Paris: UNESCO. Biennial.
This report provides worldwide statistics covering access to schooling, illiteracy rates, and pupil-teacher ratio.

Energy

See *also*: Nature/Environment

Energy Information Administration (EIA), Room BG-057, 1000 Independence Ave. SW, Washington, DC 20585, Phone: (202)586-8800, Fax (202)586-0727, E-mail: infoctr@eia.doe.gov, URL: http://www.eia.doe.gov/
The Energy Information Administration is the independent statistical and analytical agency within the Department of Energy. If you need data regarding petroleum, coal, natural gas, nuclear energy, electricity, or renewables, check this Wet site. Sample publications available on the EIA Web page and in print at many libraries and at government bookstores include:

Annual Energy Review (AER). http://www.eia.doe.gov/bookshelf.html
The statistics cover all major energy activities, including consumption, production, trade, stocks, and prices for all energy commodities, with many tables beginning in 1949.

Monthly Energy Review. http://www.eia.doe.gov/bookshelf.html
An overview of the aggregate monthly statistics on U.S. energy supply, demand, and prices. Some aggregate international statistics are also included.

State Energy Data Book: Consumption Estimates. http://www.eia.doe.gov /emeu/sep/states.html.
A look at energy consumption at both the state and national level.

International Energy Agency. http://www.iea.org/homechoi.htm

The International Energy Agency compiles energy statistics for OECD (Organization of Economic Co-Operation and Development) member countries by conducting annual studies on oil, natural gas, coal, and electricity. Many of the publications published by the IEA are not full-text on their Web page, but a few that are include: *The Monthly Electricity Survey,* supplying figures on electricity output and production; *The Monthly Natural Gas Survey,* supplying imports, exports, and consumption of natural gas; *The Monthly Price Survey,* giving recent prices of petroleum products; and *The Monthly Oil Survey,* recording imports, exports, and stock levels of oil.

Plunkett's Energy Industry Almanac. Houston: Plunkett Research, 1999.

Plunkett's offers descriptions of the size, scope, and potential of every segment of the energy industry. The Energy Industry 500 section profiles the leading electric utilities, gas utilities, pipeline companies, major and independent oil companies, refiners, offshore and onshore drillers, oil field services firms, and related technology and services companies.

Film

See also: Television and Radio

When seeking any type of information about film in a library catalog, use the phrase MOTION PICTURES instead of film. So, for example, to find information about directing, you'd do a search using the words DIRECTING or DIRECTORS combined with MOTION PICTURES.

Drew's Script-O-Rama. http://www.script-o-rama.com/

Drew's links to many full-text television and movie scripts and transcripts.

To find movie scripts in a library catalog search, do a keyword search using the word SCRIPT or SCREENPLAY and the title of the film. To buy movie or television scripts, check The Script Shop, 2221 Peachtree Rd. NE, Suite D-452, Atlanta, GA 30309, E-mail: po@scriptshop.com, URL: http://www.scriptshop.com/.

The Film Encyclopedia. 3rd edition. Ephraim Katz. New York: HarperPerennial, 1998.

The Film Encyclopedia contains biographical entries on filmmakers and performers, the history of major film industries around the world, descriptions of film organizations, and definitions and explanations of filmmaking inventions, techniques, processes, equipment, and jargon.

Film Reviews

There are several ways to locate movie reviews and commentary. Two sites on the Web are *The Movie Review Query Engine* at http://www.mrqe.com/, and *The Movie Database* at http://www.tvguide.com, which includes the contents of *The Motion Picture Guide* (New York: Cinebooks, 1985–present) and supplies reviews of thousands of films.

A number of print compendiums contain movie reviews, including *Variety Film Reviews* (V.1-16, New York: Garland; V.17-, New Providence, NJ: R.R. Bowker) which contains reviews from 1907 to the present from *Variety*, and *Magill's Survey of Cinema* (21 Volumes. Englewood Cliffs, NJ: Salem Press, 1980–1985) which critiques over three thousand international motion pictures in its original twenty-one-volume set. This set is updated with new critiques compiled yearly in *Magill's Cinema Annual.* Another resource updated yearly is the *Film Review Annual* (Englewood, NJ: Film Review Publications) which contains reviews reproduced from such publications as *The Village Voice* and *The Monthly Film Bulletin.*

Use periodical indexes to find specific film reviews in newspapers, magazines, and journals. One index that's geared to film only and will bring you to more scholarly analysis of film is the *Film Literature Index.* Also look at Appendix B and use any of the newspaper indexes. Reviews will also be indexed in the multisubject indexes described in chapter four.

Internet Movie Database (IMDb). http://www.imdb.com

> The IMDb can be searched by name of movie, actors, characters, crew members, directors, or writers. It supplies complete filmographies and everything from how to buy movies, film commentaries and reviews, and dialog from movies.

ScreenSite. http://www.tcf.ua.edu/screensite

> ScreenSite's primary purpose is to facilitate the study of film and television and is less geared to the hobbyist than many film Web sites. ScreenSite supplies information on film and TV education, scholarly societies, film festivals, production companies, online discussion groups, and access to reviews and commentary, specialized journals, and other useful documents.

Firsts

See also: Inventions, and Women

Below are lists of books that record the first occurrence of noteworthy actions and events, often notable because they were associated with a particular group of people.

Collins Dictionary of Dates. 8th edition. Audrey Butler. Glasgow: HarperCollins, 1996.

   A list of discovery/founding/starting dates of concepts, peoples, institutions and areas, birth and death dates of well-known figures, and construction dates of famous works of architecture. The dates of closures/endings are also noted.

Famous First Facts. 5th edition. Joseph Nathan Kane. New York: H.W. Wilson, 1997. Also available on CD-ROM and as a subscription database on the Web.

   Check this resource to learn of the first time notable U.S. events occurred, or when products or concepts were introduced. The first national park? Yellowstone National Park, established in 1871. The first electric blanket to warm our soles? Manufactured October 9, 1946. Indexed by years, days, and geographic location.

The Guinness Book of Records. New York: Facts on File. Annual. Also available on CD-ROM under the title *Guinness Multimedia Disc of Records.*

   Though *The Guinness Book of Records* does cover the antics and feats that show up on local news programs, such as the accomplishment of building the biggest snowman (in Yamagato, Japan, 96 feet, 7 inches) it also lists record breakers and biggest, smallest, longest (etc.) statistics for natural phenomena, sports, science, and human events.

To locate other "firsts" books in your library catalog with titles as diverse as *Connecticut Firsts* and *Maritime Firsts,* match your topic word with FIRSTS, MISCELLANEA, or CURIOSITIES WONDERS.

Food, Nutrition, and Agriculture

Department of Agriculture's National Agricultural Statistical Service (USDA NASS). Agricultural Statistics Information Hotline: (800)727-9540, URL: http://www.usda.gov/nass

   Search the USDA NASS Web site for current and historic reports, graphs, and data sets relating to agricultural baseline projections, farm sector economics, field crops, food, international agriculture, rural affairs, trade issues, livestock, dairy, poultry, inputs, technology, and weather. State-by-state agricultural reports and data are also located here. Sample publications available on this Web page and in print at many libraries and government bookstores include:

Agricultural Statistics. http://www.usda.gov/nass/pubs/agstats.htm

Find facts here on agricultural production, supplies, consumption, facilities, and costs.

Food Consumption, Prices, and Expenditures. http://www.econ.ag.gov /epubs/htmlsum/sb939.htm

This compendium presents historical data on food consumption, prices, and expenditures by commodity and commodity group, supply and use, and U.S. income and population. There are also thirty-six charts on topics such as food consumption trends and share of income spent for food.

The USDA Dietary guidelines and food pyramid are also on the *USDA* site at http://www.nal.usda.gov/fnic/. For dietary guidelines from several other countries, go to the Web page for the International Union of Nutritional Sciences at http://www.monash.edu.au/IUNS/.

Encyclopedia of Food Science, Food Technology, and Nutrition. 8 Volumes. Robert Macrae, ed. San Diego: Academic Press, 1993.

The topics in this set encompass food processing, the origin, chemical composition, and nutritive value of many foodstuffs, food additives, and the effects of nutrition on disease.

Food and Agricultural Organization of the United Nations. http://www.fao.org

An autonomous organization within the UN, the FAO, located in Rome, seeks to raise levels of nutrition, improve agricultural productivity, and to better the condition of rural populations worldwide. The FAO Statistical Database on their Web page supplies worldwide data in such areas as agricultural production and trade, food aid shipments, and fish production.

Food and Seafood Hotline. Phone: (800)332-4010 or (202)205-4314 in the Washington, DC area.

Call the Food and Seafood Hotline, managed by the FDA and the Center for Food Safety and Applied Nutrition, to hear recorded food-related informational messages on nutrition, labeling, economic fraud, additives, pesticides, contaminants, and general food safety. Representatives are available to answer questions between noon and 4 P.M., eastern standard time. Go to the *FDA* home page at http://www.fda.gov to learn of U.S. food regulations, product warnings, and information about food and nutrition.

Food Values. Many guides exist which break down the composition and nutritive value of foods, listing such characteristics as calories, protein, fat, carbohydrates, calcium, and iron. To locate these using a library catalog, try any of these keyword combinations: FOOD ANALYSIS TABLES, FOOD VALUES, NUTRITION TABLES, or FOOD COMPOSITION TABLES. These terms will pull up such titles as *Bowes and Church's Food Values of Portions Commonly Used* (Philadelphia: Lippincott, 1998). Also, see the *Calorie Calculator* at http://www.caloriecontrol.org which lists food calories and fat.

Recipes on the Web

When personal computers were first introduced, one of their supposed selling points to the stay-at-home mom was the ability to arrange all her recipes in electronic format. Now she can just read them on the Internet. *Epicurious Food* at http://www.epicurious.com contains over seven thousand recipes from *Bon Appetit* and *Gourmet* magazines. Also, if you simply search for a dish—LASAGNA, for example—using almost any search engine, recipes from grandmas and other proud chefs worldwide will appear. To find cookbooks in a library catalog, do a keyword search matching the style of cooking you're interested in with the word COOKERY.

Government

See also: Voting

Facts About the Congress. Stephen G. Christianson. New York: H.W. Wilson, 1996.

Each chapter is devoted to a Congress, beginning with the first Congress in 1789–1791. For each Congress, facts are supplied regarding the House and Senate leadership, and major bills, issues, incidents, and legislation. Also from this publisher is the book *Facts About the Presidents* (1993) and *Facts About the Supreme Court of the United States* (1996).

Irving Mann Voting and Democracy Virtual Library. http://www.nyu.edu/library/bobst/research/soc/vote.htm

This meta site points to Internet locations covering election laws, systems, and voter information.

Political Handbook of the World. Arthur S. Banks, ed. Binghamton, NY: CSA
   Publications. Annual.
      This book details the political background, current politics, and political
   parties for all countries of the world.
The United States Government Manual. Washington, DC: Government Printing
   Office. Annual. Also available at http://www.access.gpo.gov/nara/nara001
   .html.
      Discussed in chapter three, this is the "official handbook of the federal
   government," with overview information on the role of agencies of the legislative, judicial, and executive branches, as well as "quasi-official agencies, boards,
   commissions, committees, and international organizations the government is
   involved with."

 Campaign Funding and Congressional Salaries

W hat types of groups and companies are helping nudge a
candidate into office through monetary contributions?
Several Web sites will tell you, including the home page for the
Center for Responsive Politics at http://www.crp.org and *Project Vote Smart* at http://
www.vote-smart.org/. Campaign finance information is also available on the commercial database *Congressional Universe,* available at some libraries.

Health/Medical Statistics, and Facts

See also: Medicinal, Surgical, and Therapeutic Treatments; Physical Diseases and Illnesses; and Psychology/Mental
Health

AHA Hospital Statistics. Chicago: American Hospital Association, 1972–present.
   Annual.
      This annual compilation of statistical tables gathered by the American Hos-
   pital Association presents data related to U.S. hospital services, use, personnel,
   and finances.
Center for International Health Information, 1601 N. Kent St., Suite 1014,
   Arlington, VA 22209, Phone: (703)524-5225, Fax: (703)243-4669, E-mail:
   info@cihi.com, URL: http://www.cihi.com
      Health data, health trends, and basic demographic information for selected
   developing nations is available on this Web site.

National Center for Health Statistics (NCHS), 6525 Belcrest Rd., Hyattsville, MD
20782, Phone: (301)436-8500, E-mail: nchsquery@cdc.gov, URL: http://www
.cdc.gov/nchswww/

The NCHS gathers and produces data that will improve individual health
and assist in developing government health policy. *Health, United States* is an
NCHS publication that provides a profile in figures of the nation's health.
It's available in print and at http://www.cdc.gov/nchswww/products/products
.htm.

World Health Report. Geneva: World Health Organization. Annual. Excerpts are
available at http://www.who.ch/whr/.

This annual report examines global health trends. International health statistics can also be found, with some hunting, via the *World Health Organization's Statistical Information System (WHOSIS)* at http://www.who.ch/whosis
/whosis.htm.

Statistics May Lie

Educate yourself in the ways that statistics can be misused. It's
easy to misrepresent and mislead with numbers, graphs,
maps, and choice of phrasing. Books that discuss such maneuvers
include *How to Lie With Maps* (2nd edition. Chicago: The University of Chicago
Press, 1996), *Misused Statistics: Straight Talk for Twisted Numbers* (2nd edition. New
York: Marcel Dekker, 1998), and *The Data Game: Controversies in Social Science
Statistics* (2nd edition. Armonk, NY: M.E. Sharpe, 1995). A Web site that explains
basic statistical concepts is *Statistics Every Writer Should Know* at http://nilesonline
.com/stats/.

History

See: chapter eight

Homosexuality

Completely Queer: The Gay and Lesbian Encyclopedia. Steve Hogan. New York:
Henry Holt, 1998.

Completely Queer is a guide to the history, personalities, places, culture, and
ideas of lesbian and gay communities worldwide. A chronology of gay and

lesbian events from circa 12,000 BC to the present is included and cross-referenced to the text. See also the *Encyclopedia of Homosexuality* (2 Volumes. New York: Garland, 1990).

Library Q. http://carbon.cudenver.edu/public/library/libq/

Librarian Ellen Greenblatt has used her expertise in cataloging to create a comprehensive meta site pointing to pages featuring gay and lesbian events, biography, resources, news, and other information.

St. James Press Gay & Lesbian Almanac. Detroit: St. James Press, 1998.

This scholarly almanac offers a broad overview of lesbian and gay culture, history, issues, and communities in the U.S. Other almanac titles include *Out in All Directions* (New York: Warner Books, 1995) and *Gay Almanac* (New York: Berkeley Books, 1996).

Inventions

See also: Science and Engineering

How Stuff Works. http://www.howstuffworks.com/

This Web resource explains, well, how stuff works, including electronic items, parts of the human body, and finance. Still tiny compared to printed compilations with the same aim, but it's growing. Also visit http://erwin.phys .virginia.edu/Education/Teaching/HowThingsWork/, a similar site, to see the *How Things Work* page.

The MacMillan Visual Dictionary. Jean-Claude Corbeil. New York: Macmillan, 1993.

The intent of this dictionary is to link words/concepts and illustrations together to allow the drawing to assist in the defining of the term or idea. The brightly colored drawings represent such diverse items as weather satellites, household appliances, clothing, and high speed trains. A cut-away view is often provided. To find other dictionaries like this one using a library catalog, type in the subject words PICTURE DICTIONARIES.

National Inventors Hall of Fame (NIHF), 221 S. Broadway St., Akron, OH 44308-1505, Phone: (330)762-4463, E-mail: info@invent.org, http://invent.nforce .com/book/, URL http://www.invent.org/book.

Search on the NIHF home page by inventor's name or type of invention for a very brief biography with rudimentary information about the invention. Some inventors honored at this museum are Willis Haviland Carrier, inventor of air conditioning, which Carrier patented as "an apparatus for treating air," and Gertrude Belle Elion, for her work on a leukemia-fighting drug and drugs that facilitate kidney transplants.

The New Illustrated Science and Invention Encyclopedia: How It Works. 28 Volumes. Donald Clarke. Westport, CT: H.S. Stuttman, Publishers, 1994.

This is a particular favorite of mine since it covers such a wide range of apparatus and explains their workings simply, with lots of colored illustration. It's rare that I don't find what I'm looking for in here—a piano, an anchor, pistols, radios, you name it.

Patent, Trademark, and Service Mark Searching. Do you want to find out if someone has already patented an invention or process? Or to see if a word, phrase, or symbol identifying the source of goods or services has already been declared a trademark? One way to do this is to hire a lawyer or searcher specializing in patent and trademark searching. These people are experts in such work and are the best assurance against accidentally treading on someone else's property.

Information regarding how to obtain or search for patent, trademark, and service marks is on the Web at the United States Patent and Trademark Office (USPTO) Web site at http://www1.uspto.gov/. Search for both registered and pending trademarks on this page via the USTPO Web Trademark Database, and read their evolving notice concerning limitations of this database.

Almost all patents can now be searched at no charge on the Web. Using the U.S. Patent Bibliographic Database at http://www.uspto.gov/Web/menu/search.html is one option, with patents listed from 1976 to the present. Search by keyword, patent class number, or other criteria such as inventor name, application date, or inventor city.

The USPTO bibliographic database retrieves the title page of the patent but not the full patent. Drawings and diagrams are not included. Although there is full text access at this site (at the time of this writing), it is cumbersome. Full patents from 1971 to the present are easily searchable and retrievable on the Web through the *Patent Server*, maintained by the IBM corporation at http://www.patents.ibm.com/. IBM acknowledges that some patents on their database are missing fields of data and some are missing altogether because of difficulties in obtaining data, but these records represent only a tiny fraction of the database.

You can also search for patents and trademarks at a patent and trademark depository library. Libraries that are part of the Patent and Trademark Depository Program receive materials needed to help locate and apply for patents and trademarks. They may be public, state, academic, or special libraries. These libraries carry the *Official Gazette of the United States Patent and Trademark Office*, a two-volume printed set issued weekly with new trademarks featured in one volume and data about new patents in the other. The *Official Gazette* doesn't supply full patent information for each new patent, just a diagram and one "claim" about it. But patent and trademark depository libraries do have the full text of all trademarks and patents available on microfilm and/or in electronic format.

A list of patent and trademark depository libraries can be found on the Web at http://www1.uspto.gov (click on Libraries-PDTL's), or by writing or phoning the Patent and Trademark Depository Library Program, United States Patent and Trademark Office, Crystal Park 3, Suite 461, Washington, DC 20231, Phone: (703)308-5558.

Also find trademarks worldwide through the *TRADEMARKSCAN* subscription databases available on CD-ROM, through DIALOG, and SAEGIS from Thomson & Thomson.

Labor/Employment

See chapter twelve

Linguistics and Etymology

The Encyclopedia of Language and Linguistics (ELL). 10 Volumes. R.E. Asher, ed. New York: Pergamon Press, 1994.

> *ELL* offers scholarly essays about the field of linguistics. Topic areas include Apes and Language, Marathi (a major outer language of the Indo-Aryan group), and Sociophonetics, (the study of speech in its social context). The final volume contains an inventory of the languages of the world.

Human Languages Page. http://www.june29.com/HLP

> This is a meta site linking to language-related Web pages. See more about this site in chapter nine.

Oxford English Dictionary (OED). 2nd edition. 20 Volumes. Oxford: Clarendon Press, 1989. Supplemented with the *Addition Series* (2 Volumes in 1994, one in 1997). Also available on CD-ROM.

> The premier etymological dictionary of the English language, the *OED* comments on the history of English words, providing differences in meaning, spelling, pronunciation, and usage of each word over an eight hundred-year period.

Literature

Dictionary of Concepts in Literary Criticism and Theory. Wendell V. Harris. Westport, CT: Greenwood Press, 1992.

Treatments of seventy concepts of literary theory and commentary are presented in this dictionary. Sample headings include Deconstruction, Humanism, Narrative, and Semiotics.

Encyclopedia of World Literature in the 20th Century. 5 Volumes. New York: Frederick Ungar. Volumes 1-4, 1981. Volume 5 (Supplement and Index), 1993.

This encyclopedia is well known among literary researchers for its national literature surveys, biographical pieces on the writers of the world, and explanations of concepts in literary scholarship.

Literary Resources on the Net. http://andromeda.rutgers.edu/~jlynch/Lit

Major categories on his page, all literature related, include Classical and Biblical, Medieval, Renaissance, Eighteenth Century, Romantic, Victorian British, Twentieth-Century British and Irish, American, Theater and Drama, Theory, Women's Literature and Feminism, and Ethnicities and Nationalities.

Literary Criticism and Book Reviews

The line can sometimes blur between a book review and literary criticism. Generally, book reviews provide critical reaction to a piece of writing soon after its publication. Length of reviews range from a few lines to a few pages and generally include a summary of the book's plot or content. Literary criticism usually involves a more in-depth description, interpretation, and evaluation of literary writings.

When working with literary criticism, *A Handbook to Literature* by William Harmon and C. Hugh Holman is a place to check for quick definitions of genres, movements, and literary terminology (7th edition. Upper Saddle River, NJ: Prentice Hall, 1996).

Literary criticism found within books or book-length criticism can be found using a library catalog. If you're searching for overall critiques of an author's work, just do a keyword search (not an author search) using the author's name and the word CRITICISM. For example: JANE AUSTEN CRITICISM.

If you're seeking criticism on a particular piece of writing, search by the name of the piece of literature and the word criticism, e.g., COLOR PURPLE CRITICISM. If it doesn't work, go back to just using the author's name since many compilations of criticism may not list the title of each work critiqued in the online

Plot Summaries

You're probably familiar with the yellow-and-black pamphlet-like books known as *Cliffs Notes* (Lincoln, NE: Cliffs Notes) and *Monarch Notes* (Indianapolis: Macmillan General Reference). Both offer plot summaries and the analysis of plot, character, and author. Though not widely available in libraries, you'll find them in bookstores.

Salem Press publishes a series more likely found in libraries and also available on CD-ROM called *Masterplots: 1,801 Plot Stories and Critical Evaluations of the World's Finest Literature* (2nd edition. 12 Volumes. 1996). A related series from Salem is *Magill's Literary Annual: Essay-Reviews of Outstanding Books Published in the United States During (Year)*, (Pasadena, CA: Salem Press. Annual.). Note that any good-length book review also describes the plot of the book it's reviewing. I've also located helpful descriptions of books at the Web sites of online bookstores like *Amazon.com* at http://www.amazon.com.

---

record representing the book. Once you find a book of general criticism on an author, check the index for mention of the particular work you're interested in.

On the Web, try the *IPL (Internet Public Library) Online Literary Criticism Collection* at http://www.ipl.org/ref/litcrit/, a guide to over 1,300 biographical and critical Web sites about authors.

Academic libraries serving schools with literature departments and larger public libraries have compendiums in their reference collection that contain literary criticism or summaries of literary criticism. Gale publishes several titles comprising hundreds of volumes that present lengthy excerpts of criticism. Titles in the series include *Contemporary Literary Criticism, Twentieth-Century Literary Criticism, Nineteenth-Century Literary Criticism, Classical and Medieval Literature Criticism, Literature Criticism From 1400-1800, Shakespearean Criticism, Children's Literature Review, Drama Criticism, Black Literature Criticism, Hispanic Literature Criticism, Native North American Literature, World Literary Criticism From 1500 to Present*, and *Short Story Criticism*.

Chelsea House also publishes compilations of literary criticism commonly found in libraries, under such titles as *The New Moulton's Library of Literary Criticism* and *Twentieth Century American Literature*.

The premier index for locating scholarly literary writings from journals and books is the *MLA International Bibliography of Books and Articles on the Modern*

Languages and Literatures, described, along with other humanities indexes you can use for finding criticism, in Appendix B.

Book Review Indexes. Book review indexes help locate book reviews. To use indexes in their hard copy version, find the copyright date of the book you want a review for, then pull the index volume for that year and the year after and look under the author's name. The index will supply you with citations to book reviews that have appeared in magazines, journals, and newspapers.

Most Web-based book review sources show book reviews from just one publication or one genre. A great big list of links to book reviews is located at the *Needle in a Cyberstack* page at http://home.revealed.net/albee/pages/FullBook .html.

Some book review indexes:

The Book Review Digest. New York: H.W. Wilson, 1905–present. Also on CD-ROM and as a subscription database via CompuServe, FirstSearch, Ovid, and Wilson.

The Book Review Index. Detroit: Gale, 1965–present. Also available as a subscription database via DIALOG.

C.R.I.S.: Combined Retrospective Index Set to Book Reviews in History, 1838–1974. Washington, DC: Carrollton Press, 1977–. Other *C.R.I.S.* indexes cover *The Humanities, 1802–1974; Politics, 1886–1974; Sociology, 1895–1974;* and *Scholarly Journals, 1896–1974.*

Index to Book Reviews in Religion. Chicago: American Theological Library Association, 1949–present. Also available through the *ATLA Religion Database* on CD-ROM or via OCLC and OVID.

Index to Book Reviews in the Humanities. Detroit: P. Thomson, 1960–1990.

London Review of Books. New York: NYREV, 1979–present.

New York Times Index. In the print index to *The New York Times*, look under the heading BOOK REVIEWS and find the book by title. For the online version, go to http://www.nytimes.com and click on "books."

Reviews in American History. Westport, CT: Redgrave Information, 1973– present. Sample issues at http://muse.jhu.edu/journals/reviews_in_ americanhistory/index.html.

Science Fiction and Fantasy Book Review Index. San Bernadino, CA: Borgo Press, 1970–present.

TLS: The Times Literary Supplement Index, 1902–1939. Reading, England: Newspaper Archive Developments, 1978; *1940–1980* and *1981–1985.* Reading, England: Research Publications, 1982 and 1986. Later supplements from Reading, England: Primary Source Media.

Book reviews also show up in many online periodical databases, including the many produced by H.W. Wilson, including *The Readers' Guide to Periodical Literature, The Social Sciences Index, The Humanities Index, The General Science Index,* and *The Art Index.*

Medicinal, Surgical, and Therapeutic Treatments

See also: Physical Diseases and Illnesses, and Psychology/Mental Health

Alternative Medicine: The Definitive Guide. Burton Goldberg Group. Puyallup, WA: Future Medicine Publishing, 1997.

This guide is a survey of alternative therapies such as Ayurvedic medicine, flower remedies, juice therapy, and Qigong.

Current Medical Diagnosis and Treatment. Lawrence W. Way. Norwalk, CT: Appleton & Lange, 1994.

This compilation geared to health professionals discusses current knowledge related to internal medicine and other topics of interest to primary care physicians. Similarly structured texts from this publisher include: *Current Surgical Diagnosis and Treatment,* 10th edition, 1994; *Current Pediatric Diagnosis and Treatment,* 13th edition, 1997; and *Current Obstetric & Gynecologic Diagnosis & Treatment,* 8th edition, 1994.

Essential Guide to Prescription Drugs. James J. Rybacki, Pharm.D. and James W. Long, MD. New York: HarperCollins. Annual.

This is a guide to the most commonly prescribed drugs. Information supplied about each drug includes the year it was introduced, whether it's prescription or over-the-counter, a listing of any generic equivalents, the brand name(s), its benefits and risks, and how it works in the human system.

Holistic Healing Web Page. http://www.holisticmed.com/

A good starting point for links to documents, articles, association Web pages, and other sites supplying information on such holistic and alternative medical practices as chiropractic medicine, herbalism, and homeopathy.

MedicineNet. http://www.medicinenet.com

Maintained by a network of physician educators, MedicineNet includes a medical dictionary; the Diseases and Treatments Index, which lists symptoms, diagnosis, causes, procedures, and treatments for diseases; and the Pharmacy

Index, which supplies drug class and actions, proper use, precautions, interactions, and side effects of pharmaceuticals.

Merck Manual of Diagnosis and Therapy. 17th edition. Rahway, NJ: Merck, Sharp & Dohme Research Laboratories, 1999. Also at http://www.merck.com under "publications," and available on CD-ROM from MedTech USA and as part of the *PDR Electronic Library.*

    The Merck Manual offers a broad spectrum of health information, including discussions of medical disorders, treatments, symptoms, and paths to diagnosis. There's also a *Home Edition*, geared to the layperson, published in 1997. Other Merck manuals include the *Merck Manual of Geriatrics*, 2nd edition, 1995 and the *Merck Veterinary Manual*, 8th edition, 1998.

NetVet: Veterinary Resources. http://netvet.wustl.edu

    Find links to veterinary medical sites on this page.

Physicians' Desk Reference (PDR). Oradell, NJ: Medical Economics Co. Annual, plus quarterly supplements. Also available on CD-ROM.

    PDR describes thousands of pharmaceuticals and diagnostic products. The product identification section boasts glossy, colorful photos of pills, tablets, and bottles. Other *PDR* titles: *The Physicians Desk Reference for Non-Prescription Drugs, The PDR Family Guide to Prescription Drugs, The PDR Family Guide to Over-the-Counter Drugs, The PDR for Herbal Medicines, The Physician's Desk Reference for Opthamology,* and *The PDR Nurse's Handbook.*

Home Remedies. There are many books that teach you how to mix up your own medications, such as *The Herbal Medicine Cabinet: Preparing Natural Remedies at Home* (Berkeley, CA: Celestial Arts, 1997). Find them by doing a keyword search on your library's online catalog using the words FORMULAE MEDICINE.

Nonmedicinal Therapies. When looking for sources covering nonmedicinal therapies using your library's online catalog or the Web, try these word combinations: DANCE THERAPY, DRAMA THERAPEUTIC USE, MUSIC THERAPY, PHYSICAL THERAPY, PSYCHOANALYTIC THERAPY, and PSYCHOTHERAPY.

Meta Links to Reference Works on the Web

Auraria Library Virtual Reference Desk. http://carbon.cudenver.edu/public/library/reference/vl.html

    This site presents links to dozens of pages that have compiled such items as online dictionaries, thesauri, phone directories, encyclopedias, and handbooks. *Yahoo! Reference.* http://www.yahoo.com/Reference/

This Yahoo! section lists reference works on the Web under dozens of categories, including calendars, dictionaries, flags, libraries, phone numbers, postal information, and standards.

Music

There are many encyclopedias dedicated to particular musical genres. To find them, use an online library catalog and pair the word ENCYCLOPEDIAS with such genre names as BLUES, CLASSICAL MUSIC, COUNTRY MUSIC, FOLK MUSIC, JAZZ, MUSICAL THEATER, OPERA, or ROCK MUSIC.

A music encyclopedia of note is *The New Grove Dictionary of Music and Musicians* (20 Volumes. London: MacMillan, 1980). *Grove* is the first place to look for scholarly biographical and informational essays in music. More than 50 percent of the entries discuss composers, from ancient to contemporary times. Essays cover international musical concepts, influences, theories, styles, instruments, and terminology.

Finding Music Scores and Recorded Music. Sheet music, scores, and books of song compilations are available at stores that sell musical instruments; some bookstores; and libraries, especially those serving schools with departments of music. When searching in your library's online catalog for printed music of a particular style or by a particular artist, use the phrase SCORES, with the name of the artist, type of music, and/or region. Sample searches: BEATLES SCORES, FOLK SONGS RUSSIAN SCORES, or JAZZ SCORES.

If you want to find the words to the music as well as the instrumental score, do a search using the phrase VOCAL SCORES or LIBRETTO. The libretto is the text of an opera or musical. Sample searches: BILLIE HOLIDAY VOCAL SCORES or WEST SIDE STORY LIBRETTO.

Lyrics are also found in fake books, collections of songs that provide the musician with basic melodies and chords that they improvise around. Just use the word FAKE BOOK in a library catalog to locate books like *The Wedding Fake Book: More Than 150 Traditional & Popular Songs* (Miami: CPP/Belwin, 1991).

To locate recorded music or any nonmusical audio recordings such as books on tape when searching a library catalog, use the phrase SOUND RECORDING along with the name of an artist, group, or musical style, to pull up compact

Lyrics and Poems on the Web

I have had great luck finding both song lyrics and poetry on the Web. Just put a few words from the song into a search engine. Just keep in mind that the lyrics or poem you pull up may not be an "official" version. They're often placed on the Web by an aficionado so there may be inaccuracies in the transcription of the work.

discs, LPs, and cassette recordings. Sample search: ROLLING STONES SOUND RECORDING.

Who Wrote That Song? Of course, it's rather difficult to locate a song if you have no idea who performed it or what the title was. Song indexes assist in discovering who wrote a song and where you might find it when you only know the title or first line. Find these indexes in a library by combining the genre of music with the word INDEXES, e.g., DISCO MUSIC INDEXES or OPERA INDEXES. A sample song index is the *Popular Song Index* (Metuchen, NJ: The Scarecrow Press, 1975. Supplements issued in 1978, 1984, and 1989), a standard reference for finding music and lyrics appearing in songbooks and other books.

Discographies can also help when you need details about a recording such as composer of the musical piece, names of singers and musicians, and producer/label. Discographies are compilations of recorded music, describing and sometimes critiquing each recording. A sample title: *Afro-American Singers: An Index and Preliminary Discography of Long-Playing Recordings of Opera, Choral Music, and Song* (Minneapolis: Challenge Productions, 1977). Find such directories using a library catalog by combining a musical genre or the name of an artist with the word DISCOGRAPHY, e.g., CHARLIE PARKER DISCOGRAPHY or CHORAL MUSIC DISCOGRAPHY. This search method also brings some results on the Web and pulls up such guides as the *All Music Guide* at http://www.allmusic.com/ which supplies discographies for many genres.

Nature/Environment

Cool Net Sites: Ecology and Environment. http://carbon.cudenver.edu/public /library/reference/ecol.html

Librarian and environmental activist Sue Maret has compiled an unbeatable meta page to environmental resources on the Net. Look here for links to topics in all areas of environmental concern.

Environmental Protection Agency (EPA), 401 M St. SW, Washington, DC 20460,
  Phone: (202)260-7751, URL: http://www.epa.gov
  The EPA page links to full-text environmental documents and offers details
  for ordering items that are not full text online. The National Environmental
  Publications Information System (NEPIS) is on this page, a collection of over
  six thousand current and archival environmentally related documents.

Encyclopedia of Environmental Analysis and Remediation. 8 Volumes. Robert A.
  Meyers, ed. New York: John Wiley & Sons, 1998.
  This scholarly set focuses on sampling, analysis, and remediation related
  to the environment and also presents such topics as pollution sources, their
  health effects, and environmental regulations.

Statistical Record of the Environment. 4th edition. Detroit: Gale, 1998.
  This guide presents a thick volume of statistics related to areas of environmental concern culled from governmental and private resources.

United States Geological Survey, National Center, 12201 Sunrise Valley Dr.,
  Reston, VA 22092, Phone: (703)648-4460, URL: http://www.usgs.gov
  The USGS page will link you to such sites as the USGS National Earthquake Information Center, state-by-state fact sheets discussing USGS activities
  such as determining flood hazards, geologic mapping, and aquifer studies; a
  tutorial on volcanoes; and a pointer to Earthshots, satellite images of environmental change.

The Way Nature Works. Robin Rees, ed. New York: Macmillan, 1992.
  The Way Nature Works presents cross-sectional diagrams, colorful illustrations, photographs, and descriptions of creatures and phenomena in nature.
  Sample topics include causes of ice ages, how islands form, how the greenhouse
  effect warms the globe, and how birds are adapted to flight.

Older Americans

Administration on Aging. Phone: (202)619-0724, TDD: (202)401-7575,
  Eldercare Locator to find services for an older person in his or her locality:
  (800)677-1116, Fax: (202)260-1012, E-mail: aoainfo@ban-gate.aoa.dhhs
  .gov, URL: http://www.aoa.dhhs.gov/aoa/stats/statpage.html
  An impressive array of information is compiled on the Administration on
  Aging statistical information page, including demographic characteristics and
  health, social, and economic conditions of older persons. Also check this page
  to learn about programs offered to the aging.

Older American's Almanac. Detroit: Gale, 1998.

This almanac looks at the activities and needs of those in their later years, with sections devoted to such topics as retirement, volunteerism, lifelong learning, and how to make educated medical decisions. Also from this publisher: *Statistical Record of Older Americans* (1996).

Opinions

Do you want to know the number of people who favor a certain issue? Or how a percentage of a given population feels about a current trend that you're writing about? Try these compendiums of public sentiment:

American Demographics/Marketing Tools. http://www.demographics.com

Search the full-text archives of the magazine *American Demographics* (which tracks consumer trends) from 1993 to the present. For example, I did a search on the word FAT and pulled an article on fat acceptance, a look at which types of fats are "healthier," and many others. Although this site is free, the publishers consider it a shareware site—if you like it they ask that you subscribe to their magazine.

American Public Opinion Index. Louisville, KY: Opinion Research Service, 1981–present. Annual.

This is an index to the public opinion surveys conducted by a variety of market research organizations, universities, associations, and media companies. The index leads you to the accompanying microfiche set, called *American Public Opinion Data*, which provides summary results of the surveys. If you can only get hold of the *Index* and not the microfiche set, the *Index* provides the information needed to contact the pollster.

Gallup Poll Monthly. Princeton, NJ: The Gallup Poll, 1964–present. Also available at http://www.gallup.com from March 1996–present.

Gallup Poll presents results of monthly surveys that their organization conducts. About one hundred surveys are done annually. Some of the same topics repeated each year, for comparison, include surveys on religion in America, alcohol consumption, and the most admired men and women in the U.S. A survey of the president's performance is conducted bimonthly. *Gallup Poll* is indexed in the *UnCover* periodical index.

Index to International Public Opinion. Westport, CT: Greenwood Press. Annual.

This annually updated volume shows results of surveys conducted in single countries as well as groups of nations.

Public Opinion Online (POLL). Roper Center for Public Opinion Research,

1960–present. (Some questions pre-1960.) Available as a subscription database via DIALOG and Westlaw.

Each record in this online database represents a survey question, with answers usually shown as percentages. POLL covers a wide spectrum of public interest topics, including politics, international affairs, social issues and attitudes, business, and consumer issues and preferences.

Philosophy

Routledge Encyclopedia of Philosophy. 10 Volumes. Routledge, 1998. Also available on CD-ROM.

The first major print encyclopedic set on philosophy since the *Encyclopedia of Philosophy* (8 Volumes. New York: The Macmillan Company & The Free Press, 1967).

Stanford Encyclopedia of Philosophy. http://plato.stanford.edu

This Web-based encyclopedia of philosophy is from the Stanford University Center for the Study of Language and Information. Also on the Web: *The Internet Enyclopedia of Philosophy* at http://www.utm.edu/research/iep/.

World Philosophy: Essay-Reviews of 225 Major Works. 5 Volumes. Frank Magill, ed. Englewood Cliffs, NJ: Salem Press, 1982.

A compilation of essays distilling and critiquing philosophical concepts from the sixth century B.C. to 1971.

Physical Diseases and Illnesses

See also: Health/Medical Statistics and Facts; Medicinal, Surgical, and Therapeutic Treatments; Psychology/Mental Health

Complete Guide to Symptoms, Illness, and Surgery. 3rd edition. H. Winter Griffith, MD. Los Angeles: The Body Press, 1995. Also available on CD-ROM.

Each major symptom is broken down into variations of the symptom, the possible problem causing it, and what the sufferer should do. The Surgery section details common operations, and includes illustrations of each procedure. Also from this author: *Complete Guide to Pediatric Symptoms, Illness and Medication,* 1989, and *Complete Guide to Sports Injuries,* 1997.

HealthFinder. http://www.healthfinder.gov

On HealthFinder, sponsored by the U.S. Department of Health and Human Services, you can link to government fact sheets, databases, and organization/support group information related to health care and diseases.

Medical Matrix. http://www.medmatrix.org/Index.asp

Created for the health care professional but open to any of us, Medical Matrix points the user to sites related to clinical medicine. These sites are assigned a one-to-five "star" rating based on quality standards judged by the physicians and medical professionals on the editorial board.

The Surgery Book: An Illustrated Guide to 73 of the Most Common Operations. Robert Youngson, MD, and the Diagram Group. New York: St. Martin's Press, 1997.

With diagrams and simple questions and answers, frequently performed operations are described for the medical consumer. Some of the operations detailed include bone fracture treatment, leg amputation, appendix removal, hysterectomy, male sterilization and mastectomy.

Friendly Medical Books. There are many one-volume medical books meant for home use, and filled with advice on symptoms, cures, and treatments. Try a search using the words DIAGNOSIS POPULAR WORKS or POPULAR MED-ICINE HEALTH or SELF-CARE HEALTH POPULAR to find such titles as *Your Family Guide to Symptoms and Treatments* (London: Thorsons, 1997). Such guides are also now widely available on CD-ROM, such as the *Mayo Ultimate Medical Guide II* (Minneapolis: IVI Publishing, 1997). A basic textbook of health care, the *Columbia University College of Physicians and Surgeons Complete Home Medical Guide* is on the Web at http://cpmcnet.columbia.edu/texts/guide/.

Poisons, Toxic Chemicals, and Dangerous Wildlife

See also: Chemical Properties, Formulas, and Effects; Weapons; and Death

The following books are useful not only to the serious science researcher, but also the fiction researcher who wants to make sure that the poison-laced tea given to the his fictional victim does more than make the character queasy.

Deadly Doses: A Writer's Guide to Poisons. Serita Deborah Stevens with Anne Klarner. Cincinnati, Ohio: Writer's Digest Books, 1990.

Each chapter highlights a type of deadly substance, including household poisons, poisonous plants, medical poisons, snakes, spiders, other living things, and street drugs. For each toxin the author lists its common and scientific names, level of toxicity, where it can be found, which parts of it are deadly, effects and symptoms, amount of time that elapses before it takes effect, and antidotes and treatments.

Handbook of Natural Toxins. 7 Volumes. Richard F. Keeler. New York: Marcel Dekker, 1991.

This series of books, geared to the scientist, covers the many toxic pitfalls in nature. Volume titles: *Plant and Fungal Toxins; Insect Poisons, Allergens, and Other Invertebrate Venoms; Marine Toxins and Venoms; Bacterial Toxins; Reptile Venoms and Toxins; Toxicology of Plant and Fungal Compounds; Food Poisoning.* Another title covering horticultural horrors is the *AMA Handbook of Poisonous and Injurious Plants* (Chicago: American Medical Association, 1985).

Poisoning & Toxicology Compendium: With Symptoms Index. 3rd edition. Jerrold B. Leikin. Hudson, Ohio: Lexi-Comp, 1998.

This compendium explains how to treat overdoses or exposure to over one thousand toxins including medicinal agents, such as prescription drugs; nonmedicinal agents such as insecticides; biological agents, including plants and food; and such herbal agents as medicinal minerals and plants. This guide also describes diagnostic tests and procedures related to poisoning treatment.

Population/Demographics

See also: Regional U.S. Data: State, County, and City; for international population figures, chapter nine, and chapter twelve under Marketing and Advertising Data

Basic population numbers will be listed in any of the resources mentioned in the multisubject statistical compilations mentioned earlier, such as the *World Almanac* or any similar almanac. Statistical international resources like the CIA's *World Fact Book* also supply population figures.

Other important pointers to U.S. population data, including the *Census of Population: Social and Economic Characteristics* and the *Census of Population and Housing,* are described in chapter three. Other compilations of population and demographic data include:

Current Population Reports. http://www.census.gov/mp/www/pub/pop/mspop .html#CPR

There are several titles in the *Current Population Reports* series from the U.S. Census, available on the Web, in government bookstores, and in many libraries, including:

Population Characteristics, P-20. These reports are annual surveys documenting geographic residence and mobility, fertility, school enrollment, educational attainment, marital status, households and families, persons of Spanish origin, and other topics.

Population Estimates and Projections, P-25. Check these compilations for monthly estimates of the U.S. population, annual estimates of the population by age, sex, race, and geographic area, and projections for the U.S. and each state.

Demographic Yearbook. New York: Statistical Office of the United Nations. Annual.

This yearbook supplies figures related to population, natality, marriage, divorce, mortality, and migration for about 229 countries and areas.

Demographics Journal. http://www.amcity.com/journals/demographics/

Search this journal for reports and statistics on U.S. cities covering wages, employment, population trends, government, and other topics. Free at the time of this writing with a notation saying it would be subscription-based in the future.

Population Index. Princeton, NJ: Princeton University, Office of Population Research, 1935–present. Also available from 1986 to the present at http://popindex.princeton.edu/.

This is an annotated bibliography of resources related to population topics.

Psychology/Mental Health

Diagnostic and Statistical Manual of Mental Disorders (DSM-IV). 4th edition. Washington, DC: American Psychiatric Association, 1994. Also available on CD-ROM.

This is the standard source for official descriptions of psychological disorders. The *DSM-IV* identifies disorders under headings such as disruptive behavior, eating, gender identity, psychoactive substance use, anxiety, dissociative, sexual, sleep, factitious, delusional, and impulse control. A companion to this book is the *DSM-IV Casebook: A Learning Companion to the DSM-IV*, which cites actual cases and the diagnosis for each case.

The Encyclopedia of Mental Health. 3 Volumes. Howard S. Friedman, ed. New York: Academic Press, 1998.

Articles in this encyclopedia cover mental health matters of interest to the public and to researchers. Sample essays include "Behavioral Genetics,"

"Caffeine: Psychosocial Effects," and "Racism and Mental Health."

Encyclopedia of Psychology. 2nd edition. 4 Volumes. Raymond J. Corsini, ed. New York: John Wiley & Sons, 1994.

Encyclopedia of Psychology looks at the theorists and theories of psychology.

Essential Guide to Psychiatric Drugs. 3rd edition. Jack M. Gorman. New York: St. Martin's Press, 1997.

The author discusses drugs commonly used to treat such disorders as anxiety, sleeping problems, and depression, along with explanations of the disorders and what the drugs are expected to accomplish.

Mental Health, United States. Rockville, MD: U.S. Department of Health and Human Services, 1996.

Mental health facts covered in this volume include information about managed care, the prevalence of emotional disturbances in children and adolescence, and mental health services, facilities, expenditures, and personnel.

PsycSite. http://stange.simplenet.com/psycsite

PsycSite is a good choice when seeking psychology-related information on the Net. It contains links to psychology journals; online resources under such categories as clinical psychology, the psychology of art, tests and measurements; and pointers to Web resources on specific disorders, such as post-traumatic stress disorder and autism. Also on the Net, at http://www.mental health.com, is *Internet Mental Health,* a free encyclopedia of mental health information.

Regional U.S. Data: State, County, and City

See also: chapter three: under State Information; chapter nine under Facts About Countries and States; and chapter twelve under Marketing and Advertising Data

Book of the States. Chicago: Council of State Governments. Biennial. Also on CD-ROM under the name *USA State Factbook.*

Book of the States presents comparative data for the fifty states for such areas as finance and major state services. There are also essays and data on legislation, intergovernmental affairs, elections and constituents, legislatures, governors, and basic facts such as each state's motto.

County and City Data Book. Washington, DC: U.S. Department of Commerce, Bureau of the Census, 1947–present. Also available on CD-ROM under the title *County-City Plus* with additional information included. Selected contents available at http://www.census.gov/statab/www/ccdb.html.

Statistics for over 1,000 cities, all 3,141 U.S. counties, and 11,097 places of 2,500 or more inhabitants are supplied in the *County and City Data Book.* Statistical coverage includes population, health, crime, income, labor force, agriculture, wholesale and retail trade, and poverty status for U.S. counties and cities. This title and the *State and Metropolitan Data Book* (with selected contents available at http://www.census.gov/statab/www/smadb.html) are useful sources to consult between the ten-year census periods.

CQ's State Fact Finder: Rankings Across America. Harold A. Hovey. Washington, DC: Congressional Quarterly, Annual.

Using the *State Fact Finder* you can answer such questions as: Which states have the highest/lowest taxes? Which states invest in education and have high graduation rates? Rankings answering these questions and hundreds of others related to population, government, economics, geography, health, crime, transport, and welfare are included. A similar title is the *Gale City and Metro Ranking Reporter* (2nd edition. Detroit: Gale, 1997).

USA Counties. Washington, DC: U.S. Bureau of the Census. Available on CD-ROM and at http://govinfo.kerr.orst.edu/index.text.html

Find thousands of data variables related to counties, including crime statistics, information about ancestry, and health, education, population, housing, and economic data. This database includes information from both the *County and City Data Book* and the *State and Metropolitan Data Book* (see above). In its test phase at the time of this writing, the Web site at http://www.maproom.psu.edu/mapper/usa/usacounties.html from Penn State University will offer maps derived from variables in *USA Counties.*

Science and Engineering

See also: Chemical Properties, Formulas, and Effects

Basic Science and Technology Statistics. Paris: OECD, Annual.

An international data book, covering OECD (Organization of Economic Co-operation and Development) countries, that looks at each country's expenditures on research and development, and the number of patent applications generated.

Magill's Survey of Science. Pasadena, CA: Salem Press. Also available on CD-ROM.

The aim of this series is to present overviews and issues in science in a manner geared to the sophisticated nonspecialist. Titles in the series, with each base set containing five volumes, are *Space Exploration Series* (1989), *Earth Science Series* (1990, supplement 1998), *Life Sciences* (1991, supplement 1998), *Applied Sciences* (1993, supplement 1998), and *Physical Sciences* (1992, supplement 1998).

McGraw-Hill Encyclopedia of Science & Technology. 8th edition. 20 Volumes. Sybil P. Parker, ed. McGraw-Hill, 1997. Also available on CD-ROM.

Updated about every half decade, this set presents information in every field of contemporary science and technology. The entries are lengthy, and drawings, tables and graphs are included. Some subjects are updated annually in the *McGraw-Hill Yearbook of Science and Technology.* Single volumes are derived from this collection, and you'll find that some libraries buy a few of those volumes and not the entire collection. There are single volumes for *Astronomy, Chemistry, Environmental Science and Engineering,* and *Physics.*

National Science Foundation (NSF), 4201 Wilson Blvd., Arlington, VA 22230, Phone: (703)306-1234, URL: http://www.nsf.gov

Click on the "Science Statistics" option on the NSF page to pull up data and publications like the *Science and Engineering Indicators* which provides quantitative information and analysis regarding science and engineering research and education in the U.S. Available in print and on the Web, *Science and Engineering Indicators* includes such topics as trends in completion of high school science and mathematics courses, and selected characteristics and employers of those with science and engineering degrees.

ScienceNet Database. http://www.sciencenet.org.uk/first.html

ScienceNet offers explanations of scientific concepts and processes and news updates from the world of science. Pick from nine broad categories: archaeology, chemistry, engineering/technology, environment, earth science, math/computer science, biology/medicine, physics/astronomy, and social science.

To locate other encyclopedic works on specific areas in the sciences, combine the word ENCYCLOPEDIAS or HANDBOOKS with the area you want to focus on, such as AGRICULTURE, ASTRONOMY, ASTROPHYSICS, BIOLOGY, BIOCHEMISTRY, BOTANY, CHEMISTRY, COMPUTER SCIENCE, EARTH SCIENCE, ENGINEERING, GEOGRAPHY, GEOLOGY, GIS, HORTICULTURE, MATHEMATICS, PHYSICS, or ZOOLOGY.

Social Work and Sociology

Encyclopedia of Sociology. 4 Volumes. Edgar F. Borgatta, ed. New York: Macmillan, 1992.

The lengthy articles in this set cover topics of research interest to sociologists such as death and dying and quality of life; sociological concepts like replication, anomie, and alienation; and sociology as practiced in some foreign nations.

Encyclopedia of Social Work. 19th edition. 3 Volumes. Richard L. Lewis, editor. Washington, DC: National Association of Social Workers, 1995 with 1997 supplement.

This set looks at the professional needs of social workers and the many issues, cultures, and social groups that they work with.

Sports

Almost all reference sources involving sports include statistics—either player stats or records. So here I'll list just a few examples. For assistance in interpreting these figures, try Jeremy Feinberg's *Reading the Sports Page: Guide to Understanding Sports Statistics* (New Discovery Books, 1992).

Encyclopedia of World Sports: From Ancient Times to the Present. 3 Volumes. David Levinson. Santa Barbara, CA: ABC-CLIO, 1996.

This set covers historic and contemporary characteristics of three hundred sports, and the social, legal, and medicinal aspects of athletics worldwide.

ESPN.com. http://espn.go.com

Track current news, scores, league statistics, standings, schedules, and rosters for numerous sports at this ESPN site.

The Information Please Sports Almanac. Mike Meserole, ed. Boston: Houghton Mifflin. Annual. Also at http://www.infoplease.com/sports.html.

This almanac contains information on sports happenings for the current year, historical and contemporary stats for most major college and professional sporting events, and brief biographical entries for sports figures. Many statistics are tucked away in this volume, such as the capacity of major arenas and ballparks, athletic awards bestowed by journalists, and a listing of the top twenty-five horses in horse racing and the money they earned for others.

Sports Rule Books. Many of the official sports organizations regularly produce yearbooks and rule books. For example, the National Collegiate Athletic Association (NCAA) annually publishes rule books that detail dimensions of playing space, standards for equipment, a description of events and procedures, and the duties of officials for many sports activities.

General rule books are commonly found in the sports/games area of your

library's reference or circulating section; for Library of Congress that's the
*GV730*s and in Dewey Decimal look in the *790*s. Some sample titles:

*According to Hoyle: Official Rules of More Than 200 Popular Games of Skill and
Chance With Expert Advice on Winning Play.* Richard L. Frey. New York:
Fawcett Columbine, 1996.

 This guide has rules and playing strategies for board and card games.

Hopscotch, Hangman, Hot Potato, & Ha, Ha, Ha: A Rulebook of Children's Games.
Jack Maguire. New York: Prentice Hall, 1990.

 Rules for indoor, outdoor, and travel games are explained, with each entry
supplying information on where to play, the number of players required, the
equipment needed, and the object of the game.

*Rules of the Game: The Complete Illustrated Encyclopedia of All the Major Sports of
the World.* Revised edition. The Diagram Group. New York: St. Martin's
Press, 1995.

 Rules for competitive sporting events are accompanied by plenty of drawings. There are quite a variety of athletic events from around the world in
here, including surfing, snooker, aikido, and sports acrobatics.

There are subject-specific encyclopedias and handbooks for almost all sports
and recreational activities. Just match the name of a sport or activity, such as
FISHING, JUGGLING, or BASKETBALL with the word ENCYCLOPEDIAS
or HANDBOOKS and do a keyword search in your library catalog.

Television and Radio

See also: Film

International Television and Video Almanac. James D. Moser, ed. New York:
Quigley. Annual. Also on CD-ROM on the *Entertainment Industry Reference
CD-ROM.*

 This almanac looks at yearly highlights of the TV, cable, satellite, and video
industries. It supplies statistics such as the number of cable subscriptions, time
spent viewing, and Nielson TV Index Ratings for top prime-time programs,
and it lists award winners, biographies, and contact information for those in
the entertainment world. Another title with similar content for the film industry is the *International Motion Picture Almanac.*

On the Air: The Encyclopedia of Old-Time Radio. John Dunning. Englewood
Cliffs, NJ: Prentice Hall, 1998.

On the Air is a listing of the dramatic entertainment radio programs stilled by the advent of television. For each program the author lists air dates, network, sponsors, time slot, personnel, premise of the show, and biographical data for many of the shows' stars.

Old-time radio buffs should also see the *Old-Time Radio Resources* Web page at http://www.onlineinc.com/bookmark/sloden.html.

Museum of Broadcast Communications Encyclopedia of Television. 3 Volumes. Horace Newcomb, ed. Chicago: Fitzroy Dearborn, 1997.

This set contains black-and-white photographs and encyclopedic articles on television writers, producers, actors, programs, genres, technology, theories, and TV's evolution in different nations. Another title on this subject is *Les Brown's Encyclopedia of Television.* (3rd edition. Detroit: Gale, 1992).

The Ultimate TV Show List. http://www.ultimatetv.com/UTVL/

This site connects you to links and information related to over 1,400 television shows. Other meta sites to television and movies include the *Special TV Resources* at http://www.specialWeb.com/tv/ and *Cinemedia* at http://afi.cine media.org/, which also has links to radio sites.

Facts in a Flash

Surfing the Radio Waves

To tune in to worldwide radio stations of every variety on the Web, visit *vTuner* at http://www.vtuner.com.

Theater

McGraw-Hill Encyclopedia of World Drama. 2nd edition. 5 Volumes. Stanley Hochman, ed. New York: McGraw-Hill, 1984.

A standard international theater encyclopedia that presents surveys of the drama of different nations and of many genres, and critical biographies of dramatists and seminal directors.

Theatre Central. http://www.theatre-central.com

This site boasts that it offers "the largest compendium of theater links on the Internet." It includes links to sites on theater companies, playwrights, directors and actors, stagecraft, publications, and discussion groups.

Finding Plays. Locating a specific play in a library catalog isn't as straightforward as it may seem. First try a title search under the name of the play or an author search by the playwright's name. If you get no results, the library may still own the play you need. Plays included in collected works of plays are often not listed separately on a library catalog and so are somewhat elusive.

Several guides skirt this problem by telling which plays are reprinted in which specific collections. Once you know the name of the collection, you can see if your library owns that collection or if you can borrow it via interlibrary loan. Two indexes to plays are John Ottemiller's *Index to Plays in Collections* (Metuchen, NJ: Scarecrow Press, 1988) and *Play Index* (New York: H.W. Wilson, 1949–present). On the Web, try *Inter-Play: An Online Index to Plays in Collections, Anthologies, and Periodicals* at http://www.portals.org/interplay, which indexes plays not found in Ottemiller's book or the *Play Index*.

Major sellers of play scripts are Samuel French (Phone: [212]206-8990 or [213]876-0570, URL: http://www.samuelfrench.com/) or The Dramatists Play Service (Phone: [212]683-8960, URL: http://www.dramatists.com/) and The Drama Book Shop (Phone: [212]944-0595 or [800]322-0595, URL: http://www1.playbill.com/).

Transportation Statistics

See also: chapter eight for historic and contemporary descriptions of particular modes of transport, e.g., cars, planes, boats.

American Automobile Manufacturer Association (AAMA). http://www.aama.com

This page has a quarterly statistical report called Economic Indicators which supplies data related to the U.S. automobile industry, including sales figures, U.S. market share of cars and trucks, employment data, financing trends, and consumer expenditures. No statistics are provided for specific manufacturers, makes, or models of vehicles; that data can be found in AAMA print publications, including *AAMA Motor Vehicle Facts & Figures* and *World Motor Vehicle Data*. Other annually released publications providing a wide range of worldwide automotive industry statistics are *The Automotive News Market Data Book* (Detroit: Crain Communications) and *Ward's Automotive Yearbook* (Detroit: Ward's Communications).

The Aviation and Aerospace Almanac. Compiled by the editors of *Aerospace Daily* and *Aviation Daily.* New York: TAB Books. Annual.

This is an almanac of information and statistics concerning international and U.S. airlines; airports; U.S. Department of Transportation; Federal Aviation Administration; National Transportation Safety Board; Department of Defense; U.S. Air Force, Army, and Navy; NASA; and the aerospace industry. Some of the facts available in this almanac include average speed of U.S. air carriers, the market share of U.S. airports (by carrier), and the total flight hours for different types of airplanes.

Bureau of Transportation Statistics. Phone: (800)853-1351, E-mail: statistics@bts. gov, URL: http://www.bts.gov

The BTS compiles, analyzes, and makes accessible information on all types of U.S. transportation systems. Find an impressive number of transportation and travel-related statistics, surveys, and reports on this Web page answering questions ranging from "How many motorcycles were registered in the U.S. in 1970?" to "How many domestic travelers filed mishandled baggage complaints for a particular airline?" The American Travel Survey, full-text on this Web page, looks at how, why, when, and where Americans travel.

Highway Statistics. Federal Highway Administration. Washington, DC: U.S. Department of Transportation, 1945–present. Annual. URL: http://www.fhwa .dot.gov/ohim/phimstat.htm

This report presents statistics related to motor fuel, motor vehicles, driver licensing, highway-user taxation, federal and state highway finance, and highway mileage.

National Transportation Safety Board (NTSB), 490 L'Enfant Plaza SW, Washington, DC 20594, Phone: (202)314-6000, or to order reports: (202)382-6735, URL: http://www.ntsb.gov

The NTSB Web page supplies transportation accident statistics and descriptions of NTSB-investigated accidents. Facts are available regarding all civil aviation/airline disasters and major railroad, highway, marine, pipeline, and hazardous material accidents.

UFOs

The UFO Encyclopedia: The Phenomenon From the Beginning. 2 Volumes. Jerome Clark. Detroit: Omnigraphics, 1998.

An A-Z listing of UFO phenomena from ancient times to the present. Find theories, cases, hoaxes, biographies, effects on popular culture, and listings of UFO-related organizations.

UFOs: Just the Facts. Phoenix: Sky Creative Media Group, 1997.

This CD-ROM offers an extensive bibliography, documents, and commen-

tary on issues surrounding UFOs with contents updated for those who purchase the CD-ROM at http://www.ufofacts.com.

On the Web see the *ParaNet* site at http://www.paranetinfo.com.

Vital Statistics

See *also:* Death

Vital statistics are those covering human events such as death, birth, marriage
and divorce.

Accident Facts. Chicago: National Safety Council. Annual.

This is a booklet of tables, graphs, and text concerning injuries and deaths.
Examples of headings include Motor-Vehicle Deaths on Major Holidays, and
School Bus Accidents.

Vital Statistics of the United States. Washington, DC: U.S. Department of Health
and Human Services. National Center for Health Statistics, 1937–present.
Vital statistics are updated monthly at http://www.cdc.gov/nchswww
/products/catalogs/catpub.htm.

The National Center for Health Statistics produces this compendium covering
data concerning natality (fertility, live births, birth rates), mortality (infant and
fetal mortality, death by accidents, life tables), and marriage and divorce.

**How to Obtain Birth, Death, Marriage, and Divorce
Certificates**

Check the Web page maintained by the *National Center for
Health Statistics* at http://www.cdc.gov/nchswww/howto
/w2w/w2welcom.htm to find information on where you can write for vital records.
Or, look in the state government pages in your phone book and check for listings
under *vital records* or your state's Department of Health or Public Health.

Voting

The following resources cover how the public has voted for elected officials as
well as how those officials have voted on behalf of the public.

American National Election Studies Data Sourcebook: 1952–1986. Warren E.
Miller. Cambridge, MA: Harvard University Press, 1989. Updates are available
under slightly different titles. Do a keyword search in your library catalog

under AMERICAN NATIONAL ELECTION STUDIES. Also available on CD-ROM under *American National Election Studies.*

This series supplies data on the electorate and their reaction to national elections. Some elements include social characteristics of the electorate, party identification, trust/confidence in government, and involvement and turnout.

America Votes: A Handbook of Contemporary American Election Statistics. Elections Research Center. Washington, DC: Congressional Quarterly. Annual.

America Votes is arranged by state, showing the number of votes cast and the percentage of votes for major candidates in the races for governor, congress, and the presidency. Maps of state's voting districts are also provided.

Congressional Index. 2 Volumes. Chicago: Commerce Clearing House, 1930–present. Updated weekly.

This loose-leaf service reports who voted for and against bills up for enactment. Also find such roll call votes on the Web via Thomas at http://thomas .loc.gov/.

Election Statistics. http://clerkweb.house.gov/histrecs/history/elections/elections .htm

The official vote counts for federal elections from 1920 to the present are listed on this site.

Project Vote Smart. http://www.vote-smart.org/

Project Vote Smart has compiled information on state legislators, governors, congressional members, and the president, including biographical data, voting records, campaign finances, issue positions, and performance evaluations.

Voter Information Services: VIS Ratings Service. http://www.vis.org

Use this online site to see how congressional members have been rated by different advocacy groups and how they voted on different issues.

Wars and the Military

International Military and Defense Encyclopedia (IMADE). 6 Volumes. Trevor N. Dupuy, ed. Brassey's, 1993.

IMADE was developed with seventeen major subject areas in mind, including combat theory and operations, logistics, armed forces and society, leadership, command and management, defense and international security policy, material and weapons, and history and biography.

SIPRI Yearbook: Armaments, Disarmaments, and International Security. Stockholm International Peace Research Institute. New York: Oxford University Press. Annual.

SIPRI supplies international statistics on military spending, arms production and trade, and essays on timely topics for each year, such as specific peace
negotiations and major armed conflicts. Some data and graphs are also at the
SIPRI home page at http://www.sipri.se/.

World Military Expenditures and Arms Transfers. http://www.acda.gov/reports.htm

Look on this page for data on international military expenditures, armed
forces, arms transfers, and other related data from the U.S. Arms Control and
Disarmament Agency.

For every major Western war of the last few hundred years, there are one or
more encyclopedias focusing on its roots, battles, campaigns, participants, and
aftermath. Search in library catalogs under the word ENCYCLOPEDIAS or
HANDBOOKS along with the name of the war, e.g., CIVIL WAR, COLD
WAR, GULF WAR, KOREAN WAR, MEXICAN WAR, PACIFIC WAR,
REVOLUTIONARY WAR (or UNITED STATES REVOLUTION 1775–
1783), VIETNAM WAR, WORLD WAR I, or WORLD WAR II.

Weapons

Armed and Dangerous: A Writer's Guide to Weapons. Michael Newton. Cincinnati,
  Ohio: Writer's Digest Books, 1990.

Armed and Dangerous describes, in detail, the proper weapon for specific
eras and situations. No illustrations.

CIA Special Weapons and Equipment: Spy Devices of the Cold War. H. Keith
  Melton. New York: Sterling, 1993.

The devices used in the television show *Get Smart* seem tame compared to
some of the real-life gadgets in this book. Some devices listed include the
briefcase recorder (à la *Mission Impossible*), the tear-gas pen (with a range of
six feet it can "incapacitate the target long enough to allow an escape"), and,
my favorite, the dog doo transmitter (a homing beacon "camouflaged to re-
semble the excrement of a medium-size dog").

Jane's Directories.

The English publisher Jane's Information Group (founded by Fred T. Jane,
not a woman named Jane) produces directories that describe weapons, transportation systems, and combinations thereof. Each directory supplies photos of the
weapons/transport and many details about each unit. Sample titles, all starting
with the word *Jane's*, include *Jane's Air-Launched Weapons, Fighting Ships, Infantry
Weapons, Land-Based Air Defense, Military Training Systems, Military Vehicles &*

Logistics, Naval Weapons Systems, Radar and EW (Electronic Warfare) Systems, Strategic Weapon Systems, and *Underwater Warfare Systems.*

Martial Arts of the Orient. Peter Lewis. London: MMB, 1993.

This book contains action shots of karate, jiujitsu, judo, aikido, tae kwon-do, and other martial art forms. Many weapons of the martial artist are also pictured, including a chain whip, tiger fork, and rice flails.

Modern Combat Blades: The Best in Edged Weaponry. Duncan Long. Boulder, CO: Paladin Press, 1992.

A critical look at edged weaponry, including pocketknives, bowie knives, daggers, stilettos, samurai blades, kukris (knives with sloped blades created by the Nepalese), machetes, swords, battle-axes, meat cleavers, and folding shovels. Each section describes the history, construction, and use of each weapon, along with laws pertaining to its use.

 Weapon Replicas

There are companies that specialize in selling replicas of weaponry and protective clothing from days gone by. Two companies of note are *Arms and Armor,* (toll-free phone: [800]745-7345, URL: http://www.armor.com/catalog/catalog.html) and *Museum Replicas Limited Catalog,* (toll-free phone: [800]883-8838, and on the Web at http://www.museumreplicas.com.

The New Illustrated Guide to Modern Elite Forces: The Weapons, Uniforms, and Tactics of the World's Secret Special Warfare Units. David Miller, revised by Gerard Ridefort. London: Salamander Books, 1992.

The dress, trappings, and arms used by such forces as the Alpini Troops of Italy, the Commandos of Taiwan, and the U.S. Marines are described and illustrated. Other titles from Salamander Books arranged like this one are *The New Illustrated Guide to Modern Sub Hunters: The Weapons, Technology, and Techniques Used in Today's Submarine Warfare* and *The New Illustrated Guide to Modern Tanks and Fighting Vehicles.*

The Shooter's Bible. South Hackensack, NJ: Stoeger. Annual.

The Shooter's Bible supplies names, prices, specifications, and photos for foreign and domestic handguns, rifles, shotguns, and black powder guns. There's also information on ammunition and scopes.

Weapons: An International Encyclopedia—From 5,000 B.C. to 2,000 A.D. Updated edition. The Diagram Group. New York: St. Martin's Press, 1990.

This single volume contains 2,500 illustrated entries with each giving the history of the weapon and the principles by which it works.

Women

The Book of Women's Firsts: Breakthrough Achievements of Almost 1,000 American Women. Phyllis J. Read. New York: Random House, 1992.

Some of the "firsts" listed include Laura Blears Ching, the first woman to compete against men in an international surfing competition, and in 1869, Amy Bradley, the first woman to supervise a public school system. Another title on this subject is *Women's Firsts: Milestones in Women's History* (Detroit: U X L, 1998).

Statistical Record of Women Worldwide. 2nd edition. Linda Schmittroth, ed. Detroit: Gale, 1995.

This book contains a wide range of figures culled from articles, reports, studies, reference books, and newspapers. They range from opinions (e.g., How important would you say religion is in your life?) to diverse statistics (e.g., the percentage of women who hold roles on prime-time television). Another statistics compilation is the *Statistical Handbook of Women in America* (2nd edition. Phoenix, AZ: Oryx Press, 1996).

Women's Studies Section Links (WSSLINKS). http://www.library.yale.edu/wss/

Created by members of the Association of College and Research Libraries section of the American Library Association, WSSLINKS points to a wide range of Web destinations that focus on women.

Textbooks for Overview Information

Textbooks on specific subjects teach the basics of particular topics and fields of study. Unfortunately, the word *textbook* is rarely present in online library catalog records describing textbooks. Instead, the generic phrase STUDY AND TEACHING is used. So, examples of keyword searches you might try for finding textbooks: PSYCHOLOGY STUDY TEACHING or MICROECONOMICS STUDY TEACHING.

In some libraries, you'll find too many books using that technique. One trick I use when I'm looking for a textbook that will give me the basics: I do a title search using the words INTRODUCTION TO. For example, INTRODUCTION TO GEOLOGY or INTRODUCTION TO ALGEBRA.

CHAPTER 6

Experts and Quotations

Locating Experts and Using Their Words to Enhance Yours

"What a delightful thing is the conversation of specialists! One understands absolutely nothing and it's charming."

—Edgar Degas

Using Expert Information

Don't be surprised if you go into a library for information and the librarian sends you home with a phone number, fax number, address, or log-on information for a listserv. Patrons sometimes intimate that I'm shirking my duties when I tell them that they'll need to contact someone to get the answer they need, but there are many reasons to use experts:

- Information is sometimes so new that it hasn't been formally published anywhere yet.
- Sometimes you need material on an obscure topic that primarily resides in the heads of a few enthusiastic specialists.
- An expert may offer a controversial or unusual take on a topic.
- Observing experts may be necessary. Do you need a fictitious doctor to set a broken leg in a novel? Reading about it gives you an idea of the process. Watching it lets you observe the expert's technique and the patient's reaction.
- Anecdotal feedback and colorful comments from experts make your finished writing more interesting.
- Experts can supply simple explanations for processes and ideas that would be difficult to grasp in books, articles, and Web sites geared to scholars in the field.

Experts are those who have the education, work, or life experience to speak knowledgeably on a topic. Their experience may be represented by a Ph.D. or a massive collection of Barbie dolls. The person with the doctorate can be located through university directories and the collector through a doll collectors association, found in one of the directories listed later in this chapter.

An expert may also be the person who has written a number of articles on a topic or has been quoted by such articles. Periodical indexes and bibliographies will help you zero in on those who are often mentioned in relation to a topic.

Matthew Lesko, creator of the enormous directory of experts titled *Lesko's Info-Power* (Detroit: Visible Ink Press, 1996) and other directories, recommends patience when tracking experts. He says you can expect to make about seven phone calls before connecting with the person who has the information you need. He also passes on this excellent advice: Once you've politely extracted the information you need from an expert, follow up with a thank-you note. You may want to contact that expert again, and he or she will remember you.

Phone and Address Directories: Online and Off

The familiar phone book is a great place to look for hunting down experts. A few libraries still maintain a paper collection of phone books from around the world, but more often you'll be directed to the Web or a phone directory on CD-ROM or microfiche.

Directory Assistance

Good old directory assistance from your phone company is still a terrific way to find numbers when you know the name of a person or business and the location. Just dial the area code for the number you need followed by 555-1212. For toll-free numbers dial (800)555-1212. This service is also on the Web at http://555-1212.com or for toll-free numbers, at http://www.tollfree.att.net/tf.html. If you don't know the area code for the location you're calling, just dial your operator to ask.

Numerous phone and address directories are on the Web. It's a good idea to bookmark several, since you'll find that all have their drawbacks. For example, one of my long-out-of-date and useless E-mail addresses is on virtually every E-mail directory I've ever tried.

A meta-source page to directories of phone numbers, E-mail and postal addresses, and zip codes is operated by AT&T at http://www.att.com/directory/inter

net.html. This site points you to not only AT&T-created directories, but also to such sites as *Switchboard* at http://www.switchboard.com, *WhoWhere* at http://www.whowhere.lycos.com, *Big Yellow* at http://www.bigyellow.com, *Bigfoot* at http://www.bigfoot.com, and *WorldPages* at http://www.worldpages.com.

Expert Directories

There are hundreds of online and off-line directories that present the names of experts. The mother of all expert directories:

The Encyclopedia of Associations. 4 Volumes. Detroit: Gale. Annual. The companion set is the *Encyclopedia of International Associations.* Both sets are also available on CD-ROM and as subscription databases via Galenet under the name *Associations Unlimited* and through Ameritech Library Services Vista, DIALOG, and LEXIS-NEXIS.

This is often the first and last place to look for experts in any field. Associations generate statistics, carry career information, and have memberships comprised of authorities on a particular subject. Every type of association I've been able to imagine is in *The Encyclopedia of Associations*—everything from the Society for Linguistic Anthropology to the Gilligan's Island Fan Club.

For each organization named, *The Encyclopedia of Associations* provides name, address, phone, fax, year founded, number of members, membership dues, number of staff, budget, a description of the organization, publications it produces, dates and locations of upcoming conventions or major meetings, and whether it has a library and how many volumes it contains.

Directories listing experts in all areas of expertise

Besides *The Encyclopedia of Associations*, other directories with impressive all-around coverage include:

Community of Science. http://www.cos.com

Click "COS Expertise" on this home page to locate profiles of researchers and scholars in universities, government agencies, and other research and development organizations worldwide.

Lesko's Info-Power II. 3rd edition. Matthew Lesko. Detroit: Visible Ink Press, 1996. Also available through CompuServe.

A veritable library of phone numbers and addresses of experts and contacts for almost any information needed.

Research Centers Directory (RCD). Detroit: Gale. Annual. Also available as a

Locating Great Meta Pages for Specific Subjects: Associations on the Web

The home page maintained by an association representing a major field or area of interest is a great place to start when searching for subject-specific quality Web sites. So, for example, when I visit the home page for the *American Philosophical Association* at http://www.udel.edu/apa/ and click on "Web resources," I find dozens of links related to philosophy. A free Web page that lists and describes associations is the *Internet Public Library's Associations on the Net* at http://www.ipl.org/ref/AON/.

Also, you can sometimes, though not always, guess the name of an organization you need by combining the word ORGANIZATION, SOCIETY, or ASSOCIATION with a subject word. Unfortunately, sometimes this method brings up only small groups with pages that are little more than advertisements.

---

subscription database via Galenet under the name *Research Centers and Services Directories.*

RCD identifies thousands of nonprofit research organizations. Research is always being conducted in almost any field imaginable, and of course the person doing the research is, hopefully, an expert. A quick browse of the subject index shows entries for termites, famine, copper, and brambles. Other research directories from this publisher include *Government Research Directory: The Comprehensive Guide to U.S. and Canadian Government Research Programs and Facilities, Research Services Directory: A One-Stop Guide to Commercial Research Activity,* and *International Research Centers Directory.*

The Yearbook of Experts, Authorities, & Spokespersons. Washington, DC: Broadcast Interview Source. Annual. Also at http://www.YearbookNews.com.

The print edition of the *Yearbook,* also referred to as *Talk Show Guest Directory,* opens with over 150 pages of possible topic ideas, including cat allergies, corn, electric toothbrushes, hunger, living wills, sex, and Yugoslavia. Also searchable by location of speaker. Other Web pages along these lines include *Experts.com* at http://www.experts.com and *Speakers On-Line* at http://speakers.com.

Yearbook of International Organizations. 4 Volumes. Union of International Associations, ed. Brussels: K.G. Sauer. Annual. Also available on CD-ROM under the title *International Organizations and Biographies.*

Over thirty thousand worldwide organizations of all types with over ninety thousand contacts are included in the print set, both nongovernment related, e.g., the International Weightlifting Federation, and governmental, e.g., the United Nations.

Finding experts in particular fields

Below is a representative listing of sample online and off-line titles and associations geared to specific professions and subject interests.

Architects and Designers

ProFile: The Directory of U.S. Architectural Design Firms. Washington, DC: AIA Press. Annual. Also at http://www.cmdg.com/profile/.

ProFile is subdivided by state, with a separate roster of professional interest areas, identifying architectural firms with specialties in areas such as the environment, judicial buildings, and health-care facilities. There is also a search engine on the home page of the *American Institute of Architects* at http://www.e-architect.com/reference/.

Representative Organization:

American Institute of Architects, 1735 New York Ave. NW, Washington, DC 20006, Phone: (202)626-7300, Fax: (202)626-7421, URL: http://www.aia online.com

The Arts: Performing, Fine, and Visual

The Artist's Resource Handbook. Daniel Grant. New York: Allworth Press, 1996.

The names and addresses in this guide cover organizations that assist with finding careers in the field of art, professional services for artists, art associations, financial assistance outlets, artist-in-residence programs, artist communities, art councils, and public art programs.

Celebrity Access: The Directory. Thomas Burford. Mill Valley, CA: Celebrity Access Publications. Annual.

Celebrity Access furnishes names and nonhome mailing addresses of actors, actresses, and selected people in politics, science, sports, and the arts. On the Web try *Chip's Celebrity Home & E-Mail Addresses* at http://www.addresses.site 2go.com/.

Film Producers, Studios, Agents, and Casting Directors Guide. 6th edition. David M. Kipen. Los Angeles: Lone Eagle Publishing Company, 1998.

Business addresses, phone, and fax numbers are listed for most of the filmmakers in this directory. The film title index makes it simple to find the producer of a particular film, and there are also credits listed for some of the casting directors. Other directories from this publisher include *Michael Singer's Film Directors: A Complete Guide* (12th edition, 1997) and *Film Actors Guide* (3rd edition, 1996).

Musical America. New York: Musical America Publishing. Annual.

This international directory has names and addresses of managers, orchestras, opera and dance companies, choral groups, record companies, state arts agencies, those directing performing arts series and festivals, and schools for arts administration study and music study.

Stern's Performing Arts Directory. Allen E. McCormack, ed. New York: Robert D. Stern. Annual.

A directory for dance and music information with entries for dance companies, instructors, choreographers, educators, music ensembles, orchestras, composers, and conductors.

Want's Theatre Directory. Washington, DC: WANT Publishing Company. Annual.

Want's has names and numbers of about seven hundred U.S. and Canadian theaters for the performing arts, as well as some major theaters in London and Western Europe. A guide to nonprofit professional theaters in the U.S. is the *TCG Theatre Directory* (New York: Theatre Communications Group. Annual).

Representative Organizations:

American Arts Alliance, 805 Fifteenth St. NW, Suite 500, Washington, DC 20004, Phone: (202)289-1776, Fax: (202)371-6601, E-mail: aaa@tmn .com, URL: http://www.artswire.org/~aaa/

American Institute of Graphic Arts, 164 Fifth Ave., New York, NY 10010, Phone: (212)807-1990 or (800)548-1634, Fax: (212)807-1799, URL: http://www.aiga.org

Drama League, 165 W. Forty-sixth St., Suite 601, New York, NY 10036, Phone: (212)302-2100, Fax: (212)302-2254, E-mail: dlny@echonyc.com, URL: http://www.mosaic.echonyc.com/~dlny

Dramatist's Guild, 1501 Broadway, Suite 701, New York, NY 10036-9366, Phone: (212)398-9366, Fax: (212)944-0420, URL: http://www.vcu.edu /artweb/playwriting/dg.html

National Academy of Recording Arts and Sciences (NARAS), 3402 Pico Blvd., Santa Monica, CA 90405, Phone: (310)392-3777, Fax: (310)399-3090, URL: http://www.grammy.com/

Screen Actor's Guild (SAG), 5757 Wilshire Blvd., Los Angeles, CA 90036-3635, Phone: (213)954-1600, URL: http://www.sag.com/

Criminal Justice and Law

Directory of Legal Academia. http://www.law.cornell.edu/dla/

This is a directory with contact information to faculty and staff at U.S. law schools.

Judicial Staff Directory. Alexandria, VA: CQ Staff Directories. Annual.

This directory lists federal courts and the people who work in them. A directory that includes state court judges and clerks is *BNA's Directory of State and Federal Courts, Judges, and Clerks: A State-by-State Listing* (Washington, DC: Bureau of National Affairs. Annual).

Martindale-Hubbell Law Directory. 27 Volumes. New Providence, NJ: Martindale-Hubbell. Annual. Also available on CD-ROM, at http://www.martindale.com/locator/home.html under the name *Martindale-Hubbell Lawyer Locator;* at http://www.abanet.org/martindale.html, which offers the ability to limit the search to American Bar Association members; and as a commercial database via LEXIS-NEXIS.

One of the oldest and best-known directories of lawyers and law firms, supplying profiles of lawyers and law practices in the U.S. and Canada. Also search for attorneys on the Web using the *West Legal Directory* at http://www.wld.com/direct/welcome.asp.

Police Officer's Internet Directory. http://www.officer.com

Intended for the police professional, this page leads to Web sites for law enforcement agencies, organizations, suppliers, listservs, and even the personal home pages of more than a thousand police officers.

Representative Organizations:

American Bar Association, 750 N. Lake Shore Dr., Chicago, IL 60611, Phone: (312)988-5000 or toll-free: (800)285-2221, URL: http://www.abanet.org/

American Correctional Association, 4380 Forbes Blvd., Lanham, MD 20706-4322, Phone: (301)918-1800 or (800)222-5646, Fax: (301)918-1900, URL: http://www.corrections.com/aca

Education

Higher Education. University professors are usually glad to share their expertise in their particular area of study. Journalists and other writers can use the services of ProfNet, an E-mail-based service that helps pinpoint experts. ProfNet has contact

Finding Directories

When looking in an online library catalog and searching for listings of authorities in certain subjects, do a keyword search and combine the type of expert or their field of expertise with the word DIRECTORIES. For example: HISTORIANS DIRECTORIES, MATHEMATICS DIRECTORIES, PARKS DIRECTORIES, or FOUNDATIONS DIRECTORIES.

with more than 2,100 public relations officers from 800 universities. Send an E-mail to profnet@vyne.com or fax request to (516)689-1425 that includes your name, organization, address, phone number, deadline, and what you're looking for. After requests are sent, ProfNet can be reached at (800)PROFNET or (516)941-3736.

Another method of locating experts in academia is to go to a Web page that links to college home pages such as *CollegeNet* at http://www.collegenet.com/ or *College and University Home Pages* at http://www.mit.edu:8001/people/cdemello/univ.html. College home pages include the specialties of their faculty.

To find colleges that offer the type of curriculum you're interested in, you can also use *Petersons.com* at http://www.petersons.com to search colleges by keyword. You can then link to the home pages of colleges that match your criteria. Peterson's also publishes hard copy directories to colleges such as *Peterson's Guide to Graduate Programs* (Princeton, NJ: Peterson's Guides. Annual).

National Faculty Directory (Detroit, Gale. Annual) is a listing of over 600,000 faculty members around the U.S., supplying their campus addresses. *Higher Education Directory* (Falls Church, VA: Higher Education Publications. Annual) identifies names of administrators and department heads at U.S. colleges.

Print guides to colleges and universities worldwide include *International Handbook of Universities* and *World List of Universities* (both from the International Association of Universities. Paris: M. Stockton Press) and *The World of Learning* (London: Europa Publications. Annual).

Elementary and Secondary Schools

American School Directory. http://www.asd.com/.

This is an Internet directory to over 106,000 K-12 schools in the U.S., supplying contact information along with facts such as number of students, school mascot, number of Internet connections, and which school district they're a part of. Also stop at this page if you'd like to register as an alumni of one of the schools.

The Handbook of Private Schools: An Annual Descriptive Survey of Independent Education. Boston: Porter Sargent Publishers. Annual.

A standard guide to independent schools of the U.S. and a smattering of those abroad. It supplies descriptions and data for leading private schools, presented by geographic region. Comparable to this volume is the *Bunting and Lyon Blue Book: Private Independent Schools* (Wallingford, CT: Bunting and Lyon. Annual).

Patterson's American Education. Mount Prospect, IL: Educational Directories. Annual.

Found in most libraries, *Patterson's* contains contacts for educational associations, societies, and high schools, including public, Catholic, Lutheran, and Seventh-Day Adventists. Also from this publisher is *Patterson's Elementary Education.*

Representative Organizations:

American Federation of Teachers, 555 New Jersey Ave. NW, Washington, DC 20001, Phone: (202)879-4400 or (800)238-1133, Fax: (202)879-4545, URL: http://www.aft.org

National Education Association, 1201 Sixteenth St. NW, Washington, DC 20036, Phone: (202)833-4000, Fax: (202)822-7767, URL: http://www .nea.org

Environment

Amazing Environmental Organization Web Directory! http://www.webdirectory.com/ Jump to the home pages of hundreds of organizations involved in environmental issues from this page that lives up to its name.

Conservation Directory: A List of Organizations, Agencies, and Officials Concerned With Natural Resource Use and Management. Rue E. Gordon, ed. Washington, DC: National Wildlife Federation. Annual.

This directory is searchable by name, subject, and publications.

Representative Organizations:

Nature Conservancy, 4245 North Fairfax Dr., Suite 100, Arlington, VA 22203-1606, Phone: (800)628-6860 or (703)841-4220, Fax: (703)841-9692, E-mail: pwalsh@tnc.org, URL: http://www.tnc.org

Sierra Club, 85 Second St., Second Floor, San Francisco, CA 94105-3441,

Phone: (415)977-5500, Fax: (415)977-5799, URL: http://www.sierraclub
.org

Librarians and Booksellers

R.R. Bowker's American Book Trade Directory. New Providence, NJ: R.R. Bowker,
1915–present. Annual.

This directory lists contact information for over thirty thousand book and
magazine wholesalers and retailers in the U.S. and Canada, including sellers
of antiquarian and used books.

The most highly used directories to libraries are described in chapter two
under Finding Libraries: Online and Print Guides.

Representative Organizations:

American Booksellers Association, 828 S. Broadway, Tarrytown, NY 10591,
Phone: (914)591-2665 or (800)637-0037, Fax: (914)591-2720, URL:
http://www.bookweb.org/

American Library Association, 50 E. Huron St., Chicago, IL 60611, Phone:
(312)944-6780 or (800)545-2433, Fax: (312)280-3255, URL: http://www
.ala.org

Special Library Association, 1700 Eighteenth St., NW, Washington, DC
20009-2514, Phone: (202)234-4700, Fax: (202)265-9317, E-mail: sla@sla
.org, URL: http://www.sla.org/

Media

Broadcasting & Cable Yearbook. 2 Volumes. New Providence, NJ: R.R. Bowker.
Annual.

In addition to major broadcast stations, the *Yearbook* lists low-power, experimental and Spanish-language stations along with those that are college, university, or school owned. There are listings for multiple system (cable) operators, satellite owners and operators, advertising and marketing specialists, and
suppliers of programming, technical, and professional services.

MediaINFO Links Online Media Directory. http://www.mediainfo.com/emedia/
MediaINFO is an index to media, media outlets, and media-related businesses with pages on the Internet, including networks, stations, and associations. Another site of interest is *Media Online Yellow Pages* at http://www.web
com.com/~nlnnet/yellowp.html.

News Media Yellow Book: Who's Who Among Reporters, Writers, Editors, and

Producers in the Leading National News Media. New York: Monitor Leadership Directories. Semiannual. Also available on CD-ROM under the title *The Leadership Library on CD-ROM.*

The *Yellow Book* provides names, titles, and contact information for those in newspapers, cable, radio, or television, and some periodical publishers.

WRTH: World Radio TV Handbook. Andrew G. Sennitt, ed. New York: Billboard Books, 1998.

WRTH lists, country by country, long-, medium-, and short-wave broadcasters, with such extras as an hour-by-hour guide to broadcasts in English directed to particular areas, and listings of stations in frequency order.

Representative Organizations:

National Association of Broadcasters, 1771 N. St. NW, Washington, DC
    20036, Phone: (202)429-5300, Fax: (202)429-5343, URL: http://www
    .nab.org

National Press Club, National Press Building, 529 Fourteenth St. NW,
    Washington, DC 20045, Phone: (202)662-7500, Fax: (202)662-7512,
    URL: http://npc.press.org

Medical Professionals/Health Support Organizations

AMA Physician Select: On-Line Doctor Finder. URL: http://www.ama-assn.org

On the AMA home page you can search for over 650,000 doctors of medicine and doctors of osteopathic medicine searchable by name or specialty. Other online directories are the *Doctor Directory* at http://www.doctordirectory .com and the *ABMS Certified Doctor Locator Service* at http://www .certifieddoctor.com/scripts/zipsearch.asp.

Alternative Medicine Resource Guide. Francine Feuerman. Medical Library
    Association: Scarecrow Press, 1997.

This resource guide lists organizations, product suppliers, schools, journals, newsletters, and books related to such therapies as osteopathy, acupuncture, Rolfing, and the Alexander Technique.

American Dental Directory. Chicago: American Dental Association (ADA).
    Annual.

A directory to names, addresses, and credentials of U.S. dentists, including those living abroad, and affiliate, associate, and honorary ADA members. The ADA Web site is at http://www.ada.org and can be reached by phone: (312) 440-2500, Fax: (312)440-2800 or via E-mail at publicinfo@ada.org. Though this directory is not online, there are links to local dental association Web pages from their home page.

Hospital Blue Book. Atlanta: Billian Publishing. Annual.

A nationwide directory of hospitals, diagnosis-related groups (DRGs,) health care systems listings, health maintenance organizations (HMOs,) and preferred provider organizations (PPOs). Other health facility directory titles include *The Directory of Nursing Homes* (Baltimore: HCIA. Irregular), *Guide to the Nation's Hospices* (Arlington, VA: National Hospice Organization. Annual), and *Register of North American Hospitals* (South River, NJ: American Preeminent Registry. Annual).

Hotlines and Helplines.

The Self-Help Sourcebook Online at http://www.mhnet.org/selfhelp/source.htm is a database that links to information on over eight hundred national and international self-help support groups, and to ideas for starting groups. *The Self-Help Sourcebook* is also available in hard copy (order at [973]625-3037). A similar site is *Health Hotlines* at http://sis.nlm.nih.gov/hotlines/.

The Official ABMS Directory of Board Certified Medical Specialists. New Providence, NJ: Marquis Who's Who. Annual. Also available as a commercial database via LEXIS-NEXIS.

You can find brief biographical sketches of physicians in this multivolume directory by specialty, such as dermatology or family practice, and alphabetically. The specialty sections are arranged geographically.

Representative Organizations:

Alliance for Alternatives in Healthcare (AAH), P.O. Box 6279, Thousand Oaks, CA 91359-6279, Phone: (805)494-7818, Fax: (805)494-8528, E-mail: Alt HlthIns@aol.com, URL: http://www.alternativeinsurance.com

American Medical Association (AMA), 515 N. State St., Chicago, IL 60610, Phone: (312)464-5000, Fax: (312)464-5830, URL: http://www.ama-assn.org

Multicultural Resources

See also: chapter nine under Cultures and Multicultures of the United States

African Americans Information Directory. Biennial. Detroit: Gale, 1998.

More than 5,200 names of organizations, agencies, institutions, programs, and publications concerned with black American life and culture are listed in this information guide. Other publications in this series are the *Asian Americans Information Directory, Hispanic Americans Information Directory, Native American In-*

formation Directory, and *Older Americans Information Directory*.

Guide to Multicultural Resources. Alex Boyd, ed. Fort Atkinson, WI: Highsmith Press, 1997.

This directory contains multicultural resources and contacts, including arts and cultural organizations; associations; civil rights groups; colleges and universities; federal agencies; festivals; fraternities and sororities; libraries; museums; and religious, social service, and women's organizations.

Representative Organization:

Association for Multicultural Counseling and Development, division of the American Counseling Association, 5999 Stevenson Ave., Alexandria, VA 22304, Phone: (703)823-9800 or (800)347-6647, Fax: (703)823-0252, URL: http://www.edap.bgsu.edu/AMCD

The Occult

Encyclopedia of Occultism & Parapsychology. 4th edition. J. Gordon Melton, ed. Detroit: Gale, 1996.

This work lists prominent modern day and historic figures in the occult sciences, including academics, scientists, and psychologists. The Societies and Organizations heading in the topical index lists associations, groups, and academies for those with an interest in wraiths and unexplained phenomena.

To balance the above, I'll mention this title: *An Encyclopedia of Claims, Frauds, and Hoaxes of the Occult and Supernatural: James Randi's Decidedly Skeptical Definitions of Alternative Realities* (New York: St. Martin's Press, 1995; reprinted by St. Martin's Griffin, 1997).

Representative Organizations:

Committee for the Scientific Investigation of Claims of the Paranormal, P.O. Box 703, Amherst, NY 14226, Phone: (716)636-1425 or (800)634-1610, Fax: (716)636-1733, E-mail: Skepting@AOL.com, URL: http:/www.csicop.org

Ghost Research Society, P.O. Box 205, Department EA, Oak Lawn, IL 60454-0205, Phone: (708)425-5163, Fax: (708)425-3969, E-mail: dkaczmarek @aol.com, URL: http://www.ghostresearch.org

Philosophers

Directory of American Philosophers, Archie J. Bahm, ed. Bowling Green, Ohio: Bowling Green State University. Biennial.

This directory lists philosophy faculty at North American institutions of higher education. The companion volume to this is the *International Directory of Philosophy and Philosophers* which covers Europe, Central and South America, Asia, Africa, and Australia.

Representative Organizations:

American Philosophical Association, % Eric Hoffman, University of Delaware, Newark, DE 19716, Phone: (302)831-1112, Fax: (302)831-8690, URL: http://www.udel.edu/apa

Political and Judicial Figures, Agencies and Organizations—U.S.

Several online and print directories to government officials are described in chapter three. A few others:

Congressional Yellow Book: Who's Who in Congress Including Committees and Key Staff. Washington, DC: Monitor Leadership Directories, 1976–present. Updated quarterly. Also available on CD-ROM under the title *The Leadership Library on CD-ROM.*

This directory presents a page of information for each senator and representative, including a photo, contact data, names and responsibilities of staff aids, committee assignments, and brief biographical data. This publisher also produces *Federal Yellow Book, Municipal Yellow Book, Judicial Yellow Book, Foreign Representatives in the United States*, and *State Yellow Book.*

The Left Guide. 2nd edition. Ann Arbor, MI: Economics America, 1999.

This directory profiles approximately 1,300 left-leaning organizations, ranging from grassroots coalitions to Washington-based think tanks. This publisher also produces *The Right Guide*, featuring about nine hundred groups.

Municipal Year Book. The International City/County Management Association. Washington, DC: ICMA. Annual.

In *Municipal Year Book* you'll find names, addresses, and phone numbers for state municipal leagues; state, provincial, and international municipal management associations; directors of councils of government; and appointed and elected municipal officials, including fire chiefs, police chiefs, mayors, and city clerks.

National Lobbyist Directory. http://www.lobbyistdirectory.com

Search for lobbyists on this Internet page by state or by keyword describing the type of lobbying they specialize in.

Representative Organizations:

Democratic National Committee, 430 S. Capitol St. SE, Washington, DC 20003, Phone: (202)863-8000, E-mail: Use DNC Web page Guest Book, URL: http://www.democrats.org

Green Parties of North America, P.O. Box 1134, Lawrence, MA 01842, Phone: (978)682-4353, E-mail: gpusa@igc.apc.org, URL: http://www.greens.org

Libertarian Party, 2600 Virginia Ave. NW, Suite 100, Washington, DC 20037, Phone: (202)333-0008, Fax: (202)333-0072, E-mail: hq@lp.org, URL: http://www.lp.org/lp.html

National Conference of State Legislatures, 1560 Broadway, Suite 700, Denver, CO 80202, Phone: (303)830-2200, URL: http://www.ncsl.org/

Natural Law Party, 1946 Mansion Dr., P.O. Box 1900, Fairfield, IA 52556, Phone: (515)472-2040, E-mail: info@natural-law.org, URL: http://home .natural-law.org/nlp/

Reform Party, P.O. Box 9, Dallas, Texas 75221, Phone: (972)450-8800, Fax (972)450-8821, E-mail: russ.verney@reformparty.org, URL: http://reform party.org/

Republican National Committee, 310 First St. SE, Washington, DC 20003, Phone: (202)863-8500, Fax: (202)863-8820, E-mail: info@rnc.org, URL: http://www.rnc.org/

Political Figures and Government Agencies—Foreign

Diplomatic List. Washington, DC: U.S. Department of State. Quarterly. Also available at http://www.state.gov/www/about_state/contacts/diplist/index.html.

This booklet/Web site has the addresses for U.S. foreign embassies and names and titles of diplomatic staffs and their spouses.

Foreign Consular Offices in the U.S. Washington, DC: U.S. Department of State. Quarterly. Also available at http://www.state.gov/www/travel/consular_offices/ fco_index.html.

A listing of the foreign consular offices in the U.S. Located throughout the United States, consular staff act as representatives to foreign governments for a variety of purposes. They can supply business information, such as license requirements, trade quotas, and even ideas on the needs and preferences of consumers of the country the office represents.

Key Officers of Foreign Service Posts: Guide for Business Representatives. U.S. Department of State, Office of Information Services, Publishing Services Division. Updated twice a year. Also available at http://www.state.gov/www /about_state/contacts/keyofficer_index.html.

This directory lists U.S. officials at foreign service posts, including those at embassies, missions, and consulates.

Worldwide Government Directory: With International Organizations. Alan J. Day,
  ed. Washington, DC: Keesing's Worldwide. Annual.

This directory outlines, country by country, the structure of government
for almost two hundred nations with contact information for thousands of
officials in world government.

Publishers

See chapter thirteen

Representative Organization:

Publishers Marketing Association (PMA), 627 Aviation Way, Manhattan Beach,
  CA 90266, Phone: (310)372-2732, Fax: (310)374-3342, E-mail: pmaonline
  @aol.com, URL: http://www.pmaonline.org

Religion

Directory of Religious Organizations in the United States. 3rd edition. J. Gordon
  Melton. Detroit: Gale, 1993.

This directory identifies about 2,500 religious organizations of all types, including academic and theological groups, audio/video producers and distributors,
consultants, evangelical organizations, publishers, and radio and television
broadcasters.

World Guide to Religious and Spiritual Organizations. Union of International
  Associations, ed. New Providence: K.G. Saur, 1996.

A guide to 3,495 religious associations, orders, fraternities, institutes, networks, and programs.

Representative Organizations:

American Academy of Religion (AAR), 1703 Clifton Rd. NE, Suite G5, Atlanta,
  GA 30329-4019, Phone: (404)727-7920, Fax: (404)727-7959, E-mail:
  aar@emory.edu, URL: http://www.aar-site.org/

Global Congress of the World's Religions (GCWR), 10 Dock Rd., Barrytown, NY
  12507, Phone: (914)752-3087, Fax: (914)758-2156, E-mail: k4273843
  @epix.net

Scientists and Engineers

See also: Research Centers Directory and Community of Science under Directories Listing Experts in All Areas of
Expertise, earlier in this chapter.

People and Organizations. http://scilib.ucsd.edu/people-org/people.html

This meta site points to pages featuring experts and organizations in the sciences.

Representative Organizations:

American Association for the Advancement of Science, 1200 New York Ave., NW, Washington, DC 20005, Phone: (202)326-6400, E-mail: membership @aaas.org, URL: http://www.aaas.org

Federation of American Scientists (FAS), 307 Massachusetts Ave. NE, Washington, DC 20002, Phone: (202)546-3300, Fax: (202)675-1010, E-mail: fas@fas.org, URL: http://www.fas.org/

Sports and Recreation

SIRC: Sport Information Resource Center. http://www.sportquest.com/sirc/facts .html

Just choose "SportQuest" from this home page, pick a sport, and link to informational pages related to both professional and amateur recreational activities around the world.

The Sports Address Bible. Edward T. Kobak, Jr. Santa Monica, CA: Global Sports Productions. Annual.

A name and address guide to U.S. and international teams, leagues, publications, and organizations associated with virtually all sports.

Sports Halls of Fame: A Directory of Over 100 Sports Museums in the United States. Doug Gelbert. Jefferson, NC: McFarland, 1992.

With this guide you'll be able to contact the curators of such museums as the United States Bicycling Hall of Fame in Somerville, New Jersey, and Big Daddy Don Garrets' Museum of Drag Racing in Coal, Florida. Also, check this Yahoo! address for sporting halls of fame with Web pages: http://www.yah oo.com/Recreation/Sports/History/Museums_and_Halls_of_Fame/.

Representative Organizations:

National Collegiate Athletic Association (NCAA), 6201 College Blvd., Overland Park, KS 66211-2422, Phone: (913)339-1906, URL: http:// www.ncaa.org

National Association of Sports Officials (NASO), 2017 Lathrop Ave., Racine, WI 53405, Phone: (414)632-5448, Fax: (414)632-5460, E-mail: naso @execpc.com

Travel Information

See also: Transportation Statistics, and chapter nine

Department of State, 2201 C St. NW, Washington, DC 20520, Phone: (202)647-4000, URL: http://www.state gov

The Department of State home page offers answers to foreign travel questions. Look at their page or call them for information regarding passports, visas, embassies and consulates, and tips on living abroad.

State Offices of Tourism

Below is a state-by-state listing of phone numbers for state offices of tourism:

Alabama	(800)ALABAMA
Alaska	(907)465-2012
Arizona	(800)842-8257
Arkansas	(800)628-8725
California	(800)862-2543
Colorado	(800)265-6723
Connecticut	(800)282-6863
Delaware	(800)441-8846
Florida	(904)488-5607
Georgia	(800)847-4842
Hawaii	(808)586-2550
Idaho	(800)635-7820
Illinois	(800)CONNECT
Indiana	(800)289-6646
Iowa	(800)345-4692
Kansas	(800)252-6727
Kentucky	(800)225-8747
Louisiana	(800)334-8626
Maine	(800)533-9595
Maryland	(800)543-1036
Massachusetts	(800)447-6277
Michigan	(800)543-2937
Minnesota	(800)657-3700
Mississippi	(800)WARMEST
Missouri	(800)877-1234
Montana	(800)VISIT-MT
Nebraska	(800)228-4307

Nevada	(800)638-2328
New Hampshire	(800)386-4664
New Jersey	(800)537-7397
New Mexico	(800)545-2040
New York	(800)CALL-NYS
North Carolina	(800)847-4862
North Dakota	(800)HELLO-ND
Ohio	(800)BUCKEYE
Oklahoma	(800)652-6552
Oregon	(800)547-7842
Pennsylvania	(800)VISIT-PA
Rhode Island	(800)556-2484
South Carolina	(800)346-3634
South Dakota	(800)SDAKOTA
Tennessee	(800)836-6200
Texas	(800)888-8839
Utah	(800)200-1160
Vermont	(800)VERMONT
Virginia	(800)847-4882
Washington	(800)544-1800
West Virginia	(800)225-5982
Wisconsin	(800)432-8747
Wyoming	(800)225-5995
Samoa	(800)633-1091
Guam	(800)873-4826
Marianas Island	(670)234-8327
Puerto Rico	(800)866-7827
Virgin Islands	(800)774-8784

State Web Pages

The official Web page for each state in the U.S. will also quickly link you to tourism information. See the listing of URLs in chapter three under State Government Information.

Representative Organizations:

American Society of Travel Agents (ASTA), 1101 King St., Alexandria, VA 22314, Phone: (703)739-2782, Fax: (703)684-8319, URL: http://www .astanet.com

Travel Industry Association of America (TIA), 1100 New York Ave. NW, Suite
450, Washington, DC 20005, Phone: (202)408-8422, Fax: (202)408-
1255., URL: http://www.tia.org

Women

Encyclopedia of Women's Associations Worldwide. Jaqueline K. Barrett, ed. Detroit:
Gale, 1993.

Over 3,400 organizations are listed in this directory related to women and
business, politics, and social issues.

Representative Organizations:

National Organization for Women, 1000 Sixteenth St. NW, Suite 700,
Washington, DC 20036, Phone: (202)331-0066, Fax: (202)785-8576,
TTY: (202)331-9002, E-mail: now@now.org, URL: http://www.now.org

9 to 5, National Association of Working Women, 655 Broadway, Suite 300,
Denver, CO 80203, Phone: (303)628-0925 or (800)522-0925, Fax:
(303)628-3888, URL: http://www.9to5naww.qpg.com

 Experts in Cyberspace

One of the greatest uses of the Net is the ability to quickly
connect with experts—or those who profess to be—worldwide. See chapter two, under E-mail and Discussion Groups,
which goes over online discussion opportunities.

Also on the Web is a listing of people who volunteer their time to help you find
information on the Internet. They are self-proclaimed experts in all sorts of niche
subjects, such as fly fishing, employment discrimination, and the Amish. Find them
at Pitsco's *Ask an Expert* at http://www.askanexpert.com/.

Quotes

Using quotations enlivens writing. Quotations may represent the thoughts of an
expert or be the personal words of an admired celebrity. Phrases of wit and
wisdom may come from prose, poetry, or song.

Quotations on the Web

The *Quotations Page* at http://www.starlingtech.com/quotes/ is a recommended
starting point when using the Web to find quotations. Here you can search the

contents of numerous quotation collections along with quotes of the day, quotes of the week, motivational quotes, comments on quotation software, and links to plenty of other quotation sites. A list of links to quotation sites can also be found on *Yahoo!* at http://www.yahoo.com/reference/quotations/.

Did They Really Say It?

You may remember a quote and think you know the words, but actually only recall the spirit of the quote. If the final quote you find has few of the actual words you remember, don't be terribly surprised—misquotes are sometimes more famous than the quotes. For example, one book titled *They Never Said It: A Book of Fake Quotes, Misquotes, & Misleading Attributions* (Oxford University Press, 1989) confirms that James Cagney never used the line "You dirty rat!" in any of his movies.

Quotations in collections

To locate general quotation collections in the library, browse the reference and circulating stacks under 080 in the Dewey system and PN 6080–PN 6095 in the LC call number system.

In addition to well-known compilations like Bartlett's *Familiar Quotations* (Little, Brown, 1992; 1901 edition available at http://www.columbia.edu/acis/bartleby/bartlett), there are hundreds of quotation books that cover one subject, like tennis, or the utterances of those in a particular field, such as politics, or of a particular group, such as women.

Most quotation books have keyword-in-context, subject, and name (of person quoted) indexes. Just a few examples of quotation books:

From *Advice From the Masters: A Compendium for Writers* (Summerland, CA: Charters West, 1991). On Talent: "It took me fifteen years to discover I had no talent for writing, but I could not give it up because by that time I was too famous."

—Robert Benchley

From *The Bully Pulpit: Quotations From America's Presidents* (New York: Facts on File, 1988). On Courage: "I wish some of you would tell me

the brand of whiskey that Grant drinks. I would like to send a barrel
of it to my other generals."

—Ascribed to Abraham Lincoln

From *Dictionary of Musical Quotations* (New York: Schirmer Books,
1985). On Church Music: "I would earnestly entreat those who sing
ill, not to sing at all, at least in the church."

—James Beattie

From *Film Quotations* (Jefferson, NC: McFarland & Company,
1994). On Kissing: "I had a sudden, powerful, and very ignoble
desire to kiss you till your lips were somewhat bruised."

—David Niven playing a roué in *The Moon is Blue*, 1953

Facts in a Flash

Quotations From Concordances

A **concordance** is a reference book that lists, in alphabetic
order, every major word in a piece of writing, in context.
Finding a significant word is a way of finding a significant quote.
So, do a search in your library catalog under the word CONCORDANCES to pull
up titles like *A Concordance to the Poems and Plays of Federico Garcia Lorca* (Ithaca,
NY: Cornell University, 1975) or *Harvard Concordance to Shakespeare* (Cambridge,
MA: Belknap Press).

Quotations from poetry: using poetry indexes

Poetry indexes help you zero in on a poem and see where it's located. Why not
just search for a poem under the poet's name in a library catalog? Because many
poems are buried deep in collections containing the works of many authors.
Those authors' names are often not found in a library catalog record when doing
an author search. There will also be times when a poem of interest has only
appeared in a journal or magazine; poetry indexes can dig those out.

The following sources will help you in your poetry research:

Columbia Granger's Index to Poetry. 11th edition. Nicholas Frankovich. New
York: Columbia University Press, 1997. Also on CD-ROM titled *Columbia
Granger's World of Poetry*.

Granger's is the best known poetry index. You can locate a poem by its

Quotations From Speeches

A gold mine of quotes can be found in speeches since orations are written to contain clever, concise phrases. Use the techniques outlined in the previous chapter to find speeches.

title, first line, author, or subject. Once you find a poem you're interested in, look for the abbreviation codes that are near the entry. Those codes denote titles of poetry collections listed in the front pages of the book where the poem can be found.

Last Lines: An Index to the Last Lines of Poetry. 2 Volumes. Victoria Kline. New York: Facts on File, 1991.

Just as the title says, this guide offers a way of locating the titles and whereabouts for poems with memorable endings.

Poetry Index Annual: An Author, Title, First Line, and Keyword Index to Poetry in Anthologies. The Editorial Board. New York: Poetry Index Press, 1982–present. Annual.

The publishers feel this index goes beyond *Granger's* (see p. 186) by providing access to the "preponderance of anthologized poetry which is not indexed anywhere." Also, while *Granger's* is only periodically updated, this annual provides timely indexing to new collections.

Finding poetry online

To track down books by particular poets, try an author search in your library's online catalog using the poet's name. You can also try to find collections of poetry on a particular subject or from a particular area by searching the topic you're interested in and the term POETRY as a keyword search. When you use only the word POETRY with a place or topic, be prepared to get quite a few titles that are actually poetry criticism instead of books of poetry (though some sample poetry will be found in the criticism books). Sample searches: RENAISSANCE POETRY, NIGERIAN POETRY, SCOTTISH POETRY, FLOWERS POETRY, LOVE POETRY, or 17TH CENTURY POETRY.

As mentioned earlier, poems are often transcribed and placed on the Web. Put a few words of the poem into a search engine to see if it appears on the Internet. Just beware of transcription errors.

CHAPTER 7

Biographical and Autobiographical Research

Learning of the Lives of the Famous and Infamous

"I don't think anyone should write their autobiography until after they're dead."

—Samuel Goldwyn

ome books containing biographies are what I call "people directories," a.k.a. biographical dictionaries. They list the facts, ma'am, just the facts. Such guides, like the well-known Marquis *Who's Who* series, list such information as date and place of birth, awards won, colleges attended, and current mailing address.

Moving up the biographical food chain, you find biographies included in encyclopedias and biographical compendiums. These flesh out the biographical facts, adding a personal or professional perspective, usually placing the person's deeds in the context of a time period. Almost all the specialized and general encyclopedias mentioned in chapter five contain this type of substantial biographical information. So, for example, if you're looking for a quick biography of Sigmund Freud, you'd do well to consult the *Encyclopedia of Psychology*. Comments on the life of playwright Arthur Miller would surely be in the *McGraw-Hill Encyclopedia of World Drama*. And if you didn't know the titles of those encyclopedias, you could try a keyword search in a library catalog under PSYCHOLOGY ENCYCLOPEDIAS and THEATER ENCYCLOPEDIAS, respectively.

It's worthwhile to try a search on the Net for biographical information. Search by name in a search engine and indicate, if the search engine lets you, that the name is a phrase. For example, you'd search "CARY GRANT" (in quotation marks) in *AltaVista*. Including the word BIOGRAPHY is sometimes helpful. Just remember to examine the quality and authority of the Web resources you locate, since unreliable biographical sites abound.

Finally, there are full-length books about people. Some are notable for their accuracy; others are almost pure fantasy. Even when a person writes about himself or herself there's no guarantee that the facts are the facts. People both intentionally and unconsciously alter events in their lives when they put it into prose. This chapter will help you locate all varieties of biographies in many fields.

Locating Book-Length Biographies and Autobiographies

When seeking biographical information about a person, the person is the subject of your search, so to find biographies using a library catalog, do a keyword search using a person's name, a subject or discipline, and the word BIOGRAPHY, AUTOBIOGRAPHY, or PERSONAL NARRATIVE. Sample searches would be: MAO TSE-TUNG BIOGRAPHY, ANTHROPOLOGY (or ANTHRO-POLOGISTS) BIOGRAPHY, or MILITARY (or SOLDIERS) AUTOBIOG-RAPHY. If you know or suspect that a person has written an autobiography, you can also do an author search in the catalog to see if one of the titles that appears is an autobiography.

Also see the techniques discussed in chapter eight under History From Diaries and Other Published and Unpublished Primary Sources, since biographical details can of course be gleaned from first-person documents.

Biography Hidden in Books

Biographical details often hide in books that cover broader topics than biography. For example, let's say a library only owns one book about Eleanor Roosevelt called *Eleanor Roosevelt With Love* (New York: Dutton, 1984). Let's also say it's checked out. So think about what kinds of books Eleanor Roosevelt would be likely to show up in. One possibility would be a book about presidents' wives. Trying a search on an online library catalog using the phrase FIRST LADIES, or the official Library of Congress term, PRESI-DENTS' SPOUSES, could bring up a book such as *American First Ladies: Their Lives and Their Legacy* (New York: Garland, 1996). This is a good tip to keep in mind since I find that books containing hefty chapters on people will still be on the shelves when full biographies are checked out.

One of the print sources that identifies book-length biographies is the twelve-volume series titled *International Bibliography of Biography* (New York: K.G. Saur, 1988), arranged by subject and author/title. It lists approximately 100,000 biographical and autobiographical titles.

Biographies From Articles

Just as you can find articles about artichokes in magazines and journals, you can also find articles about people. Use the *Biography Index: A Cumulative Index to Biographical Material in Books and Magazines* (H.W. Wilson, 1946–present. Also available on CD-ROM and as a subscription database via WilsonWeb and OCLC's FirstSearch) to locate biographies in books, book sections, periodical articles, obituaries, letters, diaries, memoirs, and bibliographies.

Also use subject-specific indexes to find biographical information in articles. For example, you could use the *Philosopher's Index* to find articles on great thinkers, or the *Humanities Index* or *Art Index* to locate biographical articles on an illustrator. See Appendix B for a list of possible indexes.

A helpful newspaper index is the *Personal Name Index to The New York Times Index: 1851–1974* (Succasunna, NJ: Roxbury Data Interface, 1976, with updates about every five years). It's an index to an index. If you've ever tried to find information on a person in *The New York Times* indexes, you've found that names are scattered among indexes for different time periods. *Personal Name Index* quickly leads you to the specific index volumes where a person's name appears, providing the year of the index and the page number. From there, you go to *The New York Times* article(s) you need.

For example, a student in my library was having trouble finding newspaper citations regarding the alleged murderer Lizzie Borden in *The New York Times Index*. When we looked in the *Personal Name Index* we were directed to eleven entries between the years 1892 and 1968. This index is less relevant for current biographical information from *The New York Times* since indexed versions of the *Times* are available through the subscription services FirstSearch, the Information Access Company, DIALOG, DataStar, and LEXIS-NEXIS, and at http://www.ny times.com, and a name can easily be searched online.

Other biographical indexes leading to either articles and/or biographies in compendiums include:

Biography Almanac: A Comprehensive Reference Guide to More than 23,000 Famous and Infamous Newsmakers From Biblical Times to the Present as Found in Over

300 Readily Available Biographical Sources. 3rd edition. Susan L. Stetl. Detroit: Gale, 1987.

For each person listed, the *Biography Almanac* supplies birth date, birth place, death date, and listings of biographical resources where further information can be found. The *Biography Almanac* is continued by the *Almanac of Famous People* (updated irregularly and also available online through the subscription database *Gale Biographies*).

Biography and Genealogy Master Index: A Consolidated Index to More Than 450,000 Biographical Sketches in Over 95 Current and Retrospective Biographical Dictionaries. 1981–present. Annual with supplements. Also available on CD-ROM and as a subscription database via GaleNet, DIALOG under the title *Biography Master Index*, and on microfiche under the title *Bio-Base*.

The hard copy version of this directory, filled with tiny print, helps you determine which print biographical compilation has the data you're after. Sample titles of the hundreds of diverse compendiums indexed in this ongoing set are *Hollywood Baby Boomers, Polish Biographical Dictionary,* and *Contemporary Gay American Novelists.*

In Black and White: A Guide to Magazine Articles, Newspaper Articles, and Books Concerning More Than 15,000 Black Individuals and Groups. 3rd edition. 2 Volumes. Mary Mace Spradling, ed. Detroit: Gale, 1980.

The editor chose those featured in this set by scanning newspapers, magazines, books, pamphlets, calendars, and catalogs of libraries with extensive black history holdings, including New York Public Library's Schomberg Center and Howard University's Moorland.

Biographical Dictionaries

The Marquis *Who's Who* directories, and biographical dictionaries like it, are formatted in a similar fashion, providing facts about each person listed, including name, profession, vital statistics, family data, education, listings of writings and creative works, community and political activities, military service, awards, association memberships, political affiliation, religion, hobbies, home address, and office address. No photographs are included. The Marquis directories are also on the CD-ROM titled *The Complete Marquis Who's Who* (1992–date, updated quarterly). Online, these directories are available through the subscription systems DIALOG, OneSource, and LEXIS-NEXIS.

Current Marquis *Who's Who* titles are: *Who's Who in . . . America, American Art, American Education, American Law, American Nursing, American Politics,*

Asian and Australasian Politics, Finance & Industry, The East, Entertainment, Euro-pean Business, European Research and Development, International Banking, Media and Communication, Medicine and Healthcare, The Midwest Religion, Science & Engineering, South African Politics, The South & Southwest, The West, and *The World.* Also: *Who's Who of . . . American Women, Australian Writers, Emerging Leaders in America,* and *Women in World Politics.*

On the Web, see *Biographical Dictionary* at http://www.s9.com/biography/ for brief entries describing notable men and women from all walks of life. Also see *Celebsite* at http://www.celebsite.com/ for news, biographical data, and links related to contemporary celebrities.

Biographical Compendiums

Collections of full-text biographical essays exist for virtually all subject areas. You'll pull up these compilations when doing general library catalog searches using the word BIOGRAPHY and a term describing a discipline, like PSYCHOL-OGY. A few print series and databases to be aware of that cover noteworthy people of all types include:

Current Biography. New York: H.W. Wilson, 1940–present. Also available on
   CD-ROM and via the subscription database system WilsonWeb and *Wilson
   Biographies Plus.*

   This paperback publication comes out eleven times a year with a year-end cumulated and revised edition in hardcover called *Current Biography Yearbook.* From fashion designers to prime ministers, *Current Biography* provides four to six pages of coverage with references to further readings. The *Yearbook* also has a Classification by Profession Index, useful when you want a biography of someone in a particular field—but you don't know who.

The Dictionary of National Biography: From the Earliest Times to 1900. 22 Volumes.
   Sir Leslie Stephen, ed. London: Oxford University Press, 1885–1901 with
   supplements covering the years 1901 through 1970. Also available on CD-ROM.

   A standard, scholarly biographical reference set to noteworthy, deceased, British Isle and British Colony citizens and Americans of the colonial period. Extensive bibliographies are included. Patterned after this set, but focusing on American biography, is the *Dictionary of American Biography* (17 Volumes plus supplement volumes. New York: Charles Scribner's Sons, 1927; latest supplement, 1996. Also available on CD-ROM).

Great Lives From History Series. Frank Magill. Pasadena, CA: Salem Press.
   1987–1995.

Each set in this series is comprised of five volumes with almost five hundred biographical essays per set. The series titles are: *American Series, American Women Series, Ancient and Medieval Series, British and Commonwealth Series, Renaissance to 1900 Series,* and *Twentieth Century Series.*

The National Cyclopaedia of American Biography. 63 Volumes. Ann Arbor, MI: University Microfilms, 1892–1984.

The contents of this work are eloquently described on the title page: "Being the history of the United States, as illustrated in the lives of the founders, builders, and defenders of the republic, and of the men and women who are doing the work and molding the thought of the present time." This set also contains drawings and photographs and is considered one of the most comprehensive around for historic U.S. biography.

The New York Times Biographical Service: A Compilation of Current Biographical Information of General Interest. New York: The New York Times, 1970–present. Also available via the subscription database LEXIS-NEXIS.

The New York Times plucks stories and obituaries from its pages and reproduces them monthly in this series.

Newsmakers: The People Behind Today's Headlines. Sean R. Pollock, ed. Detroit: Gale. 1985–present. Monthly, with annual compilations. Also available via the subscription database *Gale Biographies.*

Those who've been spotlighted in the media are described in this collection, ranging from popular culture figures like Jenny McCarthy to unpopular political figures like Yasser Arafat. There's a cumulative index to all previous volumes in the series in each annual edition. Obituaries and citations to further information are also included.

Subject-Specific Biographical Encyclopedias

Representative titles for subject-specific biographical encyclopedias in print and online are listed below. For an impressive all-in-one listing of biographical dictionaries, use the *ARBA Guide to Biographical Sources,* compiled and edited by bibliographers Robert L. Wick and Terry Ann Mood (Englewood, CO: Libraries Unlimited, 1998). It contains citations to 1,180 biographical sources, international and national in scope, in virtually all fields and professions.

Activists and social movement leaders

American Reformers. Alden Whitman. New York: H.W. Wilson, 1985.

Covering the seventeenth century to the present, *American Reformers* describes 504 men and women involved in the evolution of American society. The essays examine the societal conditions that influenced the reformer, and offer an assessment of the activist's significance to the general reform movement in the U.S. A similar title is *American Social Leaders: From Colonial Times to the Present* (Santa Barbara, CA: ABC-CLIO, 1993).

American Women Civil Rights Activists. Gayle J. Hardy. Jefferson, NC: McFarland, 1993.

Some activities these women helped spearhead include Hispanic American rights, antilynching, adoptee/adoption rights, and consumer rights.

Aeronautics

Men and Women of Space. Douglas B. Hawthorne. San Diego: Univelt, 1992.

This book provides biographical information for every person who has received space flight training NASA astronauts and candidates, Soviet cosmonauts and candidates, X-15 military and civilian research pilots, and many others. Another book focusing on space travelers and those who helped make space travel a reality is *Space People—From A-Z* (New York: Facts on File, 1990).

NASA Astronaut Biographies. http://www.jsc.nasa.gov/Bios/astrobio.html

Biographies on this Internet site feature astronauts, astronaut candidates, cosmonauts, and payload specialists.

The Ancients

See also: chapter eight

A Dictionary of Greek and Roman Biography and Mythology. 3 Volumes. William Smith, ed. London: John Murray, 1876.

These volumes cover the lives of the "ancients" of myriad fields and professions, including jurists, artists, mathematicians, and philosophers. The writers distinguish between what is true historical biography and what is myth.

Who Was Who in the Greek World: 776 B.C.–30 B.C. Diana Bowder, ed. Ithaca, NY: Phaidon, 1982.

This compendium begins in the year of the first Olympiad when the first Olympic Games were presented. Many of the short biographies are accompanied by photographs of images on sculptures, coins, and architecture. Also compiled by the same editor: *Who Was Who in the Roman World: 753 B.C.– A.D. 476.*

Anthropologists

International Dictionary of Anthropologists. Christopher Winters, general ed. New York: Garland, 1991.

This worldwide volume interprets *anthropologists* broadly, and includes social, cultural, physical, and biological anthropologists, as well as some archaeologists, folklorists, linguists, travelers, and missionaries.

Women Anthropologists: A Biographical Dictionary. Ute Gacs, ed. Westport, CT: Greenwood Press, 1988.

Fifty-eight female anthropologists, encompassing a one-hundred-year span, are represented in this dictionary with several pages devoted to each scholar.

Architects, artists, and designers

Contemporary Designers. 3rd edition. Sara Pendergast, ed. Chicago: St. James Press, 1997.

This book presents 685 contemporary designers representing architecture, interior display, and graphic, textile, fashion, product, industrial, stage, and film design. Each entry consists of a biography, a selected list of design works, a bibliography of writings by and about the designer, and an illustration of one of his or her works. Also from this publisher: *Contemporary Artists* (4th edition, 1996), *Contemporary Architects* (3rd edition, 1994), *Contemporary Fashion* (1995), and *Contemporary Photographers* (3rd edition, 1995).

Designers International Index. 3 Volumes. Compiled by Janette Jagger. New York: Bowker-Saur, 1991.

This is an index to books and periodicals about designers of all types, including animation, computer-aided design, glass, metalwork, and even wallpaper.

Dictionary of American Sculptors: 18th Century to the Present. Glenn B. Opitz, ed. Poughkeepsie, NY: Apollo, 1984.

A compendium of basic information on over five thousand sculptors. Each brief listing supplies the artist's birth date, birth place, institution(s) of study, museums, galleries, and other exhibit areas that have shown the artist's pieces, and the area the sculptor lived or lives.

Dictionary of Women Artists. 2 Volumes. Delia Gaze, ed. Chicago: Fitzroy Dearborn, 1997.

Illustrated with black-and-white photographs of artwork, this set opens with essays covering national art movements and such topics as "Women as Artists in the Middle Ages." It moves on to biographies of several hundred female artists from medieval times through those born before 1945.

International Dictionary of Art and Artists: Artists. James Vinson, ed. Chicago: St. James Press, 1990.

    Artists names the most important artists from the thirteenth through the twentieth centuries and presents essential facts of their lives, important public and private collections of their work, bibliographies, and critical essays that discuss historical and critical aspects of their work. Black-and-white photographs of the artist's work accompany each biography.

Macmillan Encyclopedia of Architects. 4 Volumes. Adolf K. Placzek. New York: Free Press, 1982.

    These biographies include discussion of how the era of each architect, with its particular influences, contributed to the designer's ideas and approach to design. Many black-and-white photographs are included.

Museum of American Folk Art Encyclopedia of Twentieth-Century American Folk Art and Artists. Chuck Rosenak. New York: Abbeville Press, 1990.

    This volume is filled with photographs of the work of painters, sculptors, and potters recognized as the foremost twentieth-century folk artists of the U.S. The biographies supplied for each of the 257 artists include personal biographical data; general and artistic background; description of the artist's subjects, sources, materials, and techniques; and what formal recognition the artist has received.

Athletes

Biographical Dictionary of American Sports. David L. Porter. Westport, CT: Greenwood Press, 1987–1989, plus supplements every three years.

    Biographical Dictionary of American Sports is a series, with each volume highlighting a different sport: *Football, Baseball, Outdoor Sports,* and *Basketball and Other Indoor Sports.*

Great Athletes. 20 Volumes. The Editors of Salem Press. Pasadena, CA: Salem Press, 1992.

    This collection is great for basic facts, with writing geared to younger readers and large photographs accompanying each biography.

Greek and Roman Sport: A Dictionary of Athletes and Events From the Eighth Century B.C. to the Third Century A.D. David Matz. Jefferson, NC: McFarland & Company, 1991.

    The earliest known athlete listed in this book is the "stade racer" Coroebus, from the eighth century, B.C. In case you didn't know (I didn't), a stade race is a "straight Greek foot race covering approximately two hundred yards."

Autobiographies

American Autobiography, 1945–1980: A Bibliography. Mary Louise Briscoe, ed. Madison, WI: University of Wisconsin Press, 1982.

A listing of thousands of books, diaries, journals, and collected papers that U.S. citizens wrote about themselves. It doesn't say who owns them, but identifies the existence of the manuscript. Remember, just identifying a source is helpful because you can usually borrow it through an interlibrary loan service. This book serves as a companion volume to *A Bibliography of American Autobiographies* (1961), referring to autobiographical works published before 1946.

Contemporary Authors Autobiographies Series. Detroit: Gale, 1984–. Updated irregularly.

Reading an entire book that someone has written about themselves might be more than you need. Here you can look through a few pages. Writers in this series were invited to write 10,000 to 15,000 words about themselves and asked to supply family photographs that represented a range of years and a number of people who were important in their lives.

Business

The ABC-CLIO Companion to Women in the Workplace. Dorothy Schneider. Santa Barbara, CA: ABC-CLIO, 1993.

Many of the entries in this volume are biographical, touching on a variety of working women, including union organizers and those who were first in their field. This work also covers major events, organizations, and court cases that changed working conditions for women.

D&B Reference Book of Corporate Managements. 3 Volumes. Parsippany, NJ: Dun's Marketing Services. Annual.

The first two volumes of this collection are in alphabetic order by company name, with information about company officers included as part of each company entry. Information about each officer generally includes birth date, alma mater(s), a chronology of companies/organizations where the officer has worked, and military affiliation. The cross-reference volume allows searching of company officers by college/university and military affiliation.

Standard and Poor's Register of Corporations, Directors, and Executives. 3 Volumes. New York: Standard & Poor's. Annual.

This collection covers thousands of directors and executives, providing year and place of birth, college graduation dates, principle business affiliations, business and residence addresses, and fraternal memberships.

Who's Who in Finance and Industry. New Providence, NJ: Marquis Who's Who. Biennial.

This is a typical *Who's Who* publication, cramming a great deal of useful information into abbreviation-filled entries. Those profiled in this volume are from all over the world and a wide range of businesses.

Crime

Bloodletters and Badmen: A Narrative Encyclopedia of American Criminals From the Pilgrims to the Present. Jay Robert Nash. New York: M. Evans and Company, 1973.

The data section for each criminal is a litany of sequentially arranged crimes and arrests, followed by a general narrative of the criminal's life and crimes. Also from this author: *Encyclopedia of Western Lawmen and Outlaws* (New York: Paragon House, 1992).

FBI Most Wanted: An Encyclopedia. Michael Newton. New York: Garland, 1989.

This chronologically arranged compendium presents case-by-case descriptions of those named on the FBI's most wanted lists from the list's inception in 1950 through mid-1988. Find current most-wanted criminals on the FBI's home page at http://www.fbi.gov.

Film and theater

Contemporary Theatre, Film, & Television: A Biographical Guide Featuring Performers, Directors, Writers, Producers, Designers, Managers, Choreographers, Technicians, Composers, Executives, Dancers, and Critics in the United States and Great Britain. Detroit: Gale, 1984–present. Annual.

Each biographical entry in this annually updated collection lists name, personal data, addresses, career highlights, memberships, awards, honors, credits, recordings, writings, adaptations, and sources of further information. This set is a continuation of *Who's Who in the Theatre,* which began in 1912.

International Dictionary of Films and Filmmakers. 3rd edition. 5 Volumes. Nicholas Thomas, ed. Chicago: St. James Press, 1997.

There are three biographical volumes in this collection—Volume 2: *Directors,* Volume 3: *Actors and Actresses,* and Volume 4: *Writers and Production Artists.* Each volume contains *Who's Who*-type biographies, complete filmographies, a selected bibliography of works on and by the entrant, and an essay by a specialist in the field. St. James Press also publishes the *International Dictionary of the Theatre*, with one biographical volume covering *Playwrights* and another *Actors, Directors, and Designers*.

Variety Obituaries: 1905-1986. 11 Volumes. New York: Garland Publishing, 1988. Annually updated beginning with Volume 12.

Variety, billed the "official newspaper of show business," includes entertainment news items, reviews, and casting notices. This set reproduces the obituaries published in *Variety* from 1905 on, as well as articles in the newspaper that refer to deaths in show business. Some of the more unusual headlines reported include "Breaking Diet Brought Death to June Mathis" and "Freddie Welsh Died of a Broken Heart," both stories reported on August 3, 1927.

Gay and lesbian

Gay and Lesbian Biography. Michael J. Tyrkus, ed. Detroit: St. James Press, 1997.

Search by nationality, occupation, or general subject to locate biographies on 275 gay and lesbian men and women from many time periods and nations. The biographical essays in this volume supply general biographical information, and, additionally, discuss the biographee's life and importance to the gay and lesbian community.

Health professionals

American Psychiatric Association Biographical Directory. Washington, DC: American Psychiatric Press, 1989. Updated irregularly.

Data provided for each psychiatrist in this directory includes current work status, medical education and degrees, hospital affiliations, specialties, languages spoken, and writings.

Biographical Dictionary of Medicine. Jessica Bendiner. New York: Facts on File, 1990.

The authors fish through the history of medicine and offer glimpses of healers through the ages and around the world. Ancient herbalists share this volume with contemporary physicians and researchers.

Historians

Blackwell Dictionary of Historians. John Cannon, ed. New York: Blackwell, 1988.

For each scholar covered, an essay looks at the circumstances in which the person worked and to what extent his or her work was refuted or corroborated.

Great Historians From Antiquity to 1800: An International Dictionary. Lucian
   Boia, ed. Westport, CT: Greenwood Press, 1989.
      Historians from numerous nations and cultures are profiled, with entries
   arranged by country or geographic area. The companion volume is *Great Histo-*
   rians of the Modern Age: An International Dictionary (1991).

Facts in a Flash   Descriptions of Literary and Fictional Characters

There are biographies—or at least descriptions—of those who
don't exist. Sample titles include the *Cyclopedia of Literary*
Characters (New York: Salem Press, 1963, first set; 1990, second
set) which describes fictional characters from novels, short stories, plays, and classics
of world literature, arranged by title of the work; and *Imaginary People: A Who's Who*
of Modern Fictional Characters From the Eighteenth Century to the Present Day (2nd
edition. New York: World Almanac, 1996) which answers such questions as "Who
is Ignatz Mouse? John Rambo? J.R. Ewing?" *Imaginary People* includes figures from
novels, short stories, plays, opera, ballet, films, comic strips, songs, radio, and
television.

Multicultural

See also: chapter nine under Cultures and Multicultures of the United States

Contemporary Black Biography: Profiles From the International Black Community.
   Barbara Carlisle Bigelow, ed. Detroit: Gale, 1994–.
      Influential black people from a variety of countries and fields are featured
   in this regularly updated multivolume collection. Along with several pages of
   biographical coverage, a photo, mailing address, and further reading sugges-
   tions are usually included. The set is indexed by occupation and nationality,
   including American, Nigerian, and Ugandan, and has a cumulative subject
   index.

Hispanic American Almanac: A Reference Work on Hispanics in the United States.
   2nd edition. Nicolás Kanellos. Detroit: Gale Research, 1997.
      Facts, dates, biographies, and essays in this volume cover facets of Hispanic
   life in the United States. Areas covered include historic landmarks, education,
   literature, film, and religion. Other similarly structured works from Gale Re-

search: *The African American Almanac* (7th edition, 1997) and *Native North American Almanac* (1994).

Native American Women: A Biographical Dictionary. Gretchen M. Bataille, ed. New York: Garland, 1993.

This work describes American Indian women representing a diversity of roles within their culture, both contemporary and historic.

Musicians, singers, and composers

The twenty-volume *The New Grove Dictionary of Music and Musicians* (London: Macmillan, 1980), already mentioned in chapter five, is an excellent place to look for biographies of important musicians and composers. Other representative titles of specialized music biography:

All-Music Guide (AMG). http://www.allmusic.com

AMG contains biographical information on artists and bands of almost all genres except classical and opera. Additionally, *AMG* supplies discography information and over 100,000 music reviews.

Blues Who's Who: A Biographical Dictionary of Blues Singers. Sheldon Harris. New Rochelle, NY: Arlington House, 1979.

For each of the hundreds of blues figures listed, a career chronology is provided along with nicknames, quotes about those who influenced the musical style of the performer, personal data, and references for further reading.

Contemporary Composers. Brian Morton. St. James Press, 1992.

This volume presents biographies, discographies, and critical analysis of about five hundred twentieth-century composers worldwide.

Contemporary Musicians: Profiles of People in Music. Michael L. LaBlanc, ed. Detroit: Gale, 1989–.

Published twice yearly, each volume of *Contemporary Musicians* covers eighty to one hundred music writers and performers in rock, rap, pop, jazz, blues, country, new wave, New Age, folk, R&B, gospel, bluegrass, and reggae. Artists range from Desi Arnaz to the Beastie Boys. Each entry features biographical/critical essays, selected discographies, photos, and sources of additional information.

Country: Pickers, Slickers, Cheatin' Hearts, and Superstars: The Music and the Musicians. The Country Music Foundation. New York: Abbeville Press, 1988.

This thick volume supplies coverage of the stars and star makers in one of America's most popular musical genres. Stage, screen, radio, and recording personalities are all included, with more than seven hundred color and black-and-white photos of the stars in action.

International Dictionary of Opera. 2 Volumes. C. Steven LaRue, ed. Detroit: St. James Press, 1993.

Biographies of influential composers, librettists, performers, conductors, designers, directors, and producers are supplied. Each biographical outline contains the person's occupation, birth and death date, marriages and names of children, training, circle of important friends, and career data, including milestones.

Worldwide Internet Music Resources. http://www.music.indiana.edu/music_resources/

Use this site maintained by the William and Gayle Cook Music Library at the Indiana University School of Music to locate biographies and other music resources related to music of all genres.

Obituaries

See also: Variety Obituaries under Film and Theater, earlier in this chapter.

You can often learn more about a person after he or she has passed on. Check for obituaries in the local papers of communities where the deceased was born or lived. Local libraries and historical societies may have historic indexes to or files of obituaries. Compilations of obituaries include:

Annual Obituary. New York: St. Martin's Press. 1980–present.

Annual Obituaries has biographical essays on international individuals of note with sketches ranging from 500 to 2,000 words, covering basic birth/death data, events, achievements, and influences of the person's life.

Cyndi's List: Obituaries. http://www.cyndislist.com/obits.htm

Part of *Cyndi's List of Genealogy Sites on the Internet,* this section lists locations of online death notices.

Obituaries: A Guide to Sources. 2nd edition. Betty M. Jarboe. Boston: G.K. Hall, 1989.

Obituaries lists where to find death notices in newspapers, collected genealogical works, and cemetery and burial records for a variety of areas. The author has also included publications that list tombstone inscriptions.

Politicians, political theorists, and rulers

American Political Scientists: A Dictionary. Glenn H. Utter, ed. Westport, CT: Greenwood Press, 1993.

Biography From Cemeteries

Author of *Obituaries: A Guide to Sources* Betty M. Jarboe points out that "tombstone inscriptions often give valuable biographical information other than birth and death dates, as many of the older tombstones give place of birth, military service, and sometimes family relationships." For tombstones on the Net try *Find a Grave* (http://www.findagrave.com/index.html), a guide to the graves of noteworthy people. In print, consult the book *Cemeteries of the U.S.: A Guide to Contact Information for U.S. Cemeteries and Their Records* (Triennial). *Cyndi's List*, on the Web, also supplies access to information about cemeteries and funeral homes at http://www.cyndislist.com/cemetery.htm.

This dictionary presents "capsule careers" of political science scholars in the U.S.

Biographical Directory of the Governors of the United States: 1988–1994. Marie Marmo Mullaney. Westport, CT: Meckler, 1994. Updated irregularly.

Past volumes put out by Meckler, also covering governors include: *Biographical Directory of American Colonial and Revolutionary Governors: 1607–1789*, *Biographical Directory of American Territorial Governors*, and *Biographical Directory of the Governors of the United States: 1789–1983*, and *Biographical Directory of the Governors of the United States: 1983–1988*.

Biographical Directory of the American Congress: 1774–1996. Joel D. Treese, ed. Alexandria, VA: CQ Staff Directories, 1997. Also at http://bioguide.congress.gov.

This book opens with lists of all representatives and senators by state from the 1st to the 100th Congress, followed by description of each statesman arranged alphabetically by last name.

Debrett's Kings and Queens of Europe. David Williamson. Topsfield, MA: Salem House, 1988.

In *Debrett's*, you'll learn of Alphonso II the Fat, Pedro I the Severe, and Ferdinand I the Handsome. This book is a companion volume to *Debrett's Kings and Queens of Europe* (1986). Birth, marriage, ancestry, and descendants data is provided for each monarch, with an essay supplying details of each ruler's reign.

International Year Book and Statesman's Who's Who: International and National Organizations of the World and 8,000 Biographies of Leading Personalities in

Quick Facts on the Internet on Lawmakers

B asic information about state politicians currently serving terms will be on their state home page (listed in chapter three), including a listing of committees they chair or serve on and which bills they've sponsored. Also, go to the site mentioned in chapter five, *Project Vote Smart* at http://www.vote-smart.org for basic biographical information for state legislators, governors, congressional members, and the president. For politicians in the U.S. Congress, also try the Senate pages at http://www.senate.gov/ or the House pages at http://www.house.gov/.

Find biographies of all judges who have ever sat on the U.S. Supreme Court from the *Legal Information Institute* at http://supct.law.cornell.edu/supct/cases/judges .htm.

Public Life. West Sussex, England: Reed Information Services. Annual.

The first half of the book is in order by country, supplying facts and figures about each nation. The second half is comprised of thousands of short biographies arranged alphabetically by name. So, to find out a little about the prime minister of Belgium, for example, look under the country Belgium under the heading Members of Government. Once you have the name, look up the biography.

Women Who Ruled. Guida M. Jackson. Santa Barbara, CA: ABC-CLIO, 1990.

Included in this work are all women heads of state, defacto rulers, and constitutional monarchs throughout the ages, around the world. Cleopatra is in here, as is Margaret Thatcher, along with intriguing women less known to the modern world, like Zabel, also known as Isabella, ruler of Little Armenia in the thirteenth century, and Agnes of Poitou, regent for the Holy Roman Emperor Henry IV, who was characterized as being "pious and colorless . . . she gave away the duchies of Bavaria, Swabia, and Carinthia to relatives."

Religious figures

Much of the reference religious biography for the many faiths of the world show up in specialized encyclopedias, handbooks, and dictionaries. Consult chapter nine for representative religion encyclopedias.

Scientists and engineers

The Biographical Dictionary of Scientists. David Abbott, Ph.D., ed. New York: Peter Bedrick Books, 1983.

Biographical Dictionary of Scientists is a series of six books covering astronomers, biologists, chemists, physicists, mathematicians, engineers, and inventors. Each volume contains biographies, a glossary of terms of the field, and in-depth subject indexes. The entry on Charles Lutwidge Dodgson in the *Mathematicians* volume caught my eye. After reading the new book *Alice in Wonderland,* Queen Victoria requested the complete works of Lewis Carroll, a.k.a. Charles Dodgson. She was then surprised to receive in her shipment scholarly papers on mathematical subjects.

Dictionary of Scientific Biography. 15 Volumes. Charles Coulston Gillispie, ed. New York: Charles Scribner's Sons, 1970. *Supplement* (v.16), 1978. *Index* (v.17), 1980.

Though some essays are less than a page, most are substantial, ranging from several pages to over ten pages in length. This work, a standard in many libraries, covers principle mathematicians and natural scientists worldwide, from all historical periods. The bibliographical references are numerous and cover English language and non-English language works.

4,000 Years of Women in Science. http://www.astr.ua.edu/4000WS/4000WS.html

Look at this online guide for less-known but influential female scientists, pre-1900.

Notable Twentieth Century Scientists. 4 Volumes. Emily J. McMurray, ed. Detroit: Gale, 1995.

This set contains biographical essays on approximately 1,300 scientists who have been active in the twentieth century.

War figures

Biographical Dictionary of the Confederacy. Jon L. Wakelyn. Westport, CT: Greenwood Press, 1977.

In addition to biographical sketches of Southern wartime leaders, the author adds appendices that track geographical mobility before and after the war, and includes biographee's principal occupations, religious affiliations, education, and prewar and postwar political party affiliation.

Biographical Dictionary of World War I. Holger H. Herwig. Westport, CT: Greenwood Press, 1982.

Military personnel, politicians, journalists, and others for all countries involved in World War I are described.

Facts in a Flash

Requesting Military Records

The National Archives has a collection of military records for
veterans of the United States Air Force, Army, Coast Guard,
Marine Corps, and Navy, with the earliest dating from the Revolutionary War. Military record requests need to be submitted on NATF Form 80
which can be requested via U.S. mail at Reference Services Branch (NNIR), National
Archives and Records Administration, Seventh and Pennsylvania Ave. NW, Washington, DC 20408 or via E-mail at inquire@arch2.nara.gov with the word "form" on
the subject line. Put your name and address in the body of the message and the
number of copies of the form you need. Visit *Cyndi's List* at http://www.cyndislist
.com/milres.htm for much more advice on finding military records and historical
sites.

Biographical Dictionary of World War II. Christopher Tunney. New York: St.
   Martin's Press, 1972.

   The men and women profiled in this collection were military officers and
soldiers, politicians, spies, royalty, religious figures, agitators, and advisors during the second World War.

Dictionary of American Military Biography. 3 Volumes. Roger J. Spiller, ed.
   Westport, CT: Greenwood Press, 1984.

   This volume describes a wide range of biographees who have been influential in the military field, including inventors, writers, educators, physicians, and
explorers, along with, as expected, soldiers and officers. A detailed narrative
describing the person's career and influence are provided.

The Encyclopedia of Amazons: Women Warriors From Antiquity to the Modern Era.
   Jessica Amanda Salmonson. New York: Paragon House, 1991.

   This encyclopedia's author defines an *Amazon* as a woman who is a duelist
or soldier. The contents are heavy on Amazons of ancient and medieval times,
favoring, as the author says "the romance of the sword, the ax, and the bow
over the romance of the firearms." Among the Amazons listed are Cattle Kate
who was an Indian fighter and later a cattle rustler (hanged for her transgres-
sion) and Itagaki who "led a charge of three thousand warriors of the Taira
clan against ten thousand of the Heike in A.D. 119."

Who Was Who in the American Revolution. Edward L. Purcell. New York: Facts on File, 1993.

The majority of the biographies are those of American soldiers. All Continental generals are covered; but few private soldiers or noncommissioned officers. Loyalists, political leaders, British foes of the Revolution, "hessians," and French allies are also featured.

Women

See also: Activists and Social Movement Leaders; Aeronautics; Anthropologists; Architects, Artists, and Designers; Business, Multicultural; Politicians, Political Theorists and Rulers; Scientists and Engineers; and War Figures

Distinguished Women of Past and Present. http://www.netsrq.com/~dbois/index.html

Search for biographies of influential women by name or by field on this Web page. The creator of this site, Danuta Bois, works to acknowledge both well-known and lesser-known women worldwide.

An Annotated Index of Medieval Women. Anne Echols. New York: Markus Wiener Publishing, 1992.

This is an index to further readings on about 1,500 medieval women from almost thirty countries. Each entry includes a brief biographical annotation.

History of Women. New Haven, CT: Research Publications, 1977.

This is a collection on microfilm of works from the late eighteenth century to 1920 on women worldwide. Items filmed for this collection include books, pamphlets, journals, diaries, and photographs.

Lesser-Known Women: A Biographical Dictionary. Beverly E. Golemba. Boulder, CO: Lynne Rienner Publishers, 1992.

The book is arranged chronologically, beginning in 1600, with international coverage. *Lesser-Known Women* tells of people like Anne Dacier, a French translator of Greek and Latin works, noted for her 1699 translation of the *Iliad* and of the *Odyssey* some years later, and Donaldina Cameron, a native Scotswoman who worked in the late 1800s and early 1900s in San Francisco's Chinatown to turn young Chinese girls away from prostitution.

Notable American Women, 1607–1950: A Biographical Dictionary. 3 Volumes. Edward T. James, ed. Cambridge, MA: Belknap Press, 1971.

Most entries are at least a page in length and include such fascinating women as Belle Boyd, who lived from 1844–1900 and is described as a confederate spy, actress, and lecturer. This set is supplemented by a volume covering

The Modern Period (1980) and covers women who died between January 1, 1951, and December 31, 1975.

The World Who's Who of Women. Ernest Kay, ed. Cambridge, England: International Biographical Centre, 1973–present.

At the time of this writing, this set had reached twelve volumes. Earlier volumes are notable for having included small photographs of almost all of the women named; unusual for this type of who's who book. Recent editions contain only large black-and-white pictures of a few dozen women singled out in that edition for their achievements. All editions contain basic biographical data on prominent women in all careers.

Writers: fiction and nonfiction authors, journalists, and poets

Biographical Dictionary of American Journalism. Joseph P. McKerns. New York: Greenwood Press, 1989.

The appendix in the back of this work assists readers in locating journalists listed by the type of work they did, including war correspondents, radio and television, and Washington correspondents. Greenwood Press also publishes the *Biographical Dictionary of American Newspaper Columnists.*

Contemporary Authors: A Bio-Bibliographical Guide to Current Writers in Fiction, General Non-Fiction, Poetry, Journalism, Drama, Motion Pictures, Television, and Other Fields. Detroit: Gale, 1962–present. Also available on CD-ROM and as a subscription database via GaleNet under the title *Gale Literary Databases.*

This popular set is commonly recommended in libraries as a "first place to look." Typical biographical entries include personal data, career dates and highlights, organization memberships, awards, lists of writings both by and about the author, and when available, comments from the author.

The *Contemporary Authors* series is being continually updated. It's not uncommon to find an author's life recounted in one volume, an update to that narrative in another, and an obituary in a later volume. When using the print version, use the skinny paperback cumulative index to the collection. Almost identical to this title, but focusing on authors and illustrators of young adult and children's books, is the Gale series *Something About the Author.*

Contemporary Novelists. 6th edition. Lesley Henderson, ed. Chicago: St. James Press, 1996.

Selected novelists are featured in each edition. Each listing details the author's awards, the address of the literary agent, titles of publications, essays that critique and describe the author's body of work, and comments from some of the novelists themselves. St. James Press also publishes *Contemporary American Dramatists, Contemporary British Dramatists, Contemporary Literary Critics, Contemporary Poets, Contemporary Popular Writers, Contemporary Women Dramatists, Contemporary Women Poets, Contemporary Southern Writers,* and *Contemporary World Writers.*

Dictionary of Literary Biography. Detroit: Gale, 1978–present. Also on CD-ROM and as a subscription database via Galenet, under the title *Gale Literary Databases.*

At last count this multivolume series was over two hundred volumes and growing. Each volume focuses on specialized areas of the writing field, providing biographies that focus on the career of the writer (or editor, publisher, etc.) and looks at his or her work within the historical context of the time. Sample titles in this varied collection include: *American Magazine Journalists, 1900–1960,* V. 137; *Austrian Fiction Writers After 1914,* V. 85; and *Twentieth Century Spanish Poets,* V. 108.

Great Writers and Poets. http://www.xs4all.nl/~pwessel/writers.html

Maintained by antiquarian book shop proprietor Piet Wesselman of the Netherlands, this site points to biographical pages of literary prize winners, classic authors, and other pages that gather author biography. It's not fancy but it leads to worthwhile information.

IPL (Internet Public Library) Online Literary Criticism Collection. http://www.ipl .org/ref/litcrit/

Mentioned in chapter five, but worth a second reference: This Net site links to both author biographical information and literary reviews.

Journalists of the United States: Biographical Sketches of Print and Broadcast News Shapers From the Late 17th Century to the Present. Robert B. Downs. Jefferson, NC: McFarland, 1992.

Those featured in this book range from gossip columnists to major publishers with a few paragraphs to a page dedicated to each. Some of those featured include Duff Green, a Kentucky-born journalist whose inflammatory editorial involved Green in several duels in the early 1800s, and Anne Royall, who, in 1820, launched the weekly paper titled *Paul Pry,* with a stated mission of exposing "all and every species of political evil and religious fraud without fear or affection."

Literary Kicks. http://www.charm.net/~brooklyn/LitKicks.html

This Internet page is devoted to Beat authors.

World Authors: 1900–1950. Stanley J. Kunitz, New York: H.W. Wilson, 1996.

Each biography contains comments on the author's life and writings and lists his or her principle works. Other volumes in this series: *World Authors: 1950–1970, World Authors: 1970–1975,* and *World Authors: 1975–1980.* This title is also available as a subscription Web database, spanning 800 B.C. to the present.

The Writers Directory. Miranda H. Ferrara. Detroit: St. James Press. Biennial. Also available as a subscription database via *Gale Biographies.*

More than fifteen thousand living writers from Australia, Canada, Ireland, New Zealand, South Africa, the United Kingdom, and the U.S. are listed, with each entry consisting of name, pseudonym, nationality, birth year, genres, brief career information, publications, and address. This directory opens with an index to writing categories, listing the names of writers under specific genres, such as romance/historical, poetry, computers, and social commentary.

Biography in Book Reviews and on Book Jackets

There are many times when traditional biographical resources yield nothing about an author, he's not answering his phone, and the publisher, who dumped him five years ago, has nothing on file. Then it's time to use book reviews. A lengthy book review will devote a certain amount of space to a description of the author. The mention may only be brief, saying, for example, that the author is a "much-admired business professor at the University of Colorado in Denver." But it's a lead. You then call the University of Colorado to find out more. Also, check the book flaps and cover of all books by the author. These supply basic personal data.

CHAPTER 8

Historical Research

Finding Details of Different Eras

"To a historian, libraries are food, shelter, and even muse. They are of two kinds: the library of published material, books, pamphlets, and periodicals, and the archive of unpublished papers and documents."

—Barbara Tuchman

W hen looking for book-length treatments on a historical topic, the obvious choice when using a library catalog is to mix your topic word with the word HISTORY. And that's often a good choice. So, if you were looking for books about the history of modern dance, you'd do a search in a library catalog using the words HISTORY MODERN DANCE or simply HISTORY DANCE. To learn of the early days of Peru, you'd likely be successful doing searches using the terms PERU HISTORY or SOUTH AMERICA HISTORY. To find resources on the historical roots of the personal computer, a search using the words COMPUTERS HISTORY would yield useful results.

Keep in mind that historical information is also included in books that aren't specifically designated as "history" books. For example, a guide that describes points of interest when traveling in Peru should also touch on its history. To find travel books you'd use the terms DESCRIPTION TRAVEL and, in this case, PERU.

Books that discuss the biography of well-known figures are also history books since they generally discuss a person within the context of a certain period in a particular field. So a book on Martha Graham would also be a history book about modern dance, and you would locate it in a library catalog using the phrase MARTHA GRAHAM BIOGRAPHY or simply MARTHA GRAHAM. In a similar vein, finding a book that discusses a company like IBM or Apple would fit nicely with the pile of books generated by the COMPUTERS HISTORY search mentioned earlier, so doing a keyword search using a company name would be a great idea, e.g., MICROSOFT HISTORY.

Sometimes the word HISTORY won't be helpful in a library search. A book written in 1922 about fire engines is of historical interest. But it won't be cataloged with the heading HISTORY because when it was written and cataloged, it was contemporary! So try a search that simply uses your keyword, i.e., FIRE ENGINES. This will work with a specialized topic—not with a topic like WORLD WAR II.

When you want to find books that talk about archaeological sites or artifacts through a library catalog, use the name of a culture, time period, or nation combined with the word ANTIQUITIES. Examples would be VIKINGS ANTIQUITIES, BYZANTINE ANTIQUITIES, or MEXICO ANTIQUITIES.

Also, combine your topic of interest with the word HISTORIOGRAPHY on a library catalog to locate historiographic essays. Historiographies relate the views of those historians who have already written on a particular subject, creating a narrative bibliography. These help the researcher see how a topic has been previously approached, viewed, and interpreted.

To learn how to find maps and atlases of regions from historical times, go to chapter ten.

History From Diaries and Other Published and Unpublished Primary Sources

Researchers in all fields use primary sources. These can be the oral statements of individuals or writings that come from the living of everyday life and processes of business and government. They include personal letters and papers, journals, diaries, drafts of speeches, photographs, official records, and business documents. Some primary sources, like diaries, were never intended for public use. Some, like pamphlets and congressional hearings, were meant for public scrutiny. Secondary sources are those that were written after an event took place—usually looking at the happening critically, with hindsight—and includes articles and books.

When looking for a primary resource like a diary, you may find it in the attic of the writer's great-granddaughter's house, the archive of a library or historical society, or already reprinted and published in a book that's relatively simple to find.

You may think the papers in special collections have already been thoroughly mined by others. Not so. Many collections are filled with neat folders of correspondence and other writings that have been barely ruffled. Of course, it requires some dedication and expense if you live in Alabama and the papers of the person you're researching are in a collection in Oregon, since such manuscripts will usually not be loaned. If you can't travel, check with the library and ask about their photocopying service.

A useful print guide to manuscripts that can be found in collections is the *National Union Catalog of Manuscript Collections* (Washington, DC: Library of Congress, 1959–present. Annual). This is a guide to the location of personal papers and business files. The holdings of U.S. special collections, historical societies, and archives are detailed, including such items as letters, diaries, photographs, account books, and genealogies. The people whose papers are included represent many careers and lifestyles, including legislators, teachers, and pioneers. Samples of the varied holdings include: *Papers of Nancy Hamilton*, located at Smith College, known in part for her production of the documentary film *Helen Keller: Her Story*, and the records of the Fargo Rotary Club, stored at the North Dakota Institute for Regional Studies.

Another guide of interest is the *Directory of History Departments and Organizations in the United States and Canada* (21st edition. Washington, DC: American Historical Association, 1995). This publication contains descriptions of historical collections and societies throughout the U.S. A similar title is the *Directory of Historical Organizations in the United States and Canada* (Nashville: American Association for State and Local History. Biennial).

A search on the Web using the term HISTORICAL SOCIETY and the location you're interested in will often bring up the home page of a historical society.

Other print guides to archival collections, including *Subject Collections* and *Official Museum Directory*, are described in chapter two under Finding Libraries: Online and Print Guides. Chapter two also describes *WorldCat* and *Eureka*, both excellent subscription databases for finding historic materials and identifying where they're held.

Some archival collections are restricted to use only by advanced students or professional historians, so you sometimes need to justify your need for access. Also, there may be a fee for use of a special collection and costs for duplicating.

When writing a letter to request research materials from a collection or an individual, briefly outline your project and make your request as specific as possible so the person gathering resources or otherwise responding to your request understands what you're looking for. Though you can certainly phone with requests, if time allows, a letter or E-mail may be more appreciated by a library or archive with perhaps only an overworked staff of one.

The U.S. government maintains an archive at the National Archives and Records Administration (NARA). Contact information for NARA: National Archives Building, Seventh St. and Pennsylvania Ave. NW, Washington, DC 20408, Phone: (202)501-5400, URL: http://www.nara.gov. NARA is the repository for the records of dozens of government agencies such as the U.S. Senate, the Office of Censorship, the Farm Credit Administration, and the Petroleum Administrative Board. Sample items in the collection include presidential diaries and gifts and historic correspondence.

Some holdings of NARA are searchable on the Web site through the *NARA Archive Information Locator (NAIL)* at http://www.nara.gov/nara/nail.html. Selected full-text items, sound recordings, photographs and maps are on NAIL, including such items as Civil War maps and photographs from the Kennedy White House.

There are also thirteen NARA regional records services facilities:

New England	Phone: (617)647-8100
Northeast	Phone: (212)337-1300
Mid-Atlantic	Phone: (215)597-3000
Southeast	Phone: (404)763-7477
Great Lakes	Phone: (312)581-7816
Central Plains	Phone: (816)926-6272
Southwest	Phone: (817)334-5525
Rocky Mountain Region	Phone: (303)236-0817
Pacific Southwest	Phone: (714)643-4241
Pacific Sierra	Phone: (415)876-9009
Pacific Northwest	Phone: (206)526-6507
Alaska	Phone: (907)271-2441

To find personal letters and writings using an online library catalog, use the words PERSONAL NARRATIVES, CORRESPONDENCE, or DIARIES. For example, a search in the Denver Public Library online catalog using the words PIONEERS and CORRESPONDENCE brought over forty titles, including the book *Letters From Honeyhill: A Woman's View of Homesteading, 1914–1931* (Boulder, CO: Pruett Publishers, 1986).

Bibliographies will often, especially on historic topics, list primary sources. Check the bibliographies and footnotes listed in books and articles on your subject. In a library catalog, find book-length bibliographies by doing a keyword search with the term BIBLIOGRAPHY and your topic word. H.W. Wilson's *Bibliographic Index* can also assist you in locating bibliographies that deal with your topic. *Bibliographic Index* indexes bibliographies published separately or that appear as parts of books, pamphlets, or periodicals that include fifty or more citations. It's available in print and through Wilson subscription databases.

A number of directories give you the title of books containing diaries or identify what library or other special collection holds the original document, including:

American Diaries: An Annotated Bibliography of Published American Diaries and Journals. Volume 1: Diaries Written From 1492–1844; Volume 2: Diaries Written From 1845–1980. 1st edition. Laura Arkesy. Detroit: Gale, 1987.

A guide to reprints of almost ten thousand diaries found in books, periodicals, and other publications. There's a name index, geographic index, and subject index, the latter with such entries as "Marriage, Attitude Toward" and "Whaling Ships."

American Diaries in Manuscript, 1580–1954: A Descriptive Bibliography. William Matthews. Athens, GA: University of Georgia Press, 1974.

Over five thousand diaries are described with generally short statements, e.g., "Trip across the plains from Wis. to Cal.," or "Mexican War Diary." The historical society or library that houses each manuscript is identified.

And So to Bed: A Bibliography of Diaries Published in English. Patricia Pate Havlice. Metuchen, NJ: Scarecrow Press, 1987.

The majority of diaries in this bibliography were published as books, book chapters, journal articles, or dissertations. Though many nationalities are represented, all the diaries were either written in or translated to English.

Women's Diaries, Journals, and Letters: An Annotated Bibliography. Cheryl Cline. New York: Garland Publishing, 1989.

This collection identifies writings that have appeared in articles and books, and it refers to some that are not in English. There is an index of the writers by profession and a subject index.

Oral Histories

Many historians compile oral histories by interviewing and transcribing the tales and reminiscences of individuals. To learn how to conduct oral history interviews, consult the book *Recording Oral History: A Practical Guide for Social Scientists* by historian Valerie Raleigh Yow (Thousand Oaks, CA: SAGE, 1994). The book touches on interviewing techniques, legalities, and ethics surrounding the process and looks at the types of projects that might be undertaken.

The Oral History Research office of Columbia University has set up a useful Web page at http://www.columbia.edu/cu/libraries/indiv/oral/offsite.html leading to associations like the Oral History Association (at Baylor University, P.O. Box 97234, Waco, TX 76798-7234, Phone: [254]710-2764, Fax: [254]710-

1571) and links to oral history projects and programs such as the Vietnam Veterans Oral History and Folklore Project.

To locate oral histories that have already been conducted and published in print or audio format, do a keyword search on your library catalog combining your topic with the words ORAL HISTORY or PERSONAL NARRATIVES. For example, JAPANESE AMERICANS PERSONAL NARRATIVES or WAR ORAL HISTORY.

Searching for Relatives and Other Descendants to Interview When Doing Research on a Person

When searching for descendants of historical figures, check with the local libraries and archives in the town(s) where that person grew up or lived. Stan Oliner, curator of books and manuscripts for the Colorado Historical Society, has also had success browsing the phone books of the community where the person in question lived and simply calling those with the same last name and asking "Are you related . . . ?" Mr. Oliner also notes that the local postmaster or postmistress can often offer advice in regard to descendants and friends of the biographee.

History on the Web

Many worthwhile historic collections are available on the Web, including full-text historic documents, photographs, bibliographies, and reproductions of three-dimensional items.

It's worth the effort to use several search engines and simply browse for Web pages related to your historic topic. Try the keyword combinations suggested earlier for library catalogs. A history meta site to begin with:

Horus' Web Links to History Resources, a.k.a. H-GIG: Horus Gets in Gear. http://www.ucr.edu/h-gig/horuslinks.html

Maintained by the University of California, Riverside History Department, Horus leads to links on all areas of historic study worldwide.

Sample sites dedicated to particular areas of history include:

American and British History Resources on the Internet. http://www.libraries.rutgers.edu/rulib/socsci/hist/amhist.html

Scholarly U.S. and British historical resources are highlighted on this page. There are links to timelines and chronologies, biographies, maps, and full-text documents, including treaties, debates, the Constitution, the Bill of Rights, and thousands of other original writings and commentary articles.

American Memory: Historical Collections for the National Digital Library. http://lcWeb2.loc.gov/ammem/amhome.html

The National Digital Library Program is working to offer, electronically, the Americana collection held by the Library of Congress. The American Memory collections contains the digitized documents, photographs, recorded sound, and moving pictures. Sample collections include dance instruction manuals, ca. 1600–1920, the Spanish American War as shown in motion pictures, and manuscripts from the American Life Histories collection from the Federal Writers' Project, 1936–1940, offering the recollections of Americans from diverse walks of life.

Ancient World Web. http://www.julen.net/aw/

Web pages dealing with the world before A.D. 700 are spotlighted at this site. Subject headings include: alternative theories; archaeology; art, buildings, monuments, and cities; daily life; language and literature; law and philosophy; mythology and religion; and science.

Medieval Literature and History Page. http://www.shss.montclair.edu/english/furr/medieval.html

This page connects to Web sites under seven categories: Basic Medieval Resources, Chaucer, Middle English Literature, Other Medieval Literatures, Journals and Criticism, Medieval History, and Medieval Art, Music, and Culture.

History in Articles

Online periodical indexes are great for research spanning the last few decades. But what about finding articles about the Great Depression from the perspective of those who were "living" it? What did news of the Civil War look like in the newspapers of the time? Such articles show how an event was perceived at the time it occurred, as opposed to the way history now presents it. For example, articles from *The New York Times* on the Titanic from the year of the disaster, 1912, read quite differently from articles written twenty, forty, or almost a century later, reflecting upon the incident.

Articles are also of particular interest to the historian following new interpretations of history. As professor of history Anthony Brundage notes, "articles are often the format in which historians launch new interpretations. The process of revisionism would be greatly retarded if scholarly journals were not able to publish and disseminate historical findings." Specialized indexes, such as *America: History and Life*, index the contents of such journals as *Civil War History* and *Western Legal History*. For other indexes in this genre, check Appendix B under History. Also check the Appendix for periodical indexes that were being published during the time period you're interested in. For example, *Poole's Index to Periodical Literature* was published between 1802–1906.

Unfortunately, there will be times when there's simply no index to the items you want. This is particularly true of historical sources. But many of those sources are available, waiting for you to pick a time period and start browsing. *The New York Times* is commonly available, on microfilm, back to 1851 in most larger libraries. London's *Times* microfilm may go back to 1790. Additionally, it's common for historical societies and libraries to collect complete runs of local papers on microform, often with at least a rudimentary index created for them.

A major initiative funded by the National Endowment for the Humanities and the Library of Congress is the United States Newspaper Program (USNP). This program is a nationwide cooperative effort between the states and the federal government to locate, catalog, and preserve on microfilm U.S. newspapers published from the eighteenth century to the present. Once items are microfilmed, they are listed on the OCLC system (*WorldCat*), which identifies who owns the originals and the microfiche versions of the newspapers. Visit the USNP information site at http://www.neh.fed.us/html/usnp.html for contact information for the organization in each state and U.S. territory working on this project.

History on Microform

Thousands of special collections of historic newspapers, periodicals, books, and other writings and oral reminiscences have been collected by subject or time period and stored on microfilm or microfiche, some with accompanying indexes, but not all. Some are created by major publishers; others by local organizations wishing to preserve items of regional historic importance. Examples include:

> *Civil War Newspapers on Microfilm*. Wooster, Ohio: Bell & Howell. This set contains the contents of 301 newspapers published between 1861 and 1865.
> *English Literary Periodicals (ELP), 1681-1914*. Ann Arbor, MI: University Microfilms. *ELP* is comprised of 233 periodicals reflecting British life and culture.

When you locate a historic periodical title, look it up in the commercial databases *Worldcat* or *Eureka* or the Library of Congress catalog (http://lcWeb.loc

.gov/catalog/), and it may point you to a microform collection it's stored in. Also find titles of microfilm collections by checking the *Guide to Microforms in Print* (Munich: K.G. Saur. Annual) or *Microform Research Collections: A Guide* (2nd edition. Westport, CT: 1984).

Historical Encyclopedias

A specialized encyclopedia on almost any topic will include history on that topic. So, for example, the *Encyclopedia of Psychology* will look at the roots of the field and its contributors. Some representative encyclopedic titles dealing with the history of different eras:

New Dictionary of American History. 3rd edition. 10 Volumes. Stanley I. Kutler, ed. York: Macmillan Reference Library, 1999.

An A-Z compilation of the achievements and events that comprise the history of the U.S. If it happened in the United States, it's probably noted in here. Bee-keeping, black cavalry in the West, elevators, and Washington's farewell address are all included.

Historic Documents. Washington, DC: Congressional Quarterly. Annual.

A print collection of fully reproduced significant documents in foreign affairs, education, the environment, law, science, health, and culture. A CD-ROM publication that includes full-text historic writings is called *Landmark Documents in American History* from Facts on File. It contains more than twenty thousand pages of text.

Dictionary of the Middle Ages. 13 Volumes. Joseph Strayer, ed. New York: Macmillan Library Reference, 1982–1988.

The creators of this set record ideas, names, and terminology associated with art, law, literature, music, numismatics, economics, politics, philosophy, theology, technology, and everyday life in the Middle Ages, roughly A.D. 500 to 1500.

International Dictionary of Historic Places: Essays on the History of 1,000 Historic Places. Robert M. Salkin, ed. Chicago: Fitzroy Dearborn, 1994.

Each volume of this set spotlights a particular geographic region: the Americas, Northern Europe, Southern Europe, the Middle East and Africa, and Asia and Oceania. Each essay tells the historic tale of cities, buildings, monuments, parks, streets, towns, and pieces of wilderness. A similar title is the *Encyclopedia of Historic Places* (New York: Facts on File, 1984).

Larousse Encyclopedia of Archaeology. Translation of *Larousse L'Archaeologie Découvertedes Civilisations Disparues*, 1969. Gilbert Charles-Picard. New York: G.P. Putnam's Sons, 1972.

Historical Manuscripts in E-Text

To find full-text historical writings on the Internet, try a search combining the words HISTORIC DOCUMENTS, HISTORICAL DOCUMENTS, HISTORIC MANUSCRIPT(S) or HISTORICAL MANUSCRIPT(S) with words describing the type of writings you hope to locate, e.g., WORLD WAR I or COWBOYS.

History Organizations

If an event or entity is over a year old, there's probably an organization dedicated to its history. Perhaps I exaggerate—but not much. If you need an expert on the history of just about anything, you should be able to find one. There are hundreds of associations related to the history of professions, events, cultures, movements, places, and inventions. For example, the Filipino American National Historical Society, has a thousand members (Phone: [206]322-0203, Fax: [206]461-4879) and the Center for the History of American Needlework also has about a thousand members (Phone: [412]586-5325). A major historical organization with almost sixteen thousand members is the American Historical Association (AHA), 400 A St. SE, Washington, DC 20003, Phone: (202)544-2422, Fax: (202)544-8307, E-mail: aha@theaha.org, URL: http://www.theaha.org.

This one-volume work is devoted to the findings of the "detectives of the past": archaeologists. The first portion explains the work of archaeologists. The remainder examines findings from many ages, peoples, and locations, including prehistoric archaeology, Europe in the Bronze and Iron Ages, and the Etruscans. The majority of photographs are black and white.

Magill's History of Europe. 6 Volumes. Frank N. Magill, ed. Danbury, CT: Grolier Educational Corporation, 1993.

These six volumes describe, chronologically, 288 major events that shaped the Western world. Some of the events described include the Battle of Zama, a military engagement between Roman and Carthaginian armies in 202 B.C., the proclamation of Italy as a constitutional monarchy in 1861; and the recovery of Great Britain from its military intervention on the Falkland Islands.

Everyday living in days gone by

As outlined in chapter nine, there are a number of recommended Library of Congress subject headings to use in library catalogs when looking for day-to-day living habits, rituals, and customs in contemporary and historic cultures, including: SOCIAL LIFE AND CUSTOMS, CIVILIZATION, and ANTIQUITIES. Below are some sample reference works and series that examine major ancient and historic civilizations and cultures (other titles are also listed in chapter nine):

Anthropology Web Sites. http://www.anth.ucsb.edu/netinfo.html

Find links to dozens of anthropology-related Internet sites under the headings Cultural Anthropology, Archaeology, or Physical Anthropology, or by geographical region. Sample links include *Exploring Ancient World Cultures* at http://eawc.evansville.edu/index.htm and *Maya World* at http://www.steven sonpress.com/mwindex.html, an electronic magazine from the MesoAmerica Foundation.

Civilization of the Ancient Near East. 4 Volumes. Jack M. Sasson, ed. New York: Charles Scribner's Sons, 1995.

This set reconstructs culture of the ancient Near East using archaeological findings and documents. It also looks at the physical world of the ancient Near East and explores this culture's impact on succeeding cultures. Sample essays in the collection include: *Private Life in Mesopotamia, Clothing and Grooming in Western Asia,* and *The Agricultural Cycle, Farming, and Water Management.* Also from this publisher: *Civilization of the Ancient Mediterranean* (3 Volumes, 1988).

Daily Life in Victorian England. Sally Mitchell. Westport, CT: Greenwood Press, 1996.

Each chapter in this book looks at a particular aspect of daily living, including perception of social class, traditions, money, work, technology, science, government, law, housing, food, clothing, family and social rituals, education, medicine, religion, and morality. This is part of the Greenwood Press *Daily Life in . . .* series. Other books in the series: *Daily Life in . . . Elizabethan England* (1995), *Chaucer's England* (1995), *the Inca Empire* (1996), *Mayan Civilization* (1996).

What Life Was Like Among the Druids and High Kings: Celtic Ireland A.D. *400–1200.* Alexandria, VA: Time-Life Books, 1998.

Filled with color photographs of artifacts, art, and geography, this book is one in a series that describes life in bygone times. Other titles in the series include *What Was Life Like . . . on the Banks of the Nile: Egypt,*

3050–30 B.C. (1997), *in the Age of Chivalry: Medieval Europe, A.D. 800–1500* (1997), *When Rome Ruled the World: The Roman Empire, 100 B.C.–A.D. 200* (1997), *at the Dawn of Democracy: Classical Athens, 525–322 B.C.* (1997), *When Longships Sailed: Vikings, A.D. 800–1100* (1998), *in the Land of the Dragon: Imperial China, A.D. 960–1368* (1998), and *in the Realm of Elizabethan England A.D. 1533–1603* (1998).

Reenacting History

You can learn firsthand about life in different eras by joining reenactment groups, organizations of people who reenact such events as Civil War battles or fancy dress balls. Information about reenactment opportunities can be found at http://anansi.panix.com/userdirs /wlinden/enact.html, or contact the Living History Association at P.O. Box 1389, Wilmington, VT 05363, Phone: (802)464-5569, URL: http://www.geocities.com /Athens/Delphi/9463/.

The Writer's Guide to Everyday Life in the 1800s: For Writers of Historic Fiction, Westerns, Romance, Action/Adventure, Thrillers, and Mysteries. Marc McCutcheon. Cincinnati, Ohio: Writer's Digest Books, 1993.

This guide is divided into useful sections describing items and behaviors common to the eighteeenth-century citizen. Some chapter headings are: "Slang and Everyday Speech," "Money and Coinage," and "Common Food, Drinks, and Tobacco." Other guides in this vein from Writer's Digest include *The Writer's Guide to Everyday Life . . . in the Middle Ages* (1995), *in Regency and Victorian England* (1998), *in Colonial America: From 1607–1783* (1997), *in Renaissance England* (1996), *From Prohibition Through World War II* (1995) and *in the Wild West* (1999).

Modes of Transportation

To locate general books and reference books that look at modes of transportation from the horse to the supersonic rocket ship, match the type of transport with the word HISTORY, ENCYCLOPEDIAS, or DICTIONARIES. Library of Congress subject headings for different types of transport include, for four-wheeled vehicles: AUTOMOBILES, BUSES, or CARRIAGES; for air and space transport: AIRPLANES, AERONAUTICS, ASTRONAUTICS, BALLOON-ING, HELICOPTERS, ROCKETRY, or SPACE VEHICLES; for seafaring vessels: BOATS or SHIPS; for two-wheeled conveyances: BICYCLES or MOTOR-CYCLES; for rail transport: RAILROADS or STREET-RAILROADS (for trams, trolleys, and streetcars); and, for rescue vehicles: AMBULANCES, FIRE EN-GINES, or POLICE VEHICLES. The more specialized terms, such as BAL-LOONING or POLICE VEHICLES, may not need to be combined with any other terms since there will be only a few titles in most library catalogs on those subjects. The phrase LOCAL TRANSIT combined with HISTORY will also be a useful combination when researching historic modes of transport.

Some titles that illustrate the types of transportation encyclopedias available and Web sites that bring you to more information include:

Carriage Association of America. http://www.caaonline.com/Contents/contents.htm

This is the home page of an association dedicated to the preservation and restoration of horse-drawn carriages and sleighs.

Classic Car Source. http://www.classicar.com/home.htm

This site bills itself as the "world's largest online community for the classic vehicle enthusiast," and offers links to clubs, online forums, classified ads, museums, events, books, and more.

The History of the Carriage. László Tarr. New York: Arco Publishing, 1969.

A history of the origins and uses of horse-drawn carriages and chariots throughout the ages and the world, accented with black-and-white drawings of the vehicles and replicas of carriages as seen in art. Some of the groups surveyed include the Egyptians, Chinese, Greeks, Etruscans, and Europeans.

Jane's All the World's Aircraft. Paul Jackson, ed. Alexandria, VA: Jane's Information Group. Annual.

This is an annual illustrated survey of the world's aircraft that are in contin-uing production or under development. Aircraft covered include civil and military, airships, and helicopters. *Jane's* supplies information about each craft's manufacturer and specifications.

The Maritime History Virtual Archives. http://pc-78-120.udac.se:8001/WWW /Nautica/Nautica.html

This excellent meta site is maintained by a maritime history enthusiast on his work PC; we can only hope this gentleman retains his job. If not, a second choice for some links to maritime history is the page for the *National Maritime Historical Society* at http://www.seahistory.org/, Phone: (914)737-7878, E-mail: nmhs@seahistory.org.

Rails Across America: A History of Railroads in North America. William L. Withuhn, consultant ed. New York: SmithMark Publishers, 1993.

A well-illustrated accounting of the history of rail transport in the U.S. and Canada, showing trains, the men who laid the tracks, and much of the paraphernalia of trains.

Ships. Enzo Angelucci. New York: McGraw-Hill, 1975.

From animal skins sewn together and waterproofed, through nuclear-powered vessels, *Ships* traces the use of ships throughout history with each ship mentioned named and described.

TrainsOnline. http://www.kalmbach.com/trains/trains.html

This site, sponsored by *Trains Magazine,* contains selected full text from this magazine about contemporary and historic North American rail travel. Under "Rail links," pointers lead to Web pages for railroads, museums, historical societies, train suppliers, and other railroad organizations.

The World of Automobiles: An Illustrated Encyclopedia of the Motor Car. 22 Volumes. Ian Ward. Milwaukee: Purnell Reference Books, 1977.

This colorfully illustrated set covers descriptions of twentieth-century cars; a look at the notable car makes in history; concepts and workings of automobile parts and design; a who's who of race car drivers; and descriptions of racing competitions.

World Wide Web Virtual Library: Aviation. http://macwww.db.erau.edu/www_virtual_lib/aviation.html/

This Web page has links to pages related to aircraft and aviation, including aviation pioneers and history, and aviation museums, groups, and organizations. Another aviation Web page for finding plane specifications and other historic and contemporary information about more than 11,000 types of U.S. aircraft is *Aerofiles* at http://aerofiles.com.

Apparel, Fashion, and Clothing Accessories

The history of costume is important to the historian, clothes designer, theater costumer, and also to the fiction writer. (Everyone knows that a Gothic novel should feature a ripped bodice . . . but what style of bodice?)

There's no scarcity of books published that look at one type of clothing, the dress of a cultural or national group, or fashion in a certain time period. When searching your library's online catalog, remember that there are several subject headings to try, including: COSTUME (your best choice), FASHION, CLOTHING, HAIRSTYLES, or JEWELRY.

Add words for certain time periods, cultures, or geographic areas for more

specialized searches, for example: COSTUME 15TH CENTURY, FASHION
FRANCE, or HISPANIC COSTUME.

You can also do searches using words that describe particular types of apparel
or accessories, for example: KIMONOS, SHOES, GOWNS, or BRACELETS,
though this may not yield good results in library collections with small costume
book collections.

On the Internet, connect to the splendid *Costumer's Manifesto* at http://www
.costumes.org/ where there are links to history pages for dress and accessories of
all eras, chronologies of costume history, costume and textile museums, retail
outlets for items of interest to the costumer, and references to recommended
costume books. Another excellent meta page is *The Costume Page: Costuming
Resources Online* at http://members.aol.com/nebula5/costume.html.

Following are representative listings for fashion and accessory reference
sources:

Everyday dress in the U.S. and the western world

The Common Man Through the Centuries: A Book of Costume Drawings. Max
Barsis. New York: Frederick Ungar, 1973.

Simple black-and-white drawings show figures in natural poses, evoking a
feel for the variety of folks who wore these plain garments from the fourth
century B.C. through the eighteenth century. Europeans are primarily shown.

Encyclopedia of American Indian Costume. Josephine Paterek. New York: Norton,
1996.

A compilation of descriptions and cultural contexts of the traditional dress
and ornamentation of the American Indians of ten cultural regions: Southeast,
Northeast, Plains, Southwest, Great Basin, Plateau, California, Northwest
Coast, Subarctic, and Arctic.

Fashion Sourcebooks. John Peacock. New York: Thames and Hudson, 1997–.

This is a series of volumes, each dedicated to a decade, beginning with the
1900s onward. Each title contains nearly three hundred illustrations representing men's and women's day and evening outerwear, underwear, footwear,
wedding clothing, sports and leisure attire, and accessories. Note that the
author has written and illustrated many other fashion books of interest. A
similar series, from Facts on File, is the *Fashions of a Decade* series, with each
volume dedicated to a ten-year period beginning with the 1920s.

Historic Costume in Pictures. Munich: Braun and Schneider. 1861–1880. Also available under the title *History of Costume* at http://www.siue.edu/COSTU MES/history.html.

The six hundred plates in this book originally appeared over several years in the German magazine *Münchener Bilderbogen*. These plates represent historical dress from antiquity to the end of the nineteenth century, including folk dress ca.1880 from most European, Asian, and African countries. The Web site offers this caution: "One must be aware though, that these illustrations have a Victorian perspective to their designs."

The Historical Encyclopedia of Costumes. Albert Racinet. New York: Facts on File, 1988.

Based on *Le Costume Historique of 1888*, the detailed color plates featured throughout this volume make it both useful and beautiful. Details of clothing accessories and hairstyles are also easily seen in these illustrations. This resource covers clothing in the ancient world through the 1880s and contains over two thousand illustrations.

Patterns for Theatrical Costumes: Garments, Trims, and Accessories From Ancient Egypt to 1915. Katherine Holkeboer Strand. Englewood Cliffs, NJ: Prentice Hall, 1984; reprinted by Drama Book Publishers, 1993.

If you'd like to sew your own historic garb, use this volume to find the pattern.

A Pictorial History of Costume: A Survey of Costume of All Periods and Peoples From Antiquity to Modern Times Including National Costume in Europe and Non-European Countries. Wolfgang Bruhn. New York: Frederick A. Praeger, 1955.

Originally published under the title *Kostümwerk* in 1941, this book contains two hundred plates, most in color, drawn by costume researcher and painter Max Tilke. The plates present over four thousand figures drawn in costume from antiquity through the nineteenth century.

20,000 Years of Fashion: A History of Costume and Personal Adornment. François Boucher. New York: Harry N. Abrams, 1967.

The illustrations are numerous and varied and include paintings, sculpture, drawings, and photographs, in both black and white and color. The last period examined is 1939–1947.

Jewelry, shoes, hairstyles, and accessories

Antique Combs & Purses. Evelyn Haertig. Carmel, CA: Gallery Graphics Press, 1983.

Hair ornaments of all kinds are on exhibit in this volume, including hair combs carved out of tortoise shell, decorative hair pins, floral wreaths, crowns, and tiaras. Most of the handbags are embroidered, beaded, or constructed of mesh.

Collars, Stocks, Cravats: A History of Costume Dating Guide to Civilian Men's Neckpieces, 1655–1900. Doriece Colle. Emmaus, PA: Rodale Press, 1972.

This volume showcases American and European neckwear.

Corsets and Crinolines. Norah Waugh. London: B.T. Batsford, 1954; reprinted 1987.

Through patterns and photographs, this volume displays underclothing of European women from the early sixteenth century through the early twentieth century. See also *The History of Underclothes* (Boston: Faber and Faber, 1981).

The Costume Accessories Series. New York: Drama Book Publishers, 1982–1985.

This series of books highlights fashion accessories, including bags and purses, fans, gloves, hats, jewelry, shawls, stoles, scarves, shoes, socks and stockings, and umbrellas and parasols.

Fashions in Eyeglasses. Richard Corson. Chester Springs, PA: DuFour, 1967.

Fashions in Eyeglasses is a survey of eyewear, consisting of black-and-white drawings and reproductions of paintings and pictures featuring individuals wearing eyeglasses, from the Middle Ages to the middle of the 1960s.

Fashions in Hair: The First Five Thousand Years. Richard Corson. London: Peter Owen, 1971.

This book looks at hair on the face and on the head (both real and created), as worn in ancient civilizations and on through the early 1960s. The author and illustrator, who hopes his book will be of interest "to all people with hair," provides small but detailed and abundant black-and-white drawings. Also in this vein are *An Illustrated Dictionary of Hairdressing and Wigmaking* (London: B.T. Batsford, 1984), *The Mode in Hats and Headdress* (New York: Charles Scribner's Sons, 1948), and *Women's Headdress and Hairstyles in England From A.D. 600 to the Present Day* (London: B.T. Batsford, 1973).

History of Shoe Fashions. Eunice Wilson. New York: Pitman, 1969.

The author provides sketches and background for historic footwear worldwide, both fancy and plain.

Military dress

American Flight Jackets, Air Men, & Aircraft: A History of U.S. Flyers Jackets From World War I to Desert Storm. Jon A. Maguire. Atglen, PA: Schiffer Military/ Aviation History, 1994.

This book displays photographs of cloth and leather flight jackets featuring official, semiofficial, and definitely not official insignia, e.g., a Bugs Bunny look-alike holding a bomb between his feet while munching on a carrot.

American War Medals and Decorations: 1776–1967. E. Kerrigan Evans. New York: Viking Press, 1964.

This book has descriptions and illustrations of decorations, used to indicate an individual's personal heroism, and medals, showing participation in a specific military campaign.

Arms and Armour in the Western World. Bruno Thomas. New York: McGraw-Hill, 1964.

This book presents color plates of blades, armour, and firearms from the 1500s through the early 1700s. See also chapter five under Weapons.

Medieval Military Dress: 1066–1500. Christopher Rothero. Dorset: Blandford Press, 1983.

The colorful sketches of men in armor in this volume depict knights, common soldiers, and peasants.

Military Uniforms in America. John R. Elting, Colonel U.S. Army, Retired. San Rafael, CA: The Company of Military Historians.

This series of volumes illustrates uniforms of not only American soldiers, but of those who fought with and against them on U.S. soil. Titles in the series include *Era of the American Revolution: 1755–1795, Years of Growth: 1796–1851, Long Endure—The Civil War Period: 1852–1867,* and the *Modern Era: From 1868.*

Nazi Regalia. Jack Pia. New York: Ballantine Books, 1971.

This volume shows color photographs of the uniforms and decorations of the Nazis.

Ribbons and Medals: The World's Military and Civil Awards. Captain H. Tapprell Dorling; Revised, Francis K. Mason, ed. Garden City, NY: Doubleday, 1974.

Each medal and ribbon featured is accompanied by a black-and-white photograph and details of its history and appearance.

Uniforms of the United States Army. Henry Alexander Ogden, illustrator. New York: Thomas Yoseloff. 1st Series: 1959, 2nd Series: 1960.

These are two oversized volumes of description, drawings, and paintings of the uniforms worn by American soldiers during the American Revolution, the Civil War, the Spanish-American War, the Indian Wars, and other military campaigns.

Catalog Reproductions

Did you ever order merchandise from an old telephone book–sized Sears catalog? If so, you know you could buy just about anything from them, from tires to hair bows. You'll find both originals and facsimiles of older catalogs from retailers like Sears available in some libraries and bookstores. Such catalogs offer a treasure trove of examples of how many items looked and what they cost in different time periods. For example, *The 1922 Montgomery Ward Catalogue* (New York: HC Publishers, 1969), includes "warm, roomy, stylish overcoats" for men, and "cunning frocks for the miss of two to six years." A wide variety of items are pictured in this catalog, including children's Christmas postcards, milk bottle caps, an infant's hot water bottle, rat killers, violins, and duck decoys.

Toys, Games, Dolls, Hobbies, and Diversions

How did people amuse themselves when there was no Internet, video games, or, heaven forbid, television? To find general surveys of the daily diversions in times gone by, do a search in a library catalog matching the word AMUSEMENTS with the word HISTORY or the name of a country, e.g. AMUSEMENTS GREAT BRITAIN. To focus on particular types of diversions, also try more specific words such as TOYS and BOARD GAMES.

Many toys end up being collectible, and books on collectibles supply some of the best toy photographs and information. So, browse in the Dewey decimal toy collecting area of your public library–688. When doing a search in an online library catalog, use the words COLLECTIBLE, COLLECTING, or PRICES with specific toys, such as TOY SOLDIERS, MATCHBOX TOYS, or ROCKING HORSES.

Some reference books describing historical diversions include:

The Encyclopedia of Toys. Constance Eileen King. New York: Crown Publishers, 1978.

Toys of the eighteenth, nineteenth, and early twentieth century of every stripe are featured in this volume: toy theaters, prams, doll houses, exquisite toy china, and jigsaw puzzles. Also see *A History of Toys* (Delacorte Press, 1966) for a survey of the world's toys, from ancient times through the 1960s.

Games of the World: How to Make Them, How to Play Them, How They Came to Be. Frederic V. Grunfeld. Zurich: Swiss Committee for UNICEF, 1982.

This guide discusses over one hundred games from around the world, under five headings: board and table games, street and playground games, field and forest games, party and festival games, and puzzles, tricks, and stunts.

The Games Treasury: More Than 300 Indoor and Outdoor Favorites With Strategies, Rules, and Traditions. Merilyn Simonds Mohr. Shelbourne, VT: Chapters Publishing, 1993.

For each game in this illustrated treasury, the rules, rituals, historical and social contexts, and language specific to that type of game, are described.

Yesterday's Toys: 734 Tin and Celluloid Amusements From Days Gone By. Teruhisa Kitahara. New York: Black Dog & Levanthal, 1997. Originally published in three volumes by Chronicle Books.

This gorgeous compendium features tin and celluloid toys with charm that has virtually disappeared, as it says on the book's back cover, with "today's garish plastic figures and confusingly complex computer games." All 734 toys are shown in color photographs, including celluloid dolls, clowns, animals, planes, trains, boats, cars, robots, spaceships, and monsters.

The Ultimate Doll Book. Caroline Goodfellow. New York: Dorling Kindersley, 1993.

Two hundred years of worldwide dollies fill this amply illustrated volume. The dolls displayed are made of different materials, including porcelain, wood, poured wax, composition, bisque, and cloth. A modern doll that caught my eye was Judith, who looks rather Barbie-ish. She was designed in Denmark and is pregnant. Baby pops out of her tummy, at which point Judith's abdomen immediately flattens—no girdles for this doll.

Currency

Money is, of course, different from nation to nation and era to era. Coins were not invented until late seventh century B.C. in Turkey—something to keep in mind if you're writing a novel set in the sixth century. Some coin and currency compendiums:

Coin Atlas: The World of Coinage From Its Origins to the Present Day. Joe Cribb. New York: Facts on File, 1990.

Coin Atlas recounts the coinage history of each country in chronological order. There are photographs of many of the coins discussed, and small maps pinpoint the areas being examined. The arrangement of this book makes it simple to ascertain the type of coinage used in different areas and specific eras.

The Comprehensive Catalog of U.S. Paper Money: All United States Federal Currency

Since 1812. 6th edition. Gene Hessler. Port Clinton, Ohio: BNR Press, 1997.

This volume contains descriptions and photographs of paper currency throughout U.S. history, going from $1 bills to $100,000 bills. A few color illustrations are included, but they're mostly black and white. Other chapters of interest show "Unissued and Rejected Designs" and "Error Notes."

Seaby Coin Encyclopedia. Ewald Junge. London: Seaby, 1992.

An A-Z numismatic encyclopedia containing descriptions of specific coins around the world, marks, mints, coinmakers, medalists, and collectors. Mostly black-and-white photographs with some color plates. Not every coin discussed is pictured. For U.S. coins, see the *Coin World Comprehensive Catalog & Encyclopedia of United States Coins* (2nd edition. Sidney, Ohio: Coin World/Amos Press, 1998).

Standard Catalog of World Paper Money. 3 Volumes. Bruce R. Collin. Based on the original editions by Albert Pick. Iola, WI: Krause Publications. Updated irregularly.

The catalog shows photographs of paper money from all over the world. Though the pictures are black and white, the colors are described. It's released in three volumes: *Specialized Issues, General Issues,* and *Modern Issues.*

To locate books about money in your library's online catalog, try searches that pair one of the following words MONEY, COINS, COINAGE, or NUMISMATICS, with a place, an era, or simply the word HISTORY. For example, GREECE COINS or COINAGE HISTORY. The best call number areas to simply browse in the library for such titles—Library of Congress: CJ or Dewey decimal: 737.

Sample titles of specialized books about money include: *Coins of the Roman Empire* (Routledge, 1990), *A Handbook to the Coinage of Scotland* (Argonaut, 1968), and *Byzantine Coins* (Putnam, 1973).

Architecture and Decor

Books containing photographs of architecture can be found in the art and architecture collections in public, academic, and art museum libraries. The recommended call number areas for browsing in the Library of Congress are NA, which covers architecture and architectural decoration and NK, the area for Decorative Arts, including interior design, furniture and lighting. In the Dewey decimal system you'll want to browse the 700s, fine and decorative art, design, and architecture.

Historic cityscapes and landmark architecture

How can you find out what a certain area or city looked like in a specific time period? The Sanborn fire insurance maps can help. They're described in chapter ten under the Historic Maps and Atlases. While books of landmarks and specific buildings show up in ready reference sections, you'll usually need to search for resources examining cities and places of different time periods by conducting keyword searches in a library catalog or on the Web.

There are a variety of word combinations you should try if you're looking for illustration-heavy books on architecture for specific places in a library catalog. Sometimes the word HISTORY will bring up books with historical architectural pictures, e.g., HISTORY CHICAGO. Other words to match with place names are HISTORIC BUILDINGS, LANDMARKS, BUILDINGS STRUCTURES, or DESCRIPTION TRAVEL. By conducting such searches you'll uncover books like *150 Years of Chicago Architecture: 1833–1983* (Paris: Paris Art Center, 1983), an oversized volume containing photographs and illustrations of architectural plans, exteriors, and some interiors of Chicago buildings, and *Cincinnati Observed* (Columbus, Ohio: Ohio State University Press, 1992), which includes detailed descriptions of the sights of fifteen general areas in Cincinnati.

Some print resources that discuss worldwide landmark architecture and architecture design include:

Landmarks of the World's Art: The Modern World. Norbert Lynton. New York: McGraw-Hill Book Company, 1965.

Part of a series of books that surveys major artists, architects, and their works, including paintings, sculptures, and buildings. Other titles in the *Landmarks of the World's Art* series feature *The Age of Baroque, The Ancient World, The Classical World, Man and the Renaissance, The Medieval World, The Oriental World: India and Southeast Asia, Prehistoric and Primitive Man*, and *The World of Islam*.

Primitive Architecture. Enrico Guidoni. New York: Harry N. Abrams, 1979.

This title shows shelters of nonindustrialized societies. It describes the methods of building them and the beliefs and habits of the people who live(d) in them. Some of the areas where structures are shown include Mali, Nigeria, British Columbia, the U.S. (Arizona), and the Samoa Islands of Polynesia. This book is part of the *History of World Architecture* series. Other titles in the series include: *Byzantine Architecture, Late Baroque and Rococo Architecture, Oriental Architecture*, and *Romanesque Architecture*.

World Architecture Index: A Guide to Illustrations. Edward H. Teague. New York: Greenwood Press, 1991.

The *World Architecture Index* assists in tracking down photographs of specific architectural works by indexing the contents of over one hundred books. Illustrations can be located by site, architect's name, and type or name of structure, e.g., the Tower of London.

On the Web, try the Cities/Buildings archive at http://www.washington.edu /ark2/. Yahoo! points to a wide variety of architectural links at http://www.yahoo .com/arts/architecture/.

Design and architecture reference books

Following are representative titles that supply quick overviews in particular areas of decor and construction.

Antiques in general

The Encyclopedia of Collectibles. 16 Volumes. Alexandria, VA: Time-Life Books, 1978–1980.

The photographs are lustrous in this collection, allowing you to see detail of hundreds of collectibles of all types, including cash registers of the 1800s and 1900s and a tobacco humidor made of carnival glass. Museums where the collectibles may be admired are named.

Miller's Encyclopedia of Antiques. Judith Miller, ed. London: Mitchell Beazley, 1998.

Miller's gives advice on how to look at antiques and what to look for in fifteen areas of collecting: furniture, ceramics, silver, jewelry, glass, rugs and carpets, textiles, clocks and watches, arts and crafts, art nouveau, art deco, dolls and teddy bears, toys and games, postwar design, oriental works of art, and items falling under miscellaneous. Over 1,450 color photographs are provided.

The What, Where, When of Theater Props: An Illustrated Chronology From Arrowheads to Video Games. James Thurston. Cincinnati, Ohio: Betterway Books, 1992.

Though geared to the theater crowd, this book supplies simple sketches and descriptions for objects and furniture that might also adorn a room described in a novel. In addition to furniture and ornament pieces, this book goes over kitchen and household appliances, instruments of punishment, Catholic and Jewish ceremonial objects, and hearing aides.

Interior design

Authentic Decor: The Domestic Interior—1620–1920. Peter Thornton. New York: Viking, 1984.

The author looks at fifty-year blocks of time in each chapter, examining Western world home decor. Most of the numerous illustrations are drawings and paintings of rooms, painted in the time period they represent.

The Elements of Style: A Practical Encyclopedia of Interior Architectural Details From 1485 to the Present. Revised edition. Stephen Calloway, ed. 1996.

A period-by-period visual survey of interior and exterior U.S. and British architectural styles, beginning with Jacobean and Tudor styles, and finishing up with "Beyond Modern," referring to the period from 1950–1990.

Furniture and rugs

Complete Illustrated Rugs and Carpets of the World. Ian Bennet. New York: A&W Publishers, 1977.

This pictorial guide, with detailed descriptions and background, shows floor coverings of Africa, Asia, Europe, and North America.

The Encyclopedia of Furniture. 3rd edition. Joseph Aronson. New York: Crown, 1972.

This book is comprised of black-and-white photographs and line drawings of examples of furniture from many nations. Definitions are also provided for types of furniture, furniture components, and ornaments.

Lighting

Ancient Lamps. Tihamér Szentléleky. Amsterdam: Adolf M. Hakkert, Publisher, 1969.

Featured are simple black-and-white line drawings of clay and molded lamps in the style popularly associated with the story of Aladdin's lamp.

The Best of Lighting Design. Wanda Jankowski. New York: PBC International, 1987.

This book features examples of lighting design in homes, museums, churches, stores, showrooms, hotels, restaurants, and out-of-doors.

The New Let There Be Neon. Enlarged and updated edition. Rudi Stern. New York: Harry N. Abrams, 1996.

Vivé la France, the discoverers of neon! Put on your shades before you open this volume. It features neon creations worldwide—in advertisements, architecture, interior design, and art. See also *The Best of Neon: Architecture, Interiors, Signs* (Cincinnati, Ohio: Rockport Publishers/Allworth Press, 1992).

Architecture and decor magazines and journals

There are many magazines devoted exclusively to worldwide art and architecture of the present day and the past. Look for a school in your area with an architectural or interior design program to find the widest variety to browse through. Otherwise, many libraries may have the more popular titles.

Of the many dozens of architecture-related magazines and journals being published, a handful have been produced since the late nineteenth and early twentieth centuries, and are in the following list. Browsing the earliest editions of these magazines supplies a glimpse of architecture at that time. Also, check Appendix B for a listing of indexes specifically created for architecture research.

Architectural Digest: The International Magazine of Fine Interior Design. New York: Condé Nast, 1925–present. Monthly. The interiors displayed are filled with costly objects and art.

Architectural Record. New York: McGraw-Hill, 1891–present. Monthly. America's most influential architecture magazine. The magazine's main focus is on recent architectural projects, most of them in the U.S.

Architectural Review. London: MBC Architectural Press, 1896–present. Monthly. Complementary to the *Architectural Record* in that it's similar in style and content, but focuses on British and other European architectural projects.

Casabella: International Architectural Review. Milan: Elemond Periodici, 1928–present. Monthly. Published in Italy, *Casabella* focuses on public buildings and urban design worldwide.

Domus: Monthly Review of Architecture, Interiors, Design, Art. Milan: Editoriale Domus SpA, 1928–present. 11/yr. *Domus* looks at modern architecture and design worldwide. It's known for its creative layout.

House and Garden. New York: Condé Nast, 1901–present. Monthly. *House and Garden* seeks to inspire by showing current trends in interior design in well-to-do, usually professionally designed homes. Similar, but geared to a younger audience, and featuring many homes decorated by "everyday" people, is *House Beautiful* (Hearst Corporation, 1896–present. Monthly).

Landscape Architecture. Washington, DC: American Society of Landscape

Architects, 1910–present. Monthly. A look at the design of the grounds surroundings buildings.

Victorian Homes. Millers Falls, MA: Vintage Publications, 1982–present. This contemporary magazine focuses on Victorian style, with advice on how to create the Victorian aura while allowing for modern conveniences.

Searching for Books on Collectibles

Hundreds of books are devoted to the description and history of very specialized collectibles. To search for these in an online library catalog, name the type of collectible along with one of the following keywords: COLLECTIBLES, COL-LECTING, or PRICES. For example, COLLECTIBLES BASEBALL, COL-LECTING MUSIC, or PRICES ANTIQUES. Also try the name of the designer, for example: WEDGWOOD, TIFFANY, or HUMMEL. Just a few examples of books devoted to specific collectibles:

Boxes. William C. Ketchum, Jr. Washington, DC: The Cooper-Hewitt Museum, 1982.

A volume examining mostly ornate containers around the world of various shapes and sizes, including a box from China in the shape of a crab.

Luckey's Hummel Figurines & Plates. 11th edition. Carl F. Luckey. Florence, AL: Books Americana, 1997.

A pricing and identification guide for Hummel figurines, bells, plates, and other objects bearing the Hummel name, such as holy water fonts and thimbles.

A book that will help direct you to collectible experts is *Maloney's Antiques & Collectibles Resource Directory* (4th edition. Dubuque, Iowa: Antique Trader Books, 1997). It's a listing of buyers, dealers, experts, appraisers, auction houses, restorers, clubs, museums, and periodicals related to thousands of collectibles. This book illustrates just how vast and varied the collector's market is. Would you have guessed the following had collectors: menus, smurfs, tennis rackets, and potato-related collectibles (requested by the Potato Museum in Great Falls, Virginia. Their newsletter is called *Peelings*).

There are many, many pricing guides. Some volumes are devoted to a particular collectible—for example, one volume might only feature antique watches. Others, such as auction houses, provide price guides for a wide variety of collectibles. Sample titles include *Kovel's Know Your Collectibles* (New York: Three Rivers Press, 1981) and *The Lyle Official Antiques Review: The Identification and Price*

Guide (New York: Perigee Books. Annual). As far as libraries go, a public library will be your best bet for finding the best selection of price guides. For the most up-to-date information, you'll do better at a bookstore.

Identifying collectibles

The mark, or backstamp, on glassware, pottery, jewelry, and the like, is often your key to identifying the value of an item. For example, older jewelry pieces created by Monet and stamped with that name are collectible. The mark may also just be a symbol. Sample resources that will assist you in identifying marks include *A Dictionary of Marks* (5th edition. London: Barrie & Jenkins, 1992) and *Kovel's New Dictionary of Marks: Pottery and Porcelain—1850 to the Present* (2nd edition. New York: Crown Publishers, 1995).

Antiquing Online

Antique and collectible sellers and buyers will enjoy *Curioscape*, a gateway to Internet pages related to collectibles at http://www.curioscape.com/.

Either do a free text search on Curioscape by type or maker of the collectible, or search under such categories as TABLE SETTINGS, EVENTS (such as fairs, swap meets, and shows), and MEMORABILIA.

Also of interest is Ron McCoy's *CollectorWeb.com* at http://www.collectorsweb .com. and *eBay* at http://www.ebay.com.

Genealogy Tips

Genealogy, or family history research, is meant for those willing to spend time dig, dig, digging for information. I won't try to duplicate the advice of the many excellent books on the topic in the few paragraphs I can devote to this, but here are some solid starting points for the family history researcher.

Genealogical researchers should be aware of the Family History Library, operated by The Church of Jesus Christ of Latter-Day Saints (LDS). It's the world's largest genealogical/family history library, its scope going well beyond the families of the LDS community. However, a trip to the Family History Library itself (35 N. Temple St., Salt Lake City, UT 81450, Phone: [801]240-3702) probably isn't necessary when conducting genealogical research.

There are about 1,650 Family History Centers worldwide that act as satellite research centers to the Family History Library and often contain additional material of interest pertaining to the area it's in. These Centers are usually in or near LDS churches; check the yellow pages under Churches, then The Church of Jesus Christ of Latter-Day Saints. A listing of *LDS Family History Centers* can be found at http://www.genhomepage.com/FHC/.

Academic libraries rarely have genealogical collections. Almost all public libraries have, at minimum, guidebooks and handbooks for starting family history research and materials related to their community. Since there is such widespread interest in genealogy, most public libraries offer more than the minimum.

Two acclaimed genealogical meta sources on the Web are *Cyndi's List* of *Genealogy Sites on the Internet* at http://www.cyndislist.com/ and *The Genealogy Home Page* at http://www.genhomepage.com/. These sites have information useful to both beginning and experienced genealogists.

There are also many handbooks for the budding genealogist, including *Unpuzzling Your Past: A Basic Guide to Genealogy* by Emily Ann Croom (3rd edition. Cincinnati, Ohio: Betterway Books, 1995) covering home sources, interviewing, censuses, and state and federal sources, and *The Internet for Genealogists* by Barbara Renick (4th edition. La Habra, CA: Compuology, 1998).

Chronologies

Chronologies list events in date order, supplying a fact-by-fact overview of the activities of a particular group, a noteworthy event, important accomplishments in a particular discipline, or the day-by-day achievements of note in a specific country or the world.

Unfortunately, many chronologies don't supply a great deal of information for each event noted. For example, the *Timetables of American History* (New York: Touchstone Books, 1996) reports that in 1790 "John Greenwood invents foot-powered dental drill." These few words would at least indicate to a fiction writer that he can have a character in the late 1700s being operated on by a dentist who is using a foot-powered dental drill.

Multisubject chronologies like the *Timetables of American History* that look at happenings and important events in a variety of areas, such as science, the arts, and so on, help paint a quick portrait of what the world or a region was like in a particular year or for a specific time period. As James Trager says in the preface of his work *The People's Chronology* (New York: Henry Holt, 1994), chronologies "help to show interrelationships (often obscured in conventional history) between political, economic, scientific, social, and artistic facets of life."

To find chronologies using a library catalog, do a keyword search using the word CHRONOLOGY along with a word or words that describe your topic, e.g., RUSSIA CHRONOLOGY, FILM CHRONOLOGY, SCIENCE CHRONOLOGY, or AFRICAN AMERICANS CHRONOLOGY. Chronologies and timelines also show up frequently in Web documents, though some sound more promising then they are. On the Web, enter your subject with one of these terms: CHRONOLOGY, CHRONOLOGIES, TIMELINE, TIMELINES.

A chronology meta page of note on the Internet is *History Timelines From the History Beat* at http://www.search-beat.com/history.htm. This page points to Web sites offering timelines, including timelines for the Civil War, medieval times, and Chinese Americans. Also see the History on the Web section of this chapter. *Alternatime* is another Web page listing links to timelines at http://www.canisius.edu/~emeryg/time.html.

To locate birthdays, events of note, and chart-topping music by searching a particular day, go to *Those Were the Days* on the Internet at http://www.440int.com/twtd/today.html. For example, I checked September 7 (my birthday) and found dozens of memorable events, including the first appearance of the comic strip *Blondie* on September 7, 1930; the first baby to be placed in an incubator, then known as a hatching cradle, in 1888; and birthdays for John Pierpont Morgan and others. On September 7, 1949, Perry Como's "Some Enchanted Evening" topped the charts. An excellent site with similar scope but different contents is *Any Day in History* at http://www.scopesys.com/anyday/.

The Library of Congress also offers the Today in History Archive, where you can pinpoint newsy or monumental moments in American history, searchable by keyword or month and day. A similar resource in print is *The Day in American History* (New York: Neal-Schuman, 1990).

CHAPTER 9

Cultural Research

*Uncovering the Mores of Populations
Around the World*

"It's a small world, but I wouldn't want to paint it."

—Comedian Steven Wright

I frequently work with university students who step up to an online library catalog to search for materials on customs and habits in other nations and are overwhelmed by the number of books they retrieve that have little to do with their topic. They type in the name of a country, unsure of what other keyword will narrow the search. And bang—842 books about France to wade through.

To find books about habits and cultural mores, do a keyword search combining the name of a geographic area or the name of a contemporary or historic people or civilization with the Library of Congress subject heading SOCIAL LIFE and CUSTOMS. For example: AZTECS SOCIAL LIFE CUSTOMS, MEXICO SOCIAL LIFE CUSTOMS, or JEWS SOCIAL LIFE CUSTOMS. Another heading is SOCIAL CONDITIONS. Other terms to use when looking for keys to living in historic and ancient times are SOCIETY, CULTURE, CIVILIZA-TION, ANTIQUITIES, or HISTORY. For related subject headings, also see the sections Mythology and Superstition, and Religious Beliefs.

Facts About Countries and States: Overviews and Statistics

What's the major religion in Tanzania? The favorite recreational activity in Utah? There are many fast fact guides and directories that answer these sort of cultural/lifestyle questions.

A recommended site on the Web for such information is *City.net*. Located at http://www.city.net/countries/, City.net links to information about countries and territories, including historic and economic data, country profiles, cultural details, information geared to the traveler, and maps. Also see *Yahoo! Country Information* which supplies links to hundreds of international pages of interest at http://www.yahoo.com/Regional/Countries/.

Fact and statistic overviews about nations worldwide

Almanacs, like the *World Almanac*, supply statistics about nations worldwide. Two English-language almanacs originating in other countries, and so offering facts and figures most important from their national and geographic perspectives, are the *Canadian Almanac & Directory* (Toronto: Copp Clark, 1857–present. Also available on CD-ROM) and *Whittaker's Almanack* (London: J. Whitaker & Sons, 1868–present).

Following are more online and print resources containing demographic, social, and economic data:

Background Notes. Washington, DC: U.S. Department of State. Updated
  irregularly. Also at http://www.state.gov/www/background_notes/index.html.

  Background Notes succinctly covers the history, geography, culture, government, politics, economics, climate, and transportation of nations worldwide. Only selected titles are available in print, but all are on the Web site.

Country Studies/Area Handbook Program. Washington, DC: Federal Research
  Division of the Library of Congress, Department of the Army. Issued
  irregularly. Also available at http://lcWeb2.loc.gov/frd/cs/cshome.html.

  Each study in this series deals with one foreign country, describing and analyzing its economic, military, political, and social systems, and the interrelationship of those systems. Recent volumes aren't available for every nation. Available both in hard copy and on the Web.

Calling a Country Expert

There are country desk officers at the Department of State who are experts in the social, political, and economic activities of particular countries. Call (202)647-4000 and ask for the officer representing the country you're interested in. For other country contacts, see chapter six under Political Figures and Government Agencies—Foreign.

Europa Yearbook. London: Europa Publications. Annual.

  Europa supplies overviews and statistics on nations worldwide for such elements as area and population, births and deaths per one thousand, agricul-

ture data, denominations of currency, central bank reserves, trade figures,
number of tourist arrivals, principal trading partners, and number of radios,
televisions, and automobiles in use. Regional editions of *Europa* supply even
more information on each nation's geography, history, and economy.

Index to International Statistics. Washington, DC: Congressional Information
Service, 1983–present. Monthly. Also available as part of the subscription
database *LEXIS-NEXIS Statistical Universe.*

IIS indexes and describes statistical publications from about one hundred
international intergovernmental agencies around the world, including the International Labour Organization, the World Health Organization, the Food
and Agriculture Organization, and the World Tourism Organization. The
subject coverage is comprehensive, encompassing population, business and
financial activities, international trade, education, health, and other economic,
demographic, and social matters.

InfoNation. http://www.un.org/Pubs/CyberSchoolBus/menureso.htm

Use this site to view and compare statistical data for UN member countries.
Choose up to seven nations to see how data compares. Statistics include geographic figures, such as size of the largest city or average temperature; economic
data, such as GDP or unemployment; population figures, including infant
mortality and female/male ratio, and social indicators, such as number of
motor vehicles owned and illiteracy rates.

Statesman's Year-book. New York: St. Martin's Press, 1864–present. Annual.

Published for over one hundred years, this yearbook is commonly found

---

Writers Integrating Regional Facts Into Their Writing

Fictionwriters know it's not advisable to set a novel in a city
they've never seen. If they do, they'll receive letters from the
people who live there, all happy to detail every descriptive inconsis-
tency. But novels use settings in a variety of ways. Some of the traits of your characters
may stem from where they grew up or spent time. Perhaps your character, Martha,
the exceedingly shy aunt, comes to visit from Sarasota. Is there something about that
part of Florida that made her so reticent? Check out the popular Sarasota hobbies
listed in the *Lifestyle Market Analyst* (see page 244). Such statistics, figures, and brief
descriptions of areas may also be used in nonfiction works where the geography is
not the main point of the story, but can add an interesting backdrop to the subject.

in larger libraries. For every country in the world, facts and brief overviews are furnished concerning each country's history, area and population, climate, constitution and government, defense capabilities, economy, communications, religions, educational offerings, and health systems.

Statistical Abstract of Latin America. Los Angeles: UCLA Latin American Center Publications. Annual.

The *Statistical Abstract* supplies a great variety of statistics, along the lines of the United States *Statistical Abstract* described in chapter five. It covers the twenty nations of Latin America.

Statistical Abstract of the World. 4th edition. Detroit: Gale, 1998.

Each statistic-filled chapter is arranged by country with headings covering human factors, education, science and technology, government and law, labor force, production and manufacturing sectors, and finance and economics.

Statistical Yearbook. Paris: UN Educational, Scientific, and Cultural Organization. Annual.

This is a compilation of international cultural, educational, research, and media data, including figures for educational attainment, research expenditures, and viewing and production of film, radio, and television.

Statistical Yearbook for Asia and the Pacific. Bangkok: Economic and Social Commission for Asia and the Pacific, United Nations. Annual.

A wide spectrum of data is presented in this yearbook, including population figures, employment and unemployment data, trade, industry, transport, communication, wages, and prices, and some social statistics, such as education, housing, and causes of death.

World Factbook. Washington, DC: Central Intelligence Agency. Annual. Also available at http://www.cia.gov/cia/publications/factbook/index.html.

Issued by the CIA, dozens of facts are listed for all countries of the world, including geographical details, vital statistics, population variables, economic overviews, and facts about communication and transportation systems and the military.

Fact and statistic overviews for the U.S.

Comparative Guide to American Suburbs. Milpitas, CA: Toucan Valley Publications, 1997.

Suburbs surrounding the fifty largest metropolitan areas in the U.S. are rated on economics, affordable housing, crime, open spaces, education, the commute, and community/stability.

America's Top Rated Cities: A Statistical Handbook. 6th edition. Rhoda Garoogian,
ed. Boca Raton, FL: Universal Reference Publications, 1998.

This set provides a statistical profile of U.S. cities with populations over
100,000. Data presented includes imports, exports, city finances, means of
transport to work, cost of living, educational quality, climate, air and water
quality, and number of women, minority, and growing businesses.

*Cities of the United States: A Compilation of Current Information on Economic,
Cultural, Geographic, and Social Conditions.* 4 Volumes. Linda Schmittroth,
ed. Detroit: Gale, 1998.

This encyclopedic set dedicates about a dozen pages to each of over one
hundred fifty U.S. cities, covering history of the area, major industries, types
of art and cultural activities, names of local papers and newspapers, information on local taxes, and other particulars.

Guide to the Best Small Towns in America. http://www.bestsmalltowns.com

This Web page provides social, economic, cultural, and geographic information about U.S. small towns.

The Lifestyle Market Analyst. Wilmette, IL: Standard Rate and Data Service.
Annual.

LMA shows what percentage of people in a given area enjoy different types
of activities, falling under the headings "Good Life," such as gourmet cooking
and travel; "High Tech Activities," including photography and watching cable
TV; "Sports/Leisure, Outdoor, and Domestic," such as entering sweepstakes
and owning a cat or dog. For example, the 1997 *LMA* reported that the
number-one lifestyle activity for Bowling Green, Kentucky, is Bible/devotional
reading, while the top choice for Washington, DC, residents is an interest in
fashion and clothing. Demographic figures are also included.

100 Best Small Towns in America. 2nd edition. Norman Crampton. New York:
Macmillan USA, 1995.

Small towns were defined, for this source, as places with five thousand to
fifteen thousand inhabitants. The "best" were selected based on such criteria
as annual growth rate, per capita income, large 25–34 age groups, number of
physicians, crime rate, and expenditures for public education. Another title
focusing on quality of life in smaller communities is *The New Rating Guide
to Life in America's Small Cities* (Amherst, NY: Prometheus Books, 1997).

Places Rated Almanac. David Savageau. New York: Prentice Hall Travel. Updated
irregularly.

This is the rating book that makes it to the national news whenever a new edition is published. Over three hundred metropolitan areas are ranked on factors that influence the quality of life they offer. Also from this publisher and author: *Retirement Places Rated: All You Need to Plan Your Retirement or Select Your Second Home.*

Culture, Customs, and Etiquette
Cultures and multicultures of the U.S.

The United States is a big place. Though we share cultural similarities, the differences are notable. When seeking information in a library catalog about those in America with roots in the cultures of other nations, try a search using the name of the culture or nation paired with the word AMERICANS, e.g., ITALIAN AMERICANS, ARAB AMERICANS, or HAITIAN AMERICANS. Mix that phrase with the keyword that describes your query, e.g., AFRICAN AMERICANS SOCIAL CONDITIONS or HISPANIC AMERICANS WOMEN. The word ACCULTURATION is also an often-used subject heading for books about multicultural groups in the U.S., used to describe writings that talk about the adjustment of immigrants to life in America.

Some online and off-line resources that discuss the many cultural variations and religions in the U.S.:

African American Encyclopedia. 6 Volumes. Michael W. Williams, ed. New York: Marshall Cavendish, 1993; supplement, 1997.

> With entries ranging from one paragraph to several pages in length, this set examines individuals, events, organizations, and concepts within twenty broad categories, including African heritage, family life, politics and government, segregation, desegregation, integration, slavery, and visual arts. Another title from this publisher is the *Asian American Encyclopedia.*

African-American Firsts. Joan Potter. Elizabethtown, NY: Pinto Press, 1994.

> Many "firsts" books list only a line or phrase about an accomplishment. This book does a better job, with entries that run about a half page on average. Some examples of firsts: The first African American-owned company to produce serious films was The Lincoln Motion Picture Company, founded in Los Angeles in 1916; the first African American wounded in the Civil War was Nicholas Biddle, an escaped slave, in April 1861; and the first African American anchor of a TV morning news show was Bryant Gumble, who debuted in 1982 on NBC's *Today* show.

The American Culture Series: 1493–1875. Ann Arbor, MI: University Microfilms, 1941–1974.

ACS contains 5,750 American books, pamphlets, memoirs, and diaries, stored on 642 microfilm reels, all revealing glimpses of American culture of the past. The subject index, which is in hard copy, is arranged by author, title, subject, and reel number. Samples of titles in this collection are *Life on the Plains Among Indians* and *The Practical Shepherd.*

Awesome Library: Multicultural Links. http://www.awesomelibrary.org

At the Awesome Library home page, click on "Social Studies" and then "Multicultural" to find quality links to information about African Americans, Asian Americans, Hispanic Americans, Native Americans, and other selected cultures worldwide.

Bureau of Indian Affairs, Department of the Interior, 1849 C St. NW, Mail Stop 4140, Washington, DC 20240, Phone: (202)208-7315, URL: http://www.doi .gov/bureau-indian-affairs.html

This page contains a list of federally recognized American Indian tribes, explains the tribal acknowledgment and tribal federal recognition process, and presents steps for determining an individual's Native American ancestry.

Dictionary of Asian-American History. Hyung-Chan Kim. Westport, CT: Greenwood Press, 1986.

The first portion of the book is comprised of essays that discuss the history and events associated with the immigration of various Asian and Pacific groups to the U.S. Sample essay titles include *Filipinos in the United States* and *Asian Americans and the American Economic Order.* The remainder of the volume is a dictionary of "events, persons, places, and concepts that have left indelible marks on the collective experience of Asian and Pacific Americans."

Becoming a U.S. Citizen

For instructions on how to apply for naturalization, check the Internet page for the *U.S. Immigration and Naturalization Service (INS)* at http://www.ins.usdoj.gov/. Immigration statistics from 1994 to the present and state estimates of illegal alien residents and foreign-born populations are also on this site.

Encyclopedia of Southern Culture. Charles Reagan Wilson, ed. Chapel Hill, NC: University of North Carolina Press, 1989.

Focusing primarily on the eleven states of the former Confederacy, this work looks at the region's music, literature, manners, myths, life, thought, and the impact of its history and politics. There are twenty-four major topic headings, including black life, folklife, language, religion, urbanization, violence, and women's life.

Gale Encyclopedia of Multicultural America. 2 Volumes. Rudolph J. Vecoli, ed. Detroit: Gale, 1995.

This collection of multicultural information contains over one hundred essays on different ethnic, "ethnoreligious," and Native American groups. Some of the groups spotlighted include Arab Americans, Cambodian Americans, Greek Americans, Irish Americans, Sioux, and Welsh Americans. Essays cover history of the group, acculturation and assimilation, language, family and community dynamics, religion, employment and economic traditions, politics and government, and major achievements.

Handbook of American Indians. 20 Volumes. Washington, DC: Smithsonian Institution.

The editors have compiled an encyclopedic summary of the prehistory, history, and cultures of the aboriginal peoples of North America. Eleven of the twenty volumes in this compilation focus on Native Americans of particular areas (e.g., Plains, Northwest Coast) and other volumes examine Indians in contemporary society, languages, and technology and visual arts.

Handbook of Hispanic Cultures in the United States. Nicolás Kanellos, ed. Houston: Arte Pblico Press, University of Houston and Istituto de Cooperación Iberoamericana.

This is a series of four books covering, with lengthy essays, the diverse Hispanic cultures in the U.S. Titles in the series are: *Anthropology* (1994), *History* (1994), *Literature and Art* (1993), and *Sociology* (1994).

Hispanic American Almanac: A Reference Work on Hispanics in the United States. Nicolás Kanellos. Detroit: Gale Research, 1997.

Facts, dates, biographies, and essays in this volume cover facets of Hispanic life in the United States. Some areas covered include historic landmarks, education, literature, film, and religion. Other, similar works from Gale Research include *The African American Almanac* and *The Native North American Almanac.*

Hispanic American Firsts: 500 Years of Extraordinary Achievement. Nicolás Kanellos. Detroit: Gale, 1997.

Hispanic American Firsts chronologically documents first-time Hispanic achievements in art, design, business, education, film, government, labor, literature, media, the military, performing arts, religion, science and technology, sports, and theater. Here you'll find that Lee Trevino was the first Mexican American to win golf's U.S. Open in 1968, and Lasislao Lazaro was Louisiana's first Hispanic congressman in 1913.

Jewish-American History and Culture: An Encyclopedia. Jack Fischel. New York: Garland Publishing, 1992.

A broad survey of the Jewish experience in the United States, encompassing historical events and figures, literature, art, popular entertainment, and religious life. Some of the headings are Colonial American Jewry, Jewish Education, Yiddish Poetry.

LAC: The Microbook Library of American Civilization. Chicago: Library Resources, 1971–1972.

Stored on ultrafiche, an early version of microfiche, the *LAC* is 6,500,000 pages worth of pamphlets, periodicals, biographies, autobiographies, poetry, rare books, and foreign material relating to America from the country's settlement through the beginning of World War I. Sample contents include: *"Abe" Lincoln's Yarns and Stories: A Complete Collection of the Funny and Witty Anecdotes That Made Lincoln Famous as America's Greatest Story Teller* (1904) and *Abstract of a Course of Lectures on Mental & Moral Philosophy* (1840).

Statistical Record of Native North Americans. 2nd edition. Marlita A. Reddy, ed. Detroit: Gale, 1995.

There are many statistical sections in this massive volume, including historical, with population statistics from pre-1492; demographic, recording current populations of Native Americans in the U.S. and Canada; family, looking at selected characteristics of Native American families; education, which records educational attainment, enrollment, academic progress, and costs; and culture and tradition, focusing on languages spoken and occupations held. Similar titles on different cultures from this publisher include *Statistical Record of Black America, Statistical Record of Hispanic Americans,* and *Statistical Record of Asian Americans.*

Cultures of the world

Traveling to India for business? The 1998 edition of *Culturgrams: The Nations Around Us,* reports that it is not usual to shake hands with a native Indian woman in public. Learn about such customs by consulting the resources below:

Americans Traveling Abroad: What You Should Know Before You Go. 2nd edition. I. Nwanna Gladson, Ph.D. Baltimore: World Travel Institute Press, 1996.

This guide is geared to familiarizing travelers with conditions, laws, rules,

regulations, and requirements, both U.S. and foreign, that will affect a trip.
Craighead's International Business, Travel, and Relocation Guide to 81 Countries.
4 Volumes. Detroit: Gale. Annual.

A favorite resource for those preparing to travel abroad for business and pleasure. Each country report covers aspects of living in the country, including health and safety, getting around, lodging, dining, night life, and business and leisure activities.

Cultural Atlas Series. Facts on File, 1988–1998. Updated irregularly.

This series of highly illustrated volumes discusses the physical and cultural world of different nations and regions in historic and contemporary eras. Titles included in this series: *Cultural Atlas of . . . Africa; Australia, New Zealand and the South Pacific; China, Mesopotamia and the Near East; First Civilizations; France; India, Pakistan, Nepal, Bhutan, Bangladesh and Sri Lanka; Russia and the Former Soviet Union; Spain and Portugal;* and *the Viking World.*

Culturgrams: The Nations Around Us. David M. Kennedy Center for International Studies. Brigham Young University. Annual.

Each *Culturgram* in this popular collection concisely describes cultural assumptions, values, and customs for a specific nation. *Culturgrams* covers greetings, visiting, eating, gestures, personal appearance, dating and marriage, and more.

The Encyclopedia of World Cultures. 10 Volumes. Boston: G.K. Hall, 1991.

This wonderful collection, produced under the auspices of the HRAF: the Human Relations Area Files (see page 250), contains essays describing more than fifteen hundred cultural groups worldwide, including alternate names, origins, location of culture and description of the physical environment, language, population trends, economy, kin groups, rules and practices related to marriage, family, inheritance, socialization, death and the afterlife, ceremonies, arts, and religion, including practices of the present and past. Just a few of the diverse afterlife beliefs include: the Mimika of Indonesia believe that the spirits of the dead live in a beautiful underworld of sand and gardens, and the Yakan of the island of Basilan in the southern Philippines believe their dead have a one hundred-day journey to the next world.

Gestures: The Do's and Taboos of Body Language Around the World. Roger E. Axtell. New York: John Wiley & Sons, 1998.

Body language to avoid and use around the globe is the subject of this book. (Gesture information is also on the Web at the *Web of Culture: Gestures Around the World* page at http://www.Webofculture.com/edu/gestures.html.)

"And It Is Said . . ."

The proverbs, toasts, and curses worldwide illustrate cross-cultural differences. Some resources for finding proverbs include: *A Polyglot of Foreign Proverbs: Comprising French, Italian, German, Dutch, Spanish, Portuguese, and Danish With English Translations and a General Index* (London: Henry G. Bohn, 1857; reprinted, Detroit: Gale, 1968), which includes such maxims as the Dutch proverb: "A beggar's hand is a bottomless basket," and *Crisp Toasts: Wonderful Words That Add Wit and Class to Every Time You Raise Your Glass* (New York: St. Martin's Press, 1992), which offers this toast to friends: "May we have a few real friends rather than a thousand acquaintances," and the toast to overindulgence: "What would we like to drink to? To about four in the morning." On the Web, try *Sláinte! Toasts, Blessings, and Sayings* at http://zinnia.umfacad.maine.edu/~donaghue/toasts.html, a listing of primarily Irish toasts for many occasions, including, for retirees, "May the best day of your past be the worst day of your future."

Human Relations Area Files: HRAF. Pre-1994 *HRAF* information is on microfiche, 1994–present is on CD-ROM or the commercial database *Electronic-HRAF,* a.k.a. *E-HRAF.* For details on the offerings of HRAF go to http://www.yale.edu/hraf/home.htm, or contact them at 755 Prospect St., New Haven, CT 06511-1225, Phone: (203)764-9401 or (800)520-4723, Fax: (203)764-9404, E-mail: hrafmem@hrafmem.mail.yale.edu.

HRAF is a consortium of universities, colleges, and research organizations devoted to work in cultural anthropology. They offer collections of primary-source materials on societies worldwide—materials gathered up close and personal from such peoples as the Copper Eskimo, Iroquois, Lau, Tlingit, Yanoama, and hundreds of others, in a variety of formats and under several titles (for example, see earlier entry for *The Encyclopedia of World Cultures*).

National Geographic Online. http://www.nationalgeographic.com/

Use the search button to put in the name of the culture or area you're interested in, and be transported to relevant links and texts.

Web of Culture. http://www.Webofculture.com/

Written for the international business traveler, Web of Culture supplies pointers to cultural, geographical, and statistical information worldwide.

Using Travel Guides

As you probably know, bookstores and many public libraries carry guides for the traveler that detail a region's sightseeing high points, history, and restaurants and accommodations, and include titles such as *Access Visitors Guides*, *APA Insight Guides*, *Baedeker's*, *Blue Guides*, *Passport Guides*, and *Sierra Club Adventure Travel Guides*. In a library catalog, use the words DESCRIPTION TRAVEL or GUIDEBOOKS along with the name of your travel destination to find travel guides. Publishers of tour guides also hawk their books on the Web and provide a surprising amount of free information there as well. Some recommended sites include the *Lonely Planet On-line* at http://www.lonelyplanet.com, *Fodor's Travel Online* at http://www.fodors.com and *Berlitz Globetrotter* at http://www.berlitz.com.

World Cultures. http://www.wsu.edu:8080/~dee/
    Created for first-year college students, this site from Washington State University presents scholarly writings, definitions, and links related to historic and contemporary cultural study.
World Wide Web Virtual Library: Indigenous Studies. http://www.halcyon.com /FWDP/wwwvl/indig-vl.html
    Developed by the Center for World Indigenous Studies, this meta page highlights Web resources focusing on native peoples worldwide. Some of the sites noted look at one region, such as the *Western Sahara Home Page* at http:// www.arso.org/index.htm, while others have a broader scope, like the *Fourth World Documentation Project*, which offers access to fourth world documents and resources at http://www.halcyon.com/FWDP/fwdp.html.

Mythology and Superstitions

Don't comb your hair after sunset—it will bring disaster! Or so says the *Dictionary of Superstitions* (New York: Oxford University Press, 1989). The following books and databases look at the mythology of different cultures. Though many myths are often closely associated with religious beliefs, there's a separate section for resources discussing religious beliefs following this one.

    To locate book-length treatments on the mythological beliefs of different cultures, there are several different Library of Congress subject headings you might use, including FOLKLORE, MYTHOLOGY, SUPERSTITION, or TALES. For

example: ROMAN MYTHOLOGY, INDIAN FOLKLORE, CHINA SUPER-
STITION, or AFRICA TALES.

Useful meta sites to substantive mythological writings on the Web include
Myths and Legends at http://pubpages.unh.edu/~cbsiren/myth.html and the
Mythology on the Web page at http://www.angelfire.com/mi/myth. Other books and
Internet sites:

Animal-Speak: The Spiritual and Magical Powers of Creatures Great and Small.
Ted Andrews. St. Paul, MN: Llewellyn Publications, 1993.

Animal-Speak provides techniques for reading signs and omens in nature,
and it recounts both mythical associations and physical realities for over one
hundred animals, birds, insects, and reptiles.

The Book of Gods, Goddesses, Heroes and Other Characters of Mythology. http://
www.cybercomm.net/~grandpa/gdsindex.html

To find a description of a mythological being, use the index to search
alphabetically by name on this Web page. You can also search for mythological
characters, myths, and folklore under specific cultures, including African,
Asian, American Indian, Babylonian, Celtic, Egyptian, Greek, Oceanic, Roman, Russian, and Teutonic.

Bulfinch's Mythology: The Age of Fable, Age of Chivalry, Legends of Charlemagne.
Thomas Bulfinch. New York: Grosset & Dunlap, 1913. Many reprints under
many imprints over the years. Also at http://Webcom.com/shownet/medea
/bulfinch/welcome.html.

A classic writing in the field of mythology and legend. The online edition
includes annotations and useful hypertext links.

The Continuum Encyclopedia of Symbols. Udo Becker; Lance W. Garner, translator.
New York: Continuum, 1994.

Use this guide to learn of the meaning or symbolic significance of over
1,500 objects, mythological beings, and concepts in different cultures. The
items and ideas examined are quite varied. Sample entries include butterflies,
a symbol of women in Japan; a lighthouse, a representation of the heavenly
harbor the soul sails into; and the veil, a symbol of concealment and of mystery.
Unfortunately, many of the entries refer to symbolic meaning in "many"
cultures, rather than naming the specific cultures.

Dictionary of Angels, Including the Fallen Angels. Gustav Davidson. New York:
The Free Press, 1967.

Virtually all the angels named in this dictionary are culled from sources outside of the Old and New Testaments, which often refer to angels, but hardly ever name them.

A Dictionary of Dream Symbols, With an Introduction to Dream Psychology. Eric Ackroyd. London: Blandford, 1993.

This book opens with advice on how to interpret your dreams and an overview of the thoughts of both Sigmund Freud and Carl Jung on dreams. The bulk of the book is an A-Z listing of several possible meanings of dream images, for example, *hall*: (1) "A hall, particularly if large and symmetrical, may symbolize the self. (2) If the hall is a mere antechamber (like a doctor's waiting room) it may mean a large part of your psyche still remains unexplored."

Dictionary of Native American Mythology. Sam D. Gill. Santa Barbara, CA: ABC-CLIO, 1992.

Descriptions and definitions of ritual and myth of the many tribes of North America. The dictionary names a number of creatures to be wary of, including the *Ganiagwaihegowa*, a mythic, human-devouring, hairless bear. There is a cross-reference index by Tribe.

Dictionary of Satanism. Wade Baskin. New York: Philosophical Library, 1972. Republished under the title *Satanism*, New York: Carol Publishing Group, 1991.

This work discusses concepts, issues, people, places, and events associated throughout history with the concept of Satan. Includes short but scary definitions, like *Shedim*, a type of demon that has the claws of a cock, and *Hexen*, the name for witches in Germanic folklore.

Encyclopedia of Archetypal Symbolism: The Archive for Research and Archetypal Symbolism. Beverly Ann Moon, ed. Boston: Shambhala Publications, 1997.

This book examines the psychological meaning, historical and cultural context, and cross-cultural symbolism of archetypes illustrated in over one hundred color photographs of worldwide artworks/artifacts. Arranged by archetypal theme, including cosmos and creation, sacred animals, goddesses, gods, death, and transformation.

Encyclopedia Mythica: An Encyclopedia on Mythology, Folklore, and Legend. http://www.pantheon.org/mythica

This Net guide links to thousands of definitions of legendary creatures, places, objects, and gods and goddesses from folklore, religion, and myth. Another site with similar scope is *Of Gods and Men: The A to Z of Mythology and Legend* at http://www.clubi.ie/lestat/godsmen.html.

Encyclopedia of Witches and Witchcraft. Rosemary Ellen Guiley. New York: Facts on File, 1989.

Information is provided pertaining to the history, beliefs, practices, and adherents of witchcraft in Western civilization. The author also compiled the *Encyclopedia of Ghosts and Spirits* (1992), a compendium of paranormal activity worldwide.

Faiths and Folklore of the British Isles: A Descriptive and Historical Dictionary. 2 Volumes. W. Carew Hazlitt. New York: Benjamin Blom, 1965.

Covering Norman times to the end of the nineteenth century, this dictionary defines the superstitions, beliefs, and popular customs of England, Scotland, Wales, and Ireland. From these volumes you'll learn the tale of the *Chin,* an imp that resides in the chimneys of nurseries and can be called upon to take away misbehaving children.

The Golden Bough: A Study of Magic and Religion. 3rd edition. 12 Volumes. Sir James George Frazer. London: Macmillan, 1906–1915; supplement titled *Aftermath,* 1936.

More a set of books than an encyclopedic set, *The Golden Bough* is considered a classic on the topic of early religion and mythology. Sample volume titles include *The Magic Art and the Evolution of Kings* and *Balder the Beautiful: The Fire Festivals of Europe and the Doctrine of the External Soul.* A 1959 abridged edition brings elements of the original work up-to-date.

Guide to the Gods. Marjorie Leach. Santa Barbara, CA: ABC-CLIO, 1992.

Each grouping in the book is based upon the function and attributes of the gods, thereby bringing together deities from all over the world, allowing easy comparison. The entries are very brief but citations point the reader to further recommended reading. Also from this publisher, *Goddesses in World Mythology* (1993), which discusses the lives and attributes of more than 9,500 goddesses, spanning 30,000 years and dozens of cultures.

Illustrated Encyclopedia of Greek Mythology. http://www.cultures.com

This is an online guide to brief descriptions of the gods, beings, places, and beliefs from Greek mythology.

Index to Fairy Tales: Including Folklore, Legends, and Myths in Collections. Norma Olin Ireland. (Original author: Mary Huse Eastman. Original publishers: Boston Books and F.W. Faxon.) Metuchen, NJ: Scarecrow Press, 1915–1986.

This collection assists the reader in locating tales found in collections of stories. Examples of some of the collection titles: *100 Armenian Tales* (Detroit: Wayne State University, 1982) and *The Hungry Woman: Myths and Legends of the Aztecs.* (New York: William Morrow, 1984). The first and second editions are indexed by story title only. Editions beginning in with 1949–1972 also supply subject access.

Library of the Worlds Myths and Legends. New York: Peter Bedrick Books, 1982–1996.

This series of slim, well-illustrated books looks at myths and some religious beliefs of different cultures. Books in this series include: *African Mythology, Celtic Mythology, Chinese Mythology, Christian Mythology, Egyptian Mythology, European Mythology, Greek Mythology, Illustrated Dictionary of Greek and Roman Mythology, Indian Mythology, Japanese Mythology, Jewish Legends, Mexican and Central American Mythology, Near Eastern Mythology, North American Indian Mythology, Persian Mythology (Iran), Roman Mythology, Scandinavian Mythology,* and *South American Mythology.*

Man, Myth, and Magic: The Illustrated Encyclopedia of Mythology, Religion, and the Unknown. New edition. 21 Volumes. Richard Cavendish, ed. New York: Marshall Cavendish, 1997.

This set is chock-full of illustration. Use the cumulative index, the last volume, to find what you need, since there may be several mentions of a myth or belief throughout this set, buried in widely separated sections.

Motif-Index of Folk Literature: A Classification of Narrative Elements in Folktales, Ballads, Myths, Fables, Mediaeval Romances, Exempla, Fabliaux, Jest-Books, and Local Legends. 6 Volumes. Stith Thompson. Bloomington, IN: Indiana University Press, 1955; revised and enlarged, 1975. Also available on CD-ROM.

Using this set, the reader can search for thematic elements and folklore and discover which particular readings from what regions include that motif. For example, looking under the word *knots* in the index leads to references of knots that should be untied at childbirth, magic that can be unleashed by loosening knots, and others.

Spirits, Fairies, Gnomes and Goblins: An Encyclopedia of the Little People. Carol Rose. Santa Barbara, CA: ABC-CLIO, 1996.

The author briefly describes supernatural beings and "lesser" spirits found in religion, cultures, and folk beliefs, including *Olsen* of Denmark, who is responsible for all unexplained household mishaps, and *mawmets*, a euphemism in England for fairies that means "little mothers." Another title in this vein is *An Encyclopedia of Fairies: Hobgoblins, Brownies, Bogies, and Other Supernatural Creatures* (New York: Pantheon Books, 1976). On the Web, try

Faeries at http://faeryland.tamu-commerce.edu/~earendil/faerie/faerie.html, a guide to fairy lore and literature.

Religious Beliefs

In addition to the term RELIGION or the name of a particular religion, e.g., BUDDHISM, also try the terms RITES, CEREMONIES, or IDEOLOGY when using a library catalog to pinpoint books in library collections dealing with religious beliefs.

A title that will help you get ready for a personal foray into an unfamiliar religious setting is *How to Be a Perfect Stranger: A Guide to Etiquette in Other People's Religious Ceremonies.* (2 Volumes. Woodstock, VT: Jewish Lights, 1997), which explains accepted and expected behavior and dress when attending the ceremonies, services, or rituals for thirty-seven denominations.

Some religious sites and reference resources of note:

The Anchor Bible Dictionary. 6 Volumes. David Noel Freedman, ed. New York: Doubleday, 1992.

An A-Z compendium covering developments and issues in the field of bible study. There is commentary related to the Hebrew Bible, the Apocrypha, the New Testament, and references to such texts as the Dead Sea Scrolls and the Nag Hammad texts.

The Concise Encyclopedia of Islam. Cyril Glassé. San Francisco: Harper & Row, 1989.

One-volume coverage of the beliefs of Islam and its prominent persons. A chronology of Islam in maps and text is also supplied.

Encyclopedia Judaica. 16 Volumes. Jerusalem: Keter Publishing House, 1972.

A compendium of Jewish life, culture, and beliefs. This set includes eight thousand illustrations, including maps, charts, diagrams, and color photographs.

Encyclopedia of African American Religions. Larry G. Murphy, ed. New York: Garland Publishing, 1993.

This encyclopedia supplies biographical coverage of the founders of larger African American religious groups and of selected bishops serving the black community. It also includes descriptions of African American denominations, and prominent religious groups and organizations.

Encyclopedia of the American Religious Experience: Studies of Traditions and Movements. 3 Volumes. Charles H. Lippy, ed. New York: Charles Scribner's Sons, 1988.

Whether founded in America, like The Church of Jesus Christ of Latter-

Day Saints, or from other parts of the world, like the Buddhists, this encyclopedia tries to cover all religions that have been or are practiced in America.

Encyclopedia of Eastern Philosophy and Religion. Boston: Shambhala Publications,
1989.

Geared to the general reader, this volume surveys the teachers, traditions,
terminology, doctrines, and literature of Buddhism, Taoism, Zen, and Hinduism.

The Encyclopedia of the Lutheran Church. 3 Volumes. Julius Bodensieck. Minneapolis:
Augsburg Publishing House, 1965.

International in scope, this work describes the theology of the Lutheran
faith, supplies biographical information on leaders in the church, the historical
roots of the faith, recounts specific tasks and actions of Lutherans, and elabo-
rates on specific thoughts of the church on a variety of issues such as war and
prostitution.

*Encyclopedia of Mormonism: The History, Scripture, Doctrine, and Procedure of The
Church of Jesus Christ of Latter-Day Saints.* 5 Volumes. Daniel H. Ludlow.
New York: Macmillan Publishing, 1992.

This set delves into the teachings, beliefs, cultural activities, and roots of
the 160-year-old Church of Latter-Day Saints (LDS), more widely known
as the Mormons. The biographical entries cover those who were influential
contemporaries of the founder of the Church (Joseph Smith), presidents of
the Church, and some auxiliary founders. The last volume of the collection
contains a copy of The Book of Mormon and the doctrines and covenants of
the Mormons.

Encyclopedia of Native American Religions. Arlene Hirschfelder. New York: Facts
on File, 1992.

This book looks at the spiritual traditions of the native peoples in the U.S.
and Canada pre-European exposure. Sacred sites involved in public dispute are
named, as are Native American religious practitioners. Protestant and Catholic
missionaries who had influence on the Native American religious tradition are
also included.

Encyclopedia of Religion. 16 Volumes. Mircea Eliade, ed. New York: Macmillan,
1987. Reissued in 1993 in 8 Volumes.

An extensive and scholarly global survey of religious beliefs, concepts, and
practices. Using the index, the final volume in the set, it's simple to track
specific beliefs within religions. Another comprehensive encyclopedic set is *The
New Schaff-Herzog Encyclopedia of Religious Knowledge* (15 Volumes. Grand

Rapids, MI: Baker Book House, 1977, reprint; Original: Funk and Wagnalls, 1908).

Library of God (LOG). http://www.gate.net/~critch/libraryofgod/

This site aims to be a comprehensive starting point for locating religious scholarship on the Internet, including scholarly papers, bibliographies, and links related to world religions and their practices. Another meta site is the *My Facts Page: World Religion Resources* at http://www.refdesk.com/factrel.html.

The Mennonite Encyclopedia. 4 Volumes. Cornelius Krahn, ed. Scottdale, PA: Mennonite Publishing House, 1969–1973; supplement, 1990.

The original four volumes survey the Mennonite history, life, and theology worldwide from its inception in the sixteenth century through the twentieth century. The supplemental volume, in addition to supplying updated and new entries, also added more biographies of influential women Mennonites who the editors felt were underrepresented in the original set.

New Catholic Encyclopedia. 15 Volumes. William J. McDonald, D.D., Ph.D., LL.D., ed. New York: McGraw-Hill, 1967; supplements in 1974, 1979, 1989, and 1997.

International in scope, this set looks at the doctrines, institutions, and activities of the Catholic church throughout the world. Thoughts of the church on subjects as abortion and the Vietnam War are recorded. On the Web, see the *Catholic Encyclopedia*, a transcribed online edition of *The Catholic Encyclopedia: An International Work of Reference on the Constitution, Doctrine, Discipline and History of the Catholic Church* (New York: Appleton, 1907–1912) at http://www.csn.net/advent/cathen/.

Names: Books and Internet Sites

Every nation, religion, and culture has its unique names associated with particular meanings. Some places to find them:

The African Book of Names and Their Meaning. Molefi Kete Asante. Maywood, NJ: Peoples Publishing Group, 1999.

Arranged by the different geographic areas of the African continent (southern, central, eastern, western, and northern), each name is briefly defined. Some names listed include *Birago*, meaning "down-to-earth, sensible"; *Patire*, defined as "where we are"; and *Habiba*, "the beloved."

A Dictionary of First Names. Patrick Hanks. New York: Oxford University Press, 1990.

This book provides, in a few sentences for each, the linguistic root of each name, historical background, and the country in which it originated. Variations of each name are also provided.

A Dictionary of Jewish Names and Their History. Benzion C. Kaganoff. New York: Schocken Books, 1977.

The first half of the book discusses the origins and histories of naming in the Jewish religion. The second part is a dictionary of selected surnames. Names of note include the longest known Jewish family name, *Katzenellenbogen*, and a name commonly known in the U.S., *Bernstein*, which means "amber."

Dictionary of Surnames. Patrick Hanks. New York: Oxford University Press, 1988; reprinted with corrections, 1991.

A listing of European hereditary names of families passed from father to children.

The First Name Reverse Dictionary. Yvonne Navarro. Jefferson, NC: McFarland, 1993.

This volume lets you look up a meaning and then see what name or names match. For example, name choices listed under the word "heavenly" include *Celeste, Juno, Selena, Celene, Celesta,* and *Celestina.*

Phone Book: Great for Finding Names

Do remember that ultimate at-home reference source when trying to name a fictional character: the phone book. The names of those living in the United States represent peoples from all over the world, so there's no lack of variety

Hispanic First Names: A Comprehensive Dictionary of 250 Years of Mexican-American Usage. Richard D. Woods. Westport, CT: Greenwood Press, 1984.

This list of Hispanic first names provides a word or two of description for the names listed and then many cross-references to other names the name was derived from or related to.

Irish Families: Their Names, Arms, and Origins. 4th edition. Edward MacLysaght. Dublin: Irish Academic Press, 1985.

The author presents facts about Irish nomenclature and families, including over two hundred color illustrations of coats of arms.

Our Italian Surnames. Joseph G. Fucilla. Baltimore: Genealogical Publishing Company, 1949.

The names in this collection are listed within textual explanations, in chapters that describe their origin. For example, some of the chapter titles, indicating the origin of surnames, include: "Botanical Names," "Topographical Names," "Geographical Names," "Bird Names," "Occupative Names," and "Anatomical Names."

Scottish Surnames and Families. Donald Whyte. New York: Barnes & Noble, 1997.

Some names in this volume come from Irish kings, Viking warriors, and ancient Picts.

The Writer's Digest Character Naming Sourcebook. Sherrilyn Kenyon. Cincinnati, Ohio: Writer's Digest Books, 1994.

The lists of first and last names from different nations and civilizations in this book are intended to assist the writer in naming characters, places, and objects (for example, fictitious brand names).

Names on the Web

Go to http://www.aclin.org/other/community/maic/names.htm, the *What's in a Name?* list compiled by Peggy Jobe, government documents librarian at the University of Colorado at Boulder, for pointers to useful Web sites related to choosing names and learning their meaning and history. Some of the sites on Peggy's list include the *Etymology of First Names* at http://www.pacificcoast.net/~muck/etym.html, where you can look up the meaning and history of first names; the *Hall of Names* at http://www.camelotintl.com/roots/index.html, with background on over half a million European surnames; and the *Babynamer* at http://www.babynamer.com/, where you can locate first names and their meanings in myriad cultures. A database of the names of famous people is also available in Babynamer. Another excellent meta site to names is *Eponym* at http://student-www.uchicago.edu/users/smhawkin/names/.

The Culture of Language

Learning the language of a foreign culture will help you learn more about that culture. To locate foreign language learning materials in your library's online catalog, do a keyword search that combines the name of the language with the word STUDY, e.g, FRENCH LANGUAGE STUDY. Foreign language dictionaries can be found using a keyword search that combines the name of the language and the word DICTIONARIES, e.g. GERMAN LANGUAGE DICTIONARIES.

To find language study guides in audio format, do a keyword search using the name of the LANGUAGE combined with one of the phrases shown in these examples: SPANISH LANGUAGE STUDY SOUND RECORDING, DUTCH LANGUAGE STUDY AUDIO CASSETTES, or AFRIKAANS LANGUAGE SELF INSTRUCTION.

On the Internet, browse through the language-related links on *HLP: The Human Languages Page* at http://www.june29.com/HLP. The site's introduction promises connections to "online language lessons, translating dictionaries, native literature, translation services, software, language schools, or just a little information on a language you've heard about."

Slang, accents, regionalisms, and euphemisms

There are dictionaries for different professions and specialties, each revealing the jargon of the field, and guides to obscure, obsolete, slang, profane, regional and colloquial terms. In addition to their usefulness in anthropological studies, the resources in this section are of interest to anyone who writes fiction dialog. The way a person speaks says volumes about them. Likewise, the way a character speaks will influence the way a reader reacts to him. The character might occasionally say some words unique to a particular profession. Or he might use words now obsolete but common in the period in which a story is set. He may simply have an accent or manner of speech common to where he lives.

Representative books and Web pages that focus on specialized aspects of language:

British English: A to Zed. Norman W. Schur. New York: Facts on File, 1987.

> This is a lexicon of Briticisms, such as: *Bob's Your Uncle*, used at the end of instructions, it means "There you are!" or "Volià!"; *Dutch* for *wife*, used as an endearment, as in "My old dutch"; and *O.N.O.*, shorthand for *Or Nearest Offer*, seen in ads for such items as real estate and automobiles.

College Slang Research Project. http://www.intranet.csupomona.edu/~jasanders /slang/project.html

> The College Slang Research Project studies the use of slang among college students. Check this site for numerous links to U.S. and international slang language Internet pages, including *NetLingo*, a dictionary of Internet and technology-related words at http://www.netlingo.com/, and the *Dictionary of Mountain Bike Slang* at http://world.std.com/~jimf/biking/slang.html.

Dictionary of American Regional English (DARE). Frederic G. Cassidy. Belknap Press of Harvard University, 1983–1996.

> *DARE* reports the results of scholarly study, involving thousands of conversa-

tions and questionnaires with people in communities throughout the U.S., examining the way those in particular areas and social groups speak. In addition to providing word origins and characteristics of those who use specific words (i.e., age, gender, educational level), *DARE* supplies maps showing in which regions of the U.S. a word is used. Volumes 1(A-C), Volume 2 (D-H), and Volume 3 (I-O) are completed. This work is not online but information about its creation and structure is at http://polyglot.lss.wisc.edu/dare/dare.html.

Juba to Jive: A Dictionary of African-American Slang. Clarence Major, ed. New York: Penguin Books, 1994.

Terms in this book include: *griffe* (1780s–1920s), "the offspring of two mulattos or the child of black and white parents"; *machine* (1950s–1960s), "an automobile; one's car"; and *picking* (1990s), "frantically searching for particles of rock cocaine on the ground."

Maledicta Press. http://www.sonic.net/maledicta/

Maledicta: The International Journal of Verbal Aggression specializes in the origin, etymology, meaning, use, and influence of vulgar, obscene, blasphemous, and otherwise aggressive language, worldwide. On this page are recent copies of the journal and links to international Web sites specializing in "insults, curses, swearwords, blasphemies, slurs, slang, obscenities, and vulgarities."

Oxford Dictionary of Modern Slang. John Ayto. New York: Oxford University Press, 1992.

This volume pulls together slang words and phrases from throughout the English-speaking world. To find similar guides, do a search in a library catalog using the words SLANG or FIGURE OF SPEECH matched with the name of the language.

Poplollies and Bellibones: A Celebration of Lost Words. Susan Kelz Sperling. New York: Clarkson N. Potter, 1977.

This book documents some wonderful words that just don't get used much anymore, including *bellytimber*: food; *murfles*: freckles, pimples; *one-tongue*: tattle-tale; *porknella*: person as fat as a pig; and *snawk*: to smell. See also the *Random House Historical Dictionary of American Slang*, still in progress at the time of this writing.

Whistlin' Dixie: A Dictionary of Southern Expressions. Robert Hendrickson. New York: Facts on File, 1993.

Thousands of words and expressions of the historic and modern South, including *don't get cross-legged*: don't lose your temper; *make the riffle*: make the grade, succeed; and *vanity cake*: a Mississippi dessert often served at tea time. This title is part of a series called *Dictionary of American Regional Expressions*. Also in this series: *New Yawk Tawk: A Dictionary of New York City Expressions* (1997), *Happy Trails: A Dictionary of Western Expressions* (1994), *Mountain Range: A Dictionary Of Expressions From Appalachia to the Ozarks* (1997), and *Yankee Talk: A Dictionary of New England Expressions* (1996).

Wicked Words: A Treasury of Curses, Insults, Put-Downs, and Other Formerly Unprintable Terms From Anglo-Saxon Times to the Present. Hugh Rawson. New York: Crown Publishers, 1989.

This volume explains profanity through the ages, such as *boot-licker*: someone who curries favor with those in power, and *pettifogger*: a quibbling, unscrupulous lawyer.

Anniversaries, Commemorations, Holidays, Holy Days, and Festivals

Use the resources in this section to pinpoint holidays and celebrations worldwide. Freelance writers can often find a story related to anniversaries of companies, events, or places. Just remember, if you're thinking or writing about National Magic Day, which happens in October, don't submit it a week before—submit it six months earlier.

Chase's Annual Events: The Day-by-Day Directory to (Year). Chicago: Contemporary Books. Annual.

Chase's lists are arranged by days, anniversaries, holidays, birthdays, festivals, and events—unofficial, official, legal, and silly. Some events listed: January 10-16: Man Watchers Week; June: Dairy Month; September 16: Stay Away From Seattle Day; and December 2-5: The Festival of Trees, in Topeka, Kansas.

The Folklore of American Holidays: A Compilation of More Than 400 Beliefs, Legends, Superstitions, Proverbs, Riddles, Poems, Songs, Dances, Games, Plays, Pageants, Fairs, Foods, and Processions Associated With Over 100 American Calendar Customs and Festivals. 2nd edition. Hennig Cohen, ed. Detroit: Gale, 1991.

Roughly in chronological order, this volume looks at the lore and legend associated with American holidays. Some of the holidays discussed are well known, like St. Valentines Day; others are more obscure, such as Buzzard Day, which happens the first Sunday after March 15 near Hinckley, Ohio, where a flock of redheaded turkey buzzards return annually to Hinckley Ridge.

The celebration includes a pancake breakfast and souvenir selling. Also from this publisher is *The Folklore of World Holidays* (1992).

Frew's Daily Archive: A Calendar of Commemorations. Andrew W. Frew. Jefferson, NC: McFarland, 1984.

Frew's is a month-by-month listing of commemorations worldwide for each day of the year. Some are major religious and sectarian holidays, some honor events of national or international importance.

Holidays and Festivals Index. Helene Henderson, ed. Detroit: Omnigraphics, 1995.

This index can be used to locate over three thousand holidays, festivals, fairs, rituals, celebrations, commemorations, holy days, and other observances worldwide by name, ethnicity, geographic location, religion, or date. Just a few details about each occasion is supplied, including location, date celebrated, year established, and who it was named for, but citations to further reading are provided. Another title from this publisher and editor is the *Holidays, Festivals, and Celebrations of the World Dictionary* (1997).

Holidays on the Web. Web pages that compile holiday listings usually do little more than that: list them. So if you want to find Web pages *describing* particular occasions, try searching for the name of the event on a search engine.

A general holiday site, naming national and religious holidays throughout the world is at http://www.holidayfestival.com, the *Worldwide Holiday and Festival Site.*

CHAPTER 10

Geographical Research

Weather, Maps, and Geographical Details

Weather Conditions and Forecasts

Basic day-to-day weather, warnings of hazardous weather, and the ever-popular five-day forecast are simple to find in local newspapers or their Web equivalent, on television news programs or their Web equivalent, and, for cable subscribers, on the Weather Channel, which is also on the Internet at http://www.weather.com.

Weather forecast phone numbers for major cities:

Albany, NY	(518)476-1111
Albuquerque, NM	(505)821-1111
Atlanta, GA	(770)821-6800
Birmingham, AL	(205)945-7000
Bismarck, ND	(701)223-3700
Boise, ID	(208)342-8303
Boston, MA	(617)567-4670
Buffalo, NY	(716)844-4444
Caribou, ME	(207)496-8931
Charleston, WV	(304)345-2121
Cheyenne, WY	(307)635-9901
Cincinnati, OH	(513)241-1010
Cleveland, OH	(216)931-1212
Columbia, SC	(803)822-1401
Denver, CO	(303)337-2500
Des Moines, IA	(515)288-1047
Detroit, MI	(313)941-7192
Elko, NV	(702)738-3018
El Paso, TX	(915)562-4040
Eugene, OR	(503)484-1200
Fort Worth, TX	(214)787-1111
Great Falls, MT	(406)453-5469

Indianapolis, IN	(317)635-5959
International Falls, MN	(218)283-4615
Jackson, MS	(601)936-2189
Jacksonville, FL	(904)757-3311
Little Rock, AR	(501)376-4400
Los Angeles, CA	(213)554-1212
Louisville, KY	(502)585-1212
Lubbock, TX	(806)745-1058
Memphis, TN	(901)757-6400
Miami, FL	(305)229-4522
Sullivan, WI	(414)744-8000
Minneapolis, MN	(612)375-0830
New Orleans, LA	(504)465-9212
New York City, NY	(516)924-0517
Oklahoma City, OK	(405)360-5928
Omaha, NE	(402)359-9955
Philadelphia, PA	(215)936-1212
Phoenix, AZ	(602)379-4000
Pittsburgh, PA	(412)935-1212
Portland, ME	(207)713-0352
Portland, OR	(503)236-7575
Raleigh, NC	(919)515-8225
Redding, CA	(916)221-5613
Reno, NV	(702)793-1300
Salt Lake City, UT	(801)575-7669
San Antonio, TX	(210)737-1400
San Francisco, CA	(415)936-1212
Savannah, GA	(912)964-1700
Seattle, WA	(206)526-6087
Sheridan, WY	(307)672-2345
Shreveport, LA	(318)635-7575
St. Louis, MO	(314)441-8467
Topeka, KS	(913)234-2592
Washington, DC	(202)936-1212
Wichita, KS	(316)942-3102

Major Internet locales supplying weather news, data, and forecasts include the

National Weather Service from the *National Oceanic and Atmospheric Administration (NOAA)*, at http://www.noaa.gov/, and the opening page of some search engines, including *Excite* at http://www.excite.com, *Lycos* at http://www.lycos .com, and *Yahoo!* at http://www.yahoo.com. Go to the *Old Farmer's Almanac* at http://www.almanac.com/ or in print format (Dublin, NH: Yankee Publishing, 1792–present) for weather mixed with recipes, proverbs, advice, tide tables, planting charts, historical tidbits, and sunrise and sunset information. As the *Almanac*'s eighteenth-century founder Robert B. Thomas said: "Our main endeavour is to be useful, but with a pleasant degree of humour."

A gateway page to weather links on the Web is *WeatherNet*, sponsored by the University of Michigan, at http://cirrus.sprl.umich.edu/wxnet/. It offers current weather conditions, forecasts, and warnings around the world; weather maps and software; and, as the page's creators say, "the list that made us famous," WeatherSites, pointing to almost three hundred Internet weather-related Web sites. Sample links on WeatherSites include *MarineWeather.Com* at http://www .marineweather.com, with such offerings as wave height maps and sea surface temperatures; International Weather Satellite Imagery, at http://www.fas.harvard .edu/~dbaron/sat/; numerous television weather center sites; and the *Hurricane Hunters Home Page* at http://www.hurricanehunters.com/, the page featuring a Department of Defense weather reconnaissance squadron that routinely flies into the eye of hurricanes.

Some noteworthy print compilations that describe weather conditions include:
The Times Books World Weather Guide: A City-by-City Guide for Forecasting the Weather in Any Part of the World at Any Time of the Year. E.A. Pearce. Updated edition. New York: Times Books, 1990.

The tables for each city in this guide list, for cities worldwide, the average daily temperature in both Fahrenheit and centigrade, the highest and lowest recorded monthly temperatures, the relative humidity, and average monthly precipitation.
The Weather Almanac: A Reference Guide to Weather, Climate, and Related Issues in the United States and Its Key Cities. 8th edition. Richard A. Wood. Detroit: Gale, 1998.

The Weather Almanac has statistical and descriptive information about weather phenomena, listings of high and low temperatures in international cities, and record highs and lows in the U.S. (it hit 134° in Greenland Ranch, California, in 1913). This guide also lists weather characteristics for U.S. cities, including normal temperature ranges, humidity, and precipitation, and mean number of days for different kinds of weather. (Did you know that Denver, Colorado, has more sunny days than Miami, Florida?)

Weather Research

Those interested in meteorological research or in search of weather experts should know about the National Oceanic and Atmospheric Administration (NOAA) and its related agencies. The National Climatic Data Center (NCDC), under the auspices of NOAA, is charged with keeping track of weather trends and anomalies. The NCDC maintains the world's largest active archive of climatic information. Though not always easy for the layperson to decipher, plenty of weather-related data is available on their Web site at http://www.ncdc.noaa.gov/, such as graphs depicting weather elements over specified time periods, including online historical climate data beginning in the 1800s.

A monthly NCDC publication found at most government depository libraries in hard copy and available to users in government depository libraries at the NCDC Web site is *Climatological Data*. These monthly reports, published since 1976, contain reports from weather observation stations in each state of the U.S., listing daily maximum and minimum temperatures and precipitation. Some stations also report daily snowfall, snow depth, evaporation, and soil temperature data. An annual summary for each state is also produced.

For help with understanding weather maps, see the book *Weather Maps: How to Read and Interpret All the Basic Weather Charts* (Kearney, MO: Chaston Scientific, 1995).

Finding Maps and Atlases
Finding maps in hard copy

When searching for maps using an online library catalog, combine the name of a place with the word ATLAS or MAPS. An example would be: ZAMBIA MAPS. If the library had no maps of Zambia, try a broader search, e.g., AFRICA MAPS or AFRICA ATLAS. Let's say the library also lets you down when you try the Africa search. Then you might try a search using WORLD MAPS or WORLD ATLAS.

Maps also show up in books that focus on such topics as the history of a nation or a narrative describing a journey. To be sure a book contains a map, look for the word *maps* listed as part of the books' description in a library catalog. For example, in the catalog record for the book *A Walk Across England* (New

Free Foldout Maps

I t's simple to acquire foldout maps for areas worldwide for little or no fee. For the U.S., just call one of the toll-free state offices of tourism numbers listed in chapter six under Travel Information to obtain maps.

Offices of tourism also exist for hundreds of nations worldwide, and I've obtained some marvelous maps from many of them by just writing and asking. Find addresses on the Web at the *International Tourism Research Links* page at http://webhome.idirect.com/~tourism/office.html or through links from government home pages at http://www.library.nwu.edu/govpub/resource/internat/foreign.html.

Contact information for international tourism offices are also listed in the *World Travel Guide* (Roanoke, VA: SF Communications. Annual).

York: Thames & Hudson), the description notes that the book has *chiefly col. ill.* (chiefly color illustrations) and *col. maps* (color maps).

Maps are also abundant in tour books. For ideas on locating travel materials, see chapter nine under the Using Travel Guides Fact in a Flash.

Finding maps online

Online maps and mapping systems, such as the TIGER maps described later in this chapter, allow views and perspectives of geographic areas that would be impossible in print resources. Sophisticated Geographic Information Systems (GIS) software allows the user to download raw data and display it spatially in a variety of ways. The in-depth workings of advanced digital mapping databases and GIS software are beyond the scope of this book, though many of the Web sites mentioned below lead the advanced researcher to points of interest.

Note that simpler map databases allowing manipulations such as zooming in and zooming out will generally be referred to as online or electronic maps, not GIS databases. The downfall of electronic maps? You often need a high quality printer, preferably color, to replicate a hard copy of what you're looking at on-screen, and you may find yourself taping several sheets together to get the whole map.

Notable map sites on the Internet include:

Color Landform Atlas of the United States. http://fermi.jhuapl.edu/states/states.html

A shaded-relief map shows, through different shading on the map, how an area looks when the sun is shining on it from a certain direction. This helps bring to the fore such land features as mountains, valleys, rivers, and lakes. This atlas displays gorgeous shaded-relief maps (see Wyoming!).

MapQuest. http://www.mapquest.com/

Geared to the traveler looking for destination points of interest, MapQuest has maps from around the block and around the world. If you need to know how get from here to there in your automobile, try MapQuest's TripQuest, which supplies detailed directions and an accompanying map. A similar database for navigating U.S. destinations is *Maps On Us* at http://www.mapsonus .com.

National Atlas of the United States. http://www-atlas.usgs.gov/

Still in progress at the time of this writing, this atlas from the USGS offers high quality, small-scale maps with the ability to add geospatial data, such as data on soil, boundaries, volcanoes, and aquifers, and geosocial data, such as crime, population distribution, and incidence of disease.

Perry-Castañeda Library (PCL) Map Collection. http://www.lib.utexas.edu/Libs /PCL/Map_collection/Map_collection.html

The Perry-Castañeda Library at the University of Texas–Austin has created a growing database of maps from around the world, scanned from their collection of over 230,000 print maps. The online collection at the time of this writing exceeded 2,400 maps. All the maps available were in part chosen because they're not copyrighted, which means that sometimes only older maps will be available at this site.

What Does Scale Mean?

A map's scale, expressed as a ratio or a fraction, shows the relationship between a distance on a map to the corresponding distance on the ground of the feature or place it represents. So, a scale of 1:100000, expressed in inches, means that one inch on the map equals 100,000 inches on the ground. So the bigger the number, the less detail you'll get on the map, i.e., one inch representing 10,000 inches will show a lot more detail than one inch representing 100,000 inches.

TIGER Mapping Service. http://tiger.census.gov/. Also available at many government depository libraries on CD-ROM.

At the TIGER Maps site you can generate detailed maps of anywhere in the U.S., going all the way to the street level, using data from the TIGER/Line files. The TIGER database was originally created to help the Bureau of the Census with its mapping needs related to the ten-year census and other surveys. TIGER stands for Topologically Integrated Geographic Encoding and Reference system.

United States Geological Survey (USGS) National Mapping Information. http://mapping.usgs.gov/

The USGS is the top producer of maps in the U.S. They produce topographic quadrangle maps; aerial maps; satellite maps; maps of counties, states, and national parks; outline maps of the world; and others. Full and partial government depository libraries will own all or some of these maps. USGS ordering information is on their Web page and detailed in this chapter under Buying Maps.

Some gateways leading to maps and map-related information on the Web include:

Mercator's World Links. http://www.mercatormag.com/links.html

Mercator's World, subtitled The Magazine of Maps, Exploration, and Discovery, supplies links of interest to cartography aficionados, genealogists, historians, and those just hoping to find a few good maps.

Odden's Bookmarks: The Fascinating World of Maps and Mapping. http://karto server.frw.ruu.nl/html/staff/oddens/oddens.html

Odden's is a meta site to all things cartographic, encompassing online map collections of many varieties, including maps of cities, countries, regions, weather, earthquake activity, population, political divisions, geological formations, topography, and astronomical entities. Also find links on this page to geography departments worldwide, cartography journals, map sellers, and libraries.

Yahoo! Maps. http://dir.yahoo.com/science/geography/cartography/maps/

This Yahoo! category offers a listing of all kinds of maps on the Internet, for all regions.

You'll also have some success, depending on the geographic location you're interested in, in finding useful maps on the Web by just using a search engine and the term MAP or MAPS, combined with a location. For example, a search using the words KIEV MAP in *Dogpile* at http://www.dogpile.com produced a number of possibilities, including *Maps of Ukraine* at http://www.ukraine.org /maps.html.

Finding maps on CD-ROM

Maps on CD-ROM are affordable, full of bells and whistles, and relatively simple to use. Sample titles include *National Geographic Maps*, an archive of every foldout map ever published by *National Geographic Magazine*, selling for around sixty dollars at the time of this writing, and Rand McNally's *StreetFinder Deluxe*, at around forty-nine dollars. *StreetFinder Deluxe* pinpoints addresses, hotels, and restaurants on detailed street maps.

Thematic Maps and Atlases

There are special maps dedicated to showing the distribution or features of any number of tangible and intangible concepts. You probably remember atlases from when you were in third grade with a title like "Farm Products of America" showing Kansas veritably overrun with teeny icons of hay bales.

Representative categories of thematic maps and atlases:

Historic maps and atlases

There are maps that show cities, travel routes, borders, and the like, as they existed in past time periods or during historic events, worldwide. Some examples include *A Battlefield Atlas of the Civil War* (Baltimore: Nautical and Aviation Publishing Company of America, 1993), the *Atlas of Russian History* (New York: Oxford University Press, 1993), and the *Atlas of the Crusades* (New York: Facts on File, 1990).

A well-known collection of historic maps have an unlikely name—fire insurance maps. These maps were created by the Sanborn Company in the 1800s and early 1900s for areas all over the U.S. and are referred to as Sanborn Fire Insurance Maps. Though intended to show the fire hazard potential of specific buildings, these detailed and frequently updated maps list the use of every building in a town, along with its height, construction material, and location of lot lines, all of interest to historians and other researchers. The Library of Congress owns an extensive Sanborn map collection. They can also be found in selected libraries throughout the U.S.

To search for maps of different eras in a library catalog or on the Internet, combine the word MAPS or ATLAS and HISTORY or a particular time period with the name of a country, continent, or time period, for example: GERMANY HISTORY ATLAS, GERMANY MEDIEVAL MAPS, or EUROPE HISTORY MAPS.

Web sites that offer historic maps or pointers to them include *Cartographic*

Images at http://www.iag.net/%7Ejsiebold/carto.html, the *Map Collections: 1597–1988*, at http://memory.loc.gov/ammem/gmdhtml/gmdhome.html, and *Historic Maps of the United States* at http://www.lib.utexas.edu/Libs/PCL/Map_collection/histus.html.

Topographic maps

Topographic maps depict the surface features of an area along with its man-made features. Topographic maps use contour lines to depict elevation (height above sea level). The closer together the contour lines, the steeper the slope. Such maps are useful when planning a site for a new structure. Also, if you're holding a topographic map for the area you're hiking in, you'll be able to avoid the turn that will take you off a steep cliff.

The USGS produces 1:24,000–scale topographic quadrangle maps that are distributed to government depository libraries. Partial government depositories may choose to own them all or, more likely, will own those of local interest. Some topographical maps are free on the Web. Check the list of links to them at http://mcmcweb.er.usgs.gov/drg/avail.html#online.

Topographical maps are available commercially on CD-ROM via *Topo! Interactive Maps on CD-ROM* from Wildflower productions. See their home page at http://www.topo.com or call them at (415)558-8700 for prices. *TopoGuides* are also available through the Hanta Yo Company, (301)947-9319, or at http://www.topoguide.com/.

Aerial photographs, bird's-eye views, and space shots

The earth has been photographed from the sky and from space. Though some of these views feature vast expanses, others focus on surprisingly small areas. Some words to use in library catalogs when looking for maps photographed from above include AERIAL PHOTOGRAPHY, PHOTOGRAPHIC SURVEYING, PHOTOGRAMMETRY (the process of making maps or scale drawings from photographs, especially aerial photographs), or REMOTE SENSING (referring to the collection of data using instruments aboard aircraft or satellites such as the *Landsat* satellites.)

Online and print locations of satellite and aerial maps include:
The Cartographic Satellite Atlas of the World. WorldSat International. Los Angeles: Warwick Publishing, 1997.

This book is filled with color maps created from satellite transmissions.
National Aeronautics and Space Administration (NASA). http://www.nasa.gov/

From the NASA site, link to images from the Hubble telescope, space shuttle missions, weather satellites, and more in NASA's Multimedia Gallery. You can go directly to the *Hubble* page at http://oposite.stsci.edu/.

Universe Sites From the Alexandria Digital Library. http://www.alexandria.ucsb .edu/other-sites/

This meta page points to aerial and astronomical maps and mapping sites. If you feel a growing interest in cartography, take a look at the books *Map Use: Reading, Analysis, and Interpretation* (Madison, WI: JP Publications, 1992) or *Elements of Cartography* (6th edition. New York: John Wiley and Sons, 1995) to learn more.

Brushing Up on Geography

Map librarian Christopher J. J. Thiry at the Colorado School of Mines recommends keeping an atlas by the television to improve your knowledge of geography. "Then when the local news says there's a small town in Alabama that's been flooded, grab the atlas and see where that town is." An inexpensive world atlas recommended by Mr. Thiry is *Goode's World Atlas*, around twenty dollars in paperback and forty dollars in hardcover.

Gazetteers

Gazetteers are geographical dictionaries that describe physical or culturally established places. For organized, populated land areas with defined boundaries such as towns, cities, and provinces, gazetteers provide such data as latitude, longitude, population, square mileage, perhaps some information about the areas founding or creation, and notable geographic formations within its borders. For natural formations such as mountains, lakes, and oceans, descriptions include elements such as height, depth, and the like.

Sample gazetteers:

Columbia Gazetteer of the World. 3 Volumes. Saul B. Cohen, ed. New York: Columbia University Press, 1998.

The *Columbia Gazetteer* includes in its coverage: countries, provinces, regions, states, districts, capitals, cities, towns, villages, neighborhoods, special districts, continents, oceans, seas, gulfs, lakes, lagoons, rivers bays, channels, streams, islands, archipelagos, peninsulas, atolls, mountains, mountain ranges, canyons, deserts, valleys, glaciers, volcanoes, national parks, reserves and monuments, historic and archaeological sites, resorts, airports, ports, dams, nuclear plants, mines, canals, shopping malls, theme parks, stadia, military bases, fortified lines, and mythic places.

Geographic Names Information System (GNIS). http://mapping.usgs.gov/www /gnis/. Also available on CD-ROM.

GNIS is the official repository of U.S. geographic names information, with data for about two million physical and cultural geographic features. Information about each feature may include elevation, population, state and county of location, latitude and longitude, and other names by which the feature is known. For international geographic names information, go to *GEOnet Names Server* at http://www.nima.mil/ under the Maps and Geodata heading.

Omni Gazetteer of the United States of America: A Guide to 1,500,000 Place Names in the United States and Territories. 11 Volumes. Frank R. Abate, ed. Detroit: Omnigraphics, 1991.

This is a lengthy compilation of U.S. populated places, structures, facilities, locales, historic places, and geographic features.

Buying Maps
Government suppliers

The following agencies distribute maps to government depository libraries, so you can check for what you're interested in there. Maps can also be purchased through the GPO online or at their bookstores. See details in chapter three under Government Bookstores.

CIA Maps and Publications. http://www.odci.gov/cia/publications/mapspub/index .html

This site offers worldwide maps for sale from the CIA. CIA maps are also distributed to government depository libraries.

National Ocean Service, NOS Distribution Branch N/CG33, 6501 Lafayette Ave., Riverdale, MD 20737-1199, Phone: (800)638-8972 or (301)436-6990, URL: http://chartmaker.ncd.noaa.gov

NOS sells nautical, aeronautical, hydrographic charts and publications, and Flight Information Publication (FLIP) products from the National Imagery and Mapping Agency (NIMA), as well as nautical charts of coastal waterways of the continental U.S., Hawaii, Alaska, and the U.S. territories.

United States Geologic Survey, USGS Map Sales, Box 25286, Federal Center, Building 810, Denver, CO 80225, Phone: (800)USA MAPS, URL: http:// www.usgs.gov/

From the USGS Web page, choose "Products—Locating" to identify maps and mapping products, and choose "Products—Ordering" for information on how and where to buy the items.

Commercial map publishers and sellers

You can obtain maps at bookstores, travel stores and agencies, and stores specializing in maps. Look under Maps in the yellow pages. Others:

Delorme, Two DeLorme Dr., P.O. Box 298, Yarmouth, ME 04096, Phone: (800)452-5931 or (207)846-7000, Fax: (800)575-2244, URL: http://www.delorme.com/

Galaxy of Maps and Books, 5975 N. Federal Highway, Ft. Lauderdale, FL 33308, Phone: (800)388-6588, Fax: (954)267-9007, E-mail: galaxymaps@aol.com, URL: http://www.galaxymaps.com/

Maplink. 30 S. La Patera Lane, Unit #5, Santa Barbara, CA 93117, Phone: (800)962-1394, URL: http://www.maplink.com/index.html

National Geographic Store. National Geographic Society Online Store, P.O. Box 11303, Des Moines, IA 50340, Phone: (800)437-5521, TDD: (888)822-8207, Fax: (515)362-3345, URL: https://www.ngstore.com/ngstore/ngsstore.htm

Omni Resources, 1004 S. Mebane St., P.O. Box 2096, Burlington, NC 27216-2096, Phone: (800)742-2677, URL: http://www.omnimap.com

CHAPTER II

United States Legal Research

Finding the Law

"It may be true that the law cannot make a man love me, but it can keep him from lynching me, and I think that's pretty important."

—Martin Luther King, Jr.

An impressive and ever-growing amount of full-text law materials are free on the Internet at sites such as *THOMAS* at http://thomas.loc.gov. However, there are value-added elements that information providers like West Group and LEXIS-NEXIS supply that are desirable—but far from free.

The law, like other timely information that changes frequently, is well suited to online access. Print editions of all materials are listed in this chapter, but I would look for their severe reduction (definitely) and demise (probably) in a future not too far.

Some recommended meta gateways to law-related materials on the Web include:

- *FindLaw.* http://www.findlaw.com/
- *Internet Legal Resources Guide.* http://www.ilrg.com/
- *Emory Law Library: Electronic Reference Desk.* http://www.law.emory.edu /LAW/refdesk/toc.html
- *WWW Virtual Library: Law.* http://www.law.indiana.edu/law/v-lib/law index.html
- *Congressional Mega Sites.* http://lcweb.loc.gov/global/legislative/mega.html

As I define and describe specific legal publications in this chapter, I'll list the databases that contain them and the indexes that index them. Overall descriptions of these databases and indexes are then provided toward the end of the chapter under the heading Law Indexes and Databases.

When looking at the implications of a specific law or regulation, there are three ways to gather information:

- Look at the law, case, or regulation, itself.
- Examine elements that went into the creation of a law, including the original bill, congressional hearings and other official discussions that contributed to the evolution of the bill, and articles and commentary on the pending legislation.
- Find articles, related cases, and analysis after the legislation is in effect.

Before talking about where legislation can be found, let me review some of the language unique to law research.

Legal Lingo
Statutory law, administrative law, bills and resolutions, and case law

There are three major kinds of law in the U.S. **Statutory law** refers to laws enacted by bodies legally authorized to pass laws, including the U.S. Congress, state legislatures, counties, and municipalities. The precepts in the U.S. Constitution are also statutory law.

The by-products of statutory law are rules or regulations. Once laws are passed and official policies established, federal, state, and municipal agencies, such as the Federal Communications Commission or the Food and Drug Administration, are authorized to create the rules needed to support the law. These rules and regulations (one is a synonym for the other) have the force of law and are known as **administrative law**. They don't require congressional approval.

Other types of administrative law include presidential proclamations and executive orders. Executive orders are presidential mandates, usually issued to government officials. An example of an executive order from Ronald Reagan was Executive Order No. 12546, from 1986, which established a commission of "distinguished Americans" to investigate the space shuttle *Challenger* accident.

Presidential proclamations are usually associated with ceremonial matters. For example, President Clinton, in Proclamation 7145 of October 29, 1998, made comments about his administration's role in helping adopted children find safe and permanent homes and declared November of 1998 to be National Adoption Month. Obviously, this type of proclamation is meant to bring attention to the needs of adoptees—we don't all really have to formally recognize National Adoption Month. Some proclamations, though, have had far-reaching implications, such as Lincoln's Emancipation Proclamation, which officially ended slavery in the U.S.

A new law or a proposal for an amendment to an existing law is first introduced as a **bill**. It's interesting to look at historic bills to see which ones failed or to see how substantially they may have changed before becoming law. Current bills are of interest when investigating what might become law and affect our lives.

Resolutions are not essentially different than bills, but resolutions deal with such special circumstances as calling for sanctions, correcting errors in already enacted legislation, and requesting funding to keep agencies afloat in the interim period between an expiring and new budget.

Laws also come from the courtroom and are called **case law**, also known as common law or judge-made law. These are concepts and rules of action established by judges in their written opinion of a case, where they apply law to the facts of a case, explaining how the court's decision was reached. Court cases are won or lost based on different points of law. Any case may present an opinion and decision that differs from previous decisions on the same point of law or be a totally new point. This is then a precedent-setting case, one which the lower courts in the same jurisdiction will then follow. It's law. Also, many of the agencies that create rules and regulations, such as the Internal Revenue Service, may also decide cases. These administrative law hearings can spawn changes or additions to federal rules and regulations.

Legal **citations** are the shorthand abbreviations used to refer to the resource where a law or law-related document was found. There's a detailed explanation of citations later in this chapter, placed at the end since I think citations are easier to understand once you become familiar with the resources they refer to. I mention the concept now since you'll see that I mention, in brackets, next to many titles below, the way something is cited. For example, I list the *United States Code* as [cited as *U.S.C.*]

There are official and unofficial versions of laws. The official versions are the cases or statutes that are required, by law, to be published so the general public will have access to them. Official federal laws are published by the U.S. Government Printing Office (GPO), discussed in chapter three. The unofficial versions are published by private publishing companies, such as West Group, and contain the same text as the official versions, but generally have these advantages: a speedier publication process and annotations discussing the law's background, relationship to other laws, and additional information related to the law.

There are public laws and private laws. Public laws apply to and affect the general public, and they refer to the vast majority of the laws passed. Private laws affect particular people. For example, Private Law 103-8 directed that $400,577 in compensation be paid to an individual who, without his knowledge, was given LSD during his time in the Army.

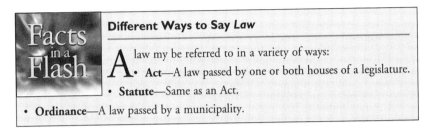

Different Ways to Say Law

A law my be referred to in a variety of ways:
- **Act**—A law passed by one or both houses of a legislature.
- **Statute**—Same as an Act.
- **Ordinance**—A law passed by a municipality.

Dictionaries and thesauri

When looking into law issues or, for fiction writers, when putting legalese in the mouth of the lawyer in your novel, I can almost guarantee there will be times when you need a law dictionary. Law is filled with jargon and abbreviations. The best-known law dictionary is *Black's Law Dictionary* (Centennial edition. St. Paul, MN: West, 1990). American and British legal terminology is covered in *Black's*, from both contemporary and ancient times. The definitions often cite authoritative cases related to the definition. Sometimes, as a layperson, I have difficulty interpreting *Black's* definitions. In those cases, I look at law dictionaries that simplify the law more.

To locate other law dictionaries, do a search on a library catalog using the phrase LAW DICTIONARIES. Legal dictionaries on the Web include *Duhaime's Law Dictionary* at http://www.wwlia.org/diction.htm, and *Shark Talk: Everybody's Law Dictionary* at http://www.nolo.com/dictionary/wordindex.cfm.

Legal encyclopedias

When I look up a famous case or a legal concept and need more than a quick definition, I turn first to a law encyclopedia geared to the layperson, such as:

West's Encyclopedia of American Law. Update of *The Guide to American Law: Everyone's Legal Encyclopedia.* 12 Volumes. St. Paul, MN: West, 1997.

The premiere layperson's law encyclopedia, *West's Encyclopedia of American Law* contains articles on most aspects of U.S. law, including overviews of major cases. Additional readings and cases are often cited.

Nolo's Legal Encyclopedia. http://www.nolo.com/briefs.html

Written for the layperson, this online encyclopedia begins with basic overviews of legal matters which then lead to more comprehensive sections through progressive links.

There are two standard law encyclopedias geared to those in the legal profession:

American Jurisprudence, 2nd: A Modern Comprehensive Text Statement of American Law—State and Federal. 82 Volumes. San Francisco: Bancroft-Whitney, 1962–present.

Updated with pocket parts and revised and expanded volumes. Also available on CD-ROM. [Cited as *AmJur2d*].

Corpus Juris Secundum: A Complete Restatement of the Entire American Law As Developed by All Reported Cases. 102 Volumes. St. Paul, MN: West, 1936–present.

Updated with pocket parts, revised volumes, and additional volumes. [Cited as *C.J.S.*]

For an overview on the Internet of the U.S. legislative process, see *How Our Laws Are Made* at http://thomas.loc.gov/home/lawsmade.toc.html and/or *Enactment of a Law* at http://thomas.loc.gov/home/enactment/enactlawtoc.html.

Other helpful, representative, law-related encyclopedias and reference materials include:

Congressional Quarterly Almanac. Washington, DC: Congressional Quarterly. Annual. Also find information about subscribing to Web versions of Congressional Quarterly publications at http://www.cq.com.

The *CQ Almanac* explains, in layperson's language, the background, progress, controversies, and provisions of major laws, and it supplies commentary on national political races. Information in the *CQ Almanac* is culled from other Congressional Quarterly publications, including: the *CQ Weekly*, which supplies news and weekly analysis of Congress and legislation, including a listing of who voted for what bill; the *CQ Daily Monitor*, a daily report on Congress and current and future activities of congressional committees; and the *House Action Reports*, which supplies timely coverage regarding legislation on the floor of the House of Representatives.

Congressional Quarterly's Guide to the U.S. Supreme Court. 3rd edition. 2 Volumes. Joan Biskupic, ed. Washington, DC: Congressional Quarterly, 1997.

This set looks at the origins and development of the Supreme Court, its members, how it works, and its influence on the populace.

Encyclopedia of the American Legal System. 2 Volumes. Joel H. Silbey. New York: Charles Scribner's Sons, 1994.

This encyclopedia examines, as it says in its subtitle, the "principal structures, processes, and policies of Congress and the state legislatures since the colonial era."

Encyclopedia of the United States Congress. 4 Volumes. Donald C. Bacon, ed. New York: Simon & Schuster, 1995.

This encyclopedia embraces such topics as campaign spending, the electoral college, and violence in Congress. Significant political figures are also profiled.

The Supreme Court Yearbook. Kenneth Jost, ed. Washington, DC: Congressional Quarterly. Annual.

All cases for the year's term are summarized in this annual volume, with excerpts from major cases and biographies of the justices supplied. Each volume also previews the upcoming term and highlights some cases in the Court's docket.

More Than a Century of Sessions

Each term of Congress runs for two years, with each Congress numbered sequentially. Generally, each newly elected Congress has two sessions, the periods of time during which Congress is scheduled to meet and handle business. The first Congress convened in 1789. Most law-related material will contain mention of the specific Congress that produced the material. For example, a hearing in the Senate cited as S. Hrg. 105-1, refers to the first hearing of the 105th Congress.

Finding the Documents and Testimonies That Lead to Laws
Finding federal bills and resolutions

Bills and resolutions, the precursors to laws and amendments, are numbered sequentially, so the three hundredth bill introduced by the Senate during a congressional session would be designated *S. 300,* and the two thousandth bill introduced by the House would be *H.R. 2000.* Published resolutions begin with *H. Res.* or *S. Res.*

The full text of federal bills and resolutions from 1989 to the present can be searched by word or bill number on *THOMAS* at http://thomas.loc.gov, with bill summaries and the legislative histories (the steps taken before the bill is vetoed or becomes law) available back to 1973. Full-text bills from 1993 to the present, updated daily, are also on *GPO Access* at http://www.access.gpo.gov/, with one-sentence summaries available back to 1983.

For those with Telnet capabilities but no Web access, try *LOCIS* at telnet://locis.loc.gov/, where you can find bill and resolution summaries from 1973 to the present. (But if you have Web access, use THOMAS, which is also free, also goes back to 1973, and is simpler to use.) You can also telnet to GPO Access through pac.coalliance.org; choose "Library Catalogs" and then "Government Publications."

Online full-text bills and bill tracking are also offered by several subscription databases, including *Congressional Universe, CQ.com On Congress, CQ's Washington Alert, ELSS, LEGI-SLATE,* LEXIS-NEXIS and Westlaw, all described in more detail under Law Indexes and Databases. The Congressional Information Service (CIS) also sells microfiche collections of the full text of all versions of House and Senate bills and resolutions.

House and Senate bills and resolutions are also available on microfiche in government depository libraries. The *Finding Aid for Congressional Bills and Resolutions* (Washington, DC: GPO), updated weekly and searchable by bill or resolution number, points users looking for a particular bill or resolution to the proper government microfiche. A finding aid is necessary because bills and resolutions are filmed as they are received—and that's not necessarily in any particular order! *The Finding Aid* won't be useful if you're seeking bills by subject.

Print indexes that help researchers find specific bills and resolution numbers, bill status, and bill history by subject include the *Congressional Index* and the *CIS Index,* both found in most larger libraries; and the *House Calendar,* the index to the *Congressional Record,* and the *Digest of Public General Bills and Resolutions,* also known as the *CRS Bill Digest,* (published from 1943–1990), all found in federal depository libraries.

Finding state bills

Each state has its own method of making bills in print format available. Find out more by calling the state's library or information office, listed in chapter three under State Home Pages and Phone Numbers.

To find information on a specific bill in state legislature and, in many cases, receive a free copy, contact one of these offices:

Alabama   Senate Bill Status, 11 S. Union, Room 716, New State House, Montgomery, AL 36130-4600, Phone: (334)242-7826.

State Legislature Home Pages

Almost all state home pages (listed in chapter three) now lead directly to the text of current state bills or to the home page of the state legislature which lists the bills. The National Conference of State Legislators supplies links to all state legislature pages on the Web at http://www.ncsl.org/public/sitesleg.htm.

Common elements that appear on the home pages of most state legislatures include:

- Current bills and where they are in the legislative process
- State statutes
- Names of legislators and information about them
- Descriptions and contact information for state agencies and departments
- Summaries or transcripts of recent legislative sessions
- Listings and descriptions of legislative committees
- A guide to unique aspects of that state legislative process, including the state constitution
- A schedule of recent and upcoming legislative activites
- Updates on new and noteworthy actions and events

	House Bill Status, 11 S. Union, Room 512, New State House, Montgomery, AL 36130-4600, Phone: (334)242-7627.
Alaska	Legislative Information, 130 Seward St., Suite 313, Juneau, AK 99801-2197, Phone: (907)465-4648.
Arizona	House of Representatives Information Desk, State House, 1700 W. Washington St., Phoenix, AZ 85007, Phone: (602)542-4221.
	Senate Information Desk, State House, 1700 W. Washington St., Phoenix, AZ 85007, Phone: (602)542-3559.
Arkansas	Office of Legislative Counsel, State Capitol Building, Room 315, Little Rock, AR 72201, Phone: (501)682-1937.
California	Office of the Chief Clerk, State Assembly, State Capitol, Room 3196, Sacramento, CA 95814, Phone: (916)445-3614.
	Secretary of the Senate, State Capitol, Room 3044, Sacramento, CA 95814, Phone: (916)445-4251.

Colorado	Legislative Information Center, 200 E. Fourteenth St., Room 022, Denver, CO 80203, Phone: (303)866-3055.
Connecticut	Bill Information Room, Law and Legislative Reference Department, State Library, 231 Capitol Ave., Hartford, CT 06106, Phone: (203)566-5736.
Delaware	Division of Research, Legislative Counsel, Legislative Hall, Dover, DE 19901, Phone: (302)739-4114 or (800)282-8545.
Florida	Legislative Information Division, 111 W. Madison St., Room 704, Tallahassee, FL 32399-1400, Phone: (904)488-4371 or (800)342-1827.
Georgia	Clerk of the House, 309 State Capitol, Atlanta, GA 30334, Phone: (404)656-5015.
	Secretary of the Senate, State Capitol, Room 353, Atlanta, GA 30334, Phone: (404)656-5040.
Hawaii	Clerk of the House, State Capitol of Hawaii, Honolulu, HI 96813, Phone: (808)586-6400.
Idaho	Legislative Services Research and Information, 700 W. Jefferson, Lower Level East, P.O. Box 83720, Boise, ID 83720-0054, Phone: (208)334-2475.
Illinois	Clerk of the House, State Capitol Building, Room 424, Springfield, IL 62706, Phone: (217)782-6010 or (800)252-6300.
Indiana	Legislative Information, Legislative Services Agency, 302 State House, Indianapolis, IN 46204, Phone: (317)232-9856.
Iowa	Legislative Information Office, State Capitol Room 16, Des Moines, IA 50319, Phone: (515)281-5129.
Kansas	Legislative Reference, State Library, State Capitol, Third Floor, 343-N, Topeka, KS 66612, Phone: (913)296-2149 or (800)432-3924.
Kentucky	Bill Status, State Capitol Annex, Room T-3, Frankfort, KY 40601, Phone: (502)564-8100 or (800)776-9158.
Louisiana	Legislative Research Library, House of Representatives, P.O. Box 94012, Baton Rouge, LA 70804-9012, Senate Docket: (504)342-2365, House Docket: (504)342-6458. Phone, during legislative session, in-state: (800)256-3793

	or out-of-state: (504)342-2456; Phone, when legislature is out of session: (504)342-4914.
Maine	Legislative Information Office, State House Station 100, Room 314, Augusta, ME 04333, Phone: (207)287-1692.
Maryland	Legislative Information Desk, Department of Legislative Reference, 90 State Circle, Annapolis MD 21401, Phone: (410)841-3886 or (800)492-7122.
Massachusetts	Citizen Information Service, 1 Ashburton Place, Sixteenth Floor, Boston, MA 02108, Phone: (617)727-7030.
Michigan	Clerk of the House, State Capitol, Lansing, MI 48909, Phone: (517)373-0135.
	Secretary of the Senate, P.O. Box 30036, Lansing MI 48909, Phone: (517)373-2400.
Minnesota	House Index Office, State Capitol Building, Room 211, St. Paul, MN 55155, Phone: (612)296-6646.
	Senate Index Office, State Capitol Building, Room 231, St. Paul, MN 55155, Phone: (612)296-2887.
Mississippi	House Docket Room, P.O. Box 1018, New Capitol Room 305, Jackson, MS 39215, Phone: (601)359-3358.
	Senate Docket Room, P.O. Box 1018, New Capitol Room 308, Jackson, MS 39215, Phone: (601)359-3229.
Missouri	House Information Bill Status, State Capitol, Room 307B, Jefferson City, MO 65101, Phone: (314)751-3659.
	Senate Research, State Capitol, Room B-9, Jefferson, MO 65101, Phone: (314)751-4666.
Montana	Legislative Counsel, State Capitol, Room 138, Helena, MT 59620, Phone: (406)444-3064.
Nebraska	Hotline, Office of the Clerk, State Capitol, Room 2018, Lincoln, NE 68509, Phone: (402)471-2709 or (800)742-7456.
Nevada	Chief Clerk of the Assembly, Legislative Building, 401 S. Carson St., Carson City, NV 89710, Phone: (702)687-5739.
New Hampshire	State Library Reference and Information Services, 20 Park St., Concord, NH 03301, Phone: (603)271-2239.
New Jersey	Office of Legislative Services—Bill Room, Executive Statehouse, Room #6, Statehouse CN 068, Trenton, NJ 08625, Phone: (609)292-6395 or (800)792-8630.

New Mexico	Legislative Counsel, State Capitol, Room 311, Santa Fe, NM 87503, Phone: (505)986-4600.
New York	Public Information Office, Room 202, LOB Second Floor, Empire State Plaza, NY 12248, Phone: (518)455-4218.
North Carolina	State Legislative Building, Legislative Library, Raleigh, NC 27601, Phone: (919)733-7779.
North Dakota	Legislative Counsel Library, State Capitol, 2nd Floor, Bismarck, ND 58505, Phone: (701)328-2916.
Ohio	Legislative Information, State House, Columbus, OH 43266-0604, Phone: (614)466-8842 or (800)282-0253.
Oklahoma	Chief Clerk, House of Representatives, State Capitol Bldg., Oklahoma City, OK 73105, Phone: (405)521-2711 or (800)522-8502.
Oregon	Legislative Library, State Capitol, S-347, Salem, OR 97310, Phone: (503)378-8871 or (800)332-2313.
Pennsylvania	Legislative Reference Bureau, History Room, Main Capitol Building, Room 648, Harrisburg, PA 17120-0033, Phone: (717)787-2342.
Rhode Island	Legislative Information Line, State House, Room #2, Providence, RI 02903, Phone: (401)751-8833 or (800)547-8880.
South Carolina	Legislative Information Systems, Room 112, Blatt Building, 1105 Pendleton St., Columbia, SC 29201, Phone: (803)734-2923 or (800)922-1539.
South Dakota	Public Information Clerk, Legislative Research Counsel, State Capitol Building, 500 E. Capitol, Pierre, SD 57501, Phone: (605)773-4498 or (605)773-4296.
Tennessee	Office of Legislative Services, Room G-20, War Memorial Building, Nashville, TN 37243, Phone: (615)741-3511.
Texas	Legislative Reference Library, P.O. Box 12488, Capitol Station, Austin, TX 78711, Phone: (512)463-1252.
Utah	Legislative Research and General Counsel, 436 State Capitol, Salt Lake City, UT 84114, Phone: (801)538-1032.
Vermont	Vermont Legislative Counsel, 115 State St., Montpelier, VT 05633-5301, Phone: (808)828-2231.
Virginia	Legislative Information, House of Delegates, P.O. Box 406, Richmond, VA 23218, Phone: (804)786-6530.
Washington	House Workroom, Legislative Building, Third Floor, Capi-

tol Campus, P.O. Box 40600, Olympia, WA 98504,
Phone: (360)786-7780 or (800)562-6000.
Senate Workroom, Legislative Building, AS32, Third
Floor, Capitol Campus, P.O. Box 40482, Olympia, WA
98504-0482, Phone: (360)786-7592 or (800)562-6000.

West Virginia   Clerk of the House, House of Delegates, 1900 Kanawha
                     Blvd. E., Building 1, Room M212, Charleston, WV 25305-
                     0470, Phone: (304)340-3200.

Wisconsin   Legislative Reference Bureau, 100 N. Hamilton St., P.O.
                     Box 2037, Madison, WI 53701-2037, Phone: (608)266-
                     0341 or (800)362-9472.

Wyoming   Legislative Service Office, State Capitol Building, Room
                     213, Cheyenne, WY 82002, Phone: (307)777-7881 or
                     (800)342-9570.
                     Senate Information Clerk or House Information Clerk,
                     State Capitol Building, Cheyenne, WY 82002, Phone:
                     (307)777-6185.

But the bill is only the beginning. Just as editors tinker with a writer's perfect and beautiful prose, congressional representatives tinker with lovely and eloquent bills. Proposed legislation goes through many permutations and leaves a useful paper trail. First, a bill is sent to a congressional committee for consideration.

Committee prints

To learn about elements in a bill they are considering, congressional committees may request research reports from the Congressional Research Service of the Library of Congress or from the committee's support staff. These reports are called committee prints, and they help policy makers understand the diverse ideas, situations, concepts, and processes that arise in proposed legislation and policy.

These varied report subjects are also of interest to the researcher on the street. Some sample titles include *Toll Roads: A Review of Recent Experience*, prepared for the Senate Committee on Environment and Public Works, and *Reducing Marriage Taxes: Issues and Proposals*, prepared for the Joint Economic Committee.

Committee prints have been government depository items since the mid-1970s, so you'll find them in your local federal depository library. They're also full text in the subscription database Congressional Universe from 1995–present.

Committee prints are indexed in the *CIS Index to Publications of the United*

States Congress (Bethesda, MD: CIS), the *Monthly Catalog to Government Publications*, and the GPO's *Sales Product Catalog* at http://www.access.gpo.gov/su _docs/sale/prf/prf.html, which includes those prints that are for sale. These indexes supply the SuDoc number needed to locate the prints, or, in the case of GPO's *Sales Product Catalog*, both the SuDoc number and information about purchasing the print. (And a reminder from chapter three: The Superintendent of Documents Classification system is used to catalog government publications, and the SuDoc number is what you use to locate the publication in your local government depository library.)

Older committee prints, from the 1830s through 1969, can be located through the *CIS U.S. Congressional Committee Prints Index* (Bethesda, MD: CIS), available in print or on CD-ROM as part of the *CIS Congressional Masterfile 1* index. The index has an accompanying set of the full-text prints—more than fifteen thousand of them—on microfiche (though some libraries may subscribe to the index but not own the microfiche collection). This index also contains a Jurisdictional Histories section, which explains the histories and charges of the subcommittees and committees that generated the committee prints.

Hearings

Hearings are a wonderful source of expert testimony, unique source material, and, in some cases, drama. As committees evaluate bills, they invite all types of experts to add to their understanding of the proposed legislation. The experts might be industry leaders, professors, government agency representatives, or just the man or woman next door with special knowledge of the situation. For example, a memorable testimony was that of the late songwriter, musician, and singer Frank Zappa testifying against music censorship, and Tipper Gore, representing the Parent's Music Resource Center (PMRC), testifying on the need for labeling music with lyrics deemed objectionable (the SuDoc number for that hearing is Y4.C73/7:S. hrg. 99-529).

The text of hearings also includes debate among committee members and items submitted to the committee for consideration, including statistical data, journal articles, and written testimony. There are a number of options for finding hearing testimony and discussion. Hearings are available in paper or on microfiche at government depository libraries. Selected current hearings can be found on the Web through *THOMAS* at http://thomas.loc.gov/, and there's a meta page to free hearings at http://www.lib.umich.edu/libhome/Documents.center/hearings.html.

Commercial databases that offer coverage of hearings include *Congressional*

Universe, CQ.com On Congress, LEGI-SLATE, and LEXIS-NEXIS. Hearing transcripts can also be purchased through the Federal News Service by calling (800) 211-4020. When it's noted that a **testimony** of a hearing is available, that includes a transcription of statements from witnesses and the question and answer session, but not reproductions of exhibits and materials produced at the hearing.

Hearings are also indexed in the *CIS Index to Publications of the United States Congress,* the *Monthly Catalog of Government Publications,* and the GPO's *Sales Product Catalog,* though the latter two don't allow for searching by those who have testified. Older hearings from the early nineteenth century through 1969 are indexed in the forty-two-volume *CIS U.S. Congressional Committee Hearings Index* (Bethesda, MD: CIS), which is also available on the *Congressional Masterfile 1* CD-ROM. The full text of these historic hearings have also been placed on microfiche by CIS.

CIS also publishes two indexes to previously unpublished hearings with a corresponding microfiche collection of full-text hearings. This collection includes hearings that had been sitting quietly in the National Archives, never before published, before standards for what had to be published had been established. The indexes are the *CIS Index to Unpublished U.S. Senate Committee Hearings* and *CIS Index to Unpublished U.S. House of Representatives Committee Hearings.*

Three Kinds of Hearings

Hearings come in three stripes:
- **Legislative hearings** consider bills and resolutions.
- **Oversight hearings** review the effectiveness of existing laws and their related policies and agencies.
- **Investigative hearings** examine events deemed important to Congress and U.S. citizens, such as Kenneth Starr's investigation of President Clinton.

Congressional reports

House and Senate committee reports are issued by committees after hearings. They detail the committee's recommendations and findings, including estimated costs of proposed programs, and thus act as a good summary of the committee's actions in regard to a bill.

House and Senate bills often emerge with notable differences for the same bill. (What a surprise, eh?) In that case, representatives from both House and

Senate serve on **conference committees** to smooth out the differences, which are explained in a conference report.

House and Senate reports, including conference reports, are numbered sequentially and identified by the Congress they are being reported in, so *H.Rept. 105-4* is the fourth House report of the 105th Congress, and *S.Rept 97-20* is the twentieth Senate report of the 97th Congress.

House and Senate reports are first published in paper or microfiche and then bound in the publication called the *Serial Set*, described later under House and Senate Documents. They are also on the Web through *GPO Access* at http://www.access.gpo.gov/, on *THOMAS* at http://thomas.loc.gov/, and available through many subscription on-line services, including *Congressional Universe*, *LEGI-SLATE*, LEXIS-NEXIS, and Westlaw. They are also indexed in the *CIS Index to Publications of the United States Congress*, the *Monthly Catalog to Government Publications*, and the GPO's *Sales Product Catalog*.

Your Friendly Neighborhood Government Documents Librarian

Libraries that maintain full or partial government depositories will have a government publications specialist on hand, so be aware that they're there should you need them. When committee reports and committee documents start blurring together, give them a call.

The *Congressional Record*

If you've ever wondered what they talk about on the floors of Congress, you'll be glad to know you can satisfy your curiosity. There is easy access to a written record of House and Senate floor debates and proceedings from the *Congressional Record*. Originally called the *Annals of Congress* from 1789–1824, the *Register of Debates* from 1824–1837 and the *Congressional Globe* through 1873, the *Congressional Record* presents daily debates and proceedings from the House and Senate floors—not to be confused with hearings, which present debate and testimony within specific committees.

The text in the *Congressional Record* is often not verbatim, since senators and representatives can insert additional information into the *Record* related to the topics being discussed or make grammatical corrections. Comments that representatives make and then regret can also be stricken if House members agree to allow it. Since 1978, a bullet (•) began to appear in the *Congressional Record* to denote comments not actually made on the floor of Congress. The Senate portion of the *Record* still uses this method. Since 1985, the House adopted the use of a different typeface to bring attention to text added after floor proceedings.

There are three sections in the *Congressional Record*. One section contains the debates of the House and debates of the Senate, as explained previously. The "Extension of Remarks" section, intended to augment the day's proceedings, is actually a hodgepodge of speeches, article clippings, odes to constituents, and even a joke and recipe or two. The third part, the "Daily Digest" section, contains schedules for committee and subcommittee hearings and summarizes congressional activities of the previous day.

Congressional Record proceedings from the 104th Congress are located at the home page of the *U.S. House of Representatives* at http://www.house.gov/ and on *GPO Access* at http://www.access.gpo.gov. The *Congressional Record* can also be found in print or on microform at all government depository libraries. It's also available full text for varying runs of years through the major commercial law databases, including *Congressional Universe, CQ.com On Congress, LEGI-SLATE,* LEXIS-NEXIS and Westlaw.

To listen to verbatim dialog during congressional proceedings, tune into the cable television network C-SPAN: The Cable Satellite Public Affairs Network, where the camera records the proceedings and the legislators sometimes play to the camera. To purchase video recordings of House and Senate proceedings, use any of the following sources:

C-SPAN On-Line Store, P.O. Box 66809, Indianapolis, IN 46266-6809, Phone: (800)277-2698, Fax: (765)423-4495, URL: http://www.c-span.org/shop/

"Every minute" of C-SPAN congressional coverage from 1979 to the present is available for purchase.

House Recording Studio. Phone: (202)225-3941.

The most recent sixty days of proceedings are available.

Library of Congress Motion Picture Broadcasting and Recorded Sound Division. Phone: (202)707-8572.

House proceedings are obtainable from 1983 to present and Senate proceedings from 1986 to present.

C-SPAN Archives. Phone: (800)277-2698, Fax: (765)497-9699, E-mail: info@ pva.purdue.edu, URL: http://www.pava.purdue.edu

The Archives records, indexes, archives, and offers for sale all C-SPAN programming from 1987 to the present.

Senate Recording Studios. Phone: (202)224-4977.

The most recent thirty days of proceedings are available.

As mentioned in chapter six in the section on quotations, wonderful commentary can be culled from both congressional hearings and the proceedings recorded in the *Congressional Record.* Some will support facts and ideas—and some will just be entertaining rhetoric, as seen in the book *Will the Gentleman Yield? The Congressional Humor Book* (Berkeley, CA: Ten Speed Press, 1987). An example from this fun book is a quote from 1963 made by democratic Representative Morris Udall of Arizona:

> "Mr. Chairman, as I rise here, I am reminded of the worn-out story of the man who was asked how he felt when he saw his mother-in-law drive his brand new uninsured Cadillac off the cliff. He answered that he had mixed emotions."

House and Senate documents

House and Senate documents are yet another class of congressional publication. They're intended to act, collectively, as a historic record of each Congress and include presidential vetoes, presidential messages that contain proposals for new legislation, annual reports to Congress from government agencies, and reports of committee studies that might also have been headed for life as committee prints if the committee had not requested they be documents. These publications are numbered sequentially by chamber, within a Congress, e.g., *H.Doc. 105-6* is the sixth document of the 105th Congress, and *S.Doc. 93-1* is the first document of the 93rd Congress.

House and Senate documents are available from 1995 to the present through both *GPO Access* at http://www.access.gpo.gov/ and through the commercial database *Congressional Universe.*

House and Senate reports and documents are reproduced in a massive and historically fascinating set of volumes called the *Serial Set.* The *House Journal* and *Senate Journal,* which compile the official records of the House and Senate, including minutes of daily sessions and a record of legislative action, motions, and votes, were also reproduced in the *Serial Set* between 1817 and 1952.

The *Serial Set* has been published since the 15th Congress. In 1832, thirty-eight volumes were retrospectively created to also cover the 1st through the 14th Congresses. These volumes are called the *American State Papers* and are considered a part of the *Serial Set*. To find items in the *Serial Set*, use the *CIS U.S. Serial Set Index*, a comprehensive index to the set through 1969, and the *CIS Index* from 1969 to the present.

Facts in a Flash

Free and Fee Congressional Publications

There are people in Washington who will send you free copies of congressional documents. Call the House Documents Room at (202)226-5200 for free copies of bills, reports, House documents, and public and private laws; contact the Senate Documents Room at (202)224-7860 for free copies of bills, reports, Senate documents, treaty documents, and laws. If you want to speak to someone else, such as an aide to the congressperson who's sponsoring a bill, call the Capitol Hill Switchboard at (202)224-3121 and ask for his or her number.

Another method of obtaining full-text copies of congressional documents is by having credit card in hand and dialing the CIS Documents On Demand service at (800)227-2477 or (301)951-4631, Fax: (301)657-3203, E-mail: cis.dod@lexis-nexis.com.

Treaties

U.S. treaties (formal, binding, international agreements) need approval by two-thirds of the Senate before they can be ratified by the president. Senate Treaty Documents (formerly called Senate Executive Documents) are issued when the president wants the Senate to ratify a treaty and they present the text of the agreement and reasons why the ratification is urged. The Senate Executive Report is issued in response to the Senate Treaty Document and contains committee recommendations regarding ratification of the treaty.

Treaties on the Web include:

Treaties on the U.S. Senate Home Page. http://www.senate.gov/activities/index.html

Treaties on this page include those under consideration or those passed during the current Congress.

Treaties in Force. http://www.acda.gov/state/

The State Department page supplies a list of active treaties and international agreements of the United States, also in print format, printed annually.

U.S. House of Representatives Internet Law Library: Treaties and International Law.
    http://law.house.gov/89.htm
        This page has links to collections of treaties and the text and discussion of
    specific treaties.

Very brief summaries of treaties are also listed in the *Congressional Index*, a
loose-leaf set published since 1930 and available at most larger libraries. Treaties
from 1818–1969 are also indexed on the *CIS Index to U.S. Senate Executive
Documents and Reports* (which is also on CD-ROM via the *Congressional Master-
File 1*) and available full-text on CIS-produced microfiche. Treaties are also indexed by William S. Hein & Co. (Buffalo, NY) in *Hein's U.S. Treaty Index on
CD-ROM*, covering 1776 to the present, and in the *United States Treaty Index:
1776-1995 Consolidation* which is updated by the *Current Treaty Index*.
    Other print titles in government depository libraries that include full-text treaties:
    Treaties and Other International Acts Series (TIAS). A series of newly approved
        treaties and agreements issued in pamphlet format.
    *Treaties and Other International Agreements of the United States of America,
        1776-1949*, which is continued by *United States Treaties and Other
        International Agreements*, with treaties and agreements from 1950–1984.
    The Serial Set, which has *Treaty Documents and Executive Reports* since 1981.
    The publisher William S. Hein also sells a microfiche collection of treaties, full
text from 1991 to present, and treaties are also on LEXIS-NEXIS and Westlaw.

Finding Statutes and Regulations

Statutory law at both the state and federal level are arranged two different ways:
- In chronological order, with each assigned a public law number based on
    the order they were passed.
- In subject order, with each law or piece of law that pertains to a subject
    placed in an appropriate subject section.

Resources listing federal laws in chronological order

When a bill becomes law it is assigned a public law number. Public laws are
assigned sequential numbers. So, the twenty-fifth law of the 103rd Congress is
cited as *P.L. 103-25*.
    In paper format, public laws first appear as slip laws—just little pamphlets or

Pocket Parts Are Important

Laws are in constant evolution. Printed sets of current laws usually consist of dozens of volumes, with each volume representing a specific legal topic. Instead of publishing a new set of all laws each time a change occurs, printed legal sets are updated with a supplementary volume or with a pocket part. **Pocket parts** are pages with updated information on them that get stuck into a little pocket in the back of the book. Always check your law in the main volume, then flip to the pocket part to be certain that no changes have occurred. Sometimes a law will be brand new and won't even show up in the main volume yet—it will just be in the pocket part.

slips of paper, each representing a law. Putting them in this format is way of getting them out to the public fairly quickly.

The slip laws are republished under the title the *United States Statutes at Large* [cited as *Stat.*]. The *Statutes at Large* contains U.S. laws listed in the order they were passed, also called session laws (i.e., laws passed in a session of Congress). The *Statutes at Large* is the "official" version released by the U.S. government. Presidential proclamations, private laws, and concurrent resolutions also appear in the *Statutes at Large*. (And there is yet another CIS index with a corresponding microfiche set, this one for orders and proclamations: the *CIS Index to Presidential Executive Orders and Proclamations*.)

The "unofficial" versions of session laws come out more quickly in print than the official ones and can be found in the *United States Code Congressional and Administrative News* from West Publishing [cited as *U.S.C.C.A.N.*]. This publication contains everything that *Statutes at Large* contains except private laws and concurrent resolutions. Additionally, *U.S.C.C.A.N.* includes all executive orders and excerpts from congressional reports of particular pertinence in a law's legislative history.

Search for laws by their public law number in any of the previous session law publications, or by public law number or the subject of a law on the Web at *GPO Access* at http://www.access.gpo.gov/ and *THOMAS* at http://thomas.loc.gov/, in the *CIS Index to Publications of the United States Congress*, and through numerous online commercial services, including *Congressional Universe*, *LEGI-SLATE*, LEXIS-NEXIS, and Westlaw.

Resources listing federal laws in subject order

The *United States Code* [cited as *U.S.C.*] is a listing of all U.S. laws currently in effect, arranged by subject. The *U.S. Code* is available in hard copy or CD-ROM in most larger libraries and free on the Web at *GPO Access* at http://www.access .gpo.gov/su_docs/aces/aaces002.html or through the *Internet Law Library* at http://law.house.gov/. It's also available, often with annotations, through sub-scription online systems, including *Congressional Universe*, *LEGI-SLATE*, LEXIS-NEXIS, and Westlaw.

The *U.S. Code* is arranged in fifty broad subject categories, each numbered and called *Titles*. For example, *Title 21* contains federal law concerning food and drugs, and *Title 43* contains law related to public lands. There's a detailed subject index that accompanies the print version. The *U.S. Code* is the official version of federal laws in subject arrangement. Two unofficial but widely used titles, both providing the identical contents of the *U.S. Code* and, additionally, interpretive materials and pointers to related laws, cases, and writings, are the *U.S.C.A.— United States Code Annotated* and the *U.S.C.S.—United States Code Service*.

In law, a code is any systematic collection of laws, rules, or regulations. So the *United States Code* is a collection of the U.S. laws that have been codified.

Remember, when you look up any law in the *U.S. Code*, there's a good chance you're looking at the dictates of many public laws. If you want to see a full original law in the order it was written, look for it in the *Statutes at Large* or using other ways explained earlier in the Resources Listing Federal Laws in Chro-nological Order section.

Resources listing state laws in subject order

All states have print collections of their laws in subject order—state codes—that are similar to the *U.S. Code*. Some put out their own collections, but all have at least one, and sometimes two, unofficial versions. Some sample titles include *Colorado Revised Statutes*, *Montana Code Annotated*, and the *General Statutes of Connecticut*. Most larger libraries will own their state's law collection.

The URL's for full-text statutes and legislation on the Internet are listed at http://www.prairienet.org/~scruffy/f.htm or on the U.S. State and Territorial Laws portion of the *U.S. Internet Law Library* at http://law.house.gov/17.htm. Laws of each state can also be found on the home pages of many state's legislatures which can be linked to via the state's home page. (See State Home Pages and Phone Numbers in chapter three). There's also a list of links to state legislatures at http://www.ncsl.org/public/sitesleg.htm.

Your Rights as a Citizen of Your State

L aw questions dealing with the rights of the citizens of a state may be answered by the office of the state attorney general for the area you are interested in. The number is available in the phone book government pages.

Regulations

Once there's a law, you generally need rules and regulations to carry it out. The federal or state administrative agencies carrying out laws and policy create these regulations.

The regulations for federal laws are first proposed in the *Federal Register* [cited as *FR*], which also contains the final versions of the regulations, presidential proclamations, executive orders, and notices of such matters as grant deadlines, and other presidential documents.

The *Federal Register*, first published in 1936, is published five days a week, Monday through Friday. It's available in print or on microfiche in government depository libraries and at no charge via *GPO Access* at http://www.access.gpo .gov/. The *Federal Register* is also available on CD-ROM and through many legal commercial databases, including *Congressional Universe, CQ.com On Congress,* DIALOG, *LEGI-SLATE*, LEXIS-NEXIS, and Westlaw.

Regulations in development are also found in the semiannual publication the *Unified Agenda of Federal Regulatory and Deregulatory Actions. Unified Agenda* is also online via the *Reginfo.gov* site http://reginfo.gov/ or via GPO Access at http:// www.access.gpo.gov/.

Final regulations are collected and codified in the *Code of Federal Regulations,* [cited as *C.F.R.*]. Presidential proclamations and executive orders are also included in the *C.F.R.* The *C.F.R.* is arranged by subject, with fifty broad subject headings, and is available through the same means and databases (except DIALOG) as the *Federal Register* described earlier.

The full contents of the print *C.F.R.* are updated annually. A researcher will find the notice of the new regulations or changes in the *Federal Register*, which is updated every weekday. (Of course it's also quite possible that the regulation you are interested in has not changed in five years and isn't expected to change any time soon.)

A publication that helps bridge the gap between when a final regulation appears in the *Federal Register* and when it's printed in the *C.F.R.* is the *List of C.F.R. Sections Affected (LSA)*. *LSA*, published monthly, lists citations to new regulations based on a *C.F.R.* citation. *LSA* is also on the Web through *GPO Access* at http://www.access.gpo.gov/nara/cfr/index.html.

The State and Federal Court Systems

There are two distinct court systems in the United States: the federal courts and the state courts.

Federal courts

These courts have jurisdiction in all cases that involve the U.S. Constitution and federal laws and treaties. The federal courts are comprised of:

- **District Courts**: It's in district court that most cases dealing with federal law both begin and end. They fall into two categories: district courts dealing with general federal jurisdiction (except bankruptcy), and bankruptcy courts.
- **Special Courts/Separate Courts**: These are courts that cater to certain specialized areas, including the U.S. Tax Court, the Court of International Trade, and the U.S. Claims Court.
- **Courts of Appeals**: When a case in a district court is appealed, it goes to one of the U.S. Courts of Appeals. A court of appeals will also hear cases from special courts such as the U.S. Tax Court, and from the rulings of regulatory agencies, such as the FCC and the National Labor Relations Board.
- **United States Supreme Court**: The "highest court in the land" may hear appeals of cases, but very few cases submitted are ever heard. The U.S. Supreme Court has discretionary power over which cases it will accept.

State courts

These courts deal with infractions of, and challenges to, state law. The names these courts go by may vary slightly from state to state.

- **Minor Courts**: Sample kinds of minor courts include municipal courts, traffic courts, and juvenile courts.
- **Trial Courts**: The bulk of major cases dealing with state law are brought to these courts, known as district, superior, or circuit courts.
- **Intermediate Appellate Courts**: This corresponds to the U.S. Court of Appeals, only at the state level. This is where appeals are heard.

- **The State Court of Last Resort**: Most states call this court the State Supreme Court. A case which has been rejected at this level may be presented to the U.S. Supreme Court for appeal if the question involves either a federal law or a constitutional question.

Not All Court Decisions Are Published

Here are the types of cases readily accessible in published versions:

At the federal level:
- All Supreme Court opinions
- Selected decisions of the U.S. Court of Appeals
- Selected decisions of the U.S. District Courts

At the state level:
- (With few exceptions) Only cases appealed to a higher court, i.e., courts of appeals or the state's supreme court

Information about cases that are not officially published may still be obtained. The location and procedure varies from state to state. Call your local state information number listed in chapter three under State Home Pages and Phone Numbers or get a head start with the guide *Find Public Records Fast: The Complete State, County, and Courthouse Locator* (Tempe, AZ: Facts on Demand Press, 1998).

Finding court cases

There are numerous locations of court cases both in print and online listed below. Also note that all federal and state cases are available through the commercial services LEXIS-NEXIS and Westlaw.

Supreme Court cases

FindLaw: Supreme Court Opinions. http://www.findlaw.com/casecode/supreme
.html

    FindLaw supplies over a hundred years worth of Supreme Court case opinions, full text, from 1893 to the present.

GPO Access. http://www.access.gpo.gov/su_docs/aces/aaces002.html

    GPO Access has online Supreme Court decisions from 1937–1975. The files that GPO Access pulls these decisions from is also accessible through http://www.law.vill.edu/fed-ct/sct.html.

Landmark Briefs and Arguments of the Supreme Court of the United States. Arlington, VA: University Publications of America, 1975–present.

This continually growing set of volumes contains lengthy presentations of the legal debates, for and against, landmark cases brought before the U.S. Supreme Court. A good source to look into if you want to analyze a specific case—but keep ye olde legal dictionary close at hand.

Legal Information Institute's Project Hermes. http://supct.law.cornell.edu/supct/

The Project Hermes site offers Supreme Court cases from 1990 to the present.

The Oyez Project: U.S. Supreme Court Multimedia Database. http://oyez.nwu.edu/

You can listen to selected opinions of the Supreme Court at this growing Northwestern University site, still in its beta stage at the time of this writing.

United States Reports. 1790–present. [Cited as *US.*]

This is the official set of Supreme Court cases from the U.S. government, containing all opinions handed down from the Court. Before the cases are bound into full volumes, they're released in pamphlet format called *Slip Opinions.*

U.S. House of Representatives Internet Law Library: Federal Court Decisions and Rules. http://law.house.gov/6.htm

This site links to many other Web locations that contain Supreme Court decisions.

United States Law Week. Washington, DC: Washington Bureau of National Affairs, 1966–present. [Cited as *U.S.L.W.*]

Several weeks after a Supreme Court decision is handed down, it's reproduced in this loose-leaf binder. *U.S. Law Week* is comprised of two sections: The Supreme Court section containing opinions and summaries of new cases and the General Law section, consisting of selected statutes, and summaries of recent federal laws and federal and state court decisions.

United States Supreme Court Reports, Lawyers Edition. Charlottesville, VA: LEXIS Law Publishing. 1754–present. [The first 100 volumes are cited as *L.Ed.* and the second series, begun in 1956, is cited as *L.Ed.2d.*] Also on CD-ROM.

This set is an "unofficial" version of the Supreme Court opinions and contains annotations and headnotes concerning the main points of law covered in each case, and summaries of the briefs of counsel prepared by the publisher's editorial staff. The *Supreme Court Reporter* (St. Paul, MN: West Publishing, [Cited as *S.Ct.*]), is another unofficial version of Supreme Court opinions.

 Parallel Citations

When you see a citation to a case or statutory law, you will often be provided with parallel citations, that is, citations to the *same* law or case appearing in *different* publications. For example, the *Employee Drug Testing Case* is cited in *Shepard's Acts and Cases by Popular Name* (an index to well-known laws and cases) as being available in three sources:

- 489 US 656—Volume 489 of the *United States Reports*, page 656.
- 103 L.Ed.2d 685—Volume 103 of the *Lawyer's Edition 2nd*, page 685.
- 109 S.Ct. 1384—Volume 109 of the *Supreme Court Reporter*, page 1384.

You will find precisely the same case in each of those volumes, except the "unofficial" versions will also be annotated, providing additional notes of interest.

U.S. Court of Appeals and District Court cases

Federal Court Locator. http://www.law.vill.edu/fed-ct/fedcourt.html

The Federal Court Locator offers access to court opinions from the Supreme Court, the courts of appeals, and the district courts. Court rules and contact information is also provided for each court.

The Federal Reporter. St. Paul, MN: West Publishing, 1st Series, 1880–1924 [Cited as *F.*]; 2nd Series, 1924–1992 [Cited as *F.2d.*]; and 3rd Series, 1993–present [Cited as *F.3d.*].

The *Federal Reporter* contains all decisions from the U.S. Court of Appeals (and for volumes from 1880–1932, decisions from the U.S. Court of Claims and the U.S. District Courts). West also publishes the *Federal Supplement* (1932–present. [Cited as *F.Supp.*]), which contains the decisions of the U.S. Customs Court, and select decisions of the U.S. District Courts, and the *Federal Rules Decisions* (1941–present. [Cited as *FRD.*]), which are decisions not included in the Federal Supplement that involve the federal rules of criminal procedure.

State Court cases

State and Local Government on the Net. http://www.piperinfo.com/state/states .html

Click on "State Courts" at the bottom of this Web page from Piper Resources to link to a state-by-state guide to court opinions available on the Web for free or through fee-based services. The Web page for each state's court also supplies contact information for each court along with other useful information about the state's court system.

The State Reporters. Each state also has its own series of reporters, which report cases for just that state. For example, in Ohio, the set that includes their supreme court cases is called *Ohio State Reports* and the volumes that include their court of appeals is called *Ohio Appellate Reports.* The cases in those volumes are the same cases for Ohio that you would find in the *North Eastern Reporter.*

There are also reporters for different regions of the United States that contain cases from each state's highest court and court of appeals. They are all "unofficial" and all published by West Publishing Company: the *Atlantic Reporter* [Cited as *A.*], *North Eastern Reporter* [Cited as *NE.*], *North Western Reporter* [Cited as *NW.*], *Pacific Reporter* [Cited as *P.* and *P2d.*], *South Eastern Reporter* [Cited as *SE.*], *Southern Reporter* [Cited as *SO.*], and the *South Western Reporter* [Cited as *SW.*].

All state cases are on the subscription services LEXIS-NEXIS and Westlaw.

Subject guides to court cases

Most online versions of court cases are searchable by subject of the case, for example, cases dealing with property rights. Another method of finding cases by subject is by using digests.

Digests are multivolume collections containing summaries of court cases, arranged by subject of the cases. Digests can also be used to match citations with case names, when you already know the case name.

Since there are two major purposes of digest—finding citations for cases and finding cases on particular subjects—there are two types of indexes for digests: word indexes (searchable by subject), and a table of cases, arranged by the name of the case, i.e., the plaintiff vs. the defendant (for example: *Smith v. United States*).

There are digests for both state and federal cases:

The Federal Digest. St. Paul, MN: West, 1960–.

Decisions of all the federal courts from 1754 to date are indexed in this series. Supplementary titles in the series are the *Modern Federal Practice Digest, West's Federal Practice Digest 2d, West's Federal Practice Digest 3d,* and *West's Federal Practice Digest 4th.*

United States Supreme Court Digest. St. Paul, MN: West, 1943–.
    This set supplies subject and case name access to Supreme Court cases, from 1754 to date.

Volumes that index state appellate court cases by subject are the *Atlantic Digest, North Western Digest, Pacific Digest, South Eastern Digest,* and the *Southern Digest.* There are also digests for forty-five individual states, such as *West's California Digest.* There are no digests for Delaware, Nevada, and Utah. West Virginia and Virginia are combined in one digest, as are North Dakota and South Dakota.
    An often-used resource, briefly mentioned above, that helps locate well-known cases (and laws, too):

Shepard's Acts and Cases by Popular Names—Federal and State. Colorado Springs, CO: Shepard's, 1968–.
    This set is a great quick look-up source for laws and cases that are fairly well known and in some cases, have come to be known by a "popular" name. If a case is famous, I don't even figure out what digest to use—I just grab this.

Another great series to use for finding in-depth analysis and critique on precedent-setting cases is the *A.L.R.: The American Law Reports* (Rochester, NY: Lawyers Cooperative Publishing. Also available through LEXIS-NEXIS and Westlaw). Each case included is summarized and discussed as it relates to other cases. If you have a law topic in mind and want to see how it's been handled in state and federal cases, this is an excellent source to turn to. The *Quick Indexes* to the *ALR* are separate volumes that lead you to the cases in the *ALR* series by topic.

Shepardizing: Determining if a Case Is Still "Good Law"

A case may lose its precedential value if its points are debunked in later court decisions. That makes the entire case, or perhaps one or two points of the case, "bad law"—they no longer set a precedent. To find out if a case's opinion is still "good," you need to see what subsequent cases said about the opinion. These later citations to the case may also be used to help further clarify or enrich your understanding of the original precedent still in force.
    This process of locating subsequent cases citing earlier cases has come to be called Shepardizing, named after the *Shepard's Citators* series published by the Shepard's Company. For example, one title in the series is *Shepard's United States*

Citations, used to Shepardize decisions of the United States Supreme Court, and federal laws and regulations. Shepard's also offers state, regional, and special citators. They are in print at most libraries with decent-sized law holdings, and available on CD-ROM or through LEXIS-NEXIS. There's a free tutorial on the Web to teach you the steps of Shepardizing at http://www.shepards.com/helpcite /tutorial.htm.

Law Indexes and Databases

Following are overviews of noteworthy databases, Web sites, and indexes, already mentioned in this chapter because of their focus on law-related publications or their collection of full-text law documents. See Appendix A for contact information for the publishers of the commercial databases. (Indexes that bring you to periodical articles focusing on law, such as the *Index to Legal Periodicals*, are described in Appendix B under Law).

CIS Index to Publications of the United States Congress. Bethesda, MD: Congressional Information Service, 1970–present. Also on CD-ROM as part of *Congressional Masterfile 2* and online as part of the subscription database *Congressional Universe.*

Found in most larger libraries, the *CIS Index* is an index to laws and publications from congressional committees, including congressional hearings, reports, documents, and committee prints. Using the Legislative Histories section of the *CIS Index,* you can look up a particular public law and find a concise listing of proceedings and materials associated with that law, sometimes dating back through a number of previous congressional sessions.

The *CIS Index* supplies a substantial description of the materials it indexes and the SuDoc number needed to locate it in government depository libraries. Additionally, the publishers of *CIS Index* produce microfiche versions of items indexed in the *CIS Index;* though, often, libraries will just own the index and offer the publications through other means.

The full text of many of the congressional materials indexed in CIS are also available on the commercial database *Congressional Universe.* The *Congressional Universe* database also has additional information not found in the *CIS Index,* including voting records, campaign finance figures, financial disclosures for members of Congress, a section of "hot" bills that have received national attention, articles from *CongressDaily,* containing time-sensitive stories on Capitol Hill legislative and campaign activity, and articles from 1977 to the present from the *National Journal,* a weekly magazine that examines federal government policy-making, identifying and tracking emerging issues.

Congressional Index. 2 Volumes per Congressional session. Chicago: CCH, 1930–present. Updated weekly. This publisher also offers a commercial online system offering material similar to that in the *Congressional Index* called *ELSS: Electronic Legislative Search System.*

Another index commonly found in larger libraries, the *Congressional Index,* in print format, is comprised of two loose-leaf volumes, updated weekly. This set contains summaries of bills in committee, enacted or vetoed, searchable by topic or name of the person who sponsored it; the action and status of each bill, descriptions of standing, select, and special committees and what bills they're working on; brief biographies of members of Congress and what bills they're associated with; voting records; and summaries of treaties, searchable by subject, name of treaty, or nation.

Congressional Masterfile 1. Bethesda, MD: Congressional Information Service.

This CD-ROM database contains the equivalent of the following print indexes: the *CIS U.S. Serial Set Index* (1789–1969), the *CIS U.S. Congressional Committee Hearings Index* (1833–1969), the *CIS Index to Unpublished U.S. Senate Committee Hearings* (1823–1972), the *CIS Index to Unpublished U.S. House of Representatives Committee Hearings* (1833–1958), the *CIS U.S. Congressional Committee Prints Index* (1830–1969), and the *CIS Index to U.S. Senate Executive Documents & Reports* (1817–1969).

CQ.com On Congress. Washington, DC: Congressional Quarterly.

Billed as a legislative tracking service, *CQ.com,* a subscription online service, offers news and analysis related to Capitol Hill legislation, full-text bills and their legislative history, roll call votes, testimonies from congressional hearings, committee reports, congressional biographies, the *Congressional Record,* the *Federal Register,* and the full text of the *CQ Weekly, The CQ Researcher,* and the *CQ Daily Monitor.*

GPO Access. http://www.access.gpo.gov/su_docs/aces/aaces002.html

Maintained by the Government Printing Office, GPO Access offers, at no charge, a useful mix of government information, including access to the *Budget of the United States,* congressional publications, bills, public laws, the *Code of Federal Regulations, Economic Indicators,* the *Economic Report of the President,* the *Federal Register,* the *Government Information Locator Service* (described in chapter three), the *Government Manual,* the *House* and *Senate Calendars,* the *House Rules Manual* and the *Senate Manual,* Supreme Court decisions from 1937–1975, the *Unified Agenda of Federal Regulatory and Deregulatory Actions,*

the *United States Code*, and the *Weekly Compilation of Presidential Documents*.
LEGI-SLATE. Washington, DC: The Washington Post Company.

This commercial online service carries full-text legislative and regulatory documents and news, with many customized tracking services available.
LEXIS-NEXIS. Dayton, Ohio: LEXIS-NEXIS.

The LEXIS-NEXIS subscription-based online information system offers full-text access to all state and federal laws and cases, citators, federal regulations, congressional documents; full-text articles from legal, business, medical, and news publications; full-text transcripts from television and radio broadcasts; access to public records; facts about the states and foreign countries; and full-text biographical information. And more. Note that law libraries with the full LEXIS-NEXIS system cannot let users who are not students or faculty members associated with the library's school use the system.

The LEXIS-NEXIS company also offers parts of its information under different database names. For example, my library subscribes to a more limited, but still incredible, permutation of the system, called *LEXIS-NEXIS Academic Universe*. Many universities now have subscriptions to this more affordable version of LEXIS-NEXIS.

If you don't subscribe to or have access to any LEXIS-NEXIS databases, you can still use their LEXIS-NEXIS Express service, where you pay for a search to be run for you. Call (800)843-6476 or (937)865-6800, ext. 5505, or E-mail lexis-nexis.express@lexis-nexis.com for more information.
MOCAT/ Monthly Catalog to Government Publications.

See chapter three.

THOMAS. http://thomas.loc.gov

Named after Thomas Jefferson and maintained by the Library of Congress, THOMAS is a free repository of congressional information and documents. THOMAS has the full text of the *Congressional Record*, a record of House and Senate roll call votes, a bill database with summaries and status going back to 1973 that can be searched by topic or bill number, a roster of bills scheduled for floor action for the current week, public laws, also back to 1973, recent committee reports, selected hearing transcripts, and quick links to historic U.S. documents.
Westlaw. St. Paul, MN: West Group.

Westlaw is a premier commercial online system for finding law information, usually available at law libraries. Its content is comparable to LEXIS-

NEXIS, described earlier. For those who don't subscribe or have access to Westlaw, they offer a fee-based document-retrieval service called *WestDoc* at http://www.westdoc.com/.

Articles and Reviews

There are times when I find that students in my library aren't actually looking for the law itself. Instead they want articles that discuss the law and its ramifications, and the public debates surrounding it.

There are hundreds of U.S. and foreign periodicals in the field of criminal justice and law. Just to show you the variety, here are some sample titles: *American Criminal Law Review, Journal of Forensic Sciences, Juvenile and Family Court Journal, Narcotics Control Digest*, and *The Police Chief*. A law review is basically a law journal, with most published by law schools. Sample law review titles include *The Harvard Law Review* and the *Villanova Law Review*.

Legal periodicals and reviews will often contain citations to cases, laws, regulations, and other legal and government documents and, alternately, law materials will often cite articles from legal periodicals and reviews. For example, 91 Colum. L. Rev. 334 (1991) refers to an article in Volume 91 of the *Columbia Law Review*, starting on page 334, from 1991.

Check Appendix B for periodical indexes that will help you find articles about laws and the criminal justice system. Just remember that many articles discussing laws and government policy won't only be in law journals, but in any magazine or journal that covers legal topics of interest to their readers. For example, discussions of laws effecting freedom of speech will show up in library science journals, and opinions about laws affecting small businesses may be included in business magazines. And of course newspapers and general newsmagazines like *Time* and *Newsweek* will be interested in almost anything that's considered news. So, when searching for law-related articles, also check multi-topic indexes, subject-specific indexes, and, definitely, newspaper indexes.

Understanding Legal Citations

The citations referring to law materials might look a bit foreign. Some examples:

    107 Stat 1909
    122 L.Ed.2d 525

Law citations appear more cryptic than they are—they're actually quite simple.

Most citations to legal materials follow a standard format consisting of three elements:

- The name of the court case, law, or law review article
- The location, consisting of the volume/title number, an abbreviation of the name of the series or volume, and the page/section number
- The date (not always included; sometimes the date will appear right after the name of the case, law, or review)

Roe v. Wade, 410 US 113 (1973)

Read as: The case *Roe vs. Wade*, which can be found in volume 410 of the *United States Reports* on page 113. The case was decided in 1973.

And, to interpret the original examples,

- *107 Stat 1909* refers to Volume 107 of the *Statutes at Large*, page 1909.
- *122 L.Ed.2d 525* refers to Volume 122 of the *Lawyer's Edition* of the *Supreme Court Reports*, 2nd series, page 525.

(Note that there are also many examples of legal citations in this chapter shown in brackets next to the titles of many legal resources.)

Different law publications may slightly alter citations. For example, some listings may drop the periods after the letter and others may drop a whole letter. Also, there are times when one abbreviation may mean several things. For example, *O.* may stand for Law *O*pinions, *O*regon, or *O*hio (among other possibilities!).

A useful collection of legal abbreviations is *Bieber's Dictionary of Legal Abbreviations: Reference Guide for Attorneys, Legal Secretaries, Paralegals, and Law Students* (4th edition. Buffalo, NY: William S. Hein, 1993). A standard guide to legal terms, abbreviations, and citations is *The Bluebook: A Uniform System of Citation* (16th edition. Cambridge, MA: The Harvard Law Review Association, 1996), also referred to as the *Harvard Bluebook*. On the Web, at http://www.law.cornell.edu/citation/citation.table.html, is the *Introduction to Basic Legal Citation* which is "based" on the sixteenth edition of the *Bluebook*.

Other legal citation elements you may run across

Sections and subsections

This symbol, §, followed by a number, refers to the section you should turn to in a law book if no page is indicated. For example, §437 means section 437. When the symbol is doubled, i.e., §§, it stands for a subsection.

And the following

The words *et seq* stand for a Latin phrase translated as "and the following." For example, here's how it would look in a citation:

> Okla. Stat. 1991, Title 62, 910 et seq.

Translation: You'll find the particular state law that this citation represents in the *Oklahoma Statutes,* the main volume of which was published in 1991, in the Title 62 volume, in section 910 and subsequent sections.

Sections denoted by two or three numbers

A section of a law may be denoted by a series of two or three numbers separated by hyphens. This is a section number. For example, here's a sample citation:

> N.M. Stat. Anno. 1978, 32-6-1 et seq

Translation: You'll find this New Mexico state law in the *New Mexico Statutes Annotated,* originally published in 1978, in section 32-6-1, and on the pages following.

Law Libraries and Beyond: Where They Keep the Law Books

An obvious answer to "where can you find law books?" would be "a law library." But a law library may not be your most convenient choice. Luckily, there are more options.

Academic Libraries and Large Public Libraries. These libraries usually offer a solid collection of law books. At the very least, they'll provide access to statutory and case law for the federal level and for the state the library is located in.

Court Libraries. Check in your town for a state- or county-sponsored library associated with the courts that carries law material for the use of lawyers and judges. It should also be open to the public.

Government Depository Libraries. All full federal depository libraries, discussed in chapter three, will have a collection of laws, cases, and government publications that must, by law, be published and distributed by the U.S. government.

Law Libraries. Academic libraries that cater to law students offer a wide spectrum of law materials. Unfortunately, most law libraries don't throw out the welcome mat to the general public. Academic law libraries usually require an entry fee, sometimes token, sometimes large, for those who aren't students or faculty associated with the library.

Feeling Loony?

If you need a break from legalese, I have just the antidote: a copy of *Loony Laws: That You Never Knew You Were Breaking* (New York: Walker and Company, 1990). Some examples: women in Minnesota may not dress up as Santa Claus on any city street—doing so will risk a twenty-five dollar fine or a thirty-day jail sentence. In Orlando, Florida, don't think that using an elephant for transportation will save you parking fees because if your pachyderm is left tied to a parking meter, you must pay the parking fee. I can only hope these laws have been repealed since revealed in this edition—but just the fact they were on the books at some point is rather delightful.

CHAPTER 12

Business Research

*Information about Companies,
Industries, and the Economy*

"The propensity to truck, barter, and exchange one thing for another is common to all men, and to be found in no other race of animals."

—Adam Smith

When you need information about a company, its products, and financial standing, you'll find some of the information from documents produced by the company itself, through its financial filings and home page, some from articles written about the company, and some from reference books and databases that compile particular kinds of information about companies, such as investment analysis. If a company is publicly-held, it will be simpler, overall, to find information about it.

A public company offers shares of its stock to the public that are traded on the open market. These publicly held companies must file specific reports with the Securities and Exchange Commission (SEC)—ones that are quite useful to the researcher. Also, because publicly owned companies tend to be larger, they're usually written about more often by outside observers.

Finding published information on companies that do not sell shares, private companies, isn't as easy, since they're not required to file information with the SEC and they're likely out of the media spotlight.

Whether a company is private or public, see if the company has a Web page. Private company pages usually just have basic information about the business; public company pages usually link directly to the financial information it's required to file with the SEC. Of course, company Web pages are maintained by the company—so don't expect any blinking arrows pointing you to information about the company's impending doom.

Finding Company Home Pages

I t's simple to just guess a company's Internet home page. It will usually be: http://www.nameofcompany.com or http://www.abbreviationofnameofcompany.com.

Some sample company URLs will give you the idea: *Reebok International* is at http://www.reebok.com, the *General Electric Company* is at http://www.ge.com, and *Newman's Own* is at http://www.newmansown.com.

A useful database that searches for company home pages is *NetPartners Company Locator* at http://www.netpartners.com/resources/search.html.

Finding Financial Reports and SEC Filings

Typically sought-after SEC filings and financial reports include:

Annual Report to Stockholders. An annual report isn't a document that the SEC requires, though all public companies produce them. These reports go to the people who've invested their money in the company through stock purchase. Annual reports are usually glossy and attractive with color photographs depicting consumers using the company's products or services. In some respects they serve as a kind of advertisement to the shareholders and potential investors. Standard elements contained in annual reports include:

- **Letter to Shareholders**. Also called the president's letter, in this document, the company's president or CEO reviews the company's past year and looks ahead to the next.

- **Financial Data**. This section includes a balance sheet, income statement, stockholder's equity statement, and cash flow statement.

- **The Auditor's Report**. This is the verification from an independent CPA of the numbers in the annual report—and sometimes the report shows that the auditor was not satisfied.

- **Management Discussion**. These are comments on how the company's actions over the last three years affected its performance and financial position, and what the numbers mean.

- **Social Responsibility Report**. The annual report sometimes includes discussion of the firm's contributions to the community, both in time and money.

10-K Reports. The 10-K includes:

- **Detailed Financial Information**. Usually more information than is found in the annual report.
- **How the Firm Does Business**. This includes a description of the company's products, where it sells, and how it distributes. Some will also discuss competition in their market, research and development activities, and patent ownership.
- **What the Firm Owns**. This section lists subsidiaries, major properties, and foreign operations.
- **Raw Materials**. This is a list of raw materials the company uses and where it obtains them.

There are no enticing photographs or illustrations in a 10-K, and this useful report usually isn't automatically sent to shareholders. The 10-Q is the quarterly financial statement that helps keep some of the company's data up-to-date for the public between the annually released 10-K.

Proxy Statements. This notice is sent to all stockholders before their annual meeting with the company. The proxy statement looks at all matters that will be voted on, including proposals from shareholders such as a socially motivated change in policy or a suggestion that the CEO take a cut in pay. The proxy statement also includes salaries of top officers and directors.

8-K Reports. The 8-K reports is filed when a company has something major to disclose since the filing of its annual report, such as information about a takeover or merger.

The reports and filings that public companies create are easy to locate. *EDGAR: Electronic Data Gathering, Analysis and Retrieval* at http://www.sec.gov is a good place to start. All companies required to file financial documents with the SEC must do so electronically, and all those reports appear on EDGAR. Though companies must submit official SEC filings to EDGAR, they don't have to submit annual reports to EDGAR. Some do, but you won't reliably find that particular report on EDGAR.

Other ways of obtaining annual reports, SEC filings, and international financial reports:

A Company's Home Page. The home page of a public firm will almost always have links to its annual report and SEC filings.

Contacting the Company Directly. Companies will usually send you a copy of the filing that you want for free.

Using Library Collections With Print Copies of Filings. It's rare anymore that a library will maintain a collection of SEC filings in print. There are too many of them. Sometimes a library makes an effort to collect a segment of the filings in hard copy, for example, only collecting annual reports for companies in their state or those listed in the Fortune 500.

Using Microfiche Collections. Large libraries catering to business researchers often maintain microfiche collections of SEC filings. Two suppliers of such collections are Q-Data (their product is called *SEC File*) and Disclosure.

Annual Reports Free on the Net. Order selected annual reports at no charge at the The Public Register's Annual Reports Service (PRARS) Web site at http://www.prars.com/. Another Web site linking to free annual report services is offered by Investor Communications Business at http://www.icbinc.com/, supplying U.S., U.K., and Canadian company reports.

Using Subscription Databases. There are many databases that contain either full or partial SEC filings, or just a good amount of company financial information, including:

Disclosure SEC Database. Bethesda, MD: Disclosure. Available on CD-ROM under the title *Compact D/SEC.* Also known as *Compact Disclosure,* this database contains financial and management information from SEC documents. It's commonly found in academic libraries catering to business schools.

Disclosure also handles a similar database purchased from another vendor called *SEC Online,* which has full-text annual reports, 10-Ks, 10-Qs, and proxy statements for all NYSE and AMEX companies, and thousands of NASDAQ companies. The *SEC Database* or *SEC Online* are available via many subscription services, including America Online, CompuServe, DataTimes, Dow Jones Interactive, DIALOG, FirstSearch, LEXIS-NEXIS, Westlaw, and others.

Other databases from Disclosure include *Compact D/Canada,* containing financials and management information for Canadian firms; *Worldscope,* with management and financial data for companies worldwide; and *Laser D/SEC,* which contains all U.S. company annual reports and SEC filings as well as data for companies on the London, Paris, Ontario, and Montreal exchanges.

FreeEDGAR. http://www.freeedgar.com.

FreeEDGAR is another version of EDGAR, described earlier. Some advantages to FreeEDGAR include the ability to pull data from SEC filings into Microsoft Excel spreadsheets, and "watch lists," which alert the user to new company filings.

OneSource Global Business Browser. Cambridge, MA: OneSource Information
   Services.

    OneSource has business news, financial reports, and analysis of companies
and industries. More than 200,000 public and private companies are covered,
including 70,000 from outside the U.S. This company also produces the *U.S.
Business Browser* and the *U.K. Business Browser.*

SEDAR: System for Electronic Document Analysis and Retrieval. http://www.sedar
   .com/

    SEDAR is the Canadian equivalent of EDGAR; a repository for securities-
related filings from public firms in Canada.

More databases and resources with company financial and investment information are described under Investment Information later in this chapter.

Facts in a Flash

Is a Company Public or Private?

Browse through the online and print directories listed in this
chapter under Business Directories. Most company directories will denote the company as public or private, listing what stock
exchange the public company is listed on and supplying its ticker symbol.

Is Your Company a Parent?

Often a company will be a subsidiary, division, or affiliate of a parent company.
For example, the National Broadcasting Company (NBC) is a subsidiary of General Electric. Unfortunately, SEC filings deal primarily with the parent company,
so you won't find an annual report issued just for NBC. You'll sometimes find
information of decent length about the subsidiaries within the SEC reports of
the parent firm, but not always.

    A multivolume title that will help you determine whether the firm you're
looking for is a parent or subsidiary is the *Who Owns Whom* series (High Wy-
combe, UK: Dun & Bradstreet. Annual), covering companies worldwide. Other
sources that list company affiliations are *America's Corporate Families & International Affiliates* (Parsippany, NJ: Dun & Bradstreet) and *The Directory of Corporate Affiliations* (New Providence, NJ: National Register Publishing. Also on
CD-ROM and as a subscription database via CompuServe, DIALOG, LEXIS-
NEXIS, National Register Publishing, and OneSource.)

Private Companies

Finding published information on private companies is more challenging, and—wouldn't you know it?—the majority of companies are private. Often, there's no published information available about a small private company.

Articles are the main source of published material on a private company, and small company articles may only show up in local newspapers. Some subscription databases that cover regional newspapers around the country include *Business Newsbank*, LEXIS-NEXIS, and ProQuest Direct (all described in Appendix B). Though I've found articles on small private companies, it's not unusual to find there are none. See more tips on article searching under Business Information From Articles later in this chapter.

A few well-placed phone calls will help you find out something about a private company. Calling the company's local chamber of commerce should reveal, at the very least, how long the company has been in business in the town. Chamber of commerce contact information is listed in the *World Chamber of Commerce Directory* (Loveland, CO: Worldwide Chamber of Commerce Directory. Annual) or on the Web at the *Global Chamber of Commerce Index* at http://www.global index.com/chamber/globcham.htm or *Find a Chamber of Commerce* at http://chamber-of-commerce.com/search.htm.

You can also contact the Better Business Bureau to see if any complaints have been filed against the company. They're on the Web at http://www.bbb.org/, or check your area phone books for listings of local offices (there are 130 of them in the U.S.).

An Internet search on the name of a private company using one or more search engines can sometimes pull up a few references to the company that ultimately add to your data—I've had success with this method.

Depending on the reasons for your research, giving the company a call is an option. See Company Directories later in this chapter for ideas on finding company phone numbers. Company directories also have basic, and sometimes more than basic, information on private firm.

NAICS and SIC Codes

Just as the Library of Congress classification system and the Dewey Decimal system arrange materials in order by subject, the North American Industry Classification System (NAICS) numerically organizes business information by product and industry. NAICS is replacing the Standard Industrial Classification (SIC) system. NAICS or SIC codes are used in business publications and databases as a way of organizing the information. So, if you're looking for information about a company or industry, find out what NAICS or SIC category it fits into. Since the SIC system was only recently replaced, it will be awhile before SIC codes are only needed for use with historic publications. But all newer publications should be using NAICS.

To determine the NAICS or SIC category for an industry, use the NAICS or SIC manual found in print or on the Web. In the print manuals, look in the back section, where types of industries are listed alphabetically. There you'll find the NAICS or SIC code. Look up that code in the front of the directory to find a more complete description of the industry so you can be sure you've made the right choice.

A list of NAICS codes and other NAICS information is on the Web at http://www.census.gov/epcd/www/naics.html. This site also translates the old SIC codes to their NAICS equivalent. Go to http://www.osha.gov/oshstats/sicser.html for a listing of SIC codes on the Web.

Company Directories

Company directories, in print and online, run the gamut between those that offer basic contact information to those that additionally supply detailed financials and company history. Most company directories have, at minimum, these elements:

Name of company and contact information   Line of business

NAICS and/or SIC code(s) appropriate for   Annual sales

the company   Number of employees

Whether the company imports or exports   Year established

Name of company officers   Ticker symbol

Whether the firm is public or private

Print versions of company directories are arranged in alphabetic order by company name. Most provide a separate index volume(s) or sections that are industry and geographic cross-references, meaning you can look under a certain geographic area or type of business to find related businesses. The industry index will usually be arranged by NAICS or SIC code.

To find U.S. company directories in libraries, do a keyword search combining the word CORPORATIONS or BUSINESS ENTERPRISES with DIRECTORIES. Add the name of a country or region to find international business listings, e.g., ASIA CORPORATIONS DIRECTORIES, or use the phrase INTERNATIONAL BUSINESS ENTERPRISE DIRECTORIES.

Below are representative Web sites you can access freely and electronic and

Business Meta Sites

Some Web pages that supply links to Internet sites for virtually all areas of business research include:

- *CEO Express!* http://www.ceoexpress.com/
- *Dow Jones Business Directory.* http://bd.dowjones.com/
- *Internet Resources on International Economics and Business.* http://dylee.keel.econ .ship.edu/intntl/index.html
- *International Business Resources on the World Wide Web.* http://www.ciber.msu .edu/busres.htm
- *Milbank, Tweed, Hadley, & McCloy Library.* http://www.milbank.com/library /library.html
- *Yahoo! Business and Economy.* http://www.yahoo.com/

Also, sign up for John McDonnell's Really Useful Business Sites. You'll receive a weekly E-mail containing one or two great sites that John has unearthed. To sign up, just send an E-mail to jaymack@ix.netcom.com with the word "Subscribe" in the subject header.

It's also worthwhile to click on the business hot button displayed at the opening page of many search engines to find links to company information.

print company directories that libraries and businesses commonly purchase. Even the smallest library should own one of these titles.

U.S. company directories covering all industries

Business USA. Omaha, NE: infoUSA. On CD-ROM.

Business USA lists over ten million company records, providing contact information, SIC/NAICS codes, estimated sales volume range, number of employees, brand names, key officers, and credit rating. Other databases from infoUSA include the *American Big Businesses Directory*, with 177,000 businesses; the *American Manufacturers Directory*, with 612,000 manufacturers; and the *4.5 Million Small Business Owners* directory. This publisher also produces company directories in hard copy.

Guidestar. http://www.guidestar.org/

Guidestar is a clearinghouse for information about nonprofit organizations with facts about the programs and finances of over half a million U.S. charities and nonprofit organizations searchable by name, keyword, mission, location, or revenue.

Hoover's Business Resources. http://www.hoovers.com

The Company Capsules section on the Hoover's Web site allows searching by company name, ticker symbol, location, industry, and sales. Each capsule provides brief information about the company, including address, Web site, officers, sales, one-year sales change, major competitors, subsidiary locations, number of employees, and links to current articles about the company. Detailed profiles are available to paying subscribers.

Hoover's Business Press (Austin, Texas) also produces many print company directories, each supplying one- to two-page company profiles that supply financials, major competitors, and discussions of company operations and history. Some titles in their expanding list include *Hoover's Handbook of American Business,* *Hoover's Handbook of Emerging Companies,* and *Hoover's Handbook of Private Companies.* These guides also include rankings for top players in different industries.

Million Dollar Directory: America's Leading Public and Private Companies.
5 Volumes. Parsippany, NJ: Dun & Bradstreet. Annual. Also available on CD-ROM and as a subscription database via Dun & Bradstreet. Company and financial databases from D&B are also on DataStar, DIALOG, and Dow Jones.

The *Million Dollar Directory* lists about 160,000 companies meeting one of the following criteria: 250 or more employees at one location, $25 million or more in sales volume, or tangible net worth greater than $500,000.

Moody's Manuals. New York: Financial Information Services. Also available on CD-ROM and as subscription databases through DIALOG, *Moody's Company Data,* and *Moody's Company Data Direct.*

The *Moody's Manuals,* covering firms on the New York and American Stock Exchanges, supply more information than the average print directory, including company history, subsidiaries, major plant locations, different lines of business the corporation deals in, capital structure, financial statements, and a Moody's rating, ranging from Aaa to C, for corporate bonds and preferred stocks. There are different manuals for different sectors, including *Moody's Bank and Finance Manual, Industrial Manual, Municipal & Government Manual, OTC Industrial Manual, OTC Unlisted Manual, Public Utility Manual,* and *Transportation Manual.* Each set is bound annually with newer information stored in loose-leaf binders updated either weekly or semiweekly, varying by title.

A set that's similar to the *Moody's* series is *Standard & Poor's Corporation Records*, a loose-leaf set that covers public companies, supplying detailed background descriptions and financial information. It's also on DIALOG.

Standard and Poor's Register of Corporations, Directors, and Executives. New York: Standard & Poor's. 3 Volumes. Annual. Also on CD-ROM and as a subscription database via *Standard & Poor's Net Advantage*, DIALOG, LEXIS-NEXIS, and OneSource.

The *Standard and Poor's Register* lists over 75,000 public and private corporations in the U.S. and some from Canada. Biographical data is also included in over 71,000 sketches of top-level managers, listing their principal business affiliations, business and home addresses, E-mail, year and place of birth (when obtainable), college and year of graduation, and fraternal memberships.

Ward's Business Directory of U.S. Private and Public Companies. 8 Volumes. Detroit: Gale. Annual. Also on CD-ROM as part of the *Companies International CD-ROM* and as a subscription database as part of *Gale Business Resources* and OneSource.

Ward's lists and ranks about 100,000 companies.

Ward's Private Company Profiles. Detroit: Gale. Updated irregularly.

The basic company data in this directory is culled from *Ward's Business Directory*, but the information for the companies in this volume is enhanced by articles and excerpts about each company from a variety of sources, including local, regional, national, and trade journals, and books, company brochures, and investment reports.

State and regional directories

Those elusive private firms often appear in directories that focus on a state, city, or region. The publisher American Business Directories produces the *State Business Directory Series*, comprised of a company directory for each of the states in the U.S., such as the *Alabama State Business Directory* and the *Alaska State Business Directory*. Dun & Bradstreet also publishes a series of company directories for each of fifty-four metropolitan areas called the *D&B Regional Business Directories*.

Your library should also have directories compiled by your chamber of commerce or a local publisher. In Colorado we have several regionally produced directories, including the *Rocky Mountain High Technology Directory* and the *Boulder County R&D/Manufacturers Directory*.

Basic Business Phone and Address Directories on the Web

Phone numbers, addresses, and driving directions are available for businesses on many of the general Web phone directories described in chapter six. A meta page to directories is operated by *AT&T* at http://www.att.com/directory/internet.html.

International company directories covering all industries

Carlson Online: Canadian Public Company Information. http://www.fin-info.com/

This free directory links to stock quotes, press releases, and company Web sites for all 4,600 firms listed on the Toronto Stock Exchange, Alberta Stock Exchange, Vancouver Stock Exchange, Montreal Stock Exchange, and the Canadian Dealing Network.

See also *Strategis* at http://strategis.ic.gc.ca/ from the Minister of Industry, which leads to directories of Canadian firms as well as industry reports and information about Canadian business laws and regulations.

Companies International CD-ROM. Detroit: Gale. Biannual.

This database contains information on 300,000 U.S. and foreign firms.

COSMOS Online—Mexican Companies. http://www.cosmos.com.mx

Search for Mexican firms by name or by product at this site in both English and Spanish.

D&B Europa. 4 Volumes. Bethlehem, PA: Dun & Bradstreet. Annual. Also available on CD-ROM.

Sixty-five thousand European firms are listed in *Europa* and ranked, by industry, in its final volume by sales within each country and for Europe as a whole. There are also ranking lists for the top five thousand companies overall ranked by sales and number of employees, and top companies for each business activity ranked by financial size.

Directory of American Firms Operating in Foreign Countries. 3 Volumes. New York: Uniworld Business Publications. Triennial.

This set lists American firms which have operations overseas and then presents listings, country by country, of the foreign operations of each American firm. This publisher also produces the *Directory of Foreign Firms Operating in the United States.*

Fax in a Flash

A print guide to U.S. fax numbers is *FaxUSA: A Directory of Facsimile Numbers for Businesses and Organizations Nationwide* (Detroit: Omnigraphics). More than 110,000 fax numbers are listed.

FP Survey—Industrials. Toronto: Financial Post DataGroup. Annual.

This is a directory to more than 2,800 publicly traded service and manufacturing firms in Canada and has a companion publication titled *FP Survey— Mines & Energy*. Additionally, the Financial Post offers the *FP 5000* on CD-ROM, with information on almost five thousand Canadian companies.

Dun & Bradstreet also publishes several directories of Canadian firms, including the *Guide to Canadian Manufacturers*, *D&B Canadian Key Business Directory*, and, on CD-ROM, *Dun's Business Locator Canada*.

Hoover's Handbook of World Business: Profiles of Major Global Enterprises. Austin, Texas: Hoover's Business Press. Annual.

This directory offers two-page overviews for 250 influential non-U.S. firms, including a history and description of each and its key competitors.

ISI Emerging Markets. Boston: Internet Securities. See http://www.securities.com/ for a demo.

ISI is a Web-based subscription database leading to company information as well as news, industry and market analysis, equity quotes, macroeconomic data, and legal and current affairs for emerging markets in Argentina, Brazil, Chile, Colombia, Ecuador, Mexico, Peru, Venezuela, China, India, the Baltic States, Bulgaria, Central Asia, Czech Republic, Hungary, Poland, Romania, Russia, Turkey, Ukraine, China, and India.

Kompass Directories. Cruet, France: Kompass International. Also available on CD-ROM, at http://www.kompass.com/ and available as subscription databases on DIALOG.

Kompass, in conjunction with publishers in other nations, publishes directories for companies and products worldwide, with each directory devoted to a specific country or region. The directories use the Kompass classification index, a unique industry/product identification system, to index companies. These directories cover a wide range of nations, including Bahrain, Croatia, Iceland, Luxembourg, Malta, Morocco, Tunisia, and Uzbekistan.

The Kompass Web page covers 1.5 million companies, 19 million product references, 2.5 million executives names, and 370,000 trade and brand names in over 60 countries. Once you register at the site, you can get worldwide company names, addresses, fax, and telephone numbers. More information is available for paid subscribers.

Major Companies of Europe. 4 Volumes. London: Graham & Whiteside, Detroit: Gale. Annual. This title and other *Major Company* directories are also on the *Major Companies Series* CD-ROM, on OneSource, and, at the time of this writing, were headed for inclusion on GaleNet.

This directory covers more than 24,000 of Europe's largest companies. Other directories in the *Major Companies* series cover *Africa South of the Sahara, The Arab World, Central and Eastern Europe and the Commonwealth of Independent States, the Far East and Australasia, Latin America and the Caribbean, Scandinavia, South East Asia,* and *South West Asia.*

Principal International Businesses. New York: Dun & Bradstreet. Annual. Also available on CD-ROM.

This directory has brief listings for 50,000 corporations in 140 countries. Dun & Bradstreet also offers a subscription database with international company information called *WORLDBASE.*

D&B publishes many company directories in print and on CD-ROM for specific countries, including *Australia's 10,000 Largest, British Business Rankings, Denmark's Top 10,000 Companies, Dun's Guide to Hong Kong Businesses, Dun's Guide to Israel, France's 30,000 Top Companies, Italy's Top 10,000 Companies, Japan 250,000 CD-ROM, Key Business Directory of India, Key Business Directory of Indonesia/Philippines/Thailand, Key Business Directory of Malaysia, Key Business Directory of Singapore, Mexico CD-ROM, Norway's Top 10,000, Principal Companies in Portugal, Spain's Top 30,000, Sweden's Top 8,000, Taiwan's Leading Corporations, Top 25,000 Companies in Netherlands, Top 25,000 Companies of Belgium and Luxembourg,* and *United Kingdom's 10,000 Largest.*

Moody's International Manual. New York: Financial Information Services. Annual with weekly updates. Also available on CD-ROM and as a subscription database via DIALOG.

Part of the *Moody's Manuals* series, described earlier, this directory includes lengthy entries that provide history, description of business and property, and financial information for 11,100 enterprises in 117 nations.

World Business Directory. Detroit: Gale. Annual. Also available on CD-ROM on *Companies International.*

Nearly 140,000 firms active in international trade in over 180 countries are listed in this directory.

Worldscope. Bethesda, MD: Disclosure. Available on CD-ROM and as a subscription database via Bloomberg Financial Markets, Bridge Data, Disclosure's *Global Access,* OCLC's FirstSearch, OneSource, and others.

This database contains business descriptions and historic and contemporary financial data for more than fifteen thousand companies in fifty nations.

Company directories for particular industries

There are thousands of directories that provide basic data on companies in specific industries. Do you want to call advertising agencies that specialize in promotions in the health industry? Check the *Standard Directory of Advertising Agencies.* Do you need to find manufacturers of bolts? Look in the *Thomas Register.* So before you check a general directory, see if there's one geared to your needs. In a library catalog, do a keyword search using the word DIRECTORIES and the industry you're interested in, such as REAL ESTATE DIRECTORIES.

Sample online and print specialized company directories include:

Accountants

CPAFirms.com. http://www.cpafirms.com/

Use this Web directory to find CPA firms worldwide. Another directory on the Internet is *Accountant Finder* at http://www.cpafinder.com/.

Emerson's Directory of Leading US Accounting Firms. Bellevue, WA: Emerson. Annual.

Five hundred top accounting firms are profiled in this directory.

Advertising/Marketing

Green Book: International Directory of Marketing Research Houses and Services. New York: New York Chapter, American Marketing Association. Annual.

The *Green Book* is a listing of names, addresses, numbers, and short statements about market research firms searchable by company specialties. The American Marketing Association also publishes the *Focus Group Directory.*

On the Web, search the *American Marketing Association's Marketing Services Guide* at http://www.ama.org/resource/msg/. Another site on the Web to search for market research firms is *Zarden's Market Research Direct-A-Net* at http://www.zarden.com/.

Standard Directory of Advertisers. Wilmette, IL: National Register Publishing.

Annual. Also available on CD-ROM and as a subscription database through the publisher.

Commonly called the *Red Book*, this directory, arranged by advertiser, lists the products each firm spends advertising dollars on and where the money goes, i.e., to cable television, billboards, radio, newspapers, consumer magazines, posters, or network television. This directory also lists the names of the sales/marketing people in a company. Companion volumes are the *Standard Directory of Advertising Agencies* and the *Standard Directory of International Advertisers & Agencies.*

Consultants

Consultants and Consulting Organizations Directory. 2 Volumes. Detroit: Gale, 1973–present. Triennial.

Both consulting firms and individual consultants are listed in this directory, with a description of their consulting specialties. A similar directory from Dun & Bradstreet is the *D&B Consultants Directory.*

HR Consultant Directory. http://memdir.shrm.org/consultants/

This site is a Web-based directory of human resources consultants, maintained by the Society for Human Resource Management.

Franchises

See the home page of the *American Association of Franchisees and Dealers* at http://www.aafd.org/, or call them at (800)733-9858 for advice on purchasing franchise businesses like Petland or Fat Boys Bar-B-Q. Other franchise resources available both in print and on the Web include *The Franchise Handbook* (Milwaukee, WI: Enterprise Magazines) at http://www.franchise1.com/, the *Franchise Annual* (Lewiston, NY: Info Franchise News) at http://infonews.com/franchise/, the *Franchise Opportunities Guide* (Washington, DC: International Franchise Association) at http://www.franchise.org/fog.asp, and, just on the Web, *Bison: The Franchise Network* at http://www.bison1.com/.

Financial Institutions

Moody's Bank & Finance Manual. 4 Volumes. New York: Financial Information Services. Annual.

This *Moody's Manual* has information about banks, insurance companies, investment firms, unit investment trusts, real estate companies, real estate investment trusts, and miscellaneous financial enterprises.

Thomson/Polk Bank Directory. 5 Volumes. Skokie, IL: Thomson Financial Publishing. Biannual. Also available on CD-ROM and as a subscription database under the name *Financial Institutions Online* from Thomson Financial.

This guide profiles banks in over 212 nations. Thomson also publishes the *Polk North American Financial Institutions Directory* with information on virtually every bank, savings and loan, and major credit union in North America, including banks and branches in Canada, Mexico, the Caribbean, and Central America.

High Tech

CorpTech Directory of Technology Companies. Woburn, MA: Corporate Technology Information Services. Annual. Also available on CD-ROM, at http://www.corptech.com, and as a subscription database via Corporate Technology Information Services, DataStar, and OneSource.

This directory identifies U.S. manufacturers and developers of technology products, including those involved in artificial intelligence, biotechnology, computer hardware and software, defense systems, photonics, robotics, test and measurement, and transportation.

Lido Telecom WebCentral. http://www.telecomwebcentral.com/

Once you register at this free site, you can search through a directory of over 1,500 high-tech companies, including Internet service providers; network equipment providers; computer hardware, software and peripheral suppliers; consultants; and telecommunication carriers and network operators.

Insurance

Best's Insurance Reports. Oldwick, NJ: A.M. Best. Annual.

There are two *Best's* reports for U.S. firms, one covering *Life-Health* insurance, the other *Property-Casualty* insurance. There is also a *Best's Insurance Reports International.* These guides look at insurance companies, and assign them each a Best's Rating, an A++ through F letter system, determined by a variety of factors. Several pages of financial data is devoted to each company, along with comment on the history, management, and operations of each company.

Manufacturers

Thomas Register of American Manufacturers. New York: Thomas Publishing. Annual. Also on CD-ROM and at http://www.thomasregister.com, with

regional editions available at http://www.thomasregional.com/newtrd/nc_
home.html.

The print version of this oversized multivolume bright green collection is
hard to miss. It's the premier all-in-one directory to U.S. manufacturers of
more than 57,000 products. Both electronic and print versions of the *Thomas
Register* are searchable by a product or company name. Thomas's also supplies
company profiles for some of the manufacturers with such information as
whether they export, asset ratings, company executives, locations of sales offices, distributors, plants, and service/engineering offices. Product catalogs are
also included for a number of the companies, supplying more detailed product
information, including specifications, drawings, photographs, and availability
and performance data.

Very Specialized Business Directories

There are hundreds of very specialized directories and mailing
lists that don't commonly show up in many libraries or
bookstores. They're directories that companies buy, or that show
up in libraries and bookstores that specialize or cater to a particular kind of business.
A guide that identifies industry-specific directories is *Directories in Print: A Descriptive
Guide to Print and Non-Print Directories, Buyer's Guides, Rosters, and Other Address
Lists of All Kinds* (2 Volumes. Detroit: Gale. Annual), also available online via
GaleNet.

Industry Information

Is there really a decline in movie attendance and a boom in video rental? Information about the health and future of industries can be culled from many types of
resources, including:

- **Industry/Market Research Reports**. There are publications and databases,
  listed on p. 329, that analyze business sectors, supplying history of an
  industry, its current prospects, competitors, and financial information.
- **Investment Reports**. Geared to the investor, these reports discuss the investment potential of specific companies and industries. See the Investment
  Information section later in this chapter.
- **Articles From Periodicals**. Seeking industry analysis from articles is often

the best choice for smaller industries that don't have nice tidy reports written about them.

Industry reports commonly found in larger libraries are:

The Encyclopedia of American Industries. 2nd edition. 2 Volumes. Scott Heil, ed. Detroit: Gale, 1998. Also available as a subscription database as part of *Gale Business Resources.*

Over a thousand manufacturing and nonmanufacturing industries are explored in these volumes. This series is unique in that it describes trends and conditions of smaller industries, such as florists, often ignored in such guides. Complementary directories from this publisher are the *Encyclopedia of Emerging Industries,* the *Encyclopedia of Global Industries,* and *U.S. Industry Profiles.*

Panorama of EU Industry. Luxembourg: Office for Official Publications of the European Communities. Annual.

This volume describes the current situation and outlook for manufacturing and service industries in the European Union.

Standard & Poor's Industry Surveys. New York: Standard & Poor's. Also available as part of the online subscription service *Standard & Poor's Net Advantage.*

Released quarterly, this publication surveys major industries such as banking, electronics, and telecommunications. Each of the surveys includes industry background, figures, trends, and outlook, as well as statistics for the leading companies in that industry. The earnings supplement section ranks companies by relative profitability.

Industry Facts and Figures From Trade Associations

Business associations are a great source of statistics related to industries and products. Find associations by using the general directories and tips recommended under Expert Directories in chapter six, or contact the American Society of Association Executives, 1575 I St., NW, Washington, DC 20005, Phone: (202)626-2723, TDD: (202)626-2803, Fax: (202)371-8825, URL: http://www.asaenet.org/. *Yahoo!* is also a good choice for locating trade associations at http://dir.yahoo.com/Business_and_Economy/Organizations/Trade_Associations/.

U.S. Industry and Trade Outlook. Formerly titled *U.S. Industrial Outlook,* 1984–1994. Published jointly by McGraw-Hill and the U.S. Department of

Commerce, International Trade Administration. Annual. Also available on CD-ROM.

Fifty manufacturing and service industries are examined in this volume, with commentary and figures related to the industry's growth potential, world-market share, trends, new technology, trade, production, and labor data. Industry reports from the *International Trade Administration* can also be found at http://www.ita.doc.gov under "Industries."

Obtaining market research reports is not always an inexpensive proposition. These reports are priced to sell to companies or potential investors who stand to earn a good deal of money. The source *Findex: The Worldwide Directory of Market Research Reports, Studies, and Surveys* (Cambridge Information Group. Annual with supplements), available in print or on the Web at http://www.findsvp.com/, lists thousands of reports available for purchase. Prices range from several hundred dollars to over ten thousand dollars.

A great resource for overseas market research reports is the *National Trade Data Bank—NTDB*, where you can find reports compiled by the International Trade Association for specific industries or products in different regions. Sample report names, to show you how specialized they can be, include *India: Hotel and Restaurant Equipment* and *Spain: Air Conditioning Service.*

All government depository libraries should have *NTDB* either on CD-ROM or offer it on the Web as part of the STAT-USA system. Many nondepository libraries as well as business people also purchase it because of the relatively low cost for the abundance of information. There's more information about STAT-USA on p. 341 under Importing, Exporting and Doing Business Overseas.

Some subscription databases offering market research reports include:

BCC Market Research, covering 80 percent U.S. firms and 20 percent non-U.S. BCC reports and newsletters. Available via DIALOG, Information Access Company, LEXIS-NEXIS, MarkIntel, and Profound.

Datamonitor Market Research, offering international coverage. Available via DataStar, DIALOG, FT-Profile, and MarkIntel. Also search for citations and order reports at http://www.datamonitor.com.

Euromonitor Market Research, covering U.S., France, Italy, Germany, Spain, and U.K. Available on CD-ROM and via DataStar, DIALOG, and FT-Profile. Also search for citations and order reports at http://www.euromonitor.com.

Freedonia Market Research, covering mostly U.S. reports. Available via

DataStar, DIALOG, FT-Profile, LEXIS-NEXIS, MarkIntel, Profound, and others. Also search for citations and order reports at http://www.freedonia group.com/.

Frost & Sullivan Market Intelligence, with international coverage. Available via DataStar and DIALOG. Full-text Frost & Sullivan reports are also part of *Investext*. Also search for citations and order reports at http://www.frost .com/.

One of the more accessible databases, *Investext*, also includes market research reports. See a full description of this database later under Investment Information.

Market Share/Rankings

What share of the high tech market is held by Microsoft? What brands of light beer sell the most?

Articles will often report on the share of the market for particular companies and top firms in different industries. Use any of the periodical indexes listed under Business in Appendix B, and try keyword phrases like MARKET SHARE, RANKING or RANKINGS combined with the name of a company, such as PEPSI, or an industry, such as BEVERAGE(S) or SOFT DRINK(S).

Trade associations may also be able to answer questions about rankings and market share. See tips for contacting industry-specific associations in the Fact in a Flash box on p. 329.

Directories and databases reporting market share and rankings include:

Asia's 7,500 Largest Companies. London: ELC International. Annual.

This directory ranks companies from the Asia-Pacific region by profits, business activity, and within country. Also from this publisher are directories *Europe's 15,000 Largest Companies* and *UK's 10,000 Largest Companies.*

Business Rankings Annual. Compiled by the Brooklyn Public Library Business Library Staff. Detroit: Gale. Annual. Also available on CD-ROM and as a subscription database via *Gale Business Resources.*

This is basically a top ten of anything related to business. The Brooklyn Library staff ransacks rankings from magazines, journals, financial services, directories, statistical compilations, and other sources to come up with this volume. The book is arranged by subject, with such diverse headings as Largest Banks in Papua New Guinea and North America's Top Ski Resorts.

D & B Business Rankings. Bethlehem, PA: Dun & Bradstreet. Annual.

This directory ranks companies by national sales and number of employees, with top companies also listed for each state and within industry categories.

Rankings Offered by Trade Journals

Many trade journals compile rankings of major companies within the industry they focus on, such as the *Inc. 500*, a ranking of small U.S. businesses, which, in addition to being a special print issue of *Inc. Magazine*, is also on the Web at http://www.inc.com/500/. Samples of other lists both in print and on the Internet include the *Private 500*, a listing of the top private U.S. companies from *Forbes* magazine at http://www.forbes .com/tool/toolbox/private500/index.htm, and the *Fortune 500* from *Fortune* magazine at http://www.pathfinder.com/fortune/fortune500/. Such lists are also part of *Price's List of Lists*, which points to company rankings on the Web at http://gwis2.circ .gwu.edu/~gprice/listof.htm.

Another way of pinpointing trade magazines that produce company rankings is by checking the *Guide to Special Issues and Indexes of Periodicals* (4th edition. Washington, DC: Special Libraries Association, 1994), which identifies special issues covering dozens of diverse topics and industries.

Many other D&B directories include rankings, including *D&B Europa*, listing top firms in Europe, and other directories listed earlier under the description of the *Principal International Businesses* directory.

FT500. London: Financial Times. Annual.

The *FT500*, a special annual issue of the *Financial Times*, is a guide to top companies in the world, the U.S., Europe, Japan and the U.K., listed by market capitalization.

Fortune Global 500. http://pathfinder.com/fortune/global500/

This listing, ranking companies worldwide by revenues and profits, is available both on the Web and in an early August issue of the print version of *Fortune* magazine.

Hoover's Business Resources. http://www.hoovers.com/

The *Hoover's* Web site and company directories, described earlier, supply company ranking lists and name company competitors.

Investext. New York: The Investext Group. Also available on CD-ROM and as a subscription database through CompuServe, DataStar, DIALOG, Dow Jones Interactive, FT-Profile, the Information Access Company, the Investext Group, LEXIS-NEXIS, OneSource, Profound, and others.

This database of investment and market research reports, described in more detail later, often includes market share data within its reports.

The Market Share Reporter: An Annual Compilation of Reported Market Share Data on Companies, Products, and Services. Detroit: Gale. Annual. Also available on CD-ROM and as a subscription database via *Gale Business Resources.*

The *Reporter* is a compilation of market share data culled from periodicals and brokerage reports. In some cases, pie charts or bar graphs are added to help the reader visualize the market share of various companies or the sales of different products or services. Don't think the product you're researching is too obscure—it might be in here. There is also an international version of this title called the *World Market Share Reporter.*

Standard & Poor's Industry Survey.

Described earlier under Industry Information.

The Times 1,000. New York: HarperCollins. Annual.

A guide to the one thousand leading companies in the U.K. and Europe, and other major companies in the U.S., Canada, Australia, South Africa, Hong Kong, Ireland, and Japan.

Ward's Business Directory of U.S. Private and Public Companies. 5 Volumes. Belmont, CA: Information Access. Annual. Also available as a subscription database as part of *Gale Business Resources* and from the Information Access Company as part of *Company ProFile* and the *General Business Database.*

In addition to being an alphabetic directory of companies, *Ward's* also ranks companies by sales within industry classification, for the nation, and state by state.

Other directories ranking companies are listed earlier under International Company Directories.

Data can also be manipulated in many online databases to create rankings. For example, on the Disclosure database, companies can be chosen and ranked by different criteria, such as choosing all companies with the industry code designated for the manufacture of paper products and then ranking them by sales.

Business Information From Articles

The answers to just about all business questions can be found in articles. Consult Appendix B under Business to see the types of business indexes available. These indexes will bring you to trade journals and newsletters devoted to a particular industry, such as *Footwear News* or *Nation's Restaurant News,* to popular general business magazines, like *Fortune* or *Forbes,* and to scholarly business journals, such as the *Journal of Management Studies*. Indexes focusing on newspapers and news services indexes will also be of particular interest in business research, so see that heading in Appendix B as well.

Remember that when using a periodical index to find business-related information:

- You can look under the name of a particular industry, like *cosmetics*.
- You can look under the name of a company or store, such as *Celestial Seasonings*.
- You can look under a person's name, like *Donald Trump*.
- You can look under a product type, for example, *ice cream*.
- Online, you can search the specific name of a product, such as *Dove Bars*.

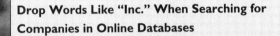

Drop Words Like "Inc." When Searching for Companies in Online Databases

When searching an online database using the name of a company, always drop the Inc., Co., Company, Corp., Corporation, PLC, and Ltd. For example, don't search with the words MAYTAG CORP. or CORPORATION—just use MAYTAG.

Investment Information

This section reviews resources that help the investor or potential investor stay away from the outer sills of tall buildings. Stock, once purchased, is often traded from one owner to another. The U.S. stock exchanges you'll see most references to are the New York Stock Exchange (NYSE) and the two that joined forces in 1998, the NASDAQ Stock Market (NASDAQ) and the American Stock Exchange (AMEX).

NASDAQ, the National Association of Security Dealers Automated Quotations, is a computerized trading system and NASDAQ dealers are not gathered in a particular place. Brokers using NASDAQ purchase stock that they specialize in, and then sell it for a markup. Most of the stocks NASDAQ works with are Over-the-Counter (OTC) stocks, referring to their not being affiliated with exchanges located in specific places, like the NYSE.

Both the NYSE and the AMEX (still maintaining its own operations despite the merger with NASDAQ) are physical places, where brokers buy and sell securities auction-style, on behalf of others. There are also regional exchanges in large cities of the U.S., including Chicago, San Francisco, Philadelphia, and Boston.

There are also OTC, or unlisted, companies, that don't meet filing requirements for major exchanges and are also not included in NASDAQ trading. These firms are not necessarily small. These companies are also referred to as pink sheet companies, in reference to a daily listing published for brokerage firms by the National Quotation Bureau that lists bid and ask prices for these companies equities.

An extensive listing of URLs for stock exchanges worldwide is at http://www .nasdaq.com/reference/onlinemarkets.stm, or at the *Stock Markets of the World* site at http://www.internationalist.com/SERVICE/Stocks.html.

Finding a Ticker Symbol

To find the ticker symbol assigned to a company—something you'll need to look up investment information on a company—look on the company's home page, in one of the print or online company directories listed above, or through a quick ticker symbol look-up page on the Web, including the one at *Yahoo!* at http://quote.yahoo.com/, or at the *CNN Financial Network* at http://cnnfn.com/markets/quotes.html.

Investment has a language of its own. Find dictionaries in libraries using the keywords INVESTMENT and DICTIONARIES. An online financial glossary supplying brief definitions is *InvestorWords* at http://www.investorwords.com/.

Stock information is listed in the business section of regional newspapers throughout the U.S., as well as papers with national coverage like *The New York Times* and *The Washington Post.*

Leading U.S. financial newspapers are *The Wall Street Journal* (http://interactive .wsj.com/), its sister publication, *Barron's*, published weekly (http://www.barrons .com/) and *Investor's Business Daily* (http://www.investors.com). In addition to economic, business, and technology news, they offer extensive, evaluative, investment information, and data.

Overseas, *The Financial Times* is the international equivalent of *The Wall Street Journal. The Wall Street Journal* also publishes the *Asian Wall Street Journal* and the *European Wall Street Journal.*

If you need daily stock prices over time, an alternative to expensive online databases or thumbing through individual daily newspapers is the *Daily Stock Price Record* series from Standard & Poor's, available at many libraries. There are separate volumes dedicated to NYSE, AMEX, and NASDAQ, each listing the volume of shares traded for the day and high, low, and closing prices.

There's no shortage of print and online resources that help investors track companies and industries. Note that almost all Web-based services supply some information for free, but then offer much-enhanced services to subscribers. All of the free services, for example, offer delayed securities quotes, with real-time quotes offered to subscribers.

Here are some of the investment services for stocks, bonds, and mutual funds available online and in print:

Bonds Online. http://www.bonds-online.com/

At Bonds Online there's information on tax-free municipal bonds, treasury/savings bonds, corporate bonds, and bond funds (with a fee for more information lurking behind every click). The Bond Professor section teaches about bonds.

Commodity Market Review. Rome: Commodities and Trade Division, Food and Agriculture Organization of the United Nations. Annual. Also available at http://www.fao.org/; click on "Economics."

The *Review* presents analysis of developments in the global economy and reviews the market situation for twenty-one commodity groups, including bananas, cocoa, forest products, cotton, and wheat. The online site for this publication includes a listing of commodity specialists that can be contacted.

Company Sleuth. http://www.companysleuth.com/

Register, at no charge, and give Company Sleuth up to ten companies you'd like to track. Sleuth then forwards to your E-mail new information that it finds on the Web related to new patents, SEC filings, earnings estimates, comments from discussion groups, stock quotes, analyst ratings, new trademarks, insider trades, job postings, and press releases.

DBC Online. http://www.dbc.com/

On the Data Broadcasting Corporation page you'll find quotes and charts for stocks and bonds, mutual fund information, news from CBS Market-Watch, and links to useful financial sites. Enhanced services are available to subscribers. Other notable sites with a mix of quotes, charts, news, and analysis include *Quicken.com* at http://www.quicken.com and *Zack's Investment Research* at http://www.zacks.com.

Dow Jones Interactive. Princeton, NJ: Dow Jones.

International in scope, this subscription database pulls news and financial data from thousands of newspapers, business publications, television transcripts, newswires, market research and financial analyst's reports, and historical financial information on more than 250,000 financial issues. *The Wall Street Journal* is also full-text on this service. Dow Jones also offers DowVision, a customizable service for timely data on companies the user chooses.

Kiplinger Online. http://www.kiplinger.com

Kiplinger Online has quotes and news for investors, along with advice on retirement, home purchasing, savings, and other personal finance topics. Kiplinger also publishes *Kiplinger' Personal Finance Magazine* and other investment and personal finance titles.

Investext. New York: The Investext Group. Also available on CD-ROM and as a subscription database through DIALOG, Dow Jones Interactive, FT-Profile, the Information Access Company, LEXIS-NEXIS, Profound, and others.

Investext includes the full text of company and industry reports created by investment banks, brokerage houses, market research firms, and trade associations. Many academic libraries with business programs subscribe to *Investext*, though their version will likely contain delayed reports.

IPO Central. http://www.ipocentral.com

This site has information on Initial Public Offerings of companies (IPOs), firms just going public or that recently went public. Search by company name, industry, underwriter, state, or metropolitan area.

Moody's Bond Publications. New York: Financial Information Services.

As mentioned earlier, corporate stocks and bonds in the company directory *Moody's Manuals* are assigned a letter rating ranging from Aaa (the best) through C, to help investors assess the issues. *Moody's Municipal and Government Manual* also rates municipal bonds. Other bond resources from this publisher include *Moody's Bond Record*, with monthly ratings and data coverage of over 68,000 issues, including corporate bonds, convertible bonds, preferred stock, and municipal bonds and notes, and *Moody's Credit Survey*, with weekly data and commentary on the economy and fixed income markets.

Morningstar Mutual Funds. Chicago: Morningstar. Monthly.

This loose-leaf service evaluates 1,700 top mutual funds. They also publish *Morningstar No-Load Funds.* The *Morningstar.Net* site at http://www.morningstar.net generates reports on more than sixteen thousand mutual funds and stocks, articles on investment and industry trends, the Portfolio X-Ray service, for evaluating your current investments, and an online discussion area.

Other print mutual fund evaluation resources commonly found in libraries include: *Investment Companies Yearbook, Mutual Funds Update* and *Mutual*

Funds Report, all from CDA/Wiesenberger (http://www.wiesenberger.com), *Mutual Fund Survey* from Value Line (http://www.valueline.com) and *Standard & Poor's Lipper Mutual Fund Profiles.*

Other recommended mutual fund sites on the Net are *Brill's Mutual Funds Interactive* at http://www.brill.com, *IBC Financial Data* at http://www.ibcdata .com, which has advice on how to select a money fund, and *FindaFund* at http://www.findafund.com.

Motley Fool. http://www.fool.com

A fun finance site? Yes. Avoiding jargon, this site is a place to learn about investing and personal finance, find the quotes and data, and chat with other investors and Motley Fool experts.

Red Chip Review. Portland: Red Chip Review. Biweekly. Also available by subscription at http://www.redchip.com/.

Red Chip, a quickly growing investment resource, supplies equity research on about three hundred small public firms. Some free information is available at their Web site. Other small cap resources are described later: the StockGuide Web site and *Walker's.*

Standard & Poor's Bond Guide and *Standard & Poor's Securities Stock Guide.* New York: Standard & Poor's. Monthly.

These booklets, issued monthly, offer data in a tabular format for stocks and bonds. The *Bond Guide* lists over 6,700 U.S. corporate bonds, 560 Canadian and foreign issues, and almost 350 convertible bonds, covering interest dates; Standard & Poor rating; eligibility for bank purchase; form of bond; call price, with beginning and ending date; sinking fund; fund restrictions; amount of issue outstanding; the original underwriter; high and low price range; last sale or bid price; yields both current and to maturity; cash and equivalent; current assets and liabilities; long-term debt; capitalization; and total debt.

The *Stock Guide,* covering more than seven thousand stock issues, lists call prices, rankings and ratings, the number of financial institutions that own shares of the stock and the number of shares owned, high and low stock price ranges, trading volume, dividend rate and latest payments, P-E ratio, the EPS five-year growth rate, the total return value, figures from company balance sheets, cash and equivalent, current assets and current liabilities, long term debt, and earnings per share. Check http://www.spsecurities.com/research.htm for more information about S&P investment databases.

Standard & Poor's Stock Reports. New York: Standard & Poor's. Quarterly. Also available on CD-ROM and as a subscription database via *Standard & Poor's Net Advantage.* Reports can also be ordered via fax for a fee; call (800)546-0300 for information.

The *Stock Reports*, available at many libraries, contain two-page reports on over 4,600 companies traded on the NYSE, AMEX, NASDAQ, and other regional and international exchanges. The reports include key income statement and balance sheet items, an analysis of the most recent earnings report, and data on dividends, stock price ranges, capitalization, management, and significant developments. There is also description and commentary on the company's business, product lines, marketing organization, and R&D efforts. Similar to these reports, covering 950 stocks, is *Moody's Handbook of Common Stocks*, issued quarterly.

StockGuide. http://www.stockguide.com

This site specializes in supplying information about OTC, pink sheet, and small capitalization (small cap) companies. A print guide to small cap firms is *Standard & Poor's SmallCap 600 Guide.*

Value Line Investment Survey. New York: Arnold Bernard. Also available on CD-ROM and as a subscription database via Value Line.

The print version of *Value Line* is in three sections. The Ratings & Reports sections, updated quarterly, present industry reviews and full-page, individual stock reports encapsulating the company's past performance, current status, and outlook, giving year-ahead and three- to five-year probable relative price performance, projections of key financial measures, and commentary on current operations and future prospects. The Summary & Index section, updated weekly, provides a key to locating the latest quarterly and supplementary reports in the Ratings and Reports section, and cites the most recent data on each of the stocks followed. The Selection & Opinion section gives *Value Line's* views on the economy, the stock market, and on stocks of interest. The standard edition of *Value Line* follows 1,700 stocks. The expanded edition adds another 1,800 stocks, mostly small cap. See the *Value Line* Internet site at http://www.valueline.com/ for information about other investment resources they offer.

Walker's Manual of Unlisted Stocks. 3rd edition. 1998.

Walker's supplies a full page of information for each of four hundred unlisted stocks and investment partnerships. Most are not profiled in other directories. Other titles from this publisher include *Walker's Manual of Penny Stocks*, highlighting companies with stocks priced under five dollars a share, and *Walk-*

er's Manual of Community Bank Stocks, devoted to banks and thrifts that are
not listed on major exchanges.

World Stock Exchange Fact Book. Austin, Texas: Meridian Securities Markets.
Annual.

There's more than twenty years of data from more than forty-five stock
markets worldwide in this fact book. Other international stock market handbooks are the *Salomon Smith Barney Guide to World Equity Markets* (London:
Euromoney) and the *Handbook of World Stock, Derivative, and Commodity
Exchanges* (London: International Financial Publications).

Small Business Start-Up/Entrepreneurship

When searching for books about starting a small business in a library catalog,
you'll find general books about business start-up by using the keywords SMALL
BUSINESS, NEW BUSINESS ENTERPRISES, ENTREPRENEURSHIP, or
SUCCESS IN BUSINESS combined with such words as CASE STUDIES,
MANAGEMENT, FINANCE, MARKETING, or a broad or specialized busi-
ness type, such as DAY CARE, RETAIL, or FLORIST.

Trade associations usually offer personal assistance and written materials for
those entering the field they represent for little or no cost. A marvelous guide to
associations, articles, guides, and seminars for specific small business types, available at many libraries, is the two-volume *Small Business Sourcebook* (Detroit:
Gale).

An Internet site full of useful links is the *Small and Home-Based Business Links*
page at http://www.bizoffice.com/index.html. It points to useful Web resources
for financing, marketing, franchising, small-business services, and how-to
information.

Web sites with sample business plans include the page for the *Small Business
Development Center* at Central Missouri State University at http://153.91.1.141
/sbdc/centsbdc/SBDC.HTM, and *Bplans*, at http://www.bplans.com/start.cfm,
which has plans for small- and medium-sized businesses. Gale also publishes a
compilation of business plans created by entrepreneurs in different industries
called *Business Plans Handbook* (5th edition, 1998).

The *Small Business Administration* also offers publications and advice on its
home page at http://www.sbaonline.sba.gov/ and through its regional, district,
and branch offices throughout the U.S. Check the government pages in your
phone book or the SBA Web site for local contacts.

To find people interested in supplying capital to get your business started, see

Tax Forms Online

There are a number of places to find tax forms online:

- *1040.com Federal Tax Forms and Instructions.* http://www.1040.com/download.htm
- *1040.com State Tax Forms and Instructions.* http://www.1040.com/stpdf.htm
- *Tax Forms From the IRS.* http://www.irs.ustreas.gov/plain/forms_pubs/forms.html

Also of interest is a site that gives tax rates by state, including sales, income, and excise taxes: *FTA—State Tax Rates and Structure* at http://www.taxadmin.org/fta/rate/tax_stru.html.

Venture Capital Online (VCOL) at http://www.vcapital.com on the Web, or *Pratt's Guide to Venture Capital Resources* and the *Fitzroy Dearborn International Directory of Venture Capital Funds* in print.

Importing, Exporting, and Doing Business Overseas

The International Trade Administration (ITA), part of the Department of Commerce, is a major source of import/export information. To talk to an expert, give the Trade Information Center a call at (800)USA-TRADE or (202)482-0543. Their fax is (202)482-4473. The ITA home page, at http://www.ita.doc.gov/, offers advice on international trade and exporting, notice of programs and events, and trade statistics. The *National Export Directory*, at http://infoserv2.ita.doc.gov/NEDHome?.nsf, helps exporters find trade contacts at the local, state, and federal levels.

A major repository of international trade information can be found on *STAT-USA*, also from the U.S. Department of Commerce, at http://www.stat-usa.gov. STAT-USA is an Internet database containing information on the U.S. economy and reams of information of interest to exporters and importers. STAT-USA has two search areas: the State of the Nation section, which has U.S. economic data and is described in detail under Economic and Financial Statistics for the U.S. and the Globus & NTDB (National Trade Data Bank) section.

The Globus & NTDB area on STAT-USA has trade-related data from over forty federal agencies, including a regularly updated listing of global business leads and trade opportunities, foreign exchange rates, market and country research reports, figures for U.S. exports and imports by commodity and country, and contact information for services related to exporting goods. Also, click on their "Trade Library" option to find writings of interest to new exporters, such as the *Basic Guide to Exporting* (also available in print in many libraries).

The country research guides on STAT-USA are called *Country Commercial Guides* (also directly accessible at http://www.state.gov/www/about_state/busin ess/com_guides/index.html). These guides, each dedicated to a nation, cover the nation's economic trends, political environment, market idiosyncrasies, leading sectors for U.S. exports and investments, trade regulations and standards, contacts, schedule of trade events, and pointers to market research.

Some of the information is free at the STAT-USA Web site, but many links are by subscription only. Check to see if your local library has STAT-USA or, to subscribe yourself, contact STAT-USA by phone: (800)782-8872 or (202)482-1986, Fax: (202)482-2164, E-mail: stat-usa@doc.gov, or via their Web site.

Facts in a Flash

Exchange Rates on the Web and by Phone

Internet sites that offer exchange rates include *The Currency Site* at http://www.oanda.com/, which has historical tables, current rates, and forecasts for world currencies, *Currency Conversion* from *Yahoo!* at http://quote.yahoo.com/m3?u; and the Fund Rates page from the *International Monetary Fund* at http://www.imf.org/external/np/tre/sdr/sdr.htm.

You can also call the Federal Reserve Bank of New York for rates at (212)720-6130. I've also had success calling a local bank for a rate.

Another government Internet site for the importer or exporter is the *U.S. Customs Service* at http://www.customs.ustreas.gov/, with links to commercial importing procedures and requirements, exporting documentation procedures, and trade rulings and regulations, including the *Harmonized Tariff Schedule of the United States* (also available in print) at http://www.customs.ustreas.gov/imp-exp/rulings/harmo niz/index.htm, which assigns a classification code to imported goods to determine things like rate of duty.

Meta sites to trade information include: *TradePort* at http://tradeport.org/, *Trade Zone* at http://www.tradezone.com/trdzone.htm, and *Country Reports On Economic Policy and Trade Practices* at http://www.state.gov/www/issues/econo mic/trade_reports/index.html.

There are several directories listing export and import companies, including *The American Export Register* (New York: Thomas Publishing), available in print and on the Web at http://www.aernet.com/, and the *Directory of United States Exporters* and *Directory of United States Importers* (New York: Journal of Commerce), available in print and on CD-ROM.

Other notable trade resources commonly found in libraries include:

The Exporters Encyclopedia. Bethlehem, PA: Dun & Bradstreet. Annual.

This guide has answers for export questions and information related to particular countries. Arranged alphabetically by country, each section presents marketing data, trade regulations, key contacts, description of communication and transportation services, and tips on business travel. It's kept up-to-date with supplements in a companion notebook called the *Fact File.*

Importers Manual USA. Novato, CA: World Trade Press. Updated irregularly. Also available on CD-ROM.

In almost nine hundred pages, *Importers Manual USA* covers how-to importing information, including facts on packing, shipping, insurance, business law, U.S. Customs entry and clearance, and international banking. This publisher also publishes *Exporting to the USA* and many other international trade titles.

Overseas Business Practices

To find books in a library catalog on how to do business in specific countries or regions, try a few keyword searches using the name of a country or region combined with one of these terms: COMMERCE, INVESTMENTS, COMMERCIAL LAW, or BUSINESS LAW. Other resources for overseas business are listed in chapter nine under Facts About Countries and States: Overviews and Statistics, and Cultures of the World.

In addition to STAT-USA, resources that list import, export, and other trade statistics include:

Direction of Trade Statistics. Washington, DC: International Monetary Fund. Annual. Also available on CD-ROM.

This guide presents, for over 150 countries, tables with the value of imports from and exports to each country's most important trading partners.

Trade Data/Trade Reports. http://www.census.gov/foreign-trade/www/tradedata .html

This site has trade statistics from the U.S. Census Bureau.

United Nations Publications.

The UN publishes several annual titles containing trade statistics, including *Commodity Trade Statistics, World Trade Annual,* and *International Trade Statistics Yearbook.*

World Trade Analyzer. http://www.tradecompass.com/trade_analyzer/

This subscription database has country trade flow data for over 190 countries and regions and 600 different commodities.

Wages and Salaries

You can find the average compensation for most professions using government and commercial resources, including:

American Almanac of Jobs and Salaries. New York: Avon. Updated irregularly.

The *Almanac* surveys dozens of occupations, supplying expected salary ranges and discussing trends in the job market.

American Salaries and Wages Survey. Marlita A. Reddy, ed. Detroit: Gale, 1997.

This survey is comprised of tables listing low, mid, and high salaries for various occupations in different cities, counties, and general areas.

America's Career Infonet. http://www.acinet.org

Visit this site to learn about trends, earnings, and training needed for specific professions nationwide and in different states.

The (Year) Geographic Reference Report: Annual Report of Costs, Wages, Salaries, and Human Resource Statistics: U.S. and Canada. Redmond, WA: BTA Economic Research Institute. Annual.

For each metropolitan area highlighted, this report lists wage/salary and cost-of-living information. It lists median salaries for specific jobs and median costs for renting an apartment or purchasing a home.

JobSmart Salary Surveys for Specific Professions. http://jobsmart.org/tools/salary /sal-prof.htm

On this Web page, click on any one of over three dozen job categories ranging from accounting to warehousing, and link to online salary surveys for that job type.

Occupational Compensation Survey: Pay and Benefits or *Pay Only.* (Formerly called *Area Wage Surveys.*) Washington, DC: U.S. Bureau of Labor Statistics. Annual.

These publications survey pay rates for a range of occupations, each dedicated to different metropolitan areas. Also see the *Bureau of Labor Statistics* Web page at http://stats.bls.gov/ for related information.

Cost of Living

Knowing a salary doesn't mean much if you don't know the cost of living in the area you'll be spending it in. Use *Cost-of-Living Comparisons* at http://www.datamasters.com/cgi-bin/col.pl to calculate what a salary in one city would be equivalent to in another city for 399 U.S. job markets. Don't use commas when you use this calculator, e.g., put $29,000 in as $29000. Similar to this resource but able to calculate comparable salaries internationally is the *Salary Calculator* at http://www2.homefair.com/calc/salcalc.html.

In print, consult the *American Cost of Living Survey* (3rd edition. Detroit: Gale, 1998) which reports prices for hundreds of products and services in over four hundred U.S. cities.

Proxy Statements.

As mentioned earlier, the proxy statement, the company filing required by the Securities and Exchange Commission, contains salaries of the top dogs at a firm.

If you'd like to see if your salary today has the same purchasing power as your salary a few years ago, look at one of the Web inflation calculators at http://www.westegg.com/inflation, or http://www.dismal.com/toolbox/cpi_index.stm. Don't cry.

Also use the techniques and resources under Careers in chapter five for more wage information.

Economic and Financial Statistics for the U.S.

When looking for indicators related to the health of the U.S. economy, here are some terms you'll see often:

Consumer Price Index (CPI). This measure shows the average change in price, over time, of what an urban consumer would pay for a fixed market basket of goods and services.

Gross National Product (GNP). This figure is a measure of the market value of goods and services generated by the labor and property of a nation, including receipts from that nation's business operation in foreign countries. The **Gross**

Domestic Product (GDP) is similar, but excludes the receipts from a nation's commercial dealings with foreign countries.

Producer Price Index (PPI). This measure tracks the rate of price change in the manufacturing, mining, agriculture, and electric utility industries.

Federal Reserve System, a.k.a. The Fed. The Congress created the Fed in 1913 to be an independent governmental entity that serves as the central bank of the U.S. It's responsible for formulating and executing monetary policy, regulating depository institutions, providing an elastic currency, assisting the federal government's financing operations, protecting consumer banking rights, and promoting community development and reinvestment. The Fed is comprised of twelve regional banks and a board of governors, all with Internet links at http://www.ny.frb.org/links.html.

Two meta sites for economic information are *The Dismal Scientist* at http://www.dismal.com/ and *Resources for Economists on the Internet (RFE)* at http://wueconb.wustl.edu/EconFAQ/sc.html.

Economic databases and print resources of note include:

Beige Book or *The Summary of Commentary on Current Economic Conditions.* Washington, DC: Federal Reserve. Also available at http://www.bog.frb.fed .us/FOMC/BeigeBook/Current.

Released eight times a year from the Federal Reserve's Board of Governors, the *Beige Book* contains anecdotal information on current economic conditions from interviews with key businesspeople, economists, market experts, and other resources.

Budget of the U.S. Government. Washington, DC: Executive Office of the President. Annual.

Also available at http://www.access.gpo.gov/su_docs/budget/index.html. This lengthy document includes actual and projected government spending for a range of fiscal years. Highlights of the budget are published in the significantly more compact *U.S. Budget in Brief.*

Bureau of Economic Analysis (BEA), Public Information, U.S. Department of Commerce, 1401 K St. NW, Room 713, Washington, DC 20230, Phone: (202)606-9900, URL: http://www.bea.doc.gov

The BEA, under the wing of the Department of Commerce, prepares reports related to national, international, and regional aspects of the U.S. economy. Their Web site features summary BEA estimates from their reports, including the latest figures on gross domestic product, personal income, and balance of payments.

The BEA monthly periodical found in government depository libraries in print, on CD-ROM, part of STAT-USA, and with full issues on the BEA Web page, is the *Survey of Current Business*, which focuses on business and economic issues and trends, supplying data and narrative on national income and product accounts, business cycle indicators, state personal income, personal income and outlays, and U.S. international trade and transactions.

The BEA also produces the *Regional Economic Information System (REIS)* available on CD-ROM and on the Web at http://fisher.lib.virginia.edu/reis/, which contains U.S. regional economic information, including personal income by major source, per capita personal income, full- and part-time employment by industry, and regional economic profiles. The disk is available at most government depository libraries.

You can also phone the BEA for recorded telephone messages summarizing key economic estimates, made available immediately after they're released and available twenty-four hours a day until the next set of estimates is released. The usual time of release (eastern standard time) and the telephone numbers to call are:

Gross domestic product, 8:30 A.M.: (202)606-5306

Personal income and outlays, 8:30 A.M.: (202)606-5303

U.S. international transactions, 10 A.M.: (202)606-5362

Economic Censuses. Washington, DC: U.S. Department of Commerce, Bureau of the Census. Also available on CD-ROM and on the Web (see information below).

The *Economic Censuses*, conducted every five years in years ending in two and seven, present data about U.S. industries, including the *Census of Agriculture, Census of Retail Trade, Census of Construction Industries, Census of Service Industries, Census of Government, Census of Transportation, Census of Manufactures, Census of Wholesale Trade*, and the *Census of Mineral Industries*. These surveys report, for different regions and using different variables, the number of establishments and firms, employment and payroll figures, sales receipts, operating expenses, capital expenditures, assets, and inventories for each industry sector. The print and CD-ROM versions of these surveys are available at most depository libraries. Specific URLs are listed below.

At my library, students studying entrepreneurship use the *Economic Censuses* as a way of determining the number of certain kinds of businesses in an area. If an area is inundated with pizza parlors, they may think twice about suggesting one be opened in that area. (Unless, of course, the residents just can't get enough pizza.) Businesspeople also use economic census figures to predict economic conditions, and analyze and forecast sales.

There are a number of publications that supplement and update some of the data appearing in *Economic Censuses*:

Census of Manufacturers. Updated by the *Annual Survey of Manufacturers* and the *Current Industrial Reports (CIR)*, a series of booklets focusing on particular manufacturing industries. Also at http://www.census.gov/econ /www/manumenu.html.

Census of Service Industries and the *Census of Transportation.* Updated annually by the *Service Annual Survey Report* in print and at http://www .census.gov/pub/svsd/www/sas.html, and the *Transportation Annual Survey*, in print and at http://www.census.gov/pub/svsd/www/tas.html.

Census of Retail Trade. Updated by the part of the *Current Business Reports* called *Monthly Retail Trade: Sales and Inventories*, which is cumulated in the publication *Annual Retail Trade*, both in print and at http://www.census .gov/econ/www/retmenu.html.

Census of Wholesale Trade. Updated, in part, by the *Monthly Wholesale Trade: Sales and Inventory* and *Annual Wholesale Trade* report, in print and at the same URL as for retail trade, http://www.census.gov/econ/www /retmenu.html.

Go to http://www.census.gov/epcd/www/92result.html for the results of the 1992 economic censuses. At the time of this writing, preliminary 1997 census data was at http://www.census.gov/epcd/www/econ97.html. If that URL doesn't work, just start at the census home page at http://www.census.gov/, and use their search tools to locate the new one.

Economic Indicators. U.S. Congress, Joint Economic Committee, 1948–present. Also at http://www.access.gpo.gov/congress/cong002.html.

This monthly report contains dozens of economic indicators, including those related to income, spending, employment, prices, money, credit, security markets, production, and business activities. Most tables present a ten-year series, with the most recent year broken down quarterly or monthly.

Economic Indicators is an update to the statistical portion of the *Economic Report of the President Transmitted to the Congress*, in print and at http://www.access .gpo.gov/eop/, which offers a review of the nation's economic conditions, documented by statistics.

Economic Statistics Briefing Room (ESBR). http://www.whitehouse.gov/fsbr/esbr .html

A good all-in-one page for finding economic statistics on the Web pulled from various federal government agency sites.

Facts & Figures on Government Finance. Washington, DC: Tax Foundation. Annual.

This guide supplies figures for government expenditures and revenue at the federal, state, and local levels. Sample tables include: federal expenditures by state, federal tax burden by type of tax and state, state and local taxes by type, per capita, and state and local debt.

FAIRMODEL. http://fairmodel.econ.yale.edu/

Geared to the economist, teacher, and economics student, FAIRMODEL supplies a U.S. macroeconometric model or a multicountry econometric model to do economic forecasting, policy analysis, and examination of historical episodes.

Federal Reserve Bulletin. Washington, DC: Board of Governors of the Federal Reserve System, 1915–present.

This monthly periodical provides commentary and regularly updated statistics on financial conditions in the United States and financial developments in foreign countries. Many statistics appear on the *Federal Reserve* Web page at http://federalreserve.gov/.

Federal Reserve Economic Data (FRED). http://www.stls.frb.org/fred/

FRED, created by the Federal Reserve Bank of St. Louis, provides historical U.S. economic and financial data, including daily U.S. interest rates, monetary and business indicators, exchange rates, and regional economic information for Arkansas, Illinois, Indiana, Kentucky, Mississippi, Missouri, and Tennessee.

STAT-USA. Washington, DC: U.S. Department of Commerce. http://www.stat-usa.gov. Some information on STAT-USA is free on the Web, but most is by subscription. Check your local library for ownership.

The State of the Nation part of STAT-USA contains current and historic U.S. economic data. It includes general economic indicators, including the consumer price index, producer price index, gross domestic product, and national income and product accounts; housing and construction data, including housing starts and building permits, new construction figures, and new home sales; employment indicators, including the employment cost index, local area employment and unemployment, and the weekly unemployment claims report; reports on manufacturing and industry, including retail sales, manufacturing, trade, inventories, industrial production and capacity utilization, and current industry reports; and monetary statistics, including selected interest rates, foreign exchange rates, bank credit, and money stock.

U.S. Bureau of Labor Statistics (BLS). http://stats.bls.gov

The BLS collects and publishes labor-related statistics and reports. On their Web site you'll find their most-requested data, including time series data related to employment, unemployment, hours, earnings, payrolls, prices, labor relations, benefits, occupational safety and health, and productivity. The BLS also publishes *Monthly Labor Review* (1918–present), a journal that supplies a wide variety of current labor statistics, updated monthly.

A good place to check for state economic and business statistics are the labor offices of each state. Each state maintains a department charged with gathering labor market data for the region. Much of it ends up being reported in federal documents, but you may get more detailed data that's more up-to-date when you contact the office itself. These offices track employment, unemployment, and wages, yearly and monthly, by county and by occupation. Other information available from these offices includes number of businesses in an area in a particular SIC/NAIC code, the types of benefits offered employees, and forecasts of demographic and economic trends. (Information available may vary from state to state.)

These offices also produce regional publications documenting their research. You'll find some of the statistics they produce on home pages of the labor departments; link to them via state home pages listed in chapter three.

Contact information for State Labor Offices:

Alabama	Department of Industrial Relations, Research and Statistics Division, 649 Monroe St., Montgomery, AL 36130, Phone: (205)242-8855
Alaska	Department of Labor, Research and Analysis, P.O. Box 25501, Juneau, AK 99802, Phone: (907)465-4500
Arizona	Department of Economic Security West, Research Administration, 1789 W. Jefferson, Site Code 733A, Phoenix, AZ 85007, Phone: (602)542-3871

Arkansas	Employment Security Department, Labor Market Information Section, P.O. Box 2981, Little Rock, AR 72203, Phone: (501)682-3197
California	Employment Development Department, Labor Market Information Division, 7000 Franklin Blvd., #1100, Sacramento, CA 95823, Phone: (916)262-2237
Colorado	Department of Labor and Employment, Labor Market Information Section, 393 S. Harland St., Lakewood, CO 80226, Phone: (303)937-4935
Connecticut	Department of Labor, Office of Research and Information, 200 Folly Brook Blvd., Wethersfield, CT 06109, Phone: (203)566-3472
Delaware	Labor Department, Occupational and Labor Market Information Office, P.O. Box 9029, University Office Plaza, Newark, DE 19714, Phone: (302)368-6962
DC	Employment Services Department, Labor Market Information, Room 201, 500 C St. NW, Washington, DC 20001, Phone: (202)724-7214
Florida	Department of Labor and Employment Security, Bureau of Labor Market Information, Suite 200, Hartman Building, 2012 Capital Circle SE, Tallahassee, FL 32399, Phone: (904)488-1048
Georgia	Department of Labor, Labor Information Systems, 148 International Blvd. NE, Atlanta, GA 30303, Phone: (404)656-3177
Hawaii	Labor Market and Employment Services Branch, Labor and Industrial Relations Department, Research Division, 830 Punchbowl St., Honolulu, HI 96813, Phone: (808)586-8999
Idaho	Department of Employment, Research and Analysis Bureau, 317 Main St., Boise, ID 83735, Phone: (208)334-6469
Illinois	Employment Security Bureau, Research and Analysis, 401 South State St., Chicago, IL 60605, Phone: (312)793-2316
Indiana	Employment Security Division, Labor Market Information, 10 N. Senate Ave., Indianapolis, IN 46209, Phone: (317)232-7701
Iowa	Department of Employment Services, Labor Market Information Unit, 1000 E. Grand Ave., Des Moines, IA 50319, Phone: (515)281-8182

Kansas	Department of Human Services, Division of Employment and Training, Research and Analysis Section, 401 SW Topeka Blvd., Topeka, KS 66603, Phone: (913)296-5058
Kentucky	Department for Employment Services, Research and Statistics, 275 E. Main St., Frankfort, KY 40601, Phone: (502)564-7976
Louisiana	Department of Employment Security, Research and Statistics Unit, P.O. 94094, Baton Rouge, LA 70804, Phone: (504)342-3141
Maine	Bureau of Employment Security, Division of Economic Analysis and Research, 20 Union St., Augusta, ME 04330, Phone: (207)287-2271
Maryland	Department of Human Resources, Research and Analysis, Employment and Training, 1100 N. Eutaw St., Baltimore, MD 21201, Phone: (410)333-5007
Massachusetts	Massachusetts Division of Employment and Training, 19 Staniford St., Boston, MA 02114, Phone: (617)626-6003
Michigan	Employment Security Commission, Bureau of Research and Statistics, 7310 Woodward Ave., Detroit, MI 48202, Phone: (313)876-5439
Minnesota	Department of Jobs and Training, Research Office, 390 N. Robert St., St. Paul, MN 55101, Phone: (612)296-8716
Mississippi	Employment Security Commission, Labor Market Information Department, P.O. Box 1699, Jackson, MS 39215, Phone: (601)961-7424
Missouri	Division of Employment Security, Research and Analysis, P.O. Box 59, Jefferson City, MO 65104, Phone: (314)751-3602
Montana	Department of Labor and Industry, Research and Analysis Bureau, P.O. Box 1728, Helena, MT 59624, Phone: (406)444-2430
Nebraska	Department of Labor, Labor Market Information, 550 S. Sixteenth St., Lincoln, NE 68509, Phone: (402)471-2600
Nevada	Employment Security Department, Research Section, 500 E. Third St., Carson City, NV 89713, Phone: (702)687-4550
New Hampshire	Employment Security Department, Economic Analysis and Reports and Labor Market Information Bureau, 32 S. Main St., Concord, NH 03301, Phone: (603)224-3311

New Jersey	Labor Department, Labor Market Information Office, John Fitch Plaza, CN056, Trenton, NJ 08625, Phone: (609)292-7376
New Mexico	Department of Employment Security, Economic Research and Analysis, P.O. Box 1928, Albuquerque, NM 87103, Phone: (505)841-8645
New York	Department of Labor, Division of Research and Statistics, State Office Building, Campus #12, Albany, NY 12240, Phone: (518)457-3800
North Carolina	Employment Security Commission, Labor Market Information Division, P.O. Box 25903, Raleigh, NC 27611, Phone: (919)733-2936
North Dakota	Job Service, Research and Statistics, P.O. Box 5507, Bismarck, ND 58502, Phone: (701)224-3048
Ohio	Bureau of Employment Services, Labor Market Information Division, 145 S. Front St., Columbus, OH 43216, Phone: (614)466-4636
Oklahoma	Oklahoma Employment Security Commission, Economic Analysis, 2401 N. Lincoln Blvd., Oklahoma City, OK 73105, Phone: (405)557-7104
Oregon	Employment Division, Research and Statistics, 875 Union NE, Salem, OR 97311, Phone: (503)378-8656
Pennsylvania	Department of Labor and Industry, Research and Statistics Division, 300 Capital Associates Building, Harrisburg, PA 17120, Phone: (717)787-2114
Rhode Island	Department of Employment Security, Research and Statistics, 101 Friendship St., Providence, RI 02903, Phone: (401)277-3706
South Carolina	Employment Security Commission, Labor Market Information Division, P.O. Box 995, Columbia, SC 29202, Phone: (803)737-2660
South Dakota	Department of Labor, Labor Market Information Center, P.O. Box 4730, Aberdeen, SD 57402, Phone: (605)622-2314
Tennessee	Department of Employment Security, Research and Statistics Division, Eleventh Floor, James Robertson Parkway, Nashville, TN 37245, Phone: (615)741-3639
Texas	Texas Employment Commission, Economic Research and

	Analysis Department, Room 208-T, TEC Building, Austin, TX 78778, Phone: (512)463-2616
Utah	Utah Department of Employment Security, Labor Market Information Services, P.O. Box 45249, Salt Lake City, UT 84147, Phone: (801)536-7800
Vermont	Department of Employment and Training, Labor Market Information, P.O. Box 488, Montpelier, VT 05601, Phone: (802)229-0311
Virginia	Virginia Employment Commission, Labor Market and Demographic Analysis Section, P.O. Box 1358, Richmond, VA 23211, Phone: (804)786-8222
Washington	Employment Security Group, Labor Market and Economic Analysis Branch, P.O. Box 9046, Olympia, WA, 98507, Phone: (206)438-4804
West Virginia	Employment Security Department, Labor and Economic Research, 112 California Ave., Charleston, WV 25305, Phone: (304)558-2660
Wisconsin	Department of Industry, Labor and Human Relations, Employment and Training Library, P.O. Box 7944, Madison, WI 53707, Phone: (608)267-9613
Wyoming	Employment Security Commission, Research and Analysis, P.O. Box 2760, Casper, WY 82602, Phone: (307)265-6732

Economic and Financial Statistics for the World

Handbook of International Economic Statistics. Washington, DC: GPO. Annual. Also at http://www.odci.gov/cia/publications/pubs.html.

This handbook from the CIA presents basic worldwide statistics for comparing the economic performance of major countries and regions.

International Financial Statistics. Washington, DC: International Monetary Fund (IMF). Monthly. Also available on CD-ROM and as a subscription database through the IMF. Data is compiled annually in the *International Financial Statistics Yearbook.*

This is a standard source of international statistics on all aspects of international and domestic finance. Covering most countries of the world, it supplies data needed in the analysis of international payments and inflation and deflation, including data on exchange rates, international liquidity, international

Financial Planning Calculators

How much of a home mortgage payment can you afford? Are you saving enough to retire comfortably? Use financial calculators on the Web to help answer those type of questions. *FinancCenter* at http://www.financenter.com/indexjs.html, has over one hundred calculators and definitions related to autos, homes, retirement, credit cards, credit lines, savings, budgeting, insurance, and investment. Another personal finance site is the *MoneyAdvisor* at http://www.moneyadvisor.com/.

banking, money and banking, interest rates, prices, production, imports and exports, and national accounts.

The IMF publishes many world economic and financial surveys and statistical compilations, including: *Government Financial Statistics*, containing statistical data on government financial operations; *Balance of Payments Statistics*, with balance of payments and international investment position data; and *World Economic Outlook*, with commentary and statistics on the world economy, which is available in print or full text on the IMF home page at http://www.imf.org/, along with many other IMF publications.

Main Economic Indicators. Organization for Economic Co-operation and Development. Monthly.

Main Economic Indicators supplies economic data for the OECD member countries: Austria, Australia, Canada, Belgium, Denmark, Finland, France, Germany, Greece, Iceland, Ireland, Italy, Japan, Luxembourg, Mexico, Netherlands, New Zealand, Norway, Portugal, Spain, Sweden, Switzerland, Turkey, the United Kingdom, and the United States.

Monthly Bulletin of Statistics. United Nations: Statistical Office. Monthly. Also available online as a subscription database via the UN under the title *MBS Online.*

This bulletin has economic and social statistics for more than two hundred countries and territories, including population, food, trade, production, finance, and national income. There are also monthly features on special topics such as fuel imports, industrial output, and world ship-building. The UN also publishes the *Statistical Yearbook* which presents world economic, demographic, and social data.

World Competitiveness Yearbook. Lausanne, Switzerland: Institute for
  Management Development. Annual.).

The *World Competitiveness Yearbook* ranks the capacity of a country's economic structure to promote growth. Forty-six countries are ranked. The index
of competitiveness is based on 244 indicators under eight broad headings:
domestic economy, internationalization, government, finance, infrastructure,
management, science and technology, and people. Another survey of international competitiveness is the *Global Competitiveness Report* (Geneva: World
Economic Forum. Annual.).

World Development Report. Washington, DC: The World Bank. Also available at
  http://www.worldbank.org/.

Each yearly report has a unique subtitle, with essays on a particular subject,
but the same indicators are updated in each new edition, including data on
production, agriculture, manufacturing, energy, education, consumption, investment, government finance, money, interest rates, trade, foreign aid, debt,
flow of capital, population, health, urbanization, and women.

You can also find economic reports and news for specific countries in the Market
and Country Research section of STAT-USA.

Marketing and Advertising Data

Marketers can pull information from many of the information resources discussed
earlier in this book and in this chapter. For example, check chapter five for
pointers on finding public opinion and regional U.S. data. Ideas for finding
industry and investment reports, and economic statistics, detailed previously, will
also be of interest.

A resource for finding the cost of advertising in periodicals and broadcast
media is the *Standard Rate and Data (SRDS)* series. *SRDS* supplies advertising
rates and circulation figures in the U.S., Canada, and overseas for business publications, newspapers, consumer magazines, radio, television, and cable.

For an overview of costs of advertising in international markets, look at the
Market & MediaFact pocket book series (London: Zenith Media). There are four
books in the series covering Africa/Middle East, the Americas, Asia Pacific, and
Europe.

Other directories that include advertising costs, such as the *Bacon's* directories,
are described in chapter thirteen under Market Directories.

Some reference titles of note for marketers and advertisers include:

Encyclopedia of Major Marketing Campaigns. Detroit: Gale, 1999.

This encyclopedia looks at five hundred major marketing and advertising campaigns from an historical perspective. Gale also publishes the *Major Marketing Campaigns Annual,* highlighting one hundred marketing initiatives of the previous year.

International Marketing Data and Statistics. London: Euromonitor. Also available on CD-ROM. Other titles in the series include *China Marketing Data & Statistics* and *European Marketing Data and Statistics.*

These Euromonitor resources supply demographic and socioeconomic indicators for nations worldwide, including per capita consumption and sales of many products and services, costs of selected food and drink items, and cultural indicators such as number of movies attended and types of books published.

Sourcebook of Zip Code Demographics. La Jolla, CA: CACI Marketing Systems. Annual. Also available on CD-ROM under the title *Sourcebook America,* which also includes their publication *Sourcebook of County Demographics.*

Using this book, you can zero in on one of over thirty thousand zip codes and find more than seventy demographic variables for that area, including population characteristics, income, and the likelihood of someone in a zip code area purchasing a type of product, service, or entertainment. CACI also has other subscription databases geared to marketers; see their site at http://demographics.caci.com/.

What's the Chat About a Company or Product?

It can be interesting to "eavesdrop" on Internet conversations about companies and products. Services like Company Sleuth, described earlier, automatically dig up comments from some online discussion groups about companies. But you can also do your own search. Put the name of a company or product in a search engine like *DejaNews,* which searches discussion forums, at http://www.dejanews.com. A search on BOSTON CHICKEN brought almost three hundred messages. Will all the people on these lists be credentialed experts? Definitely not. But the comments, ranging from nasty to thoughtful, can lead to other discoveries.

CHAPTER 13

Authorship Research

The Business and Pleasure of Writing

"Writing only leads to more writing."

—Collette

I f you intend to use your information gathering skills to put your findings into writing, this chapter will be of interest. It focuses on resources for writers of term papers, scholarly tracts, business communications, articles, or the great American novel; resources that offer advice and instruction on writing techniques, manuscript format, proper language usage, and finding avenues of publishing or disseminating your writing.

Finding Library Materials About Writing

When searching for library books on the art and craft of writing, the word AUTHORSHIP is the keyword to be aware of when doing a subject search. It's often used to describe books that offer instruction on writing and getting published.

Other standard Library of Congress subject headings that deal with writing:

To find books that offer guidance on writing a college paper and teach how to write well: REPORT WRITING, ENGLISH LANGUAGE WRITING, or EXPOSITION RHETORIC.

To find writings that assist the fiction writer: Combine the word AUTHORSHIP with the name of the genre of writing you're interested in, for example: ROMANCE AUTHORSHIP, POETRY AUTHORSHIP, or SCIENCE FICTION AUTHORSHIP. Other subject headings of interest include: CHILDREN'S LITERATURE TECHNIQUE, CREATIVE WRITING, CRIME WRITING, DRAMA TECHNIQUE, FICTION TECHNIQUE, MOTION PICTURE AUTHORSHIP, ONE-ACT PLAYS TECHNIQUE, PLAYWRITING, PLOTS, POPULAR MUSIC WRITING (writing song lyrics), RADIO AUTHORSHIP, or TELEVISION AUTHORSHIP.

To find books that assist the nonfiction writer: FEATURE WRITING,

JOURNALISM AUTHORSHIP, or TECHNICAL WRITING. You can also combine the word WRITING with the name of a major type of nonfiction writing, such as TRAVEL WRITING, SPORTS WRITING, or FASHION WRITING.

To locate books on how to prepare writings that will be offered to agents or publishers: BOOK PROPOSALS, AUTHORSHIP QUERIES, or AUTHORSHIP MARKETING.

To find books that help with the wording of writing needed in day-to-day business and day-to-day living: BUSINESS WRITING, COMMERCIAL CORRESPONDENCE, COMMUNICATION IN MANAGEMENT, LETTER WRITING, PUBLIC SPEAKING (for writing speeches), SPEECHWRITING, or THANK YOU NOTES.

Online and Print Magazines and Newsletters for Writers

If you'd like to read articles purely for your own growth as a writer, you'll find there are many. You might choose to subscribe to a writing magazine, seeing what they have to offer each month. Or you could use periodical indexes to look up particular topics you want to read more about. You can also peruse the following list of online newsletters and the specialized Web sites described in the next section, Web Sites for Writers.

The most popular writing magazines, such as *Writer's Digest*, are found in bookstores and libraries. But many of the following publications for writers may be in only a few libraries or available only through subscription.

American Journalism Review, formerly *Washington Journalism Review*, University of Maryland, 1117 Journalism Building, College Park, MD 20742-7111, Phone: (800)827-0771 or (301)405-8803 Fax: (301)405-8323, E-mail: editor @ajr.umd.edu, URL: http://www.ajr.org. Covers issues related to print and broadcast journalism in the U.S. Monthly. $24/yr. Selected contents on the Web page.

American Writer, NWU National Office/East, 113 University Place, Sixth Floor, New York, NY 10003, Phone: (212)254-0279, Fax: (212)254-0673, E-mail: nwu@nwu.org. The magazine of the National Writers Union. Quarterly. Included in membership. Also available full text at http://www.nwu.org/aw /awhome.htm.

ASJA Contracts Watch, American Society of Journalists and Authors, 1501 Broadway, Suite 302, New York, NY 10036, Phone: (212)997-0947, Fax: (212)768-

7414, E-mail: asja@compuserve.com, URL: http://www.asja.org. Free E-mail bulletin that keeps freelancers informed about contract specifics related to different publishers. Sign up on their Web site.

Authorship, The National Writer's Association, 3140 Peoria, #295, Aurora, CO 80014, Phone: (303)841-0246, Fax: (303)751-8593, URL: http://www.national writers.com. Discusses creative and compositional techniques. Bimonthly, $20/yr. or included in membership.

BookFlash. This Web page, at http://www.bookflash.com/, features news and events related to publishing, including new title announcements. Their E-mail bulletin is free.

Book Publishing Report, 11 Riverbend Dr. S., P.O. Box 4234, Stamford, CT 06907-0234, Phone: (800)307-2529 or (203)358-9900. Fax: (203)358-5824, E-mail: info@simbanet.com, URL: http://www.simbanet.com. The business of book publishing and distribution from a strategic, product, financial, and marketing perspective. 50/yr. $525/yr. North America, $575/yr. elsewhere.

The Bookwoman, Women's National Book Association, 160 Fifth Ave., New York, NY 10010, Phone: (212)675-7805, Fax: (212)989-7542. Covers major topics of interest to publishers, librarians, educators, writers, and agents in the book world. 3/yr. Price included in membership.

Byline, P.O. Box 130596, Edmond, OK, 73013-0001, E-mail: bylinemp@aol .com, URL: http://www.bylinemag.com/. Presents articles on the craft or business of writing and also publishes short stories and poetry. 11/yr. $22/yr. U.S., $26/yr. Canada and Mexico, $38/yr. overseas. Excerpts on Web site.

Canadian Author, Canadian Authors Association, P.O. Box 419, Campbellford, ON, Canada, KOL 1LO, Phone: (705)653-0323, Fax: (705)653-0593. Canada's national writer's magazine. Quarterly. $18/yr. Canada, $28/yr. U.S. and elsewhere.

Children's Book Insider, 901 Columbia Rd., Ft. Collins, CO 80525, Phone: (970)495-0056, E-mail: mail@write4kids.com, URL: http://www.write4kids .com/. Geared to aspiring and working writers of children's fiction and nonfiction. Monthly. $29.95/yr. U.S., $34.95/yr. Canada, $42.95/yr. elsewhere.

Comedy Writer's Association Newsletter, % Robert Makinson, Box 023304, Brooklyn, NY 11202-0066, Phone: (718)855-5057. Looks at the creation and marketing of jokes, humorous scripts, and stories. Semiannual. $6/issue, $24/yr. with membership.

Creativity Connection, University of Wisconsin at Madison, Department of Liberal Studies and the Arts, 610 Langdon St., Room 622, Madison, WI 53703,

Phone: (608)262-4911, Fax: (608)265-2475, E-mail: marshall.cook@ccmail .admin.wisc.edu. Profiles, how-to articles, and listings of conferences and workshops for writers and small-press publishers. Quarterly. $18/yr.

Creative Screenwriting, 6404 Hollywood Blvd., Suite 415, Los Angeles, CA 90028, Phone: (213)957-1405, Fax: (213)957-1406. Devoted to the scholarly study of screenwriting. $35/yr.

Cross & Quill: The Christian Writers Newsletter, Rt. 3 Box 1635, Clinton, SC 29325, Phone: (803)697-6035, URL: http://members.aol.com/cwfi/writers .htm. How-to's and help for writers. Bimonthly. $20/yr. nonmembers U.S., $21/yr. elsewhere; $35/yr. members U.S., $40/yr. elsewhere.

DarkEcho Newsletter. Free weekly E-mail newsletter supplying market, genre, and publishing news for horrorwriters. Subscribe at http://www.darkecho.com /darkecho/newsletter/index.html.

The Eclectic Writer. Free online newsletter at http://www.eclectics.com/writing /writing.html. Supplies advice articles for writers of all genres and maintains a discussion board and links to other Web pages, arranged by writing genre.

The Editorial Eye, EEI Press, 66 Canal Center Plaza, Suite 200, Alexandria, VA 22314, Phone: (800)683-8380 or (703)683-0683, Fax: (703)683-4915. Focuses on standards and practices for editors, writers, and publication managers. Monthly. $99/yr.

EFA Newsletter, Editorial Freelancers Association, 71 W. Twenty-third St., Suite 1910, New York, NY 10010, Phone: (212)929-5400, Fax: (212)929-5439, E-mail: info@the-efa.org, URL: http://www.the-efa.org/index.html. News of the concerns and activities of the Editorial Freelancers Association. Bimonthly. Price included in membership or $20/yr. for nonmembers. Sample articles on the Web page.

Empire: Zine. This elegant-looking E-zine presents pieces about writing and writers of the past and present of all genres, including songwriting, poetry, and erotica. It's free at http://www.spydersempire.com/empirezine/.

Fiction Writer, F&W Publications, 1507 Dana Ave., Cincinnati, OH 45207, Phone: (800)289-0963, E-mail: wdweb@fwpubs.com, URL: http://www.writ ersdigest.com/. A quarterly magazine for writers who want advice on how to hone their skills and sell their fiction. $5.25/issue.

Fiction Writer's Guidelines, Fiction Writers Connection, P.O. Box 4065, Deerfield Beach, FL 33442, Phone: (954)426-4705, E-mail: BCAMENSON@aol.com, URL: http://www.fictionwriters.com. For those who want to learn how to write fiction and get it published. $21/yr. or free with membership. The Fiction Writers Connection also offers two free E-mail newsletters called *Tidbits* and *Little Bits*. Sign up for them at the URL listed above.

Food Writer, P.O. Box 156, Spring City, PA 19475-0156, Phone: (610)948-6031, E-mail: FoodSleuth@aol.com. Marketing tips and resources for freelance food-writers, cookbook authors, publishers, and editors. Quarterly. $30/yr.

Freelance Success, 801 NE Seventieth St., Box IK, Miami, FL 33138, Phone: (305)754-8854, Fax: (305)757-8857, E-mail: freelance-succes@usa.net, URL: http://www.freelancesuccess.com. A marketing and management guide for experienced freelance writers. Monthly. $97/yr. for E-mail version, $120/yr. for print. Sample issue at Web site.

Gothic Journal, P.O. Box 6340, Elko, NV 89802, Phone: (800)7-GOTHIC or (702)738-3520, Fax: (702)738-3524, E-mail: kglass@GothicJournal.com, URL: http://gothicjournal.com/romance/gothic.html. For readers, writers, and publishers of romantic suspense, romantic mystery, and gothic, supernatural, and woman-in-jeopardy romance novels. 6/yr. $24/yr., U.S., $30/yr. Canada, $36/yr. elsewhere. Information of interest on the Web page.

Hellnotes: Your Insider's Guide to the Horror Field, 27780 Donkey Mine Rd., Oak Run, CA 96069, Fax: (530)472-1050, URL: http://www.hellnotes.com/. For those interested in horror writing. Weekly. $10 for an E-mail subscription or $40/yr. for print. Some articles are also free on their Web page.

Hollywood Scriptwriter, P.O. Box 10277, Burbank, CA 91510, Phone: (818)842-3912, Fax: (818)842-6618, Practical answers, advice, and guidance from working professionals. Monthly. $44/yr. U.S., $50/yr. elsewhere.

Inklings, 55 McCaul St., Box 123, Toronto, ON, Canada, M5T 2W7, E-mail: editor@inkspot.com or asstedit@inkspot.com, URL: http://www.inkspot .com. Free, online biweekly newsletter for writers. Has market leads, interviews with writing experts and authors, and recommended online and off-line resources. To subscribe, send an E-mail to adminfaq@inkspot.com. It's also on their Web page.

Inscriptions. This free weekly E-zine features how-to articles; interviews with writers, editors, and publishers; and listings of job opportunities, paying markets, and contests. Subscribe at their Web site at http://members.aol.com/maiden fate/Inscriptions.html.

Locus: The Newspaper of the Science Fiction Field, Locus Publications, P.O. Box 13305, Oakland, CA 94611, Phone: (510)339-9198, Fax: (510)339-8144. Science fiction news, people, and issues of interest to publishers, writers, and others. Monthly. $43/yr. U.S., $48/yr. elsewhere.

National Writers Monthly. A free E-mail report of markets and articles about writing. Find back issues and sign up for news ones at http://www.writersmarkets .com/index-wm.htm.

Network, International Women's Writing Guild, P.O. Box 810, Gracie Station, New York, NY 10028-0082, Phone: (212)737-7536, Fax: (212)737-9469, E-mail: iwwg@iwwg.com, URL: http://www.iwwg.com/. News of, by, and for women writers. Bimonthly, $35/yr. U.S., $45/yr. elsewhere.

The New York Screenwriter Monthly, 655 Fulton St., Suite 276, Brooklyn, NY 11217, Phone: (800)418-5637, E-mail: info@nyscreenwriter.com, URL: http://www.nyscreenwriter.com/. Offers articles on getting scripts read, represented, and produced. Monthly. $35/yr. includes a free copy of the *Annual Screenwriter's Guide*. Some articles are full text at their Web site.

NovelAdvice. This is a "cyberjournal for writers devoted totally to the craft of writing" at http://www.noveladvice.com/.

Novelists' Inc., The Newsletter, P.O. Box 1166, Mission, KS 66222-0166, URL: http://www.ninc.com/. For members of Novelists' Inc. Criteria to join: You need to have published two novels by "bona fide professional publishers." Some free articles at the Web site.

On Second Thought, Center for Professional Writing, 200 University Ave. W., Waterloo, ON, Canada, N2L 3G1, Phone: (519)725-0279, Fax: (519)884-8995. Presents information on professional writing. Quarterly. Free.

Papyrus: The Writer's Craftletter Featuring the Black Experience, P.O. Box 270797, West Hartford, CT 06127-0797, URL: http://www.readersndex .com/papyrus/. Features market guidelines, information on black writers, and craft-oriented columns on writing. Quarterly. $8/yr. Some content is on their Web page.

Poets and Writers Magazine, 72 Spring St., New York, NY 10012, Phone: (212)226-3586; Fax: (212)226-3963, E-mail: pwsubs@pw.org. Discusses topics of interest to established and beginning writers, including commentary on publishing issues, interviews with authors, information on grants, calls for writing, and awards. Some information of interest is on the home page at http://www.pw .org/mag/. Bimonthly. $19.95/yr.

Publishers Weekly, 245 W. Seventeenth St., New York, NY 10011, Phone: (800)278-2991 or (310)978-6916, Fax: (310)978-6901, URL: http://www .bookwire.com/pw/pw.html. The international news magazine of book publishing and bookselling. Weekly. $169/yr. U.S., $217/yr. Canada, $299/yr. elsewhere. Many interesting features are on their Web site.

The Quill, The Society of Professional Journalists, 16 S. Jackson St., Greencastle, IN 46135-1514, Phone: (317)653-3333, Fax: (317)653-4631. National magazine for professional journalists and students and teachers of journalism. 9 times/yr. $27/yr. U.S., $32/yr. elsewhere.

The Quill Magazine. An online magazine for beginning writers at http://www.the quill.com.

Quill and Quire, Key Publishers, 70 The Esplanade, Suite 210, Toronto, ON, Canada M5E 1R2, Phone: (416)360-0044, Fax: (416)955-0794, E-mail: quill @idirect.com. Articles and features on bookselling, publishing, and Canadian libraries for writers, booksellers, publishers, and librarians. Monthly. $56.03/ yr. Canada, $85/yr. U.S. and other countries.

Romance Writers Report, Romance Writers of America, 3707 F.M. 1960 West, Suite 555, Houston, TX 77068, Phone: (713)440-6885, Fax: (713)440-7510, E-mail: info@rwanational.com, URL: http://www.rwanational.com/. Provides romance writers with information and support by publishing agents' special reports, author profiles, and how-to articles. Price included in membership.

Scavenger's Newsletter: The Monthly Marketletter for SF/Fantasy/Horror/Mystery Writers & Artists, Janet Fox, 519 Ellinwood, Osage City, KS 66523-1329, E-mail: foxscav1@jc.net, URL: http://www.cza.com/scav/index.html. Each issue contains market information, commentary, and small-press reviews. $17/yr. U.S., $20/yr. Canada, $26/yr. elsewhere.

ScienceWriters, National Association of Science Writers, P.O. Box 29, Greenlawn, NY 11740, Phone: (516)757-5664, Fax: (516)757-0069, URL: http://nasw .org/. Covers the preparation and interpretation of science news for the public. Quarterly. Price included in membership. Sample articles on their Web page.

Script, 5638 Sweet Air Rd., Baldwin, MD 21013, Phone: (410)592-3466, Fax: (410)592-8062. Each issue features articles on the craft of screenwriting and an interview with a screenwriter. The January/February issue contains a comprehensive listing of contests. Bimonthly. $29.95/yr. U.S., $37.95/yr. Canada, $49.95/yr. elsewhere.

Science Fiction Chronicle, P.O. Box 022730, Brooklyn, NY 11202-0056, Phone: (718)643-9011, Fax: (718)522-3308, E-mail: SF_Chronicle@compuserve .com, URL: http://www.sfsite.com/sfc/home.htm. Includes market listings and news about science fiction and fantasy writings and writers. Bimonthly. $42/yr. U.S., $45/yr. Canada, $49/yr. elsewhere. No contents online; just information about the publication.

SFWA Bulletin, Department H, Wildside Press, 522 Park Ave., Berkeley Heights,

NJ 07922, E-mail: execdir@sfwa.org, URL: http://www.sfwa.org. Information, insights, and insider news on fantasy and science fiction from the Science Fiction and Fantasy Writers of America. Quarterly. $15/yr. Some contents are also available on their Web page.

The Short Order. This is the free online newsletter of the Short Mystery Fiction Society at http://www.thewindjammer.com/smfs/newsletter/, updated quarterly. To subscribe to the E-mail version, send E-mail to rkfoster@ix.netcom .com with a brief note asking to be subscribed.

Speechwriter's Newsletter, Ragan Communications, 212 W. Superior St. #200, Chicago, IL 60610, Phone: (800)878-5331, or order at http://www.ragan .com/pubs/order_SN.html. Offers practical information on speech writing and delivery for full- and part-time speechwriters in business, government, associations, and education. Monthly. $287/yr.

Talking Agents, Agent Research & Evaluation, Department WS, 334 E. Thirtieth St., New York, NY 10016, URL: http://www.agentresearch.com/services .html. Looks at literary and dramatic rights agents from the writer's point of view. Published every month except June and December. $29.95/yr. U.S. for online or print version, $32/yr. Canada, $39/yr. elsewhere.

Travelwriters.com. Sign up for a free E-mail-based travelwriters marketing newsletter at this Web site: http://www.travelwriters.com. Other useful information for travelwriters at this site.

A View From the Loft, 66 Malcolm Ave. SE, Minneapolis, MN 55414, Phone: (612)379-8999, Fax: (612)951-4423, E-mail: loft@loft.org, URL: http://www .loft.org/view.htm. Each issue carries articles about writing, a listing of publications and contests seeking submissions, and a listing of Internet sites of interest to writers. Monthly, except July. Comes with membership, $40/yr. for individuals, $20/yr. low income.

Working Writer. Free bi-weekly E-mail newsletter for writers. Sign up at http:// www.freelancewriting.com.

Write Market Webzine, 3500 Mira Loma Dr., Cameron Park, CA 95682. This free title, at http://www.writemarket.com/, supports the genre and small-press industry by supplying free market listings to magazine and publisher Web pages and by supplying reviews of new books and magazines. Monthly.

Write On Newsletter, Box 66064, Heritage PO, Edmonton, AB, Canada T6J 6T4, Phone: (403)438-6335, URL: http://www.duban.com/writeon/help .htm. How-to techniques and ideas, best-available writers markets, and writers guidelines. Bimonthly. $20/yr. U.S. or Canada.

The Writer, 120 Boyleston St., Boston, MA 02116, Phone: (617)423-3157. Magazine for aspiring professional writers. Each issue features articles by experts in the publishing and writing field, up-to-date market information, and tips on manuscript submission. Monthly. $28/yr. U.S., $39/yr. elsewhere.

Writer's Block. A free Web newsletter, at http://www.niva.com/writblok/index .htm, containing articles of interest to many types of writers.

Writer's Digest, F&W Publications, 1507 Dana Ave., Cincinnati, OH 45207, Phone: (800)289-0963, E-mail: wdweb@fwpubs.com, URL: http://www.writers digest.com/. Articles on writing techniques, on how to become successful and maintain success in all writing genres, profiles of authors, and market listings. Monthly. $23.96/yr. U.S., $33.96/yr. Canada, $58.96/yr. elsewhere. You can also sign up for a free E-mail newsletter, *Writer's Digest Update*, on the Web site.

Writer's Guidelines: A Roundtable for Writers and Editors, HC 77, P.O. Box 608, Pittsburg, MO 65724, Phone and Fax: (417)993-5544. News and how-to pieces that help writers get published. Bimonthly. $45/yr.

Writers Guild of America, East—Newsletter, 555 W. Fifty-seventh St., New York, NY 10019, Phone: (212)767-7800, URL: http://www.wgaeast.org/. Informs members of news and information concerning the broad range of Guild-related activities and services, from contract negotiations and organizing efforts to union benefits. 11/yr. Free with membership or $22/yr. for nonmembers.

Writer's Journal, Val-Tech Media, P.O. Box 394, Perham, MN 56573-0394. Information on style, technique, editing, publishing, copywriting, research, marketing, copyright law, and other topics. Bimonthly. $17.97/yr. U.S., 21.97/yr. Canada, $30.97/yr. overseas.

Writers Write Internet Writing Journal. Contains writers guidelines to online publications, writing and publishing news, message boards, and job listings. Free on the Web at http://writerswrite.com/.

Writing for Dollars. A free monthly E-mail newsletter focusing on the business details of writing. To subscribe send an E-mail to editor@awoc.com with the word "subscribe" in the subject header, or subscribe at their Web site at http:// www.awoc.com/WFD.cfm.

Writing That Works, 7481 Huntsman Blvd., Suite 720, Springfield, VA 22153-1648, Phone: (703)643-2200, Fax: (703)643-2329, E-mail: concepts@writing thatworks.com, URL: http://writingthatworks.com. Business writing techniques, including editing, style, and usage; publication design and production; and marketing strategy. Monthly. $99/yr.

Written By: The Journal of the Writer's Guild of America West, 7000 W. Third St., Los Angeles, CA 90048, Phone: (888)WRITNBY, URL: http://www.wga .org/. Written by and for television and film writers on the art, craft, and business of writing in Hollywood. Monthly. $40/yr. U.S., $45/yr. Canada, $50/yr. elsewhere. Selected articles also appear at the Web site.

Writer's Web Sites

Numerous sites on the Net offer a wide variety of writing information, including writing advice, publishing news, interviews with writers, tips on doing research, lists of markets resources, associations, award opportunities, newsletters, and conference announcements. Is there crossover between sites? You bet. I'm listing representative sites here—play around with a few and see which ones you tend to go back to.

Meta sites covering multiple writing genres

Authorlink! http://www.authorlink.com
Bookwire. http://www.bookwire.com
The Eclectic Writer. http://www.eclectics.com/writing/writing.html
Fiction Writer's Connection. http://www.fictionwriters.com/
Inkspot.com: The Writer's Resource. http://www.inkspot.com/
Publishers Weekly Interactive. http://www.bookwire.com/pw/pw.html
The Writer's Internet Resource Guide. http://www.novalearn.com/wirg/
Writer's Net. http://www.writers.net/
The Writer's Nook. http://www.twnn.com
Writers on the Net. http://www.writers.com
Writer's Realm Webring. http://www.geocities.com/Athens/Oracle/2060/
Writers Write. http://writerswrite.com/
Zuzu's Petals Literary Resources. http://www.zuzu.com/

Web sites covering particular genres
Academic

Textbook and Academic Authors. http://taa.winona.msus.edu/taa/
Association of American University Presses Online Catalogs.
   http://aaup.pupress.princeton.edu/

Business and technical

Association for Business Communication.
   http://courses.sha.cornell.edu/orgs/abc/

Business Writing Links. http://owl.ccd.cccoes.edu/owl/links/bus.html

Internet Resources for Business and Technical Writers.
   http://www.english.uiuc.edu/cws/wworkshop/ww_tech.html

John Hewitt's Technical Writing Center.
   http://www.azstarnet.com/~poewar/writer/pg/tech.html

Children's

Canadian Children's Book Centre.
   http://www3.sympatico.ca/ccbc/mainpage.htm

Children's Writing Resource Center from the *Children's Book Insider* (see p. 360).
   http://www.write4kids.com/

Purple Crayon. http://www.underdown.org/

The Society of Children's Book Writers and Illustrators. http://www.scbwi.org/

Christian

Christian Writers Fellowship International.
   http://members.aol.com/cwfi/writers.htm

OHZone Community Center: Where Christian Writers Meet.
   http://www.ohzone.net/

Writers Information Network: The Professional Association for Christian Writers.
   http://www.bluejaypub.com/win/

Crime and mystery

American Crime Writers Leagues. http://www.klew.com/acwl.html

ClueLass—A Mystery Lover's Notebook. http://www.cluelass.com

Internet CrimeWriting Network.
   http://hollywoodshopping.com/Crime/index.html#crime

*The Mysterious Home Page: A Guide to Mysteries and Crime Fiction on the
   Internet.* http://www.webfic.com/mysthome/

The Mystery Writer's Forum. http://www.zott.com/mysforum/default.html

Electronic publishing

Association of Electronic Publishers. http://welcome.to/AEP

EPIC: The Electronically Published Internet Connection.
   http://www.eclectics.com/epic/

Historical fiction

Historical Fiction. http://falcon.jmu.edu/~ramseyil/historical.htm
Soon's Historical Fiction Site. http://uts.cc.utexas.edu/~soon/histfiction/

Humor, stand-up

Business of Comedy. http://208.8.220.10/shayne-michael/comics.htm
Creating Comics. http://www.cadvision.com/dega/creating.htm
The Humor and Life, in Particular Web Site.
    http://www.geocities.com/SoHo/Gallery/4111/menu.html
Sitcom Format 101.
    http://home.earthlink.net/~chuckat/sitcom/sitcom_101.html
Stand-Up Comedy FAQ. http://rampages.onramp.net/%7Estevebo/faq.html
Writing for Television Comedy.
    http://tvcomedy.miningco.com/msubwrite.htm

Journalism, freelance

AJR Newslink. http://ajr.newslink.org/
American Society of Journalists and Authors. http://www.asja.org/
Columbia Journalism Review. http://www.cjr.org/
Freelance Online. http://www.freelanceonline.com/
Internet Newsroom. http://www.editors-service.com/
National Press Club. http://npc.press.org
Write This! Free-lance Writers Online. http://www.shutup101.com/writethis/

Playwriting and screenwriting

In Hollywood. http://www.inhollywood.com
New Dramatists Home Page.
    http://www.itp.tsoa.nyu.edu/~diana/ndintro.html
Playbill On-Line/Theatre Central. http://www1.playbill.com/playbill/
Playwrights on the Web.
    http://www.stageplays.com/writers.htm
Playwrights Project. http://users.vnet.net/phisto/
The Playwriting Seminars. http://www.vcu.edu/artweb/playwriting/
Screaming in the Celluloid Jungle. http://www.celluloidjungle.com
Screenwriter.Com. http://screenwriters.com/hn/writing/screennet.html
Screenwriters Cyberia. http://members.aol.com/swcyberia/
Screenwriters Homepage. http://home.earthlink.net/~scribbler/

Screenwriters/Playwrights Home Page.
  http://www.teleport.com/~cdeemer/scrwriter.html
Screenwriters Utopia. http://www.screenwritersutopia.com/
SCRNWRiT: Motion Picture and Television Screenwriting Home Page.
  http://www.panam.edu/scrnwrit/
Writer's Guild of America. http://www.wga.org/

Poetry

Academy of American Poets. http://www.poets.org
Poetry Today Online. http://www.poetrytodayonline.com/
Poetry World Home Page. http://news.std.com/poetryworld
The Semantic Rhyming Dictionary.
  http://www.link.cs.cmu.edu/dougb/rhyme-doc.html
W3PX Poetry Exchange. http://www.w3px.com/Index.htm

Romance

Gothic Journal (Excerpts). http://gothicjournal.com/romance/gothic.html
Romance Central. http://romance-central.com/
Romance Novels and Women's Fiction.
  http://www.writepage.com/romance.htm
Romance Writers of America. http://www.rwanational.com/
Romantic Times. http://www.romantictimes.com/
Useful Links for Romance Writers and Readers.
  http://www.jacklynreding.com/links

Science fiction, fantasy, and horror

Critter's Workshop. http://www.critique.org/critters/index.html
DarkEcho Horror. http://www.darkecho.com/darkecho/index.html
Horror Writer's Association. http://www.horror.org/
Pegasus Online Writer's Corner.
  http://www.pegasusonline.com/writers-corner/writers-corner.html
Science Fiction and Fantasy Workshop.
  http://www.sff.net/people/Dalton-Woodbury/sffw.htp
Science Fiction and Fantasy Writers of America. http://www.sfwa.org/
Science Fiction Resource Guide. http://sflovers.rutgers.edu/Web/SFRG/
Science Fiction Writers of Earth. http://www.flash.net/~sfwoe/

Speculative Fiction: Resource Network.
http://www.speculativevision.com

Who Will Publish Your Writing?

Whether you write science fiction screenplays, rhyming poetry for greeting cards, or scholarly missives, there's a publisher interested in your genre.

There are many directories that will help you find a market for an article, book, or script, and they come in a few varieties. Some are geared to writers. They provide answers to such questions as: "Should I send a full manuscript or query?" and "What type of material is the editor particularly interested in?" Other guides, also useful to writers, are geared to advertisers or consumers. These guides emphasize items such as advertising cost, description of the program or publication, and the demographics of its readers or viewers. The useful thing about these directories is that they may include titles neglected by directories geared just to authors.

Both types of guides just described are listed below. (Market resources are also included in many of the Web sites, magazines, and newsletters previously listed).

Market directories

The Association of American University Presses Directory. New York: The
  Association of American University Presses. Annual.

> This is a guide, indexed by subject, to 114 U.S., Canadian, and overseas scholarly presses who annually publish nearly nine thousand books and eight hundred periodicals. Each entry supplies contact data, responsibilities of key staff, and advice to authors concerning the submission of materials.

American Directory of Writer's Guidelines. Fresno, CA: Quill Driver Books, 1997.

> This listing has submission guidelines for more than 450 magazine and book publishers.

Bacon's Magazine Directory. Directory of Magazines and Newsletters. Chicago:
  Bacon's Information. Annual.

> Each magazine entry in *Bacon's* lists circulation, description, frequency of publication, types of press releases and publicity items it accepts, whether it's full-text on an online database, subscription rate, basic advertising rate, lead time for writers, and a listing of names, titles, and direct phone numbers for editors. There are also *Bacon's* directories for newspapers (including news services and syndicates), radio/TV/cable, international media, business media, computer and hi-tech, and medical and health publications.

Benn's Media Directory: United Kingdom—The Guide to United Kingdom Newspapers, Periodicals, Television, Radio, and Other Media. Tonbridge, Kent, U.K.: Benn Business Information Services. Annual.

One edition of *Benn's* covers the United Kingdom; the other is an international edition. Each publisher entry includes contact information, frequency of publication/program, topics covered, type of readership, circulation, and advertising rates. Another guide to U.K. and international print media is *Willings Press Guide* (Teddington, Middlesex, U.K.: Hollis Directories. Annual).

Big Guide to Guidelines. http://writersdigest.com/

The Big Guide to Guidelines, from Writer's Digest, acts as an update to the *Writer's Market* (see p. 376), giving details about the writing needs of specific publications. This Web site also offers a Hot List of desirable publications to write for and a Market of the Day.

Cabell's Directory of Publishing Opportunities in Accounting, Economics, and Finance. 7th edition. 2 Volumes. David W. Cabell. Beaumont, Texas: Cabell, 1997.

The scholarly journals listed in these volumes don't pay writers. In fact, some charge a review or publishing fee. Geared to academics, the hundreds of journals in this guide are accompanied by information on acceptance rate, editorial guidelines, the review process, time required for review, and the type of reader the journal attracts. Other titles published by Cabell include *Cabell's Directory of Publishing Opportunities in Education* and *Cabell's Directory of Publishing Opportunities in Management and Marketing.*

Christian Writer's Market. Sally E. Stuart. Wheaton, IL: Harold Shaw, 1998.

This guide points to over one thousand markets for writers of Christian fiction and nonfiction, including greeting cards and specialty markets.

The Deadly Directory. Kate Derie. New York: Deadly Serious Press, 1998.

Find listings of booksellers, publications, and organizations related to the mystery genre in this directory.

Directory of Literary Magazines: Complete Information on More Than 500 U.S. and Elsewhere Magazines That Publish Poetry, Fiction, and Essays. The Council of Literary Magazines and Presses. Wakefield, RI: Moyer Bell. Annual.

The magazines listed in this directory are the kinds of publications where writers like Ezra Pound and Ralph Ellison got their first exposure. Each entry provides descriptions of the magazines, the types of materials published, the number of unsolicited manuscripts received, what the writer's payment is (for most of these small magazines, payment is in copies), and subscription information.

Directory of Poetry Publishers. Len Fulton, ed. Paradise, CA: Dustbooks. Annual.

More than two thousand magazine and book publishers interested in acquiring poetry are described. There's usually a quote from editors commenting on the type of work they want along with contact data, payment and submission information, and percentage of poetry published out of the total amount submitted. The subject index clusters publishers under such topics as Alaska, Erotica, Men, Surrealism, and Zen. Also from this publisher and editor is the annually updated *International Directory of Little Magazines and Small Presses,* geared to the writer.

Dramatist's Guild Directory. New York: Dramatist's Guild. Annual.

This directory lists theatrical agents, attorneys, artists' colonies, Broadway and off-Broadway producers, conferences, festivals, emergency funds, fellowships, grants, organizations, non-Equity institutional theaters, contests, residencies, and workshops. The *Dramatist's Guild* Web page is at http://www.vcu.edu/artweb/playwriting/dg.html. Other directories for playwrights include the *Dramatist's Sourcebook: Complete Opportunities for Playwrights, Translators, Composers, Lyricists, and Librettists* (New York: Theatre Communications Group) and *The Playwright's Companion: A Submission Guide to Theatres and Contests in the USA* (New York: Feedback Theatrebooks. Annual).

Editor & Publisher International Year Book. New York: Editor & Publisher. Annual.

"The encyclopedia of the newspaper industry." The *Year Book* supplies information about newspapers of all varieties: daily, weekly, special (military, black, gay, lesbian, ethnic, religious, and college), and tabloid from all over the world, listed in geographic order. For each paper, information such as circulation, price, advertising costs, and names of editors and managers is supplied. Also search for media outlets at Editor & Publisher's *Media Links Online Media Directory* at http://www.mediainfo.com/emedia/.

Encyclopedia of Associations. 4 Volumes. Detroit: Gale. Annual.

Described earlier, the *Encyclopedia* can also be used to find special publications. Locate an association for the topic you're interested in and then see whether they produce a specialized newsletter or other outlet for writing. Most do.

Gale Directory of Publications and Broadcast Media. 4 Volumes. Detroit: Gale.

Annual, plus updates. Also available online via GaleNet through the *Gale Database of Publications and Broadcast Media.*

The *Gale Directory* lists, state by state and province by province, North American newspapers, magazines, journals, radio and television stations, and cable systems indexed by subject, format, and intended audience. Some elements of the publication entries include key personnel, description, and circulation; the broadcast listings include format, operating hours, and cities served.

Greeting Card Publishers. http://www.greetingcard.org/gca/linksPublishers.htm

This page has names, addresses and numbers for greeting card publishers— but no guidelines for writers.

The Literary Market Place (LMP): The Directory of the American Book Publishing Industry. New Providence, NJ: R.R. Bowker. Annual. Also available as a subscription database through Bowker. At the time of this writing you could also sign up for a free trial run of *LMP* at http://www.bowker.com/.

This is a key one-stop directory for book publishing services in the U.S. and Canada. Book publishers are listed, with the larger and/or more established presses indexed by subject, type of publication, and geographic location. You'll find contact information for publicity, agents, awards, wholesalers, and desktop publishers. The *International Literary Market Place* is also released annually.

Market Info For Writers. http://www.inkspot.com/bt/market/

This terrific Inkspot site offers a meta list of free online market resources, including the *Writers' Guidelines Database* at http://mav.net/guidelines/ and *AWOC.com: The Writer's Place* at http://www.awoc.com/Guidelines.cfm.

The Market List: A Resource for Writers of Science Fiction, Fantasy, and Horror. http://www.marketlist.com/

This free Web site provides genre fiction writers with market leads and advice.

MLA Directory of Scholarly Presses in Language and Literature. 2nd edition. James L. Harner. New York: Modern Language Association, 1998.

The *MLA* Directory describes the fields of interest, submission requirements, contract provisions, and editorial procedures of 315 publishers of scholarly books on the study of language and linguistics. Publishers from thirty-four countries are included. Note that these publishers are interested in books *about* literature, not works of fiction.

Newsletters

Directories listing newsletter titles include *Newsletters in Print* (Detroit:

Gale. Also available online via GaleNet and DIALOG), *Community, Specialty & Free Publications Year Book* (New York: Editor & Publisher), *Oxbridge Directory of Newsletters* (Oxbridge Communications. Annual. Also available on CD-ROM), *Hudson's Subscription Newsletter Directory* (Rhinebeck, NY: Hudson Associates. Annual), and on the Internet, *Newsletter Access*, at http://www.newsletteraccess.com.

Publishers' Catalogues Home Page. http://www.lights.com/publisher/
   This is a free list of links to publishers' home pages worldwide.

Publishers Directory. Detroit: Gale. Annual.
   More than twenty thousand North American publishers are listed in this directory.

The Small Press Net. http://www.io.org/~gutter/#spn
   This Web page supplies a list of links to small presses.

Travel Publications Update. Oldsmar, FL: Marco Polo Publications. Annual.
   Travel Publications Update supplies information on over six hundred travel magazines and more than two hundred newspaper travel sections and can be ordered at http://www.travelwriters.com/ or by calling (727)785-1845.

Ulrich's International Periodicals Directory. 5 Volumes. New Providence, NJ: R.R. Bowker. Annual with supplements. Also available on CD-ROM and online as a subscription database via DIALOG, EBSCO, Gale, OCLC, and Ovid. Limited content is also searchable at no charge at http://www.publist.com.
   Ulrich's, a standard source at all libraries, briefly describes international magazines, journals, and newspapers in over one hundred subject classification areas—great for unearthing niche publications. *The Serials Directory* (Birmingham, AL: EBSCO. Annual, with supplements. Also online via EBSCOhost) is similar to *Ulrich's*.

Working Press of the Nation. 3 Volumes. New Providence, NJ: National Register Publishing. Annual.
   This set lists newspapers, including dailies, weeklies, and special interest, as well as magazines, internal publications and television and radio stations. Entries supply staff member names and titles, writing deadlines, freelancer pay (though unfortunately this can often say "varies.")

Write Markets Report. http://www.writersmarkets.com/.
   Each edition of this online bimonthly report, available by subscription, supplies more than fifty potential markets for writers and articles on how to earn money writing. A free issue can be requested at their Web site.

Writers' and Artists' Yearbook. London: A&C Black. Annual.

This guide supplies market information for articles, books, scripts, poetry, illustrations, photographs, and music, primarily in the U.K., but also for publishers and other buyers from Australia, Canada, Ghana, Hong Kong, India, Ireland, Kenya, Malaysia, New Zealand, Nigeria, Singapore, South Africa, Tanzania, the U.S., and Zimbabwe.

Writers and Photographers Guide to Global Markets. Michael H. Sedge. New York, Allworth Press: 1998.

This directory describes hundreds of worldwide markets for authors and photographers.

Writer's Guide to Book Editors, Publishers, and Literary Agents. Jeff Herman. Rocklin, CA: Prima Publishing. Annual. Also available with CD-ROM.

A mix of instructional articles and listings of book publishers and literary agents. Each publisher entry consists of a description of the genres the publisher is most interested in, their recent publications and better-known authors, and a listing of acquisitions editors and their interests.

The Writer's Handbook. Sylvia K. Burack. Boston: The Writer. Annual.

This handbook, from *The Writer* magazine, supplies market listings, interviews with successful writers, and articles on the craft of writing.

Writer's Market: Where & How to Sell What You Write. Cincinnati, Ohio: Writer's Digest Books. Also available with CD-ROM. Annual.

One of the most popular market guides, *Writer's Market* is published annually with interim updates included in *Writer's Digest* magazine and on-line at no charge at the *Big Guide to Guidelines* at http://writersdigest.com/guidelines/index.htm. *Writer's Market* lists outlets for short stories, novels, plays, television and film scripts, articles, greeting cards, fillers, and nonfiction books, listing necessary information for writers. The book also includes practical advice for professional writers; interviews with authors, editors, and publishers; and listings and descriptions of agents.

Writer's Digest Books also publishes market directories that focus on specialty markets, including *Artist's and Graphic Designer's Market, Children's Writer's and Illustrator's Market, Novel and Short Story Writer's Market, Photographer's Market, Poet's Market,* and *Songwriter's Market.*

Style and Format

Both teachers and editors expect writings to be presented in standard formats. A teacher will usually let you know the preferred format, telling you, for example, to follow the MLA style book. Other times you'll need to decide what the accepted standard is for a type of writing. The following resources list suggested manuscript guidelines for different types of writing and standard formats along with other writing-related advice.

The Associated Press Stylebook and Libel Handbook. Norm Goldstein, editor. Reading, MA: Perseus, 1998.

The *AP Stylebook*, geared to journalists, presents the AP's rules on grammar, spelling, punctuation, and word usage. It also includes advice on how writers can guard against libel and copyright infringement.

Chicago Manual of Style. 14th edition. Chicago Editorial Staff. Chicago: University of Chicago Press, 1993.

This manual recommends manuscript formats and offers advice on punctuation, grammar, spelling, typeface, capitalization, and citations.

Columbia Guide to Online Style. Janice Walker and Todd Taylor. New York: Columbia University Press, 1998.

The authors provide rules for citing electronic resources and supply guidelines for formatting documents for online publication and for electronically preparing texts for print publication. The guidelines can be applied to such styles as MLA, APA and Chicago.

A meta site to pages on the Internet with tips for citing electronic documents is *Internet Citation Guides* at http://www.library.wisc.edu/libraries/Memorial/citing.htm.

Elements of Style for Screenwriters. Paul Argentini. Los Angeles: Lone Eagle Publishing, 1998.

This guide presents the principles of screenplay formatting, structure, and style for screenwriters.

The Grammar Hotline Directory. http://www.tc.cc.va.us/writcent/gh/hotlinol.htm

This is an online list of experts you can call to assist with tricky grammar queries.

MLA Handbook for Writers of Research Papers. 4th edition. Joseph Gibaldi. New York: The Modern Language Association, 1995.

A guide to preparing and citing research papers. It includes information on grammar and punctuation, on using computers for research and writing, and on citing electronic publications. Also from MLA is the *MLA Style Manual and Guide to Scholarly Publishing* (1998).

Prentice Hall Style Manual: A Complete Guide With Model Formats for Every Business Writing Occasion. Mary Ann De Vries. Englewood Cliffs, NJ: Prentice Hall, 1992.

Spelling Not Your Strength?

There are dictionaries that help you spell. They list thousands of possible misspellings for the spelling-impaired to locate, followed by the accepted spelling. An example of this type of book is *NTC's Spell It Right Dictionary* (Lincolnwood, IL: National Textbook Company, 1992). To find other dictionaries like this one, do a keyword search on your library's on-line catalog using the phrase ENGLISH LANGUAGE SPELLING DICTIONARIES.

This book supplies two hundred model correspondences in 125 categories.

The Songwriter's Market Guide to Song & Demo Submission Formats. Donna Collingwood, ed. Cincinnati, Ohio: Writer's Digest Books, 1994.

This guide offers instructions for packaging and pitching songs and music.

Formatting & Submitting Your Manuscripts. Jack and Glenda Neff, Don Prues, and the editors of *Writer's Market.* Cincinnati, OH: Writer's Digest Books, 1999.

This guide shows sample formats for numerous sources in both their query and finished stages, including books, scripts, poetry, greeting cards, and even recipes, photographs, and anecdotes.

Writing Centers Online. http://departments.colgate.edu/diw/NWCAOWLS.html

This is a directory to academic Writing Centers and Online Writing Labs, a.k.a. OWLs. Though created for registered students, many contain tutorials, advice, guides, and links of interest to authors and researchers. Some sample centers include *Dakota State University OWL* at http://www.dsu.edu:80/depart ments/liberal/cola/OWL/ and *Purdue University's OWL* at http://owl.english .purdue.edu

Finding Agents

Literary agents are experts in the marketing of writers manuscripts. If they sell the manuscript, they can also work with the publisher and writer to hammer out contractual details. Agents are listed in a number of the resources listed previously, including *Literary Market Place* and *Writer's Market.* Other online and off-line places to dig up information on agents:

Agent Research & Evaluation. http://www.agentresearch.com

This company publishes and sells the *New Agent List;* the *Fisher Report,* which identifies "dubious" agents; and a newsletter (see *Talking Agents,*

p. 365). They also offer such fee-based services as finding the names of the agents of particular authors.

The Annual Screenwriter's Guide. New York: New York Screenwriter's Monthly. Annual.

This guide lists products and services of interest to screenwriters along with listings of agencies and production companies open for screenplay submissions. It's free with a paid subscription to *The New York Screenwriter Monthly,* or it can be purchased separately.

The Association of Authors' Representatives (AAR). http://www.bookwire.com/AAR/

This is the home page for the not-for-profit organization of independent literary and dramatic agents, listing their code of ethics and members.

Guide to Literary Agents. Donya Dickerson. Cincinnati, OH: Writer's Digest Books. Annual.

This yearly guide is divided into two sections, literary agents and script agents, and then further divided by those who charge a fee and those who don't. Each entry describes the agent's specialties and lists contact information, any fees charged, comments from the agents, recent titles represented, and any conferences the agent plans to attend. There's also overall advice on how to snag an agent.

Guild Signatory Agents and Agencies. http://www.wga.org/agency.html

The free listings on this site, supplying agent names and addresses, represent those agents who have agreed to abide by the standards established by the Writer's Guild of America regarding the representation of writers.

Hollywood Access Directory. http://hollydex.com/Search/index.html

Agents for screenwriters can be searched at this Web site.

Hollywood Agent's and Manager's Directory. Los Angeles: Hollywood Creative Directory, 1998.

This guide lists names and contact information for those in agencies and management firms. Also from this publisher is the *Hollywood Creative Directory,* a who's who of people at studios, networks, and production companies, and the *Spec Screenplay Sales Directory,* listing who sold scripts on spec and for how much.

Writers Net Literary Agents. http://www.writers.net/agents.html

This directory lists agents that do not charge reading fees.

Appendix A
Commercial Online Database Vendors

These vendors provide access to subscription databases that they create or lease. Though their primary subscribers have traditionally been businesses, libraries, and other institutions, more and more are offering plans for individuals that make access affordable.

This is not a listing of all the databases and systems these publishers and distributors handle; only titles listed in this book. Each listing includes:

- Name of the provider
- Contact information
- Name(s) of databases or resources they include in their services (in italics) or the names of the umbrella service(s) they offer that include many databases and resources (not in italics) mentioned in *Facts in a Flash*.

ABC-CLIO, Phone: (800)368-6868 or (805)968-1911, Fax: (805)685-9685, URL: http://www.abc-clio.com
America: History and Life

American Mathematical Society, P.O. Box 6248, Providence, RI 02940-6248, Phone: (800)321-4267 (U.S. and Canada), Fax: (401)455-4046, E-mail: cust-serv@ams.org, URL: http://www.ams.org/
MathSciNet

Bloomberg Financial Markets, 499 Park Ave., New York, NY 10022, Phone: (212)318-2000, Fax: (212)980-4585, URL: http://www.bloomberg.com
Business Wire, PR Newswire, WorldScope

R.R. Bowker, Reed Reference Publishing Group, 121 Chanlon Rd., New Providence, NJ 07974, Phone: (908)464-6800, Fax: (908)464-3553, E-mail: info@bowker.com, URL: http://www.reedref.com/bowker/
Books in Print, International Literary Market Place, Literary Market Place

CCH, Inc., 2700 Lake Cook Rd., Riverwoods, IL 60015, Phone: (847)267-7000 or (800)248-3248, Fax: (800)224-8299, URL: http://www.cch.com

ELSS: Electronic Legislative Search System

Chadwyck-Healey, Inc., Regional Office, 1101 King St., Suite 308, Alexandria, VA 22314, Phone: (800)752-0515 or (703)683-4890, Fax: (703)683-7589, E-mail: info@chadwyck.com, URL: http://www.chadwyck.com/

> *ABELL: Annual Bibliography of English Language and Literature, International Index to Music Periodicals, International Index to the Performing Arts,* Literature Online, *Periodicals Contents Index*

Compuserve, Inc., 5000 Arlington Centre Blvd., P.O. Box 20212, Columbus, OH 43220, Phone: (614)457-8600, URL: http://www.compuserve.com

> *America: History & Life, Book Review Digest, Business Index, Computer Database, Corporate Affiliations, Dissertation Abstracts, Disclosure, F&S Index, Health Periodicals Database, Investext, Lesko's Info-Power, National Newspaper Index, Newsletter Database, NTIS, PROMT, PsycInfo*

Congressional Information Service, Inc., 4250 East-West Highway, Bethesda, MD 20814-3389, Phone: (800)638-8380 or (301)654-1550, Fax: (301)654-4033, URL: http://www.cispubs.com.

> *American Statistics Index, CIS History Universe, Congressional MasterFile 1, Congressional MasterFile 2, Congressional Universe, Enviroline, Statistical MasterFile, Statistical Universe*

Congressional Quarterly, Inc., 1414 Twenty-second St. NW, Washington, DC 20037, Phone: (202)887-6272 or (800)432-2250, ext. 272, URL: http://www.cq.com

> *CQ.com On Congress, CQ Researcher*

Corporate Technology Information Services, 12 Alfred St., Suite 200, Woburn, MA 01801-1915, Phone: (800)333-8036 or (781)932-3100, Fax: (781)932-6335, E-mail: sales@corptech.com, URL: http://www.corptech.com

> *Corptech Directory of Technology Companies*

DataStar (owned by the DIALOG Corporation), DIALOG/Datastar, Haymarket House, 1 Oxendon St., London, SW1Y 4EE England, Phone: 44-171-930-7646, Fax: 44-171-930-2581, URL: http://www.dialog.com

> *ABI-INFORM, Arts & Humanities Citation Index, Biosis, Business & Industry, Business Index, CINAHL, Computer Database, COMPENDEX, Corptech, Datamonitor Market Research, Disclosure, Dissertation Abstracts, Enviroline, Euromonitor Market Research, Extel Cards, Freedonia Market Research, Frost & Sullivan Market Intelligence, IAC Computer Database, IAC F&S Database, IAC Health Periodicals Database, IAC Legal Resources, IAC Magazine Database, IAC Newsletter Database, ICC reports, InfoTrac SearchBank, INSPEC, Investext,*

Medline, National Newspaper Index, New York Times, PAIS, PROMT, PsycInfo, SSCI, Sociological Abstracts, SportDiscus, National Newspaper Index, Science Citation Index, Social Sciences Citation Index, Who Owns Whom

DIALOG Corporation, 2440 W. El Camino Real, Mountain View, CA 94040-1400, Phone: (800)334-2564 or (650)254-7000, Fax: (650)254-7070, URL: http://www.dialog.com/

ABI/INFORM, Accounting & Tax Index, Aerospace Database, America: History & Life, Architectural Publications Index, Arts & Humanities Citation Index, Biosis, Brands and Their Companies, Business and Industry, Business Index, COMPENDEX, Complete Marquis Who's Who, Computer Database, Datamonitor Market Research, DataStar, DIALOG, *Dissertation Abstracts, Dun's Electronic Business Directory, Dun's Financial Records Plus, Dun's Market Identifiers, EconLit, Euromonitor Market Research, European Dun's Market Identifiers, EventLine, F&S Index, Freedonia Market Research, Frost & Sullivan Market Intelligence, GeoRef, Global Corporate Linkages, Health Periodicals Database, ICC data, International Dun's Market Identifiers and European Financial Records, Linguistics and Language Behavior Abstracts,* Medline, *Microcomputer Abstracts, National Newspaper Index, Newsletter Database, New York Times, Philosopher's Index,* Profound, *PR Newswire, PROMT, Science Citation Index, Social Sciences Citation Index, Sociological Abstracts, Ulrich's*

Disclosure, Inc., 5161 River Rd., Bethesda, MD 20816, Phone: (800)236-6997, ext. 300 or outside the U.S.: 44-171-278-8277, URL: http://www.disclosure.com

Compact D/Canada, Compact D/Laser, Compact D/SEC, Disclosure SEC, Global Access, ICC data, Worldscope

Dow Jones Information Service, P.O. Box 300, Princeton, NJ 08543-0300, Phone: (800)522-3567 or (609)520-4000, Fax: (609)520-5757, URL: http://www.dj.com/ or http://djinteractive.com

Business Index, Computer Database, Dow Jones Interactive, DowVision, *Ethnic NewsWatch, F&S Index, Health Periodicals Database, National Newspaper Index, Newsletter Database, PR Newswire, PROMT*

Dun & Bradstreet, One Diamond Hill Rd., Murray Hill, NJ 07974-1218, Phone: (800)526-0651, ext. 3030, or (908)665-5000, Fax: (908)665-5803, URL: http://www.dnb.com/

D&B Million Dollar Database, Who Owns Whom, WORLDBASE

EBSCO Information Services, 10 Estes St., Ipswich, MA 01938, Phone:

(800)653-2726 or (978)356-6500, Fax: (978)356-6565, E-mail: ep@epnet
.com, URL: http://www.ebsco.com

> *Books in Print, CINAHL,* EBSCOhost, *Medline, Newspaper Source, Psyc-Info, Ulrich's*

Encyclopedia Britannica, Phone for online product: (800)522-8656, Phone for other products: (800)747-8503, URL: http://www.eb.com

> *Encyclopedia Britannica*

EINS (European Information Network Services), The British Library Science Information Service, 25 Southampton Buildings, London, WC2A 1AW, Phone: 011-44-171-412-7946, Fax: 011-44-171-412-7954, URL: http://www.eins.org

Financial Information Services, 60 Madison Ave., Sixth Floor, New York, NY 10010, Phone: (800)342-564, ext. 7601 or (212)413-7601, Fax: (212)413-7777, E-mail: fis@fisonline.com, URL: http://www.fisonline.com/

> *Moody's Company Data, Moody's Company Data Direct*

Financial Times Information, Ltd., 13-17 Epworth St., London EC2A 4DL, England, Phone: 011-44-171-825-8000, Fax: 011-44-171-608-3514, URL: http://netserve.ft.com

> *Business Index, Computer Database, Extel, F&S Index,* FT-Profile, *Health Periodicals Database, ICC data, Investext, National Newspaper Index, Newsletter Database, PROMT*

FT-PROFILE. *See* Financial Times Information, Ltd.

Gale Research, 27500 Drake Rd., Farmington Hills, MI 48331-3535, Phone: (800)347-4253 or (248)699-4253, Fax: (248)699-8061, E-mail: galeord@gale
.com, URL: http://www.gale.com

> *Associations Unlimited, Biography and Genealogy Master Index, Books in Print, Contemporary Authors, Encyclopedia of American Industries, Gale Biographies, Gale Literary Databases,* GaleNet, *Ulrich's*

Grolier Electronic Publishing, Inc., Sherman Turnpike, Danbury, CT 06816, Phone: (203)797-3500, Fax: (203)797-3835.

> *Academic American Encyclopedia*

Grove's Dictionaries, Inc., 345 Park Ave. S., New York, NY 10010-1707, Phone: (800)221-2123 or (212)689-9200, Fax: (212)689-9711, E-mail: grove
@grovereference.com, URL http://www.macmillan-reference.co.uk

> *Grove Dictionary of Art*

Infonautics Corporation, 900 W. Valley Rd., Suite 1000, Wayne, PA 19087-1830, Phone: (800)304-3542, E-mail: info@infonautics.com, URL: http://
www.infonautics.com or http://www.elibrary.com

Electric Library, Ethnic NewsWatch

Information Access Company (IAC), part of the Gale Group, 362 Lakeside Drive, Foster City, CA 94404, Phone: (800)227-8431 or (650)378-5200, Fax: (650)378-5369, E-mail: info@informationaccess.com, http://www.information access.com/

Books in Print, Computer Database, Business Index, Expanded Academic Index, F&S Index, Health Periodicals Database, Infotrac Searchbank, *National Newspaper Index, Newsletter Database, New York Times, PAIS International, PROMT, PsycInfo, SIRS Researcher, Sociological Abstracts*

infoUSA, Inc., 5711 S. Eighty-sixth Circle, P.O. Box 27347, Omaha, NE 68127, Phone: (800)321-0869, Fax: (402)537-6065, E-mail: internet@infousa.com, URL: http://www.abii.com/

American Big Businesses Directory, American Manufacturers Directory, Business USA, 4.5 Millions Small Business Owners

Institute for Scientific Information (ISI), 3501 Market St., Philadelphia, PA 19104, Phone: (800)336-4474, URL: http://www.isinet.com

Arts & Humanities Citation Index, Science Citation Index, Social Science Citation Index, Web of Science

International Monetary Fund, Headquarters, 700 Nineteenth St. N.W., Washington, DC 20431, Phone: (202)623-7430, Fax: (202)623-7201, E-mail: publications@imf.org, URL: http://www.imf.org

International Financial Statistics

Internet Securities, 695 Atlantic Ave., Boston, MA 02111, Phone: (617)204-3100, Fax: (617)204-3101, E-mail: jbyram@securities.com, URL: http://www.securities.com/

ISI Emerging Markets

Investext Group, 40 W. Fifty-seventh St., Suite 1000, New York, NY 10019, Phone: (800)662-7878 or (212)484-4700, Fax: (212)484-4720, URL: http://www.investext.com/

Investext

LEGI-SLATE, Inc., 10 G St. NE, Suite 500, Washington, DC 20002, Phone: (202)898-2300, Fax: (202)898-3030, URL: http://www.legislate.com

Legi-Slate

LEXIS-NEXIS, P.O. Box 933, Dayton, OH 45401-0933, Phone: (937)865-6800 or (800)227-9597, URL: http://www.lexis-nexis.com/

ABI/INFORM, Business Index, Complete Marquis Who's Who, Computer Database, Ethnic NewsWatch Facts on File, F&S Index, Health Periodicals Database,

ICC data, LEXIS-NEXIS, *National Newspaper Index, Newsletter Database, New York Times Biographical Service, Official ABMS Directory of Board Certified Medical Specialists, PR Newswire, PROMT, Standard & Poor's Register of Corporations, Statistical Masterfile*

MarkIntel. *See* Thomson Financial

MedTech USA, 6310 San Vicente Blvd., Suite 425, Los Angeles, CA 90048, Phone: (800)260-2600, Fax: (800)671-8100, E-mail: mail@medtech.com, URL: http://www.medicalamazon.com

Merck Manual on CD-ROM

National Register Publishing, 121 Chanlon Rd., New Providence, NJ 07974, Phone: (908)464-6800, URL: http://www.reedref.com.

Standard Directory of Advertisers

NewsBank, Inc., 58 Pine St., New Canaan, CT 06840-5426, Phone: (800)223-4739 or (203)966-1100, Fax: (203)966-6254, URL: http://www.newsbank.com

Business Newsbank, Newsbank

OCLC: Online Computer Library Center, Inc., 6565 Frantz Rd., Dublin, OH 43017-3395, Phone: (800)848-5878 or (614)764-6000, Fax: (614)764-6096, E-mail: oclc@oclc.org, URL: http://www.oclc.org

ABI/INFORM, Applied Science and Technology Abstracts, Art Abstracts, ArticleFirst, Arts & Humanities Citation Index, Biography Index, Biological and Agricultural Index, Biosis, Books in Print, Business & Industry, Business Periodicals Index, CINAHL, Disclosure, Dissertation Abstracts, EconLit, Education Abstracts, ERIC, Ethnic NewsWatch, Eventline, FirstSearch, *General Science Abstracts, GeoRef, Health Reference Center, Humanities Abstracts, Index to Legal Periodicals and Books, Library Literature, Linguistics and Language Behavior, Abstracts Medline, Microcomputer Abstracts, MLA International Bibliography of Books and Articles on the Modern Languages and Literatures, Newspaper Abstracts, The New York Times, PAIS International, Periodicals Abstracts, Periodicals Contents Index, PapersFirst, ProceedingsFirst, PsycInfo, Reader's Guide Abstracts, RILM Abstracts of Music and Literature, SIRS Researcher, Social Sciences Abstracts, Sociological Abstracts, Ulrich's, WorldCat, Worldscope, World Almanac, World Book Encyclopedia*

OneSource Information Services, Inc., 150 Cambridge Dr., Cambridge, MA 02140, Phone: (800)554-5501 or (617)441-7000, Fax: (617)441-7058, URL: http://www.onesource.com

Business Browser, *CorpTech Directory of Technology Companies, Directory of Corporate Affiliations, Global Business Browser, Hoover's Guides, ICC* data, *Investext, Marquis Who's Who, Reuters, Standard & Poor's Register of Corporations,* U.K. Business Browser, U.S. Business Browser, *Ward's Business Directory, Worldscope*

Ovid Technologies, Inc., 333 Seventh Ave., New York, NY 10001, Phone: (800)950-2035, ext. 249, or (212)563-3006, Fax: (212)563-3784, E-mail: sales@ovid.com, URL: http://www.ovid.com

ABI/INFORM, BIOSIS, Books in Print, Business Periodicals Index, CINAHL, COMPENDEX, Dissertation Abstracts, INSPEC, Linguistics and Language Behavior Abstracts, Medline, PsycInfo, Sociological Abstracts, SportsDiscus, Ulrichs

Profound. *See* DIALOG

ProQuest. *See* UMI

Questel·Orbit, Regional Office, 8000 Westpark Dr., McLean, VA 22102, Phone: (800)456-7248 or (703)442-0900, Fax: (703)893-4632, URL: http://www.questel.orbit.com/

Business Index, COMPENDEX, Computer Database, Enviroline, Dun's directories, *Eventline, F&S Index, GeoRef, Health Periodicals Database, INSPEC, Medline, Merck Index Online, National Newspaper Index, Newsletter Database, PROMT*

Research Libraries Group, 1200 Villa St., Mountain View, CA 94041-1100, Phone: (800)537-7546, Fax: (650)964-0943, E-mail: bl.ric@rlg.org, URL: http://www.rlg.org/

Avery Index to Architecture Periodicals, Bibliography of the History of Art, Chicano Database, CitaDel, Eureka, *Handbook of Latin American Studies, Hispanic American Periodicals Index, Index to Foreign Legal Periodicals*

Standard & Poor's, 25 Broadway, New York, NY 10004, Phone: (212)208-8340, Fax: (212)412-0422, URL: http://www.standardandpoors.com/

Standard & Poor's Net Advantage, *Standard & Poor's Register Databases*

STN International/Chemical Abstracts Service, 2540 Olentangy River Rd., P.O. Box 3012, Columbus, OH 43210-0012, Phone: (614)447-3600, Fax: (614)447-3713, E-mail: help@cas.org, URL: http://www.cas.org

ABI/INFORM, Biosis, Business Index, Chemical Abstracts, COMPENDEX, Computer Database, Eventline, F&S Index, GeoRef, Health Periodicals Database, INSPEC, Medline, National Newspaper Index, Newsletter Database, PROMT, Science Citation Index, WorldCat

Thomson & Thomson, 500 Victory Rd., North Quincy, MA 02171-3145,

Phone: (800)692-8833 or (617)479-1600, Fax: (617)786-8273, URL: http://
www.thomson-thomson.com

SAEGIS, *TRADEMARKSCAN*

Thomson Financial Publishing, 4709 W. Golf Rd., Skokie, IL 60076-1253,
Phone: (800)321-3373, Fax: (847)933-8101, E-mail: customerservice@tfp
.com, URL: http://www.tfp.com/

MarkIntel

UMI Company (now called Bell & Howell), 300 N. Zeeb Rd., Ann Arbor, MI
48106-1346, Phone: (800)521-0600 or (313)761-4700, E-mail: info@umi.c
om, URL: http://www.umi.com

*ABI/INFORM, Accounting & Tax Index, Applied Science and Technology
Index, General Science Index, INSPEC,* ProQuest Direct, *ProQuest Discovery,
Social Sciences Index*

UnCover Company, 3801 E. Florida Ave., Suite 200, Denver, CO 80210,
Phone: (800)787-7979 or (303)758-3030, Fax: (313)758-5946, E-mail:
uncover@carl.org, URL: http://uncweb.carl.org

UnCover

United Nations, United Nations Publications, Subscriptions Office, P.O. Box
361, Birmingham, AL 35201-1943, Phone: (800)633-4931 (U.S. & Canada
only) or (205)995-1567, Fax: (205)995-1588, URL: http://www.un.org/
Pubs/sales.htm

MBS Online (Monthly Bulletin of Statistics)

Value Line Publishing, Inc., 220 E. Forty-second St., New York, NY 10017,
Phone: (800)634-6583 or (212)907-1500, Fax: (212) 818-9747, URL: http://
www.valueline.com/

Value Line Investment Survey

West Group, 610 Opperman Dr., Eagan, MN 55123, Phone: (800)328-4880,
Fax: (612)687-6674, URL: http://www.westgroup.com

*Business Index, Computer Database, F&S Index, Health Periodicals Database,
National Newspaper Index, Newsletter Database, PROMT,* Westlaw

H.W. Wilson Company, 950 University Ave., Bronx, NY 10452-4224, Phone:
(800)367-6770 or (212)588-8400, Fax: (718)590-1617, URL: http://www
.hwwilson.com

*Applied Science and Technology Index, Art Index/Abstracts, Bibliographic In-
dex, Biography Index, Biological & Agricultural Index, Book Review Digest, Business Periodicals Index, Current Biography, Education Index, Essay and General
Literature Index, General Science Index, Humanities Index, Index to Legal Period-*

icals and Books, Library Literature, Readers' Guide, Social Sciences Index, Vertical File Index, Wilson Biographies Plus, WilsonWeb

World Book Publishing, 525 W. Monroe Street, Twentieth Floor, Chicago, IL 60661, Phone: (312)258-3600, URL: http://www.worldbook.com

   World Book Encyclopedia

Appendix B
Periodical Indexes

B elow is a listing of indexes to articles in magazines, journals, newspapers, and newsletters commonly found in larger public and/or academic libraries, arranged by subject. Most of the online indexes, in addition to being accessible through one or more commercial vendors, can also be purchased on tape to load on to local computer networks. There may be slight variations in names of databases in their print, CD-ROM, and online formats. Periodical indexes that cover multiple subject areas are listed in chapter three.

Subject headings:

Art, Architecture, Dance, Literature, Music, and Theater
ABELL: Annual Bibliography of English Language and Literature. Leeds, England: Maney & Son, 1920–present. Also available as a subscription database via Chadwyck Healey's *Literature Online.*

Abstracts of scholarly articles, dissertations, books, and reviews.

Architectural Publications Index. London: RIBA Publications, 1933–present. Also
available on CD-ROM and as a subscription database via DIALOG.

Indexes architecture journals worldwide with an emphasis on literature,
projects, and designs in Great Britain.

Art Index. New York: Wilson, 1929–present. Also available on CD-ROM and
as a subscription database via OCLC and Wilson.

Covers all aspects of art and art research, including archaeology, architecture, and photography.

Arts & Humanities Citation Index (A&HCI). Philadelphia: ISI, 1976–present.
Also available on CD-ROM and as a subscription database via DataStar, DIA-
LOG, OCLC, and ISI on their *Web of Science.*

Index to journals in all arts and humanities fields, including dance, film,
radio, television, music, and literature. Additionally, offers more reference possibilities by listing the authors and articles cited by each article it indexes.

Avery Index to Architecture Periodicals. Boston: G.K. Hall, 1963–1990; New York:
MacMillan, 1991–present. Also available on CD-ROM and as a subscription
database via the Research Libraries Group. A limited number of years of *Avery*
is also available free at http://www.ahip.getty.edu/aka/.

Indexes periodicals in architectural design, the history and practice of architecture, landscape architecture, historic preservation, interior design, and city
planning.

Bibliography for the History of Art (BHA). Cedex, France: Centre National de la
Recherche Scientifique. Also available as a subscription database via DIALOG
(called *Art Literature International)* and the Research Libraries Group.

Supplies abstracts from worldwide literature on European and American
art from late antiquity to the present. In 1990, the index *International Repertory
of the Literature of Art (RILA)* merged with its French counterpart, the *Réper-
toire d'Art et d'Archéologie (RAA)* to form BHA. *RILA* from 1975–1989, is
available both in print or free via the *Getty Information Institute* at http://
www.ahip.getty.edu/aka.

Essay and General Literature Index. New York: Wilson, 1900–present. Also available on CD-ROM and as a subscription database via Wilson.

Index to writings published in books of collected essays, primarily in the
fields of the humanities and social sciences. Useful for finding essays buried
in anthologies and collections.

Film Literature Index. Albany, NY: Film and Television Documentation Center, 1973–present.

International index to articles about film, television, and video.

Humanities Index. New York: Wilson, 1974–present. Formerly called the *International Index to Periodicals*, 1907–1955, the *International Index*, 1955–1965, and the *Social Sciences and Humanities Index*, 1965–1974. Also available on CD-ROM and as a subscription database via OCLC and Wilson.

Indexes four hundred humanities periodicals. The online full-text version includes full-text articles for about a quarter of the journals indexed.

International Index to Music Periodicals. Cambridge, England: Chadwyck-Healey.

This subscription database contains abstracts of articles from over 375 international music periodicals.

International Index to the Performing Arts. Cambridge, England: Chadwyck-Healey.

There are article abstracts from more than 130 international periodicals related to the performing arts in this subscription database.

Linguistics and Language Behavior Abstracts (LLBA). Also available on CD-ROM and as a subscription database via DIALOG, OCLC, and Ovid.

Presents abstracts of articles from more than two thousand international journals, plus coverage of books, book chapters, occasional papers, monographs, technical reports, dissertations, and book reviews.

MLA International Bibliography of Books and Articles on the Modern Languages and Literatures. New York: The Modern Language Association of America, 1921–present. Also available on CD-ROM and as a subscription database via OCLC.

The premier scholarly index of languages and literature.

Music Index. Warren, MI: Harmonie Park Press, 1949–present. Also available on CD-ROM.

Topics indexed include the history of music, different forms and types of music, musical instruments, biographies, and reviews of recordings and performances.

Periodicals Contents Index. Cambridge, England: Chadwyck-Healey. Available as a subscription database via Chadwyck-Healey's *Literature Online* and OCLC.

Indexes articles from humanities and social science periodicals.

RILM Abstracts of Music Literature. New York: RILM Abstracts, 1969–present. Also available on CD-ROM and as a subscription database via OCLC.

An international bibliography of scholarly writings on music in over two hundred languages.

Business

ABI/INFORM. New York: UMI, 1971–present. Available on CD-ROM and via DataStar, DIALOG, LEXIS-NEXIS, OCLC, Ovid, ProQuest Direct, STN International, and others.

An electronic database that indexes business periodicals, including scholarly business publications. Has selected full text.

Accounting & Tax Index. Ann Arbor, MI: UMI, 1920–present. Formerly called the *Accountants' Index.* Also available on CD-ROM and as a subscription database via DIALOG and ProQuest Direct.

Supplies citations to accounting and tax writings, including articles, tax publications, pamphlets, books, dissertations, and theses.

Business and Industry. Beachwood, OH: Responsive Database Services. Available on CD-ROM under the title *B&I OnDisc* and as a subscription database via DIALOG and OCLC.

Indexes articles from business trade publications, newspapers, newsletters, and business dailies, supplying summaries and selected full text.

Business Index. Foster City, CA: Information Access Company, 1981–present. Available as a subscription database via CompuServe, DataStar, DIALOG, Dow Jones, FT-Profile, IAC, LEXIS-NEXIS, Questel-Orbit, STN International, Westlaw, and others.

Online index to business journals, trade magazines, and newspapers with selected full text.

Business Periodicals Index (BPI). New York: Wilson, 1958–present. Formerly titled *The Industrial Arts Index,* 1913–1957. Also available on CD-ROM and available as a subscription database via OCLC, Ovid, and Wilson.

Indexes about three hundred business journals and magazines. The online full-text version includes selected full text articles.

CNNFN. http://www.cnnfn.com.

The day's top financial stories appear on this free Web site. Another site with timely full text financial news is *Business Wire* at http://www.businesswire .com.

Dow Jones. Princeton, NJ: Dow Jones.

Dow Jones offers many online information resources geared to business researchers of all types, with in-depth investment data and news and information on companies, industries, and products.

Predicast's F&S Index: United States. Foster City, CA: Information Access Company, 1960–present. Also available on CD-ROM and via CompuServe, DataStar, DIALOG, Dow Jones, FT-Profile, IAC, LEXIS-NEXIS, Questel-Orbit, STN International, Westlaw, and others.

  Index to company, product, and industry information from trade publications, business-oriented newspapers, and special reports. Non-U.S. versions of this index are *Predicast's F&S Index: Europe* (1978–present) and *Predicast's F&S Index: International* (1967–present). *F&S Index Plus Text* on CD-ROM contains full text.

PROMT: Predicast's Overview of Markets and Technology. Foster City, CA: Information Access Company. Available as a subscription database via CompuServe, DataStar, DIALOG, Dow Jones, FT Profile, IAC, LEXIS-NEXIS, Questel-Orbit, STN International, Westlaw, and others.

  Supplies business-related abstracts and full text from journals, magazines, newsletters, investment reports, and government publications.

Computer Science, Information Systems, and Library Science

See also: Science

Computer Database. Foster City, CA: Information Access Company. Available via CompuServe, DataStar, DIALOG, Dow Jones, FT-Profile, IAC, LEXIS-NEXIS, Questel-Orbit, STN International, Westlaw, and others.

  Online index to publications covering computers, electronics, telecommunications, and other high-tech topics. The ASAP version includes selected full-text articles.

Computer Literature Index. Formerly titled *Quarterly Bibliography of Computers and Data Processing.* Phoenix, AZ: Applied Computer Research, 1971–present.

  Citations in this index, relating to computers and data processing, are culled from articles, books, and reports.

Library Literature. New York: Wilson, 1921–present. Also available on CD-ROM and as a subscription database via DIALOG, OCLC, and Wilson.

  Contains references to literature from journals and books of interest to library and information professionals and those interested in such topics as censorship, copyright legislation, preservation of materials, and the Internet.

Microcomputer Abstracts. Formerly titled the *Microcomputer Index.* Medford, NJ: Information Today, 1980–present. Also available on CD-ROM and as a subscription database via DIALOG.

Indexes and summarizes articles concerning the use of microcomputers as well as new product announcements and hardware and software reviews.

Education

Education Index. New York: Wilson, 1929–present. Also available on CD-ROM and as a subscription database via OCLC, ProQuest Direct, and Wilson.

Covers over four hundred journals dealing with all levels of education. The full-text version online includes full-text articles for about a third of the journals indexed.

ERIC: Educational Resources Information Center. Also available on CD-ROM and free through *AskEric* at http://www.askeric.org or through *ERIC Search Wizard* at http://ericae.net/scripts/ewiz/amain2.asp. Also available as a subscription database via DIALOG, OCLC and Ovid.

The print version of *ERIC,* the premier education index/database, is divided into two parts. The first, *Resources in Education (RIE),* 1966–present, contains current research findings, projects, technical reports, speeches, conference proceedings, unpublished manuscripts, and books. An accompanying set of full text *RIE* microfiche is available. The second part, *Current Index to Journals in Education (CIJE),* 1969–present, covers hundreds of education magazines and journals. The *ERIC* database combines both sections.

Energy/Environment

Energy Research Abstracts. Department of Energy, Office of Scientific and Technical Information. Washington, DC: GPO, 1976–present. Also available as a subscription database via DIALOG and STN International.

Indexes Department of Energy technical reports from its laboratories, energy centers, and contractors as well as articles, conference papers, books, patents, and theses.

Environment Abstracts Annual. Bethesda, MD: Congressional Information Service, 1971–present. Also available on CD-ROM and as a subscription database via DataStar, EINS, DIALOG, LEXIS-NEXIS, Questel-Orbit, and others.

Covers all aspects of environmental research. The online version is called *Enviroline.*

Wildlife Review. Washington, DC: GPO, 1935–present. Also available on CD-ROM.

Supplies indexing to the natural resource and wildlife literature in books, journals, and symposia proceedings.

Health, Medicine, and Physical Education

Cumulative Index to Nursing and Allied Health Literature (CINAHL). Glendale, CA: CINAHL Information Systems, 1956–present. Also available as a subscription database via DataStar, EBSCOhost, OCLC, and Ovid.

Index to the literature from the nursing and allied health fields, covering topics such as health administration, biomedicine, consumer health, ethics, protocol, technology, and psychology.

Health Periodicals Database. Foster City, CA: Information Access Company. Available as a subscription database via CompuServe, DataStar, DIALOG, Dow Jones, FT-Profile, IAC, LEXIS-NEXIS, Questel-Orbit, STN International, Westlaw, and others.

Provides broad, topical coverage of health, medicine, fitness, and nutrition from consumer health magazines, professional medical journals, and health pamphlets, with selected full text.

Index Medicus. National Library of Medicine. Washington, DC: GPO, 1960–present.

The standard medical index, geared to medical professionals, supplying indexing to thousands of English and foreign-language journals. It's online version is *Medline*, available through the National Library of Medicine at no charge at http://www.nlm.nih.gov/ and via several subscription services, including DataStar, DIALOG, EBSCOhost, OCLC, Ovid, and STN International.

Physical Education Index. Cape Gerardeau, MO: BenOak Publishing, 1978–present. Also available on CD-ROM.

Index to articles in the field of physical education, such as dance, health, physical therapy, recreation, sports, and sports medicine.

SportDiscus. Formerly called the SPORT database. Ontario: Sport Information Resource Center. Available on CD-ROM and as a subscription database via DataStar, DIALOG, and Ovid.

Online index with summaries and citations for articles, books, conference proceedings, and other materials in all areas of sport and recreation, both scholarly and applied.

History/Anthropology

Abstracts in Anthropology. Amityville, NY: Baywood Publishing Company, 1970–present.

> Covers topics in the fields of archaeology, cultural and physical anthropology, and linguistics.

America: History and Life. Santa Barbara, CA: ABC-CLIO, 1954–present. Also available on CD-ROM and as a subscription database through ABC-CLIO, CompuServe, and DIALOG.

> An index to the literature of the history and culture of the United States and Canada from prehistoric times to the present.

The Anthropological Index Online. http://lucy.ukc.ac.uk/AIO.html

> A free Web index to periodicals in the Museum of Mankind Library, incorporating the former Royal Anthropological Institute library.

Anthropological Literature. Cambridge, MA: Harvard University. 1979–present. Also available on CD-ROM and via the Research Libraries Group.

> Covers archaeology; linguistics; and biological, physical, cultural, and social anthropology.

Historical Abstracts. Santa Barbara, CA: ABC-CLIO, 1955–present. Also available on CD-ROM.

> Covers all branches of world history from 1450 to the present for the world *except* the United States and Canada.

Law and Criminal Justice

See also: chapter eleven

Criminal Justice Abstracts. Monsey, NY: Willow Tree Press, 1968–present. Also available on CD-ROM and via West Group.

> Compilation of citations and abstracts of books, journal articles, dissertations, unpublished papers, and governmental and nongovernmental agency reports on criminology and criminal justice worldwide.

Criminal Justice Periodical Index. Ann Arbor, MI: UMI, 1973–present.

> Indexes criminal justice magazines and journals.

Current Law Index. Foster City, CA: Information Access Company, 1980–present. Also available as a subscription database via DIALOG, LEXIS-NEXIS, Ovid, and West Group.

> Indexes law journals from the United States, Canada, the United Kingdom, Ireland, Australia and New Zealand.

Index to Foreign Legal Periodicals. Berkeley, CA: University of California Press, 1960–present. Also available on CD-ROM and as a subscription database via the Research Libraries Group.

Covers more than four hundred legal and business periodicals from fifty-nine countries.

Index to Legal Periodicals and Books. Bronx, NY: Wilson, 1908–present. Also available on CD-ROM and as a subscription database via LEXIS-NEXIS, OCLC, Ovid, West Group, and Wilson.

Provides indexing to articles and monographs discussing all aspects of law and legal research for the United States, Canada, Great Britain, Ireland, Australia, and New Zealand.

Index to Periodical Articles Related to Law. Dobbs Ferry, NY: Glanville Publishers, 1958–present.

Covers all articles of a legal nature that are not covered by *Current Law Index, Foreign Legal Periodicals, Index to Legal Periodicals,* or *LegalTrac.*

LegalTrac. Foster City: Information Access Company. Formerly known as the *Legal Resources Index.* Available on CD-ROM and via CompuServe, DIALOG, Dow Jones, LEXIS-NEXIS, OVID, Questel-Orbit, STN International, and West Group.

Indexes law journals, legal newspapers, and law articles from other periodicals.

NCJRS: National Criminal Justice Reference Service. Rockville, MD: NCJRS. Available on CD-ROM and free at http://www.ncjrs.org/.

An online index supplying summaries of criminal justice books; U.S. federal, state, and local government documents; journals; unpublished research reports; and program descriptions and evaluations.

Multiculture Topics

Chicano Database on CD-ROM. Includes the *Chicano Index,* formerly titled the *Chicano Periodical Index,* 1981–1989. Berkeley, CA: University of California at Berkeley, 1990–present. Available on CD-ROM and as a subscription database via the Research Libraries Group.

Comprehensive database on all aspects of Latino culture, economics, politics, and literature.

Ethnic NewsWatch. Stamford, CT: SoftLine Information. Available on CD-ROM and via Dow Jones, *Electric Library,* LEXIS-NEXIS, OCLC, and Profound.

Online database of full-text articles, including editorials and reviews, from over two hundred magazines, newspapers, and journals published by the ethnic and minority press in the Americas.

Handbook of Latin American Studies. Hispanic division of the Library of Congress. Washington, DC: Library of Congress, 1935–present. Also available free under the title *HLAS Online* at http://lcweb2.ocl.gov/hlas/ and as a subscription database via the Research Libraries Group.

    Annotated bibliography of works on Latin America.

Hispanic American Periodicals Index (HAPI). Los Angeles: Latin American Studies Center Publications, University of California, 1974–present. Also available on CD-ROM and as a subscription database via the Research Libraries Group.

    Indexes periodical articles about Latin America, the Carribean, and Hispanics in the United States.

Index to Black Periodicals. Thorndike, ME: MacMillan, 1960–present.

    Index to African-American periodicals of general and scholarly interest.

Newspaper, Newsletter, and Newswire Indexes

See also: chapter four under Newswires and Daily News

Note that a number of high-circulation newspapers have their own indexes, including *The New York Times, The Wall Street Journal, The Washington Post,* and *The Christian Science Monitor.*

DIALOG. Mountain View, CA: DIALOG Corporation.

    The DIALOG commercial online system offers access to many national, regional, and local newspapers.

National Newspaper Index. Foster City, CA: Information Access Company. Available on CD-ROM and as a subscription database via CompuServe, DataStar, DIALOG, Dow Jones, FT-Profile, IAC, LEXIS-NEXIS, Questel-Orbit, STN International, Westlaw, and others.

    Online index to citations from the last five years of five major newspapers: *The Wall Street Journal, The Christian Science Monitor, New York Times, The Los Angeles Times,* and *The Washington Post.*

Newspaper Source. Ipswich, MA: EBSCO. Available on CD-ROM and as a subscription database via EBSCOHost.

    Supplies full-text access to regional, national, and international newspapers.

NewsBank. New Canaan, CT: NewsBank, 1970–present.

    Newsbank has several CD-ROM and online products that index hundreds of regional newspapers around the United States—good for subjects not easily found in national publications. Most include full text. *Business Newsbank* covers regional business publications and the business sections of local newspapers.

Newsletter Database. Foster City, CA: Information Access Company. Available via CompuServe, DataStar, DIALOG, Dow Jones, FT-Profile, IAC, LEXIS-NEXIS, Questel-Orbit, STN International, Westlaw, and others.

Database comprised of more than six hundred full-text industry and company newsletters from around the world.

Newspage. http://www.newspage.com

Newspage filters news, based on each subscriber's choices, from over six hundred newswires, newspapers, newsletters, and magazines, categorizing it into 2,500 news topics. Basic service is free. Premium service, including full access to full text, is by subscription.

Proquest Full-Text Newspapers. Ann Arbor, MI: UMI. Available as a subscription database via UMI.

This database offers the full text of newspapers. Which newspapers? It all depends on what choice the subscriber has made. Regional, state, and national packages are available.

Philosophy and Religion

ATLA Religion Database. Evanston, IL: American Theological Library Association. Also available on CD-ROM and as a subscription database via OCLC and Ovid.

The premier index to journal articles, book reviews, and collections of essays in all fields of religion. Its print equivalents are the *Religion Index One: Periodicals*; *Religion Index Two: Multi-Author Works*; and the *Index to Book Reviews in Religion.*

The Philosopher's Index. Bowling Green, OH: Philosopher's Information Center, 1967–present. Also available on CD-ROM and as a subscription database via DIALOG.

An index to major philosophy journals and books from more than forty countries.

Political Science/Public Policy

ABC POL SCI—A Bibliography of Contents: Political Science and Government. Santa Barbara, CA: ABC-CLIO, 1969–present. Also available on CD-ROM.

Index to international periodical literature in the field of political science and government as well as the related disciplines of law, sociology, and economics.

Public Affairs Information Service (PAIS). New York: Public Affairs Information Service, 1914–present. Also available on CD-ROM and as a subscription database via DIALOG, EBSCOhost, Infotrac, OCLC, and Ovid.

Indexes literature covering contemporary public issues and the making and evaluating of public policy.

Social Sciences: Sociology, Psychology, and Economics

EconLit. Nashville: American Economic Association. Available on CD-ROM and as a subscription database via DIALOG and OCLC.

This online database supplies indexing and abstracts to economic articles, books, and dissertations.

Journal of Economic Literature. Nashville: American Economic Association, 1963–present. Also available on CD-ROM.

This review of economic research includes an index to scholarly economic subjects in English-language journals.

Psychological Abstracts. Washington, DC: American Psychological Association, 1927–present. Also available on CD-ROM, called *PsycLit,* and as a subscription database called *PsycInfo* via DataStar, Infotrac, EBSCOhost, OCLC, Ovid, and others.

The premier scholarly index to the literature of psychology. The electronic versions also index books.

Social Sciences Citation Index. Philadelphia: ISI, 1969–present. Also available on CD-ROM and as a subscription database via DataStar, DIALOG, and ISI on their *Web of Science.*

Index to more than 1,700 journals in all social sciences fields, and, additionally, lists the authors and articles cited by each article it indexes.

Social Sciences Index (SSI). New York: Wilson, 1974–present. Previously called *Social Sciences and Humanities Index* (1965–1974), *International Index* (1955–1965), and *International Index to Periodicals* (1907–1955). Also available on CD-ROM and as a subscription database through OCLC, ProQuest Direct, and Wilson.

Provides indexing from more than four hundred periodicals on a wide spectrum of social science topics. The online full-text version includes selected full-text articles.

Sociological Abstracts. San Diego: Sociological Abstracts, 1953–present. Also available on CD-ROM (*SocioFile*) and as a subscription database via DIALOG, OCLC, and Ovid.

Scholarly index to journal citations and abstracts in sociology.

Science: Agriculture, Biology, Chemistry, Electronics, Engineering, Geosciences, Mathematics, and Physics

Agricola. Baltimore, MD: National Agricultural Library. Available free at http://www.nal.usda.gov/.

The records in *Agricola* describe publications and resources encompassing all aspects of agriculture and its allied disciplines.

Applied Science and Technology Index. New York: Wilson, 1958–present. Formerly called the *Industrial Arts Index* (1913–1957). Also available on CD-ROM and as a subscription database through OCLC, ProQuest Direct, and Wilson.

Indexes over 350 journals in the areas of science, engineering, and technology.

Biological Abstracts. Philadelphia: Biosis. Also available on CD-ROM and as a subscription database called *BIOSIS* via DataStar, DIALOG, OCLC, Ovid, and STN International.

Presents references, abstracts, and indexes to the world's life sciences research literature.

Biological and Agricultural Index. New York: Wilson, 1964–present. Formerly called *The Agricultural Index* (1916–1964). Also available on CD-ROM, as a subscription database through OCLC, ProQuest Direct, and Wilson.

Covers 250 key journals in the life sciences and agriculture.

Chemical Abstracts. Columbus, Ohio: The American Chemical Society, 1907–present. Available on CD-ROM and via STN International.

The standard index for chemists, *Chemical Abstracts* indexes and abstracts scientific and technical papers, books, dissertations, conference proceedings, and journals containing new information of chemical or chemical engineering interest. Information can be searched by topic, author, or chemical formula.

Engineering Index Monthly. Hoboken, NJ: Engineering Information, Inc., 1896–present. Also available on CD-ROM and as a subscription database under the title *COMPENDEX* via DataStar, DIALOG, Ovid, Questel-Orbit, STN International, and others.

Covers such areas as chemical engineering, civil engineering, computers and electrical engineering, metals, mining, and mechanical engineering.

General Science Index. New York: Wilson, 1978–present. Also available on

CD-ROM and as a subscription database via OCLC, ProQuest Direct, and Wilson.

 General Science Index covers a wide range of science topics and indexes 150 journals. The online full-text version includes selected full-text articles.

GeoRef. Alexandria, VA: American Geological Institute, 1966–present. Available on CD-ROM and as a subscription database via DIALOG, OCLC, Questel-Orbit, STN International, and others.

 The most comprehensive index to literature in the geosciences. Its print version is called the *Bibliography and Index of Geology.*

INSPEC: Information Service for Physics, Electronics, and Computing. London: Institution of Electrical Engineers. Also available as a subscription database via DataStar, Ovid, Questel-Orbit, STN International, and others.

 INSPEC, a subscription database, contains citations with abstracts to physics, electronics, electrical engineering, computers, control engineering, and information technology literature worldwide. The print indexes that are the equivalent of the *INSPEC* database are *Physics Abstracts, Electrical & Electronics Abstracts,* and *Computer & Control Abstracts.*

Mathematical Reviews. Providence, RI: American Mathematical Society, 1940–present. Also available on CD-ROM, titled *MathSciDisc,* and as a subscription database called *MathSciNet* via the American Mathematical Society.

 Supplies reviews of the world's mathematical literature, classified according to the mathematics subject classification.

Science Citation Index. Philadelphia: ISI, 1961–present. Also available on CD-ROM and as a subscription database via DataStar, DIALOG, STN International, and ISI on their *Web of Science.*

 Provides access to current bibliographic data and cited references from about 3,500 scientific and technical journals.

Bibliography

Bremser, Wayne. "The Best Things in Life Are Almost Free (The Best Shareware and Freeware in Several Categories.)" *Computer Life* 4.7 (July 1997); 60p.

Brundage, Anthony. *Going to the Sources: A Guide to Historical Research and Writing.* 2nd edition. Wheeling, IL: Harlan Davidson, 1997.

Busiel, Christopher and Tom Maeglin. *Researching Online.* Adapted from *Teaching Online: Internet Research, Conversation, and Composition.* New York: Longman, 1998.

Crawford, Walt. "Paper Persists: Why Physical Library Collections Still Matter." *Online* 22.1 (January–February 1998): 42–.

Forte, Eric. "Plugging Into Capitol Hill." *Colorado Libraries* 24.1 (Spring 1998): 26-29.

Herman, Edward. *Locating United States Government Information: A Guide to Sources.* 2nd edition. Buffalo, NY: William S. Hein, 1997.

Katz, William. *Introduction to Reference Work.* 7th ed. 2 Volumes. New York: McGraw-Hill, 1997.

Koutnik, Chuck. "The World Wide Web is Here: Is the End of Printed Reference Sources Near?" *RQ* 3 (Spring 1997): 422–425.

Krol, John, editor. *Information Industry Directory.* 20th edition. Detroit: Gale. Annual.

Lake, Matt. "The Best Free Stuff Online." *PC World* 16.4 (April 1998) p.104–.

Lane, Carole. *Naked in Cyberspace: How to Find Personal Information Online.* Wilton, CT: Pemberton Press, 1997.

Larsgaard, Mary Lynette. *Map Librarianship: An Introduction.* 3rd edition. Englewood, CO: Libraries Unlimited, 1998.

Lavin, Michael R. *Understanding the Census: A Guide for Marketers, Planners, Grant Writers and Other Data Users.* Kenmore, NY: Epoch Books, 1996.

Maloy, Timothy K. *The Writer's Internet Handbook.* New York: Allworth Press, 1997.

Maze, Susan, David Moxley and Donna J. Smith. *Authoritative Guide to Web Search Engines.* New York: Neal-Schuman Publishers, 1997.

Morris, Evan. *The Book Lover's Guide to the Internet*. New York: Fawcett Columbine, 1996.

Pagell, Ruth A. and Michael Halpern. *International Business Information: How to Find It, How to Use It*. 2nd edition. Phoenix, AZ: Oryx Press, 1998.

Plewe, Brandon. *GIS Online: Information Retrieval, Mapping, and the Internet*. Santa Fe, NM: OnWord Press, 1997.

Quercia, Valerie. *Internet in a Nutshell: A Desktop Quick Reference*. Cambridge, MA: O'Reilly, 1997.

Rodrigues, Dawn. *The Research Paper and the World Wide Web*. Upper Saddle River, NJ: Prentice Hall, 1997.

Steffens, Henry J. and Mary Jane Dickerson. *Writer's Guide: History*. Lexington, MA: D.C. Heath, 1987.

Taylor, Maureen K. "The World at Your Fingertips: Maps on the Internet." *Colorado Libraries* 24.2 (Summer 1998): 41–43.

INDEX

NOTE: Boldface denotes resources available free on the Internet or organizations with Web pages.